CRIMINAL JUSTICE, LAW ENFORCEMENT AND CORRECTIONS

Paralysing International Criminal Justice

Criminal Justice, Law Enforcement and Corrections

Additional books and e-books in this series can be found on Nova's website under the Series tab.

Human Rights: Contemporary Issues and Perspectives

Additional books and e-books in this series can be found on Nova's website under the Series tab.

CRIMINAL JUSTICE, LAW ENFORCEMENT AND CORRECTIONS

Paralysing International Criminal Justice

Farhad Malekian

nova science publishers
New York

Library of Congress Cataloging-in-Publication Data

Names: Malekian, Farhad, author.
Title: Paralysing international criminal justice / Farhad Malekian, Uppsala, Sweden.
Other titles: Paralyzing international criminal justice
Identifiers: LCCN 2020044021 (print) | LCCN 2020044022 (ebook) | ISBN 9781536187427 (hardcover) | ISBN 9781536187823 (adobe pdf)
Subjects: LCSH: Criminal justice, Administration of. | Victims of crimes (International law) | International criminal courts. | International Criminal Court. | Palestinian Arabs--Crimes against--Israel. | Discrimination in criminal justice administration--Israel. | Palestinian Arabs--Civil rights--Israel. | United Nations. Security Council.
Classification: LCC K5001 .M347 2020 (print) | LCC K5001 (ebook) | DDC 345--dc23
LC record available at https://lccn.loc.gov/2020044021
LC ebook record available at https://lccn.loc.gov/2020044022

Published by Nova Science Publishers, Inc. † New York

A man visited his friend for a night. In the morning he asked his friend: "Where is your rooster which sings with ancient words at dawn?" His friend replied, "well, we cut his neck." "Why?" "Because he was waking up people and disturbing the powerful neighbours." The friend then added, unprompted, "since then I have understood that everything which wakes up people with the truth, has to be killed."

Ancient Proverb

CONTENTS

Preface		**xiii**
Chapter 1	Struggling for Companionate Justice	**1**
	1. Justice without Philosophy	*1*
	2. Justice against the Biblical Code	*4*
	3. Justice Facing Injustice	*6*
	4. Justice with False Principles	*8*
	5. Funeral of Justice	*11*
	6. Conspiracy against Justice	*13*
	7. The Path of Injustice	*15*
	8. Violating Our Own Justice	*16*
	9. Justice against the Defenceless	*18*
	10. Misinterpretation of Justice	*21*
	11. Wedding of Injustice	*24*
	12. Authentic Justice	*25*
	13. Facing Justice	*39*
	14. Morally Correct Justice	*41*
Chapter 2	Crimes of Justice	**45**
	1. Ridding the Stem of Membership	*45*
	2. Committing Injustice	*48*
	3. Illegal Annexation	*50*

	4. The Policy of Non-Completion	*53*
	5. Promoting Injustice	*55*
	6. Violating Pacta Sunt Servanda	*57*
	7. Violation of Chief Principles	*60*
	8. Powerless Prosecutors	*61*
	9. Ignoring the UN's Report	*63*
	10. Violation of Litigations	*64*
	11. Legalising the Illegal	*67*
	12. Misleading Jus Cogens	*69*
	13. Impeachable Duties	*70*
	14. Injustice by Superior States	*72*
	15. Crucifying Self-Determination	*75*
Chapter 3	The Notion of International Legal Personality	**83**
	1. The Notion of Personality	*83*
	2. Subjects of Personality	*85*
	3. Criteria of Personality	*85*
	4. Legal Personality of Palestine	*86*
	5. Establishing Legal Personality	*87*
	6. Membership in International Organisations	*88*
	7. Breach of Personality	*89*
	8. Monopolisation of Legal Personality	*89*
	9. Violation of Personality	*91*
	10. Legal Capacity in International Legal Personality	*93*
	11. Right to Jurisdiction	*93*
	12. Consensus Facit Legem	*94*
	13. Customary Right	*95*
Chapter 4	Traditional Recognition of Palestine	**97**
	1. Consent to Recognition	*97*
	2. Resolution Confirming Personality	*98*
	3. Recognition through Resolutions	*103*
	4. Constitutive Recognition	*105*
	5. Arguments Facing Recognition	*106*
	6. Criteria for Recognition	*107*

7. Owning Statehood Conditions *109*
8. Permanent Population *110*
9. Legitimacy of Statehood *112*
10. Territorial Acquisition *113*
11. Conditions of Defined Territories *114*
12. Statehood through Self-Determination *116*
13. Inalienable Right of Self-Determination *117*
14. Full Statehood of Palestine *119*
15. Judgments of Courts *120*

Chapter 5 Violations of International Peremptory Criminal Law **123**
1. Problem of Law-Making Treaties *123*
2. Mishandling of the Concept *126*
3. Validity of Treaties Ratified by Palestinians *127*
4. Palestine Constituting Jus Cogens Norms *128*
5. Palestine in the International Court of Justice *130*
6. Accountability *132*
7. Expansion of Settlements *133*
8. Settlements against Peremptory Norms *136*
9. Violations of Jus Cogens Norms *140*
10. Recurrence of Serious Crimes *143*
11. Crimes within the ICC Authority *147*
12. Reasonable Basis for Investigation *149*

Chapter 6 The *Mens Rea* of Political Laundering Crucifying *Al-Quds/Jerusalem* **155**
1. Introduction *155*
2. Civilization on Palestinian Soil *156*
3. International Criminal Law Regarding Brutality *157*
4. Ignominy by Crucifixion *159*
5. The Leading Masters of International Criminal Justice *161*
6. The Weakness of the ICC *163*
7. Mens Rea in the Unilateral Illegal Declaration *167*
8. Negation of International Criminal Law *171*

	9. The Immoral Force of the Declaration	*173*
	10. Mens Rea of a Magic Show	*174*
	11. Legitimising Illegality	*176*
	12. The Codex of Prejudice Covering Mens Rea	*179*
	13. Mens Rea with Intent	*183*
Chapter 7	*Actus Reus* of the Declaration Implying the Guilty Mind	**189**
	1. International Criminal Laws Condemning Mens Rea	*189*
	2. Equal Seats in Courtrooms	*194*
	3. The Position of Actus Reus in Law	*195*
	4. Violations of the Basic Principles of Criminal Laws	*196*
	5. Predominantly Oblivious Declaration	*197*
	6. Violations of the Rights of Occupied Countries	*198*
	7. The Advisory Opinion of the International Court of Justice	*200*
	8. Inclination in Political Mens Rea	*201*
	9. The Hidden Mens Rea	*204*
	10. A One-Eyed Justice	*205*
	11. The Actus Reus of the Declaration	*208*
	12. Preliminary Sanctions in Resolution 181	*210*
	13. Solving the Dilemma Created by Great Britain	*210*
Chapter 8	Characterising Dignity through the Exploitation of Legal Personality	**213**
	1. Limiting the Recognition of the Dignity of Europeans	*213*
	2. Instrumentality of Human Rights Law	*215*
	3. Impunity Constituting the Principle of Unity	*218*
	4. Membership Paralyzing Justice	*220*
	5. Big Powers Institutionalising the Decision Makers	*221*
	6. Security Council Imposing Justice	*223*
	7. Dealing the Principles of Justice	*226*

	8. The Powerful Game of Justice	*228*
	9. Instrumentality of the Principles of Legality	*229*
	10. Oppressor of Injustice in Palestine	*233*
Chapter 9	Conclusion	**237**
Appendices		**243**
	Resolution 181 (II). Future Government of Palestine	*243*
	Plan of Partition with Economic Union	*245*
	Appendix: Human Rights Council Twenty-Fifth Session	*271*
References		**305**
Index		**337**

PREFACE

The system of international law is not pure, but rather is influenced by power and politics. The most major parts of the system were created as a result of the signature of unjust treaties imposed upon the vanquished states by victorious states after a war. Therefore, since there was no stage of ratification of treaties at the time of their formulation, international law as a result reflects the conditions of war. This is because the ratification process allows for further evaluation of the provisions of the treaty by states, in order to prevent the enforcement of certain unequal provisions. For instance, the Treaty of Versailles was not respected due to a considerable number of political considerations and strife between the big political parties which sought to divide the wealth of the world among themselves, and ensure that some states had more rights and privileges than the others. This is also true concerning the monopolised legal personality of the Security Council and certainly, the situation of Palestine up until today.

The system of international law was, is, and will continue to be, a manifestation of the use of force. That is why Article 2 (4) of the UN Charter attempts to abolish the use of force. However, since the ratification and establishment of the monopolised body of the Security Council, this notion has developed strongly and aggressively under the power of big political parties in the world. Concerning Palestine, the British colonial power imposed the Balfour Declaration for the creation of a homeland for the Jews, and for their own economic benefit. A similar phenomenon can be seen in the provisions of the secret Sykes-Picot Agreement of 1916, according to which the territory of the Middle East was divided between two colonised authorities—that of the United Kingdom and that of France.

This book discusses the questions of justice side by side with the serious violation of the international legal personality of Palestine which was agreed through political dealings between a number of states such as the United States, the United Kingdom, Israel, Egypt, Saudi Arabia, and the United Arab Emirates. The concept of international legal personality governs the legal statute of an international organisation or a state, which has the *capacity* of concluding law-making treaties. The book explores various discussions surrounding the concept of personality, with particular focus on Palestinian statehood. It concludes that, regardless of the various arguments made around the negotiation table between the members of the United Nations concerning the statehood of Palestine, Palestine has always maintained its international legal personality despite violation and obstruction by the militarily powerful nations.

The reality is, it is almost impossible to separate the intention of the rule of law from certain moral principles. Inequality is a major cause of unequal justice and indicates the violation of the primary essence of human dignity. The word 'injustice' indicates a departure from pure negotiation and the application of ideological modalities through military force. Thus, people are forced from their homelands, homes are destroyed, and people are disrespected, imprisoned, killed, and hunted like beasts. When nations only sign certain agreements and do not ratify them, they are then able to escape from their international legal obligations. They have the ability to ignore international principles whenever they deem fit, and to regain political power through the use of force. This means that they disrespect the legal and moral requirements of international conventions. Furthermore, the silence of the international community is historically equivalent to support of criminal acts of governments against many peoples such as the Jews, Vietnamese, Rwandans, Iraqis, Syrians, Yemenis, and Palestinians. All these crimes paralyse international criminal justice.

The rights of Palestine concerning full sovereign independence and its territories are an integral part of *jus cogens* and *erga omens* obligations. They constitute an integral part of peremptory international human rights law. They are consequently of concern to all states of the international legal and political community. However, it seems that justice has been manipulated by political powers with the assistance of lawyers, cooperative bodies, and states for the benefit of their own personal or intergovernmental incomes. This can be seen clearly through the conducts of certain permanent members of the Security Council.

If the central organisation of the world does not keep its legal virginity, if the well-known international lawyers have not moral virginity based on their private economic interests, if the international political powers ignore Victims of Gross Violations of International Human Rights Law and Serious Violations of International Humanitarian Law than the politics of the world run with the power of one-eyed justice. Malcolm X correctly asserts "If you're not careful, the newspapers will have you hating the people who are being oppressed, and loving the people who are doing the oppressing." Today, the notion of justice in the United Nations organisation is like a house of cards.

The content of the book does not only support the Palestinian cause, because if the Palestinians were Jewish or the Americans were Vietnamese my arguments would certainly remain the same.

Written with love for justice in the territory of united essence of humankind, 2020.

F. Malekian
f.malekian.in.crim.l@telia.com

Chapter 1

STRUGGLING FOR COMPANIONATE JUSTICE

1. JUSTICE WITHOUT PHILOSOPHY

The question of what is encompassed by the term "philosophy of justice," and what its principles, norms, and frameworks constitute, are very complicated questions.[1] This is simply because when we speak of the philosophy of justice, we are also simultaneously speaking about the philosophy of law, philosophy of coexistence, philosophy of trust, and most importantly , the philosophy of telling the truth in practice, which refers to the fight for the truth through our strength and bringing justice to unjust order.[2] Due to these factors, the definition of the term "philosophy of justice" is very demanding and sophisticated, particularly when we face violations of the system of international criminal law and international criminal justice

---

[1] Farhad Malekian, 'Emasculating the Philosophy of International Criminal Justice in the Iraqi Special Tribunal', 38:3*Cornell International Law Journal* (2005), pp. 673-723; Farhad Malekian, 'Armenian Genocide and the Questions of Responsibility of the Turkish Government' (*House of Commons Conference on the Armenia Genocide*, Nor Serount Publications, 2007), pp. 31-39; Farhad Malekian, 'The Homogeneity of International Criminal Court with Islamic Jurisprudence', 9 *International Criminal Law Review* (2009), pp. 595-621; Farhad Malekian, *International Criminal Law: The of Somebodiness - The Law of Nobodiness* (New York: Nova Sciences Publishers, 2021).

[2] See Alan Hart, Open letter to British Conservative Party leader David Cameron, in August 2007www.alanhart.net/zionism-open-letter-to-british-conservative-party-leader-david-cameron/

through various forms of genocide. It seems that genocide is not a new phenomenon, and that the systems of international criminal law and international criminal justice, and the body of international human rights law can be violated by anyone, even those who were once themselves victims of inhumane violations by European states. That is why the term 'philosophy of justice' must be interpreted taking into consideration the history of human civilisation.

The term 'philosophy of justice' does not only refer to legal requirements, but also, and more obviously, to moral necessities. The latter may be an essential reason for why the definition of "philosophy of justice" is more controversial than it appears at first glance, since there are no clear principles to identify what constitutes the scope of moral requirements. Martin Luther King correctly asserted that "A man dies when he refuses to stand up for that which is right. A man dies when he refuses to stand up for justice. A man dies when he refuses to take a stand for that which is true."[3]

In addition, the word "moral" is itself subject to debate, and its definition varies from culture to culture, nation to nation, and from year to year, as what is considered moral one day, or in one culture, may be considered immoral the next, or in another culture. When the word justice accompanies moral attitudes, the explanation may become much more personal. Aside from this, the concept of justice has also been heavily influenced by the evolution of the history of jurisprudence.[4] Nevertheless, we must find a way to avoid personal justice, and avoid violating the principle of universal morality in the interpretation of justice by using our own understanding of the principle of morality. As it has been stated:

---

[3] Apr 3, 1998.

[4] See also *Issues in Contemporary Legal Philosophy: The Influence of H.L.A. Hart* (Ruth Gavison, ed., 1987); Heidi Hurd, '*Challenging Authority,'* 100 *Yale Law Journal* 1611 (1991); G. Hughes, 'Validity and the Basic Norm,' 59 *California Law Review* 695 (1971); H.L.A. Hartart, *Essays in Jurisprudence and Philosophy* (1983); Joseph Raz, *The Morality of Freedom* (1986); J.W. Harris, *Legal Philosophers* (2nd edn.,1997); Johan Austin, *The Province of Jurisprudence Determined and the Uses of the Study of Jurisprudence* (1954); Postema Gerald J., *Bentham and the Common Law Tradition* (1986); Julie Dickson., *Evaluation and Legal Theory* (2001); H.L.A. Hart., *The Concept of Law* (1961). H.L.A. Hart., *The Concept of Law* (2nd edn, P.A. Bulloch and J. Raz eds., 1994).

> But if, on the other hand, there be in nature no such principle as justice, no such principle as honesty, no such principle as men's natural rights of person or property, then all such words as justice and injustice, honesty and dishonesty, all such words as mine and thine, all words that signify that one thing is one man's property and that another thing is another man's property, all words that are used to describe men's natural rights of person or property, all such words as are used to describe injuries and crimes, should be struck out of all human languages as having no meanings; and it should be declared, at once and forever, that the greatest force and the greatest frauds, for the time being, are the supreme and only laws for governing the relations of men with each other; and that, from henceforth, all persons and combinations of persons—those that call themselves governments, as well as all others—are to be left free to practice upon each other all the force, and all the fraud, of which they are capable.[5]

As I have also indicated in my recent work on moral norms and their relations to justice:

> We do understand that justice is very difficult to uphold, and that justice may take different perspectives. What is peculiar to human beings concerning the proper definition of justice is not the definition itself, or principles, but the manner of treatment by nations with different vocabularies for the definition of justice. If the definition of international human rights is torment, misery, destruction of our homes, and the killing of our children, then all nations should share the same principles. We should not only kill the Afghan, Syrian, Vietnamese, Iraqi, Libyan, but also the children of permanent members of the Security Council and their allies. Obviously, this is a very silly argumentation and has to be rejected immediately. However, if the definition of justice means heavenly rights, bliss, happiness, sincere commitment, and respect for all individuals of all

---

[5] Lysander Spooner, *Natural Law or the Science of Justice: A Treatise on Natural Law, Natural Justice, Natural Rights, Natural Liberty, and Natural Society; showing that all Legislation whatsoever is an Absurdity, a Usurpation, and a Crime*. Part First. [1882] Available online at http://oll.libertyfund.org/titles/spooner-natural-law-or-the-science-of-justice-1882.

nations that too should certainly be provided to our neighbours near and far.[6]

Certainly, the intention of justice is to prevent the killing, destruction, humiliation of a group, and to prevent the restriction of rights of one group to give them to another. When we strip justice down to a certain set of principles, we do not limit the boundaries of justice, but rather wish to create a balance between the means and the end.

2. Justice against the Biblical Code

St. Thomas Aquinas was a leading European philosopher of the Middle Ages. His philosophy about justice is the most dominant in the Catholic tradition, and is an integral part of the modern school of moral and political theory based on his thoughts, known as Thomism. His ideas are still powerful today, and serve as the framework for many philosophical discussions, including those concerning the concept of justice. Aquinas stripped justice down to its fundamental concepts in order to uncover the basic truth of the principle. Thomas Aquinas' argumentation is based on a system of justice emanating from the principle of proportional reciprocity, meaning that each person should respect justice and should define it based on what they give and receive.

Aquinas encouraged the awareness that we live in a community of human beings, and consequently, that we have to make sure that our actions do not harm the community. All this means that he encouraged the stripping down justice to find its true virtue. According to Aquinas, the basic principles of justice can only be understood by stripping down the virtues of justice, so that any individual of any faith can recognise justice and act on it. Thus, Aquinas accepted pre-Christian and even Islamic thought in Europe at

---

[6] Farhad Malekian, *Classical Morality in International Peremptory Criminal Law* (Cambridge Scholars Publishing, 2018), pp.211-2. See *also* Malekian Farhad, *International Criminal Law of Children* (New York: Nova Sciences Publishers, 2021).

a time when Christian thought dominated, and Christian thinkers rejected other forms of thought. Thus, stripping down justice was not seen as necessary to identify our own interests, but rather to identify the interests of the whole community of humankind. Aquinas believed that working toward certain interests may seem good at first glance, but that doing so may harm the virtue of justice, and thus we have to strip down justice in order to preserve the necessary moral grounds for its cultivation.

It is rightly indicated in the Bible that governments react like wolves, invisible wolves. They often destroy the identity of a nation for their own benefit all while calling it the implementation of legislation:

> The Sins of Israel's Leaders: 23The Lord spoke to me again. 24"Mortal man," he said, "Tell the Israelites that their land is unholy, and so I am punishing it in my anger. 25The leaders are like lions roaring over the animals they have killed. They kill the people, take all the money and property they can get, and by their murders leave many widows. 26 The priests break my law and have no respect for what is holy. They make no distinction between what is holy and what is not. They do not teach the difference between clean and unclean things, and they ignore the Sabbath. As a result, the people of Israel do not respect me. 27The government officials are like wolves tearing apart the animals they have killed. They commit murder in order to get rich. 28The prophets have hidden these sins like workers covering a wall with whitewash. They see false visions and make false predictions. They claim to speak the word of the Sovereign Lord, but I, the Lord, have not spoken to them. 29The wealthy cheat and rob. They mistreat the poor and take advantage of foreigners. 30I looked for someone who could build a wall, who could stand in the places where the walls have crumbled and defend the land when my anger is about to destroy it, but I could find no one. 31So I will turn my anger loose on them, and like a fire I will destroy them for what they have done." The Sovereign Lord has spoken.[7]

[7] https://biblehub.com/gnt/ezekiel/22.htm. Bible also says "Whoever says to the guilty, "You are innocent," will be cursed by peoples and denounced by nations…But it will go well with those who convict the guilty, and rich blessing will come on them."

Therefore, we must strip down justice with good intentions, and without harming anyone, which is exactly what Immanuel Kant posited with his idea of justice. He based his idea on enlightenment thought and asserted that we should treat all people as ends in themselves, and not as tools to be used to achieve our own desires. His theory, as we will see, greatly supports universal moral philosophy. Consequently, when Kant stripped down justice, he sought to find out whether or not there were moral reasons which justify our actions as correct. He did not question the quality or the quantity of our actions or conducts, but rather if said conducts carried out by human beings are correct and just. What I am focusing on here is not only proportional justice, but also our actions to create a qualified distributive justice for all members of our environment or universe. For instance, destroying a forest in the territory of another state may not only harm that state, but the world in general. Thus, in order for an action to be just, it must have the same impact on all, and benefit everyone.

3. Justice Facing Injustice

The truth is, it is almost impossible to separate the function of law from certain moral principles. Suppose that when we hear about the implementation of capital punishment in different parts of the world, we listen, protest, and express our criticism of the relevant mechanism of justice, and the responsibility of the judges and the jury for the application of capital punishment. This is because our criticism is not directed solely at the law, but also at the people who are responsible for the implementation of it.[8]

When nations only sign certain agreements and do not ratify them, they are then able to escape from their international legal obligations whenever they want. They have the ability to ignore international principles whenever

---

[8] Michael J. Sandel, *Justice: What's the Right Thing to Do?* (2010); Brian Barry, 'Justice as Reciprocity' in Eugene Kamenka and Alice Erh-Soon Tay (eds.), *Justice* (1979); Abtahi Hirad and Gideon Boas (eds.), *The Dynamics of International Criminal Justice - Essays in Honour of Sir Richard May* (2005).

they deem fit and to regain political power through the complete ignorance of the principles of international criminal law, international criminal justice, and international human rights principles. That is why many governments do not ratify certain important conventions of international human rights law and argue that they are not bound to the provisions of the relevant international conventions. This means they can ignore the legal and moral requirements of those conventions. However, Kant believed something else:

> Kant favoured a very high moral choice in expressing his moral, political, or legal theories. Kant was against any immoral conduct that increased injustice in the den of iniquity. He was therefore against lying, theft, cheating, suicide, and murder, for example. He certainly prohibited all these acts, not only in the personal realm, but also all collective and joint actions, which, for our purpose, also includes the United Nations Security Council. This vehement philosophy of Kant in international criminal law, in human rights law, and – for us – within the resolutions of the Security Council means exactly this, even in cases in which our lying, stealing, cheating, and murder would bring about more contentment than the alternative. Kant therefore puts two serious questions to our sense of morality or to the permanent members of the Security Council. He simply asks that, whenever we take decisions at home or around the negotiation table of the Charter, two basic moral philosophies must have core functions before taking any decision: *i)* Is it reasonable that everyone act as I intend to act? If the answer is no, then it is obvious that we should avoid performing such an action. *ii)* Does my personal or self-made action respect the natural integrity of human beings rather than simply utilising them for my own ends? Naturally, if our answer is no again, then we are definitely obliged not to implement it. Kant's conclusion, under consideration of self-interests, self-love, and self-tactics with the sole intention of evil terror, can also be addressed to the Security Council members. All this introspection means that Kant would intend to prohibit immoral acts in the den of iniquity of the Security Council.[9]

[9] Farhad Malekian, *The Mirage of International Criminal Law, Kant Metaphysics of Mens Rea* (Cambridge Scholars Publishing, 2018), pp.61-2.

However, the fact is that the non-ratification of international conventions does not necessarily mean that a state evades the obligation of respecting the basic provisions of the relevant human rights conventions because certain international conventions have become part of customary international law or customary international criminal law, meaning that regardless of whether or not a state is a party to an international convention, they are still obliged to respect the specific significant provisions. For instance, a state cannot claim that since they are not party to the convention on genocide or the convention on the prohibition of torture that they are allowed to commit the acts criminalized within these conventions which violate basic human rights.

4. Justice with False Principles

Overall, we want to strive to freely interpret the principles of justice and what we believe to be good or not for the health of national and international power. This means that we have different interpretations, and subsequently definitions, of the principle of justice. One may assert that our political understanding influences most definitions of criminal justice, and our political understanding is tied to the political understanding of our allies. Thus, differences in perceptions lead to inconsistencies in the system of justice, despite the basic principles remaining the same. Therefore, the term 'justice' may sometimes be separated from the universal centre of justice, and have different meanings which are far from the real definition of justice or the real principle of universal morality. This also means that the term justice may split from its own components and be mixed with false principles. Otherwise,

> If there be in nature such a principle as justice, such a principle as honesty, such principles as we describe by the words mine and thine, such principles as men's natural rights of person and property, then we have an immutable and universal law; a law that we can learn, as we learn any other science; a law that is paramount to, and excludes, everything that conflicts

> with it; a law that tells us what is just and what is unjust, what is honest and what is dishonest, what things are mine and what things are thine, what are my rights of person and property and what are your rights of person and property, and where is the boundary between each and all of my rights of person and property and each and all of your rights of person and property. And this law is the paramount law, and the same law, over all the world, at all times, and for all peoples; and will be the same paramount and only law, at all times, and for all peoples, so long as man shall live upon the earth.[10]

The fundamental principles of justice can be traced back to the notions of national, regional, and international social solidarity, mutual assistance, support, interaction among constituent parts or members, and equal dignity. For Rawls, the stability of a society constitutes justice. This means that we strip down justice and uncover its origins such that the members of the society feel secure. This implies the fact that they are treated justly, and stripping it down reveals the virtue of its existence. In other words, if the members of our national society or international society, or even our neighbours, feel as though they are not being treated equally, then there must be something wrong, and there is not an equal division of justice.

This may then concern the false interpretation of justice. Rawls believed that the members of a national community are connected, and therefore many factors in their life are interdependent. With the stripping down of justice, we refer to the attempt to uncover the hidden facts and to reach pure justice with the bare truth. Thus, as Immanuel Kant expressed, human beings are created equal in essence, and this equality must also be respected concerning their dignity. In other words, all human beings deserve to be treated equally. Inequality is primary cause of unequal justice and indicates the violation of primary human dignity. This implies that the concept of justice is the core principle of humanity, and of love for equality with due regard to consideration of morality and respect for the dignity of man.

---

[10] Lysander Spooner, *Natural Law or the Science of Justice: A Treatise on Natural Law, Natural Justice, Natural Rights, Natural Liberty, and Natural Society; showing that all Legislation whatsoever is an Absurdity, a Usurpation, and a Crime*. Part First. [1882] Available online at http://oll.libertyfund.org/titles/spooner-natural-law-or-the-science-of-justice-1882.

Dworkin states, "Without dignity our lives are only blinks of duration. But if we manage to lead a good life well, we create something more. We write a subscript to our mortality. We make our lives tiny diamonds in the cosmic sands."[11] Professor Ronald Dworkin describes the effect of injustice in his work *Justice for Hedgehogs* by asserting that:

> Cultures have tried to teach a malign and apparently persuasive lie: that the most important metric of a good life is wealth and the luxury and power it brings. The rich think they live better when they are even richer. In America and many other places they use their wealth politically, to persuade the public to elect or accept leaders who will do that for them. They say that the justice we have imagined is socialism that threatens our freedom. Not everyone is gullible: many people lead contented lives without wealth. But many others are persuaded; they vote for low taxes to keep the jackpot full in case they too can win it, even though that is a lottery they are almost bound to lose. Nothing better illustrates the tragedy of an unexamined life: there are no winners in this macabre dance of greed and delusion. No respectable or even intelligible theory of value supposes that making and spending money has any value or importance in itself and almost everything people buy with that money lacks any importance as well. The ridiculous dream of a princely life is kept alive by ethical sleepwalkers. And they in turn keep injustice alive because their self-contempt breeds a politics of contempt for others. Dignity is indivisible.[12]

If stripping down justice demonstrates that not all individuals are being treated equally, then our criteria for the treatment of the principles of justice must be wrong. The stripping down of justice must not only reveal that all people are being treated as equals, but also that the general social welfare is being looked after. When stripping down justice does not reveal the expression of our mutual recognition, then basic dignity comes under serious question.

---

[11] Ronald Dworkin, *Justice for Hedgehogs* (Harvard University Press, 2011), pp.423.

[12] *Id*. P.422.

5. FUNERAL OF JUSTICE

Plato, in a hypothetical dialogue with other philosophers, formulated the concepts of justice and injustice as follows:

> They say that to do injustice is, by nature, good; to suffer injustice, evil, but that the evil is greater than the good. And so when men have both done and suffered injustice and have had experience of both, not being able to avoid the one and obtain the other, they think that they had better agree among themselves to have neither; hence there arise laws and mutual covenants, and that which is ordained by law is termed by them lawful and just. This they affirm to be the origin and nature of justice, it is a mean or compromise, between the best of all, which is to do injustice and not be punished, and the worst of all, which is to suffer injustice without the power of retaliation, and justice, being at a middle point between the two. It is tolerated not as a good, but as the lesser evil. It is honoured by reason of the inability of me to do injustice. For no man who is worthy to be called a man would ever submit to such an agreement if he were able to resist; he would be mad if he did.

Wherever the force of the gun issues justice, the basic principles of justice have altered their nature and become principles of injustice. The word injustice indicates a departure from pure negotiation and the application of ideological modalities through military force. People are forced from their homelands, homes are destroyed, and people are disrespected, imprisoned, killed, and hunted like animals. However, we should not forget that all the instances of injustice mentioned above are identical, and present the true nature of our understating of justice. The term "funeral of justicc" may initially be defined as the end of legality, the end of morality, and the end of happiness. The term also refers to the severe brutality of international conflicts, the high number of killings, and the final stage of humanity. This is because our human rights are combined with the principles of human rights law, with the provisions of humanity, and with the obligations to follow all human rights principles. This means that when we have a funeral of justice, we have a funeral of the principles of legality, *de lege lata,* or of the principle of theorizing justice with our military strength at the same time. From another perspective:

> What I have not given due weight to so far is the power of Hume's negative arguments. What drives Hume to the conclusion that morality must be understood in terms of, explained and justified by reference to, the place of the passions and desires in human life is his initial assumption that either morality is the work of reason or it is the work of the passions and his own apparently conclusive arguments that it cannot be the work of reason. Hence he is compelled to the conclusion that morality is a work of the passions quite independently of and prior to his adducing of any positive arguments for that position. The influence of negative arguments is equally clear in both Kant and Kierkegaard. Just as Hume seeks to found morality on the passions because his arguments have excluded the possibility of founding it on reason, so Kant founds it on reason because his arguments have excluded the possibility of founding it on the passions, and Kierkegaard on criterionless fundamental choice because of what he takes to be the compelling nature of the considerations which exclude both reason and the passions.[13]

The funeral of justice refers to the burial of the most significant principles of justice. This is based on the fact that an appropriate legal order is based on three basic norms – legality, morality, and love. When love is buried with unjust decisions and conducts, two norms remain, however, they are not complete without the presence of the third norm, which is the love for justice. Thus, the term "funeral of justice" implies the burial of the norm of love, and the ignorance of the other principles of justice, including fair judgments. Thus, we give full political and legal power to the principle of injustice, which has been so widely practiced throughout the history of mankind, that it has developed its own unique identity. In fact:

> There are two types of laws, those that are just and those that are unjust. A just law is a man-made code that squares with the moral law. An

[13] Alasdair Macintyre, *After Virtue: A Study in Moral Theory* (University of Notre Dame Press, 2007), p.49.

> unjust law is a code that is out of harmony with the moral law...Any law that uplifts the human personality is just. Any law that degrades human personality is unjust. All segregation statutes are unjust because segregation distorts the soul and damages the personality.[14]

The idea of justice here provides several examples for the interpretation of justice as seen through the practices of different governments in their international relations. The governments may lose their own moral goals due to fear of losing their political leverage with militarily and economically strong powers. For instance, it reveals how governments, in the name of democracy, have worked to prevent Palestinian membership to various bodies of the United Nations, and consequently, how they thus cause the destruction of the Palestinian identity, with its territorial, cultural, and political facets.[15] Thus, when we peel back their notion of justice, it appears that there is no virtue of love left, and that injustice has been replaced with justice.

6. Conspiracy against Justice

Unfortunately in international relations there are two principles which exist in tension with one another—those of justice and injustice. Any solution which attempts to straddle the two is only a temporary balancing of the principles in the given situation. Take for example when experts of law gather and collectively discuss many principles of economic crimes, but do not spare a single word about the gross violations of international criminal law and justice caused by the trading of weapons.[16] They certainly do not consider this trade a crime or at least, are silent about its grossly inhumane economic nature. In this case, their silence is equivalent to support for the criminal acts of governments against many peoples such as the Palestinians,

---

[14] Martin Luther King.

[15] Noura Erakat, *Justice for Some: Law and the Question of Palestine* (Stanford University Press, 2019).

[16] Farhad Malekian, *Trading Virginity of International Criminal Justice* (Nova Sciences Publishers, 2020), pp.2, 4, 31 and 34.

Jews, Vietnamese, Iranians, and Libyans etc. Our silence is thus a criminal conspiracy as we sit back and watch criminal activities and human rights abuses being carried out by our governments against other groups of people.

What is meant by criminal conspiracy? When one commits criminal conspiracy, governments know that acts were being committed which violated human rights law and UN law, and although they had the obligation and responsibility to intervene, they chose not to. One is aware of historical criminal activities, for instance in Germany against the Jews, but governments still remained or remain silent, not because they do not know the difference between right and wrong, but because they are defending their own interests. As Immanuel Kant expressed, morality is not something which we chase after or which we hope to satisfy, but something which when practiced universally prevents immorality and malfeasance. The virtue of our morality should not violate the virtues of universal norms. If morality can violate the universal law of man, then we have a weak moral foundation.

> It may then be high time for the United Nations to examine the problem, not from the view of law or morality but also from the perspective of what is actually erroneous in the policy of all the treaties that are supposed to prevent national, regional, or international criminal violations. It should also examine what is wrong with the policies of the Security Council and the General Assembly of the United Nations and with the extensive overlapping norms of international human rights law, international humanitarian law of armed conflict, and statutes of international criminal justice. One could certainly believe that the transformative policy of the norms of law and morality into international conventions or organisations must not be accurate. Otherwise, why has the average number of violations increased? Why have the elements of peace brought us solely elements of injustice? In addition, why has the contemporary human historical evolutionary context resulted in us being armed more heavily than ever before?[17]

[17] Farhad Malekian, *Judgments of Love in Criminal Justice* (Springer: 2017), pp.32-33.

7. The Path of Injustice

The term "criminal justice" may be defined differently, depending on the way in which one views justice, and approaches its components. However, regardless of how the term justice is defined, it is obvious that through our unjust decisions and conducts, we may kill justice, eradicate rights, kill happiness, and we may reach the highest stage of brutality between men. This can be seen with what happened against the Jews in Germany, with the brutal crimes in Rwanda, and the barbarity of the crimes against Russians under Stalin. Further examples include the grave atrocities committed against Afghans, the waging of bloody war against the people of Vietnam, the inhumane crimes against the Iraqi population, and both the direct and indirect involvement of big powers in killing the population of Yemen.

This was the situation for the children of Rwanda, where serious brutal acts committed against children constituted crimes against humanity and genocide. The victims of genocide may not even have been born at the time of commission of crimes against humanity or genocide, and yet could still be recognised as victims afterwards.[18] One clear example is that in the instance of rape, the children born as a result of this crime are also considered victims. This also means that there exist victims of genocide beyond the physical genocide itself. For example:

> the UN initially estimated that 5,000 children were born of rape in the 1994 genocide, but the Survivors' Fund – a British charity working in Rwanda – believes the number might be nearer 20,000. Unlike genocide orphans, children of rape do not qualify for government assistance and many live in poverty. Aid programmes have tended to concentrate on the plight of the raped women, paying little attention to the children, who have grown up feeling rejected by their mothers and stigmatised by the wider community. In Rwanda, ethnicity comes through the father's line, so Tutsi

[18] 'Towards a New Convention on Crimes against Humanity: The Way Forward', *Indian Journal of Law and International Affairs,* http://ijlia.in/towards-a-new-convention-on-crimes-against-humanity-the-way-forward/.

> survivors call the children *Interahamwe* and "son of a snake," while the relatives of the Hutu rapists often tell the children that their mothers are wicked for testifying against their fathers and putting them in jail.[19]

The act of rape kills the act of legal love and buries the philosophy of love for justice alive. In the case of Palestinian rights, the criminal conducts of groups and states are targeted at one nation. This means that we have been successful in our criminal policy against the weaker groups and we have put law into force, and force behind the gun, which is used against justice and fairness and buries them in graves. When we speak about the funeral of the love for justice, then all goodness and all rights have been killed, and at the same time, all injustices, all illegal rights, and immorality are protecting and controlling the power of injustice. One clear example of this is the tragedy of the Second World War and the killing of millions of Jews as a result of injustice, immorality and inhumanity.[20]

8. Violating Our Own Justice

We not only criticise those that carry out the orders, but also the prosecutors, judges, and the entire personnel who aid in the process of administering justice. Within our personal judgement we not only struggle against fanatical provisions of law, but also against those who assist in implementing ill rules of law or the rules of capital punishment. Our reaction is more serious and even more powerful when the implementation of capital punishment relates to children. This is because it is an almost universally accepted general principle of law, as well as a part of customary and conventional international law, that children should be protected by criminal

---

[19] Rwanda 20 years on: the tragic testimony of the children of rape https://www.theguardian.com/world/2014/jun/08/rwanda-20-years-genocide-rape-children. See also Malekian, *International Criminal Law of Children*, note 6.

[20] Mohammad Gholi Majd., *A Vctorian Holocuast: Iran in the Great Famine of 1869 and 1873* (Hamilton Books, 2017). Mohammad Gholi Majd, T*he Great Famine & Genocide in Iran: 1917-1919* (2nd ed., University Press of America, 2013); Mohammad Gholi Majd, *Great Britain & Reza Shah: The Plunder of Iran, 1921-1941* (University Press of Florida, 2001).

justice, and should not be subjected to capital punishment. All this comes from our general knowledge, and from our general sense of justice which teaches us that minors are minors, and the tools of justice and different social antagonisms against their international protected position should not ignore their age. An old ancient proverb indicates "True teaching is not an accumulation of knowledge; it is an awaking of consciousness which goes through successive stages."

If the illegal occupation of Palestine has been deemed legal, if the occupation of Palestine was supported by a correct interpretation of justice, if the demolishing of the houses of Palestinians is legal, then we should assert that all the immoral and brutal conducts of the Nazis were also morally and legally correct.[21] Moreover, those brutal conducts at the time did not violate the universal rights of man, nor the rights of Jews on their own land in Germany. We are not trying to say that these two immoral, illegal, and brutal periods are the same, but rather that we should judge every matter of justice by its consequences.

During the Nazi period we did not yet have the United Nations, but rather the very weak system of the League of Nations. Certainly, no wise man can assert that the consequences of the criminal actions of the Germans were morally right, customarily correct, and legally acceptable. A legislation which does not respect the first principles of justice, a legislation that is based on one eyed-justice, and a legislation, or even a government, which

---

[21] For instance, the serious crimes committed against Palestinian civilians in Sabra and Shatila in Beirut in 1982. See the Security Council Resolution 521 (1982), which reads, "*Condemns* the criminal massacre of Palestinian civilians in Beirut." Similar reaction can be seen in the General Assembly Resolution (37/123D). It reads that the General Assembly: "*Recalling* its resolution 95 (I) of 11 December 1946, *Recalling* also its resolution 96 (I) of 11 December 1946, in which it, inter alia, affirmed that genocide is a crime under international law which the civilised world condemns, and for the commission of which principals and accomplices - whether private individuals, public officials or statesmen, and whether the crime is committed on religious, racial, political or any other grounds - are punishable, *Referring to* the provisions of the Convention on the Prevention and Punishment of the Crime of Genocide, adopted by the General Assembly on 9 December 1948, *Recalling* the relevant provisions of the Geneva Convention relative to the Protection of Civilian Persons in Time of War, of 12 August 1949, *Appalled* at the large-scale massacre of Palestinian civilians in the Sabra and Shatila refugee camps situated at Beirut, *Recognising* the universal outrage and condemnation of that massacre, *Recalling* its resolution ES-7/9 of 24 September 1982, 1. Condemns in the strongest terms the large-scale massacre of Palestinian civilians in the Sabra and Shatila refugee camps; 2. Resolves that the massacre was an act of genocide."

only focuses on the will of one race, one religion, or one cultural group certainly violates universal moral law, and therefore has a satanic character. A similar conclusion may be drawn concerning the situation of the Palestinians, Iraqis, and Afghans on their own lands. How can the Israeli government assert that its actions are correct and are in accordance with the principles of the United Nations Charter? There is no doubt that we are seriously violating the entire concept of justice, regardless of the name of our legislation or legislators.

9. Justice against the Defenceless

We cannot accept injustices against those whom are almost completely defenceless due to their age, and who are under protection of a number of international conventions, including the 1948 Geneva Conventions relating to armed conflict, the 1985 United Nations Standard Minimum Rules for the Administration of Juvenile Justice (The Beijing Rules), and the 1989 Convention on the Rights of the Child. We have a shared responsibility concerning the implementation of these international conventions everywhere, including in occupied territories.

This is what I call the responsibility of justice, the responsibility of our police forces, the responsibility of our politicians, the liability of our criminal lawyers, and the responsibility of our judges. The fact is, we are used to ignoring many provisions of international human rights law and asserting that we do not have the territorial or political jurisdiction necessary to do anything about what is occurring in Palestine. This is the most disappointing feature of criminal justice, as it is blind to the plights and sufferings abroad, as it asserts that if such acts happen outside our jurisdiction, we cannot do anything to help.

> a law that is uninformed by philosophy and that systematically and wilfully ignores scholars is both unethical and a danger to the lives lived in it or subject to it. An ethics in the Aristotelian sense, of which Ramist logic or dialectic is a distant branch, does not exist to teach mere rules, norms or

> mores. It is not simply a morality, it is habitual and comprehensive: through the law men should learn to desire, through repetition and through learning, to do the right thing in the right place at the right time; they should come to desire justice and as lawyers their lives should embody a true law, a lived law, authentic justice pragmatically located in a specific place and time.[22]

Obviously, national criminal justice, a public criminal court, an international prosecutor, a group of lawyers, and the philosophy of judges would all have a large impact on the policy of our politicians, if they understood the proper definition of justice. *If we are really working for justice, we are forced to have the courage and bravery to tell the truth and to fight for the rights of the suffering population using our offices. No government in the world could reject the strong will of its national authorities if they went against the unjust conducts of other nations - - even if only with their words and in writing. However, the biggest issue facing justice is that we are afraid of losing our own position and our hold on our interests. This means we are the real enemies of justice.*

This is where we really trade criminal justice and become the dealers of the truth. This is what I call the naked truth, the misery of justice, and the protection of the strong through our silence. It refers to crimes between us and justice, between truth and fairness, and between the limit of our morality for personal interests and possible advantages to be gained. It also references grave criminal violations of the system of international human rights law by governments which kill to protect their own interests. An old ancient proverb indicates "whoever has walked with truth generates life." Plato was correct in his dialogue when he stated:

> have you never heard that forms of government differ; there are tyrannies, and there are democracies, and there are aristocracies? Yes, I know. And the government is the ruling power in each state? Certainly. And the different forms of government make laws democratically, aristocratically, tyrannical, with a view to their several interests; and these

---

[22] Peter Goodrich, *Languages of Law: From Logics of Memory to Nomadic Masks* (Weidenfeld and Nicolson, 1990), pp. 22-23.

> laws, which are made by them for their own interests, are the justice which they deliver to their subjects, and him who transgresses them they punish as a breaker of the law, and unjust. And that is what I mean when I say that in all states there is the same principle of justice, which is the interest of the government; and as the government must be supposed to have power, the only reasonable conclusion is, that everywhere there is one principle of justice, which is the interest of the stronger.[23]

Under article 2(2) of the International Covenant on Economic, Social and Cultural Rights the States parties are obliged "to guarantee that the rights enunciated in the present Covenant will be exercised without discrimination of any kind as to race, colour, sex, language, religion, political or other opinion, national or social origin, property, birth or other status." According to the provisions of the International Covenant on Civil and Political Rights, the states parties to the International Covenant on Economic, Social and Cultural Rights also must seek, by virtue of article 3, "to ensure the equal right of men and women to the enjoyment of all economic, social and cultural rights set forth in the present Covenant." Article 7(a) (i), contains the principle of non-discrimination and guarantees "fair wages and equal remuneration for work of equal value without distinction of any kind, in particular women being guaranteed conditions of work not inferior to those enjoyed by men, with equal pay for equal work." Similarly, Article 7(c) of the Covenant protects the right to "equal opportunity for everyone to be promoted in his employment to an appropriate higher level, subject to no considerations other than those of seniority and competence."

One can find similar protection of rights in the provisions of the International Convention on the Elimination of All Forms of Racial Discrimination. According to Article 1(1), "the term 'racial discrimination' shall mean any ethnical discrimination." It states further, "any distinction, exclusion, restriction or preference based on race, colour, descent, or national or ethnic origin which has the purpose or effect of nullifying or impairing the recognition, enjoyment or exercise, on an equal footing, of human rights and fundamental freedoms in the political, economic, social,

---

[23] Plato, The Republic, p.190.

cultural or any other field of public life." Article 2 specifically makes clear that the provisions of the Convention does not, "apply to distinctions, exclusions, restrictions or preferences made by a State Party ... between citizens and non-citizens."

Article 3 provides that nothing in the Convention "may be interpreted as affecting in any way the legal provisions of States Parties concerning nationality, citizenship or naturalization, provided that such provisions do not discriminate against any particular Nationality." It is also significant that the Convention only refers to discrimination that takes place in the "field of public life." What "public life" exactly refers to is a very serious question of legal moral law, particularly when it comes to the rights of people. States parties also have the obligation to eliminate racial discrimination as put forth in Article 5. Civil, political, economic, social, and cultural rights must be available to everyone "without distinction as to race, colour, or national or ethnic origin." Consequently, the simple question that has to be asked at all times is whether or not the rights of people in occupied territories are being respected, and how occupation can even be justified to begin with. All these conventions taken together thus imply that the principles of justice, equality, and love in the implementation of equal rights are essentially significant.

10. Misinterpretation of Justice

Naturally, we would expect that even a dictatorial regime, a non-democratic society, or a fanatical group would set certain restrictions on the use of capital punishment, and would realise that a child is a child, which means that they therefore cannot receive severe punishment for violations they have committed or any harm they have caused.[24] For instance, when we hear about the implementation of capital punishment against minors in Iran, we see it as disgraceful, and condemn the Iranian machinery of justice

---

[24] Farhad Malekian, Kerstin Nordlöf (eds.), *Sovereignty of Children in Law* (Cambridge Scholars Publishing, 2012); Farhad Malekian, Kerstin Nordlöf., *Confessing the International Rights of Children: The Basic Documents with Analysis* (Cambridge Scholars Publishing, 2012).

because we believe that the bodies of justice, and even human morality, have been violated by their shameful conduct.[25] We may express a similar sentiment about the application of capital punishment against children in Afghanistan, China, Iraq, Saudi Arabia, Sudan, Yemen, Pakistan, the United States and other countries.[26]

Here I am referring to the Convention on the Rights of the Child, Article 2(1) of which provides that: "States Parties shall respect and ensure the rights set forth in the present Convention to each child within their jurisdiction without discrimination of any kind, irrespective of the child's or his or her parent's or legal guardian's race, colour, sex, language, religion, political or other opinion, national, ethnic or social origin, property, disability, birth or other status." According to the provisions of Article 2(2) of the Convention, States parties are required to take "all appropriate measures to ensure that the child is protected against all forms of discrimination or punishment on the basis of the status, activities, expressed opinion, or beliefs of the child's parents, legal guardians, or family members."

Furthermore, the provisions of Article 30 of the Convention on the Rights of the Child protect minority rights in different social circumstances. Although the terms used in this article are similar to the provisions of Article 25 of the International Covenant on Civil and Political Rights, they are not identical. They have the intention of providing justice concerning the rights of children. Article 30 reads that "in those States in which ethnic, religious or linguistic minorities or persons of indigenous origin exist, a child belonging to such a minority or who is indigenous shall not be denied the right, in community with other members of his or her group, to enjoy his or her own culture, to profess and practice his or her own religion, or to use his or her own language." All this means that all states have responsibility to protect the rights of children in certain significant spheres.

---

[25] Sanaz Alasti, *Cruel and Unusual Punishment: Comparative Perspective in International Conventions, the United States and Iran* (2009).

[26] *Id.* Raymond Paternoster, *Capital Punishment in America* (1992); en.wikipedia. org/wiki/Capitalpunishment; See *also* Malekian, *International Criminal Law of Children*, note 6.

Our reaction to, and explanation of these practices, may be to say that the legislation of the aforementioned countries and their legislators are not sufficiently familiar with the principles of international human rights law, or that their governments are fanatical, dictatorial, or do not understand European norms of justice.[27] With these various explanations, we imply that these countries are suffering from a serious misinterpretation of justice due to their cultures, social norms, religions, or authorities. Often, after evaluating the standard of criminal justice in these nations we condemn the heavy influence of Islamic rules within the criminal systems of those states, and perhaps rightfully so.

The reason is again very simple. We strongly believe and trust that religious rules should not have any power within civil or criminal law, and should therefore be limited to personal understanding and not be a public phenomenon. Although this theory appears true and logically acceptable given significant developments of various branches of public international law, in particular human rights law, it may not be correct nor have any ethical foundation due to the view of those governments which have come into power through the use of force. This is because in such nations, the constitutions are biased and do not contain properly developed human rights principles, liberal rules, and democratic norms, which are present in constitutions of countries such as Australia, Sweden, Denmark, Finland, Norway, Germany, the United Kingdom, and the United States.[28] Here, the intention is solely to refer to the actual content of the constitutions, and not the practices and relevant policy of the aforementioned states. All these countries criticise the constitutions and practices of those countries, however they do not see that their own politics kill millions of people in other countries including children and adults.

---

[27] Schabas William A, *The Abolition of the Death Penalty in International Law* (2002 and 2003).

[28] David Arter, *Democracy in Scandinavia: Consensual, Majoritarian or Mixed?* (Manchester University Press, 2006). Farhad Malekian, *Condemning the Use of Force in the Gulf Crisis* (Almqvist & Wiksell International, 1st ed. (1992), 2nd ed. (1994).

11. Wedding of Injustice

Have you ever analysed injustice, and if so, have you looked its virtue? Our expectation is that the countries which are proud to be democratic, and whose constitutions are based on the modern concepts of positive and natural law, would also follow democratic decisions in national or international matters which affect our common fate and common interests. This may concern the *horrible holocaust against the Jews* in the Second World War at the hands of the Nazis, or *the shameful occupation of Palestinian* territories over several decades by the descendants of the same Jews.[29] Hanan Ashrawi stated, "Our goal isn't outrageous. We simply want to live in dignity on our own land, see a just solution for the refugees, and closure to fifty-five years of injustice and denial of our own existence."

In particular, our expectations are higher when it comes to democratic countries such as Sweden, Denmark, Finland, Norway, the United Kingdom, or the Netherlands which are seen, at least politically, as banners of peace and the embodiment of international human rights law through their establishment of many international human rights law institutes.[30] Thus, the question is: are we analysing justice with the right norms or are we cultivating the seeds of tyranny for the rights of the victims?

> there is the just man neglecting his affairs and perhaps suffering other losses, and getting nothing out of the public, because he is just; moreover he is hated by his friends and acquaintance for refusing to serve them in unlawful ways. But all this is reversed in the case of the unjust man. I am speaking, as before, of injustice on a large scale in which the advantage of the unjust is most apparent. My meaning will be most clearly seen if we turn to that highest form of injustice in which the criminal is the happiest of men, and the sufferers or those who refuse to do injustice are the most miserable–that is to say tyranny, which by fraud and force takes away the property of others, not little by little but wholesale; comprehending in one, things sacred as well as profane, private and public; for which acts of

---

[29] www.spectator.co.uk/coffeehouse/3553206/conway-of-tehran.thtml.
[30] *Id.*

> wrong, if he were detected perpetrating any one of them singly, he would be punished and incur great disgrace–they who do such wrong in particular cases are called robbers of temples, and man-stealers and burglars and swindlers and thieves. But when a man besides taking away the money of the citizens has made slaves of them, then, instead of these names of reproach, he is termed happy and blessed, not only by the citizens but by all who hear of his having achieved the consummation of injustice. For mankind censure injustice, fearing that they may be the victims of it and not because they shrink from committing it. And thus, as I have shown, Socrates, injustice, when on a sufficient scale, has more strength and freedom and mastery than justice; and, as I said at first, justice is the interest of the stronger, whereas injustice is a man's own profit and interest.[31]

There is therefore a certain limit on the implementation of the provisions of law that must be respected and should not be violated. This norm of non-violation is not only based on legal necessity, but also upon moral requirements. Thus, regardless of whether or not we accept a law, we are still evaluating the principles of the law using moral principles, and by referring to the principle of proportionality. In other words, the elements of law, the principles of morality, and the conditions of proportionality are linked to our judgements and to our understanding of the rules of law.

12. Authentic Justice

Producing authentic justice not only demonstrates our knowledge or understanding of a case, but also our basic attitude towards the appropriate solution to the case at hand.[32] Naturally, the way we react is a manifestation

---

[31] Plato, The Republic, p.196.

[32] Some instruments of international law implying the right to justice, equality and peace are Charter of the United Nations, 1945; Universal Declaration of Human Rights, 1948; The Four Geneva Conventions of 12 August 1949; The 1977 Protocols Additional to the Geneva Conventions of 12 August 1949; International Covenant on Civil and Political Rights, 1966; International Covenant on Economic, Social and Cultural Rights, 1966; International Convention on the Elimination of All Forms of Racial Discrimination, 1965; Convention on

of our attitudes. This interpretation of justice is relatively similar across individuals, groups, governments, and states. That is why we are divided into different political groups. One usually joins a political group with ideas and policies which align with their own. However, this does not necessarily mean that the basic understandings of the principles of justice differ between individuals. Certain principles of justice may be similar across the board, and are thus unable to be modified by individual, collective, or political decisions.

Plato in his long dialogue with philosophers examined justice and its virtue, rules, misunderstanding, functions and results. He asserted:

> May I ask, Cephalus, whether your fortune was for the most part inherited or acquired by you? Acquired! Socrates; do you want to know how much I acquired? In the art of making money I have been midway between my father and grandfather: for my grandfather, whose name I bear, doubled and trebled the value of his patrimony, that which he inherited being much what I possess now; but my father Lysanias reduced the property below what it is at present: and I shall be satisfied if I leave to these my sons not less but a little more than I received. That was why I asked you the question, I replied, because I see that you are indifferent about money, which is a characteristic rather of those who have inherited their fortunes than of those who have acquired them; the makers of fortunes have a second love of money as a creation of their own, resembling the affection of authors for their own poems, or of parents for their children, besides that natural love of it for the sake of use and profit which is common to them and all men.
>
> And hence they are very bad company, for they can talk about nothing but the praises of wealth.
>
> That is true, he said.
>
> Yes, that is very true, but may I ask another question?–

---

the Elimination of All Forms of Discrimination against Women, 1979; Declaration on the Elimination of All Forms of Intolerance and of Discrimination based on Religion or Belief, 1981; Convention on the Rights of the Child, 1989; Statute of the International Tribunal for the Former Yugoslavia, 1993; Statute of the International Tribunal for Rwanda, 1994; Rome Statute of the International Criminal Court, 1998; Declaration on the Rights of Persons Belonging to National or Ethnic, Religious and Linguistic Minorities, 1992.

What do you consider to be the greatest blessing which you have reaped from your wealth? One, he said, of which I could not expect easily to convince others.

For let me tell you, Socrates, that when a man thinks himself to be near death, fears and cares enter into his mind which he never had before; the tales of a world below and the punishment which is exacted there of deeds done here were once a laughing matter to him, but now he is tormented with the thought that they may be true: either from the weakness of age, or because he is now drawing nearer to that other place, he has a clearer view of these things; suspicions and alarms crowd thickly upon him, and he begins to reflect and consider what wrongs he has done to others. And when he finds that the sum of his transgressions is great he will many a time like a child start up in his sleep for fear, and he is filled with dark forebodings.

But to him who is conscious of no sin, sweet hope, as Pindar charmingly says, is the kind nurse of his age: 'Hope,' he says, 'cherishes the soul of him who lives in justice and holiness, and is the nurse of his age and the companion of his journey;– hope which is mightiest to sway the restless soul of man.'

How admirable are his words! And the great blessing of riches, I do not say to every man, but to a good man, is, that he has had no occasion to deceive or to defraud others, either intentionally or unintentionally; and when he departs to the world below he is not in any apprehension about offerings due to the gods or debts which he owes to men. Now to this peace of mind the possession of wealth greatly contributes; and therefore I say, that, setting one thing against another, of the many advantages which wealth has to give, to a man of sense this is in my opinion the greatest.

Well said, Cephalus, I replied; but as concerning justice, what is it?– to speak the truth and to pay your debts–no more than this? And even to this are there not exceptions? Suppose that a friend when in his right mind has deposited arms with me and he asks for them when he is not in his right mind, ought I to give them back to him?

No one would say that I ought or that I should be right in doing so, any more than they would say that I ought always to speak the truth to one who is in his condition.

You are quite right, he replied.

But then, I said, speaking the truth and paying your debts is not a correct definition of justice.

Quite correct, Socrates, if Simonides is to be believed, said Polemarchus interposing. I fear, said Cephalus that I must go now, for I have to look after the sacrifices, and I hand over the argument to Polemarchus and the company.

Is not Polemarchus your heir? I said.

To be sure, he answered, and went away laughing to the sacrifices.

Tell me then, O thou heir of the argument, what did Simonides say, and according to you truly say, about justice?

He said that the repayment of a debt is just, and in saying so he appears to me to be right. I should be sorry to doubt the word of such a wise and inspired man, but his meaning, though probably clear to you, is the reverse of clear to me. For he certainly does not mean, as we were just now saying, that I ought to return a deposit of arms or of anything else to one who asks for it when he is not in his right senses; and yet a deposit cannot be denied to be a debt.

True.

Then when the person who asks me is not in his right mind I am by no means to make the return?

Certainly not. When Simonides said that the repayment of a debt was justice, he did not mean to include that case? Certainly not; for he thinks that a friend ought always to do good to a friend and never evil. You mean that the return of a deposit of gold which is to the injury of the receiver, if the two parties are friends, is not the repayment of a debt,– that is what you would imagine him to say?

Yes.

And are enemies also to receive what we owe to them?

To be sure, he said, they are to receive what we owe them, and an enemy, as I take it, owes to an enemy that which is due or proper to him– that is to say, evil. Simonides, then, after the manner of poets, would seem to have spoken darkly of the nature of justice; for he really meant to say that justice is the giving to each man what is proper to him, and this he termed a debt.

That must have been his meaning, he said.

By heaven! I replied; and if we asked him what due or proper thing is given by medicine, and to whom, what answer do you think that he would make to us?

He would surely reply that medicine gives drugs and meat and drink to human bodies.

And what due or proper thing is given by cookery, and to what?

Seasoning to food.

And what is that which justice gives, and to whom?

If, Socrates, we are to be guided at all by the analogy of the preceding instances, then justice is the art which gives good to friends and evil to enemies.

That is his meaning then?

I think so.

And who is best able to do good to his friends and evil to his enemies in time of sickness?

The physician.

Or when they are on a voyage, amid the perils of the sea?

The pilot.

And in what sort of actions or with a view to what result is the just man most able to do harm to his enemy and good to his friend? In going to war against the one and in making alliances with the other. But when a man is well, my dear Polemarchus, there is no need of a physician?

No.

And he who is not on a voyage has no need of a pilot?

No.

Then in time of peace justice will be of no use? I am very far from thinking so.

You think that justice may be of use in peace as well as in war?

Yes.

Like husbandry for the acquisition of corn?

Yes.

Or like shoemaking for the acquisition of shoes,–that is what you mean?

Yes.

And what similar use or power of acquisition has justice in time of peace?

In contracts, Socrates, justice is of use.

And by contracts you mean partnerships?

Exactly.

But is the just man or the skilful player a more useful and better partner at a game of draughts?

The skilful player.

And in the laying of bricks and stones is the just man a more useful or better partner than the builder?

Quite the reverse.

Then in what sort of partnership is the just man a better partner than the harpplayer, as in playing the harp the harp-player is certainly a better partner than the just man? In a money partnership.

Yes, Polemarchus, but surely not in the use of money; for you do not want a just man to be your counsellor in the purchase or sale of a horse; a man who is knowing about horses would be better for that, would he not?

Certainly.

And when you want to buy a ship, the shipwright or the pilot would be better?

True.

Then what is that joint use of silver or gold in which the just man is to be preferred?

When you want a deposit to be kept safely.

You mean when money is not wanted, but allowed to lie?

Precisely.

That is to say, justice is useful when money is useless?

That is the inference.

And when you want to keep a pruning-hook safe, then justice is useful to the individual and to the state; but when you want to use it, then the art of the vine-dresser?

Clearly.

And when you want to keep a shield or a lyre, and not to use them, you would say that justice is useful; but when you want to use them, then the art of the soldier or of the musician?

Certainly.

And so of all other things;–justice is useful when they are useless, and useless when they are useful?

That is the inference. Then justice is not good for much. But let us consider this further point: Is not he who can best strike a blow in a boxing match or in any kind of fighting best able to ward off a blow?

Certainly.

And he who is most skilful in preventing or escaping from a disease is best able to create one?

True.

And he is the best guard of a camp who is best able to steal a march upon the enemy?

Certainly.

Then he who is a good keeper of anything is also a good thief?

That, I suppose, is to be inferred.

Then if the just man is good at keeping money, he is good at stealing it.

That is implied in the argument.

Then after all the just man has turned out to be a thief. And this is a lesson which I suspect you must have learnt out of Homer; for he, speaking of Autolycus, the maternal grandfather of Odysseus, who is a favourite of his, affirms that 'He was excellent above all men in theft and perjury.' And so, you and Homer and Simonides are agreed that justice is an art of theft; to be practised however 'for the good of friends and for the harm of enemies,'– that was what you were saying?

No, certainly not that, though I do not now know what I did say; but I still stand by the latter words.

Well, there is another question: By friends and enemies do we mean those who are so really, or only in seeming?

Surely, he said, a man may be expected to love those whom he thinks good, and to hate those whom he thinks evil.

Yes, but do not persons often err about good and evil: many who are not good seem to be so, and conversely?

That is true.

Then to them the good will be enemies and the evil will be their friends? True.

And in that case they will be right in doing good to the evil and evil to the good?

Clearly.

But the good are just and would not do an injustice?

True.

Then according to your argument it is just to injure those who do no wrong?

Nay, Socrates; the doctrine is immoral.

Then I suppose that we ought to do good to the just and harm to the unjust?

I like that better.

But see the consequence:–Many a man who is ignorant of human nature has friends who are bad friends, and in that case he ought to do harm to them; and he has good enemies whom he ought to benefit; but, if so, we shall be saying the very opposite of that which we affirmed to be the meaning of Simonides.

Very true, he said: and I think that we had better correct an error into which we seem to have fallen in the use of the words 'friend' and 'enemy.'

What was the error, Polemarchus? I asked.

We assumed that he is a friend who seems to be or who is thought good.

And how is the error to be corrected?

We should rather say that he is a friend who is, as well as seems, good; and that he who seems only, and is not good, only seems to be and is not a friend; and of an enemy the same may be said.

You would argue that the good are our friends and the bad our enemies?

Yes.

And instead of saying simply as we did at first, that it is just to do good to our friends and harm to our enemies, we should further say: It is just to do good to our friends when they are good and harm to our enemies when they are evil?

Yes, that appears to me to be the truth. But ought the just to injure any one at all?

Undoubtedly he ought to injure those who are both wicked and his enemies.

When horses are injured, are they improved or deteriorated?

The latter.

Deteriorated, that is to say, in the good qualities of horses, not of dogs?

Yes, of horses.

And dogs are deteriorated in the good qualities of dogs, and not of horses?

Of course.

And will not men who are injured be deteriorated in that which is the proper virtue of man?

Certainly.

And that human virtue is justice?

To be sure.

Then men who are injured are of necessity made unjust?

That is the result. But can the musician by his art make men unmusical?

Certainly not.

Or the horseman by his art make them bad horsemen?

Impossible.

And can the just by justice make men unjust, or speaking generally, can the good by virtue make them bad?

Assuredly not.

Any more than heat can produce cold?

It cannot.

Or drought moisture?

Clearly not.

Nor can the good harm anyone?

Impossible.

And the just is the good?

Certainly.

Then to injure a friend or anyone else is not the act of a just man, but of the opposite, who is the unjust?

I think that what you say is quite true, Socrates.

Then if a man says that justice consists in the repayment of debts, and that good is the debt which a just man owes to his friends, and evil the debt which he owes to his enemies,–to say this is not wise; for it is not true, if, as has been clearly shown, the injuring of another can be in no case just.

I agree with you, said Polemarchus.

Then you and I are prepared to take up arms against anyone who attributes such a saying to Simonides or Bias or Pittacus, or any other wise man or seer?

I am quite ready to do battle at your side, he said.

Shall I tell you whose I believe the saying to be?

Whose?

I believe that Periander or Perdiccas or Xerxes or Ismenias the Theban, or some other rich and mighty man, who had a great opinion of his own power, was the first to say that justice is 'doing good to your friends and harm to your enemies.'

Most true, he said.

Yes, I said; but if this definition of justice also breaks down, what other can be offered?

Several times in the course of the discussion Thrasymachus had made an attempt to get the argument into his own hands, and had been put down by the rest of the company, who wanted to hear the end. But when Polemarchus and I had done speaking and there was a pause, he could no longer hold his peace; and, gathering himself up, he came at us like a wild beast, seeking to devour us. We were quite panic-stricken at the sight of him. He roared out to the whole company: What folly, Socrates, has taken possession of you all? And why, sillybillies, do you knock under to one another? I say that if you want really to know what justice is, you should not only ask but answer, and you should not seek honour to yourself from the refutation of an opponent, but have your own answer; for there is many a one who can ask and cannot answer. And now I will not have you say that justice is duty or advantage or profit or gain or interest, for this sort of nonsense will not do for me; I must have clearness and accuracy.

I was panic-stricken at his words, and could not look at him without trembling. Indeed I believe that if I had not fixed my eye upon him, I should have been struck dumb: but when I saw his fury rising, I looked at him first, and was therefore able to reply to him. Thrasymachus, I said, with a quiver, don't be hard upon us. Polemarchus and I may have been guilty of a little mistake in the argument, but I can assure you that the error was not intentional. If we were seeking for a piece of gold, you would not imagine that we were 'knocking under to one another,' and so losing our chance of finding it. And why, when we are seeking for justice, a thing more precious than many pieces of gold, do you say that we are weakly yielding to one another and not doing our utmost to get at the truth? Nay, my good friend, we are most willing and anxious to do so, but the fact is that we cannot. And if so, you people who know all things should pity us and not be angry with us.

How characteristic of Socrates! he replied, with a bitter laugh;–that's your ironical style! Did I not foresee–have I not already told you, that whatever he was asked he would refuse to answer, and try irony or any other shuffle, in order that he might avoid answering?

You are a philosopher, Thrasymachus, I replied, and well know that if you ask a person what numbers make up twelve, taking care to prohibit him whom you ask from answering twice six, or three times four, or six times two, or four times three, 'for this sort of nonsense will not do for me,'–then obviously, if that is your way of putting the question, no one can answer you. But suppose that he were to retort, 'Thrasymachus, what do you mean? If one of these numbers which you interdict be the true answer to the question, am I falsely to say some other number which is not the right one?–is that your meaning?'–How would you answer him?

Just as if the two cases were at all alike! he said.

Why should they not be? I replied; and even if they are not, but only appear to be so to the person who is asked, ought he not to say what he thinks, whether you and I forbid him or not?

I presume then that you are going to make one of the interdicted answers.

I dare say that I may, notwithstanding the danger, if upon reflection I approve of any of them.

But what if I give you an answer about justice other and better, he said, than any of these? What do you deserve to have done to you?

Done to me!–as becomes the ignorant, I must learn from the wise–that is what I deserve to have done to me.

What and no payment! A pleasant notion!

I will pay when I have the money, I replied.

But you have, Socrates, said Glaucon: and you, Thrasymachus, need be under no anxiety about money, for we will all make a contribution for Socrates.

Yes, he replied, and then Socrates will do as he always does–refuse to answer himself, but take and pull to pieces the answer of someone else.

Why, my good friend, I said, how can any one answer who knows, and says that he knows, just nothing; and who, even if he has some faint notions of his own, is told by a man of authority not to utter them? The natural thing is, that the speaker should be someone like yourself who professes to know and can tell what he knows. Will you then kindly answer, for the edification of the company and of myself? Glaucon and the rest of the company joined in my request, and Thrasymachus, as any one might see, was in reality eager to speak; for he thought that he had an excellent answer, and would distinguish himself. But at first he affected to insist on my answering; at length he consented to begin. Behold, he said, the wisdom of Socrates; he refuses to teach himself, and goes about learning of others, to whom he never even says Thank you. That I learn of others, I replied, is quite true; but that I am ungrateful I wholly deny. Money I have none, and therefore I pay in praise, which is all I have; and how ready I am to praise anyone who appears to me to speak well you will very soon find out when you answer; for I expect that you will answer well.

Listen, then, he said; I proclaim that justice is nothing else than the interest of the stronger. And now why do you not praise me? But of course you won't.

Let me first understand you, I replied. Justice, as you say, is the interest of the stronger. What, Thrasymachus, is the meaning of this? You cannot mean to say that because Polydamas, the pancratiast, is stronger than we are, and finds the eating of beef conducive to his bodily strength, that to eat beef is therefore equally for our good who are weaker than he is, and right and just for us?

That's abominable of you, Socrates; you take the words in the sense which is most damaging to the argument.

Not at all, my good sir, I said; I am trying to understand them; and I wish that you would be a little clearer.

Well, he said, have you never heard that forms of government differ; there are tyrannies, and there are democracies, and there are aristocracies?

Yes, I know.

And the government is the ruling power in each state?

Certainly.

And the different forms of government make laws democratical, aristocratical, tyrannical, with a view to their several interests; and these laws, which are made by them for their own interests, are the justice which they deliver to their subjects, and him who transgresses them they punish as a breaker of the law, and unjust. And that is what I mean when I say that in all states there is the same principle of justice, which is the interest of the government; and as the government must be supposed to have power,

> the only reasonable conclusion is, that everywhere there is one principle of justice, which is the interest of the stronger.
>
> Now I understand you, I said; and whether you are right or not I will try to discover. But let me remark, that in defining justice you have yourself used the word 'interest' which you forbade me to use. It is true, however, that in your definition the words 'of the stronger' are added.
>
> A small addition, you must allow, he said.
>
> Great or small, never mind about that: we must first enquire whether what you are saying is the truth. Now we are both agreed that justice is interest of some sort, but you go on to say 'of the stronger'; about this addition I am not so sure, and must therefore consider further.[33]

The above should also be the intention of the United Nations Charter, which should further consider the function of justice and injustice in connection with various interests of the states parties, and the intentions behind the founding of the institution. It is not without reason that Articles 1(2) and (3) of the Charter state that the intentions of the United Nations are, inter alia, "to develop friendly relations among nations based on respect for the principle of equal rights and self-determination of peoples." The intention is also "to achieve international co-operation in solving international problems of an economic, social, cultural, or humanitarian character, and in promoting and encouraging respect for human rights and for fundamental freedoms for all without distinction as to race, sex, language, or religion." Thus, the Charter provides that the respect of justice, equality, and peace are superior to any other principles. The United Nations "Organization is based on the principle of the sovereign equality of all its Members"[34] and the element of non-discrimination in the observance of international human rights law is reaffirmed in Articles 13(1)(b), 55(c) and 76(c).

Thus, the Charter gives appropriate weight to the definition of justice, and prohibits the violation of this important principle. It is for this reason that the Charter testifies to the fact that international peace and security

---

[33] Plato, Republic, pp.180-190. Available online at http://www.literaturepage.com/read/therepublic-34.html.

[34] Article 2(1).

depend largely on "universal respect for, and observance of, human rights and fundamental freedoms for all without distinction as to race, sex, language, or religion."[35] In other words, human rights principles should not only be respected by all members of the UN, but should also serve to protect non-members as well because human rights principles are universal.

For instance, if the Russians had completely occupied Finland during the Second World War and integrated it into the Union of Soviet Socialist Republics' territories and it remained so until today, the position of the Finnish population would not have been different from its current iteration. The international legal personality of Finland would have been the same as before occupation, even though the resolutions of the Security Council of the United Nations would have been blocked by the USSR,[36] China, Cuba, North Korea, and others.

The members of the international community would reject any occupation of Finland by any country of the world, including the USSR, based on international law. There would be strong protests against any governmental decisions which violated the self-determination, or the independence of the Finnish population and the integrity of their territories. Swedish experts would not only support this theory based on human rights law, but the Swedish government would do the same.[37] It would also be very surprising to see Sweden claiming any right over Norwegian territories. Thus, I am insisting that we have a great responsibility to the populations of occupied countries whose territories have been seized by one or several members of the United Nations.

---

[35] Article 55 (c).

[36] The USSS was established in 1922 and dissolved officially in 1991, but practically its political position stopped in 1989.

[37] More obviously and theoretically, if any part of Finnish territories would have been separated from it by use of force and would have been annexed by the USSR, the only government, which would have had the right to legitimize it, was the Finnish government itself and not any other state of the world, even the United Nations Organization. Similar basic philosophy can be expressed about the Palestinian population territories. See Alan Hart available online at www.alanhart.net/zionism-open-letter-to-british-conservative-party-leader-david-cameron/.

13. FACING JUSTICE

The notion of justice is one of the most significant moral and political notions ever to be discussed in the history of human civilisation. The term "justice" originates from the word "jus," which implies the notion of law. The word justice has been used to evaluate our conducts and actions, and thus we categorize people, governments, entities, and international decisions as just or unjust. The same terms are used when discussing the decisions of international organisations such as the various bodies of the United Nations, namely the Security Council.

Thus, when one considers the nature of justice, or the content of a UN resolution, one considers not only the provisions and principles within it, but whether or not those provisions have moral or political aspects. Still, the notion of politic is itself evaluated again with the very significant term "morality." Thus, justice is bound with the notion of morality. The definition of morality is not very straightforward as it depends on the context of the case. However, the general understanding of the term refers to a desirable quality of cultural understanding of human essence, human virtue, human protection, and the humanisation of inhumane actions that have been committed against victims by another political party. If you kill a spider in your garden at home, you may not consider it as a generally unjust act, even though it could be considered as such when you looked at the case from the point of view of the respect for natural life and animals.

Consequently, protecting certain species of animals is fair conduct, and the destruction of their environment may certainly be considered as unjust. Humans continue to destroy these environments, despite understanding that what we are doing is unjust and unfair. Obviously, justice has not only a moral virtue, but also a collective one. This means that we react to certain matters that are against our collective interest. Thus, even if a person's unjust actions may not directly harm us, we may still protest, because such unjust conduct should never be carried out against anyone. Similar duties exist regarding unlawful and discriminatory conducts carried out against the individuals of other nations, in particular those in occupied countries. The prohibition of discrimination is based on the high value of equality between different *races, sexes, languages, and religions* proscribed in the Charter of the United Nations. The theories within in the Universal Declaration of Human Rights and the Convention on the Prevention and Punishment of the Crime of Genocide in 1948 demonstrate the importance of the recognition, identification, and consolidation of the principle of equality.

Article 1 of the Universal Declaration proclaims, "All human beings are born free and equal in dignity and rights." According to the provisions of Article 2, everyone is entitled to all the rights and freedoms set forth in the Declaration

> without distinction of any kind, such as race, colour, sex, language, religion, political or other opinion, national or social origin, property, birth or other status. Furthermore, no distinction shall be made on the basis of the political, jurisdictional or international status of the country or territory to which a person belongs, whether it be independent, trust, non-self-governing or under any other limitation of sovereignty.

Article 7 of the Declaration also concerns equal rights for all individuals and maintains that "All are equal before the law and are entitled without any discrimination to equal protection of the law. All are entitled to equal protection against any discrimination in violation of this Declaration and against any incitement to such discrimination." Furthermore, this significant right of equality is strengthened by the provisions of Article 2 of Universal Declaration which prohibits "*distinctions of any kind,*" that is, any inequality. This means that racism cannot be legally tolerated, and that the United Nations Security Council is responsible for protecting the rights of all individuals and populations of all countries, even those who are not members.

Various provisions of international conventions protect the right to equality and to freedom from discrimination. A clear example of this are the provisions of the International Covenant on Civil and Political Rights. Article 2(1) states that each State party: "undertakes to respect and to ensure to all individuals within its territory and subject to its jurisdiction the rights recognized in the present Covenant, without distinction of any kind, such as race, colour, sex, language, religion, political or other opinion, national or social origin, property, birth or other status." Article 26 of the Covenant serves as the basis for protection against discrimination under the legal body of the Covenant. It reads,

> All persons are equal before the law and are entitled without any discrimination to the equal protection of the law. In this respect, the law shall prohibit any discrimination and guarantee to all persons equal and effective protection against discrimination on any ground such as race, colour, sex, language, religion, political or other opinion, national or social origin, property, birth or other status.

In particular, Article 26 provides "an autonomous right" of equality and "prohibits discrimination in law or in fact in any field regulated and protected by public authorities." Article 20(2) obliges States parties to criminalize any "advocacy of national, racial or religious hatred that constitutes incitement to discrimination, hostility or violence." This means that the Covenant also protects the rights of self-determination, of independence, and the legal personality of states. Thus, states should not violate the territorial integrity of states, which is an integral part of self-determination.

14. Morally Correct Justice

When we witness grave crimes, we should react in defence of our own rights, own moral standards, and our own social standards. This implies the way in which we see the ethical and social decision-making. Similarly, we apply this form of judgment to the value of the moral standard of punishment, disobedience, equality between races, right to property, to the enslavement of human beings, and all matters concerning the international humanitarian law of armed conflicts. We should not forget the fact that the whole idea behind the recognition of core international crimes in the statute of the International Criminal Court is grounded it moral philosophy.

There are certain principles that should not be violated by any person or authority no matter what. That is why we say that justice is not for sale and that justice should not be traded through occupation, or the use of military force. That is why Kant compared the terms "moral" and "moral duties," both of which are based on the principle of "ought to." According to Kant, it is actually the universal principle of 'right' which pushes us towards a correct notion of justice or the fulfilment of the concept of morality. According to this philosophy, any action is able to be considered as 'right', if it can coexist with each individual freedom, and does not violate the freedom of others. The concept of justice is thus a reciprocal duty which has to be respected by all. Even so, unilateral intimidation cannot supply a genuine and lawful basis for the enforcement of rights.

Philosophers of law, moral ethics, and of natural/positive law are surely aware of the fact that the virtue of love for justice, love for humanity, love for peace, and love for the eradication of radical evil has to be the model of humanity we practice– if injustice is not going to be the decision-maker of international relations. I will demonstrate here that the pure, sheer love for justice is the only principle that can prevent injustice, and injustice is the only toxin which stimulates the propensity to express radical innate evil in human nature and in the nature of the United Nations Charter. As Kant purported, we must treat our human mentality and freedom properly.[38] Kant went further and illustrated that:

> now a unilateral will cannot serve as a coercive law for everyone with regard to possession that is external and therefore contingent, since that would infringe upon freedom in accordance with universal laws. Therefore, it is only a will putting everyone under obligation, hence only a collective general (common) and powerful will that can provide everyone with this assurance. However, the condition of being under a general

---

[38] Malekian, *The Mirage of International Criminal Law*, note 9, pp.82-83. Henry Allison, *Kant's Theory of Freedom* (Cambridge University Press, 1990), 2-3, 11-12; Sharon Anderson-Gold, *Unnecessary Evil: History and Moral Progress in the Philosophy of Immanuel Kant* (SUNY Press, 2001), 15-17.

> external (i.e., public) lawgiving accompanied with power is the civil condition. So only in a civil condition can something external be mine or yours.

Therefore, the will of the society or international society to make just decisions and promote rights is called *justice*. As we saw, the justice supposedly exercised by Germany against the Jews was not correct, and similarly we can see that the humiliating framework of justice used by Israel regarding the Palestinians violates all conceptions of justice. However, this is not our core discussion. There is more to justice than this. Kant has properly asserted that:

> A man reduced to despair by a series of misfortunes feels wearied of life, but is still so far in possession of his reason that he can ask himself whether it would not be contrary to his duty to himself to take his own life. Now he inquires whether the maxim of his action could become a universal law of nature. His maxim is: "From self-love I adopt it as a principle to shorten my life when its longer duration is likely to bring more evil than satisfaction." It is asked then simply whether this principle founded on self-love can become a universal law of nature. Now we see at once that a system of nature of which it should be a law to destroy life by means of the very feeling whose special nature it is to impel to the improvement of life would contradict itself and, therefore, could not exist as a system of nature; hence that maxim cannot possibly exist as a universal law of nature and, consequently, would be wholly inconsistent with the supreme principle of all duty.[39]

[39] Immanuel Kant, *Fundamental Principles of the Metaphysic of Morals, 1724-1804. Available online at https://ebooks.adelaide.edu.au/k/kant/immanuel/k16prm/chapter2.html.*

Chapter 2

Crimes of Justice

1. Ridding the Stem of Membership

The Crimes of Jerusalem: The Lord spoke to me. "Mortal man," he said, "are you ready to judge the city that is full of murderers? Make clear to her all the disgusting things she has done. Tell the city what I, the Sovereign Lord, am saying: Because you have murdered so many of your own people and have defiled yourself by worshiping idols, your time is coming. You are guilty of those murders and are defiled by the idols you made, and so your day is coming, your time is up! That is why I have let the nations make fun of you and all the countries sneer at you. Countries nearby and countries far away sneer at you because of your lawlessness. All Israel's leaders trust in their own strength and commit murder. None of you in the city honours your parents. You cheat foreigners and take advantage of widows and orphans. You have no respect for the holy places, and you don't keep the Sabbath. Some of your people tell lies about others in order to have them put to death. Some of them eat sacrifices offered to idols. Some are always satisfying their lusts. Some of them sleep with their father's wife. Some force women to have intercourse with them during their period. Some commit adultery, and others seduce their daughters-in-law or their half sisters. Some of your people murder for pay. Some charge interest on the loans they make to other Israelites and get rich by taking advantage of them. They have forgotten me." The Sovereign Lord has

> spoken. "I will bring my fist down on your robberies and murders. Do you think you will have any courage left or have strength enough to lift your hand when I am finished with you? I, the Lord, have spoken, and I keep my word. I will scatter your people to every country and nation and will put an end to your evil actions. And so the other nations will dishonour you, but you will know that I am the Lord."[40]

For decades the Palestinian population has struggled to establish an independent, sovereign state in the West Bank (including East Jerusalem and the Gaza Strip), which has been occupied by the Israeli armed forces since the Six-Day War in 1967.[41] In 1993, with the continuous support of Norway, the Palestine Liberation Organization (PLO) and Israel signed the Oslo Accord. In this accord, both sides agreed to mutual recognition. However, since then, no specific settlement has been reached between the two conflicting parties-- actually on the contrary as the Palestinians have been the target of heavy military attacks by the Israeli armed forces.

Among the various moves made by the PLO, was their move to request *membership to the United Nations Educational, Scientific and Cultural Organization (UNESCO)* in 2011. A vote was carried out regarding this request. It is interesting to note that 107 states parties voted in favour of Palestine's request,[42] 52 countries abstained, and 14 states voted against Palestinian membership, namely: the United States of America, Canada, Germany, Sweden,[43] Australia, Czech Republic, Israel, Lithuania, the Netherlands, Palau, Panama, Samoa, the Solomon Islands, and Vanuatu.

The question is, how could these governments vote against Palestinian membership in UNESCO when they claimed to work for national, regional, and international democracy? This claim of democracy was even enhanced by their motto of protecting human rights principles for the global equality of humankind. It is not hard to see how the policy of Germany has evolved

---

[40] https://biblehub.com/gnt/ezekiel/22.htm.

[41] Farhad Malekian, 'Judging International Criminal Justice in the Occupied Territories,' 12 *International Criminal Law Review* (2012), 827–869.

[42] In addition, 21 states could not vote because their membership fees were not paid.

[43] The other states which voted against were Australia, Czech Republic, Israel, Lithuania, the Netherlands, Palau, Panama, Samoa, Solomon Islands, and Vanuatu.

since 1939, and how the German government has followed the policy of give and take at regional and international political tables. It is also not hard to understand why the Swedish government, who laundered money to the Nazis during the Second World War, and who betrayed the innocent Jews, would reject Palestine's membership, thus diminishing the value of the struggle of the Palestinian population for self-determination and independence. Nor is it irrelevant to mention that quite a large number of Swedes were working either directly or indirectly in Adolf Hitler's criminal system.[44]

It is not important to which degree different states prevented Palestine's membership in UNESCO, but that it demonstrates how we modify the history of suffering nations to favour the strong. To impute an act to any government is to say that the relevant government is the origin and executor of said act. That is, no state is responsible for the acts of those who voted against membership, except those states themselves. Here, we are not focusing on the United States of America, or Canada themselves, but on the fact that they have always taken the side of Israel for the protection of economic interests. However, we also call into question the policy of the other countries which voted against Palestinian membership.

Human rights law must be respected at all times, and democratic rules have to be given priority in all situations, even when justice is manipulated by political parties. Thus, the cause of an international criminal conduct may include factors which are related to the context of international politics within which the decisions were made. A state is obviously responsible for

---

[44] Although one may not make any claim against the humanitarian assistance which was granted to the Jews at the end of the war, the question remains as to why the Swedish government helped indirectly in the process of the genocide of innocent Jews during the war. It was not by accident that Hans Göran Person the Prime Minster of Sweden (1996-2006) stated clearly in Gothenburg, in his apology speech to the Jews of Europe, that the Swedish government very regretfully acknowledged the collaboration of the Swedish government with the Nazis during the Second World War. Some of the classic crimes recognized by the Nuremberg Tribunal against accused persons were war crimes, crimes against peace, and crimes against humanity. Of course, the integration of these three categories of crimes could lead to the chief crime against the Jews, namely genocide. However, the Major German War Criminals were not punished according to the Convention of Genocide because the Convention did not exist as it was formulated in 1948. Many crimes in Europe committed by the Germans were identified in other countries in this year as well.

acts and decisions which have been carried out by false interpretation or tactics. We are not condemning the decision of relevant states, but rather are highlighting the fact that they are responsible for their decisions which they made freely and willingly.

2. Committing Injustice

Although we are aware that many governments have modified their positions to be in favour of Palestine that may still not be enough. The parallel question is whether the vetoes of 31 October 2011 by governments such as those of the United States of America, Canada, Sweden, Australia, Czech Republic, Israel, Lithuania, the Netherlands, Palau, Panama, Samoa, the Solomon Islands, and Vanuatu, harmed the political situation of the Palestinians. Additionally, one cannot help but wonder if the vetoes did not help in the continuation of brutal crimes against humanity and war crimes in the Gaza Strip, including those which occurred in 2014.

One should not disregard the fact that permission for the commission of international crimes is always expressed indirectly rather than directly. Furthermore, it is doubtful that governments plan to explain their negative votes against Palestinian membership to UNESCO, which has led to the total occupation of Jerusalem. Of course, this is not the case, since full recognition of the Palestinian population would first have to be carried out and be recognised by the United Nations, and future governments would have to accept the responsibility of their predecessors for their role in the destruction of the Palestinian state.

It would also be relevant to know whether governments are up-to-date concerning the development of international rules, and in particular concerning the resolutions of the General Assembly or the Security Council. Alternatively, the question would be whether governments intentionally decided against certain very vital questions relating to the existence of the Palestinian population. For instance, the United Nations Security Council

Resolution 478,[45] with fourteen votes for to none against (with the abstention of the United States), officially condemned the Israeli government's claim concerning the annexation of East Jerusalem from the West Bank and recognized the annexation as invalid.[46]

This resolution put forward the most significant views of the United Nations. It reads:

> The Security Council,
>
> Recalling its resolution 476 (1980),
>
> Reaffirming again that the acquisition of territory by force is inadmissible,
>
> Deeply concerned over the enactment of a "basic law" in the Israeli Knesset proclaiming a change in the character and status of the Holy City of Jerusalem, with its implications for peace and security,
>
> Noting that Israel has not complied with resolution 476 (1980),
>
> Reaffirming its determination to examine practical ways and means, in accordance with the relevant provisions of the Charter of the United Nations, to secure the full implementation of its resolution 476 (1980), in the event of non-compliance by Israel,
>
> 1. Censures in the strongest terms the enactment by Israel of the "basic law" on Jerusalem and the refusal to comply with relevant Security Council resolutions;
>
> 2. Affirms that the enactment of the "basic law" by Israel constitutes a violation of international law and does not affect the continued application of the Geneva Convention relative to the Protection of Civilian Persons in Time of War, of 12 August 1949, in the Palestinian and other Arab territories occupied since June 1967, including Jerusalem;
>
> 3. Determines that all legislative and administrative measures and actions taken by Israel, the occupying Power, which have altered or purport to alter the character and status of the Holy City of Jerusalem, and in particular the recent "basic law" on Jerusalem, are null and void and must be rescinded forthwith;

---

[45] Resolution 478 was adopted on 20 August 1980.

[46] The resolution became the reason that states having embassies in Jerusalem relocated their embassies to other cities.

4. Affirms also that this action constitutes a serious obstruction to achieving a comprehensive, just and lasting peace in the Middle East;

5. Decides not to recognize the "basic law" and such other actions by Israel that, as a result of this law, seek to alter the character and status of Jerusalem and calls upon:

(a) All Member States to accept this decision;

(b) Those States that have established diplomatic missions at Jerusalem to withdraw such missions from the Holy City;

6. Requests the Secretary-General to report to the Security Council on the implementation of the present resolution before 15 November 1980;

7. Decides to remain seized of this serious situation.

Adopted at the 2245th meeting by 14 votes to none, with 1 abstention (United States of America).

3. Illegal Annexation

East Jerusalem has been and will remain forever the capital of Palestinians population. The annexation of East Jerusalem was protested against by most states in the world. According to the Security Council, the annexation violated elements of international law and international human rights law. Therefore, the question is whether or not the governments which voted against Palestine's membership had examined all aspects of the Palestinian case, the relevant resolutions, and many other vital questions of justice before deciding on their negative vote, thereby leaving a problem unsolved and indirectly ignoring the rights of the Palestinians. Today such policy is very controversial and thoughtlessly harmful to the philosophy of justice and humanity.

States that were not actively contributing to the humiliation of the rights of the Palestinians, such as Sweden, should have been informed by their experts on international law and international relations about the judgements of the advisory opinion of the International Court of Justice and Resolution 478. The ICJ declared that all states were under an internationally recognized *obligation* to not take actions which may be interpreted as accepting the illegal and immoral situation in and around East Jerusalem. Here we are focusing on the apartheid, or racial segregation wall there.[47] According to the advisory statement, the Israeli authorities had not only gravely infringed upon international human rights law, but also needed to be held responsible for the reparation of all consequent damages.[48]

It is of high importance to note here the letter of the Republic of Guinea addressed to the International Court of Justice.[49] It reads:

> Referring to the Order issued on 19 December 2003 entitled "Legal Consequences of the Construction of a Wall in the Occupied Palestinian Territory" and pursuant to Article 66, paragraph 2, of the Statute of the International Court of Justice, I have the honour to inform you, on the orders of my Government, as follows:
>
> Israel's construction of the separation wall in the occupied Palestinian territory, which is at odds with the relevant resolutions of the Security Council and General Assembly of the United Nations, is an illegal measure under international law.
>
> Far from satisfying the need for security of the Israeli populations, the continued construction of this wall leads to reinforcing the feelings of frustration and hate of the put-upon Palestinian populations and, by extension, to deepening the lack of understanding between the two parties. It imperils the very core of the painstakingly negotiated Road Map of the Quartet, whose implementation is just beginning.
>
> There should be no doubt that the sole purpose in constructing this separation barrier, whose route cuts seriously and deeply into Palestinian territories, is to pursue, by pernicious means, the settlement of the occupied territory and to deprive the Palestinian people of a territorial element that is essential to the full exercise of its sovereignty. It is the expression of a policy known as "bantustanization," whose objective is to create enclaves that are not viable, thus denying any freedom of movement to the

---

[47] Zwelivelile Mandela says Israeli apartheid is the worst form of apartheid ever witnessed https://www.aljazeera.com/news/2019/07/nelson-mandela-grandson-slams-israeli-apartheid-190707053146087.html.

[48] *Legal Consequences of the Construction of a Wall in the Occupied Palestinian Territory, International Court of Justice Advisory Opinion*, 9 July 2004, para.163.

[49] Letter to the President of the Court from the Permanent Representative of the Republic of Guinea to the United Nations dated 15 January 2004.

> Palestinian people and robbing it of the most fertile and most productive lands, for the sole benefit of the Israeli occupier.
>
> This is an enterprise doomed to failure, being counter to elementary standards of international law, human rights and humanitarian law and intends to undermine the very basis of the peace process in the Middle East. It clearly runs counter to historical development and to the universally accepted vision of two States, Palestinian and Israeli, living side by side, within secure and internationally recognized borders. Worse, it is the most flagrant manifestation of the denial to the Palestinian people of the exercise of their right to full sovereignty within the framework of an independent, free and viable State.
>
> Confident in the foregoing, the Republic of Guinea, committed to defending the legitimate rights of the Palestinian people, unequivocally condemns the ongoing construction of the separation wall. It urges the Israeli Government to demonstrate common sense by immediately ending this deplorable practice and by restoring to the Palestinian people the territories arbitrarily confiscated from them, which would be the sign of a greater readiness to contribute to a just and lasting solution to the crisis in the Middle East.
>
> Accordingly, the Republic of Guinea reiterates its support for the application of resolution A/RES/ES-10/14 adopted on 8 December 2003 by the Resumed Tenth Emergency Special Session of the United Nations General Assembly on the illegal Israeli actions in Occupied East Jerusalem and the rest of the Occupied Palestinian Territory. It joins the many peace-loving nations of the world in requesting the International Court of Justice urgently to render an advisory opinion on the consequences arising under international law from the construction by the Israeli Government of the separation wall in the occupied Palestinian territory.[50]

This apartheid system is planned by the Israeli governments and is assisted by the United States Presidents as well as the United Kingdom prime ministers like David Cameron or Boris Johnson and some authoritarian Arab states such as Saudi Arabia, United Arab Emeritus as well as Egypt. Just recently, a new deal for the ethnic cleansing of Palestine and violations of international criminal justice has been again announced

---

[50] https://www.icj-cij.org/en/case/13.

between Israel and the United Arab Emeritus called by the United States president "Huge breakthrough" and a "Historic Peace Agreement between our two Great friends." Rashida Tlaib, an American politician and Lawyer responses this aggressive apartheid system by asserting that "We won't be fooled by another Trump/Netanyahu deal.[51] We won't celebrate Netanyahu for not stealing land he already controls in exchange for a sweetheart business deal. The heart of the issue has never been planned, formal annexation, but ongoing, devastating apartheid."[52] The statement above certainly keeps its objectivity which means the concept of truth independent from her subjectivity. It is not caused by her personal emotions nor her perception. It is the face of legal truth in international criminal law and international criminal justice.

4. The Policy of Non-Completion

One cannot deny the fact that the states which voted against the membership of Palestine in the United Nations (2011) such as the governments of the United States of America, Canada, Sweden, Australia, Czech Republic, Israel, Lithuania, the Netherlands, Palau, Panama, Samoa, and the Solomon Islands, had surely already read and understood the judgment of the Permanent International Court. But to what extent, if at all, the opinion of the Court in The Hague played a role in their decision varies from state to state and is not entirely clear, since even if governments put faith in the opinion, they may still have considered its recommendations to be non-compulsory.

---

[51] The six-member Gulf Cooperation Council (GCC) or shall to say, the allied states working side by side of the United States, the United Kingdom and the Israeli governments, are some other serious problems endangering the Palestinian population. GCC consists of Bahrain, Kuwait, Oman, Qatar, Saudi Arabia, and the United Arab Emeritus. They are in the rank of Jordan, and Egypt. The authorities in these states are similar to a Saddam Hussein dictatorship.

[52] https://theglobepost.com/2020/08/14/israel-uae-ties/.

For instance, it is documented that the Swedish government has, on several occasions, received warnings concerning their policy of non-fulfilment concerning their international obligations, such as in the European Court of Justice. Sweden has even avoided incorporating the International Convention on the Rights of the Child and its protocols into their domestic legislation. They are still reluctant to incorporate it, even after the advice received from the Commission of Human Rights.[53] Their argument is that the state of the rights of the child in Swedish legislation is preferable and sufficient.[54] Our argument is more or less the same concerning other governments. The question is therefore, if the situation was the other way around, how we would proceed? That is if Palestine was in the position of Israel and vice versa, would those governments have acted towards Israel in the same way they did towards Palestine? Although this question may seem difficult to answer, the fact is that none of those big powers would let Palestine occupy the territories of Israel, because they supported the creation of Israel at the expense of the destruction of Palestine.

However, there are cases which demonstrate the non-completion of the Convention on the Children Rights by the Swedish government. This non-completion of the provisions of the Convention should also be designated in connection with their voting policy against the rights of children in the Gaza Strip. According to the reports of international organizations such as Human Rights Watch, over 1,550 people were killed in the attack on Gaza in 2008, including several hundred children. In fact, supporting the International Humanitarian Law of Armed Conflict originated from the provisions of the four Geneva Conventions of 1949, their Protocols of 1977, and many other international instruments is a duty of all states. The merit of these instruments should not be ignored by any state due to their hidden political laundering.

---

[53] However, slow movements are happening.

[54] Kerstin Nordlöf, *The Sovereignty of Children in Law in* Farhad Malekian & Kerstin Nordlöf, *Sovereignty of Children in Law* (Cambridge Scholars Publishing, 2012), p.62. However, some modifications have been adopted. Malekian, *International Criminal Law of Children*, note 6.

5. Promoting Injustice

Promoting injustice occurs when we know that certain acts are wrong, but we still adopt policy which violates the principles of international law, including international human rights law. In particular, here we are speaking about the system of international criminal law and the core crimes as identified by the international criminal court, the merit of which are significant and should not be violated in any case. The members of the United Nations, in particular those governments which present themselves as neutral states, must be aware of their particularly sensitive duties.[55] According to a consolidated principle of international customary law, states have duties towards the international legal and political community as a whole, including the ratification of the most significant international treaties. According to the Report of the United Nations Fact Finding Mission on the Gaza Conflict, all the aforementioned conventions were gravely violated in 2008 in the Gaza Strip by the Israeli armed forces, which would have been common knowledge for governments when they voted against the membership of Palestine in UNESCO in 2011.[56] These governments should have known that the Israeli authorities could interpret their vote as an indirect endorsement of the criminal activities in the Gaza Strip. In addition, the Reporter of the United Nations Report, Richard Goldstone, was widely acclaimed by the public of some of those countries which voted against the membership of Palestine in 2011. Hanan Ashrawi summarised the world policy by saying that, "We are the only people on Earth asked to guarantee the security of our occupier...while Israel is the only country that calls for defence from its victims."

Do governments respect the system of international law at all? The fact that the governments of the world are silent concerning Palestine requires further inquiry. Similar questions would be raised if the situation were the other way around. *Here, I am not simply protecting a Muslim population, if*

---

[55] *Examine* DeAnna Emerson, Mars/Earth Enigma: A Sacred Message to Mankind (1996), 238; Hans *Blix*, *Sovereignty, Aggression and Neutrality* (1970).

[56] For the report, see Report of the United Nations Fact Finding Mission on the Gaza Conflict, A/HRC/12/48, 15 September 2009.

the Palestinians were Jewish or had no faith at all, my arguments would remain the same. Thus, the question is not about religion, but rather about the ethics of law and legal order. If we say that the rules of law are rules of law, then they have to apply to every nation, both large and small. It is indeed very critical to note that governments do nothing for the Palestinian population. When one examines the provisions of Article 8 of the Statute of the International Criminal Court (ICC) governing war crimes or other core crimes in other relevant articles of the Statute, one sees the fact that these provisions have been gravely violated in the territories of the Gaza Strip. Concerning human rights in Palestine Richard Falk states:

> In the face of the unequivocal opinion of the International Court of Justice, and of General Assembly resolution ES-10/15, in which the Assembly called on Israel to comply with the advisory opinion, Israel has defiantly acted as if international law and international judicial authority has no bearing on its policies and behaviour. With the tenth anniversary of the advisory opinion approaching, it is time again to examine what legitimate action by the international community can be taken to achieve compliance with international law, as set out by the International Court of Justice. It is often supposed that because the legal findings of the Court were embedded in an "advisory opinion" it has no bearing on the status of the legal obligations of Israel.[57]

Why can our governments not agree that the wilful killing of civilians or the wilful causing of great suffering or serious injury are serious crimes? The widespread destruction and appropriation of properties, which were not justified by military necessity and were carried out illegally and wantonly, are sufficient to convince any government to call for the protection of the rights of the victims. Moreover, it should be clear to the decision makers and government experts that many of the principles of the Statute of the ICC were seriously violated in the Gaza Strip, as indicated in the UN Report.[58]

---

[57] Report of the Special Rapporteur on the situation of human rights in the Palestinian territories occupied since 1967. United Nations, General Assembly, A/HRC/25/67 (13 January 2014).

[58] Article 8 of the Statute of the ICC. John Dugard, 'Lifting the Guise of Occupation and Recourse to Action before the ICJ and ICC', Palestine Yearbook of International Law, Vol. 17, 2013–

6. VIOLATING *PACTA SUNT SERVANDA*

The decision by governments to ratify the Statute of the ICC was a significant step towards the improvement of the world of justice. In particular, the voting record clearly shows that certain governments are entirely opposed to war crimes, crimes against humanity, genocide, and 'aggression'. States examined the positions of all these crimes in a Review Conference that took place in Kampala, Uganda in June 2010. Moreover, the attribution of international criminal responsibility to the perpetrators of the crime of aggression may soon become one of the significant duties of the Court.

This means that governments, with their participation in the Review Conference and ratification of the Statute of the ICC in its very early stage of formulation, proved that they would not allow injustice and the ignorance of the law by certain states, entities, or individuals, and would give priority to the rules of law and work to prevent impunity. Those governments believed, and still believe, in the fulfilment of the principle of *pacta sunt servanda*--a basic element of civil and international law. This principle encourages all state parties to international agreements, conventions, declarations, pacts, treaties, covenants, protocols, or statutes, to fulfil the given provisions in the given international agreement. This even includes certain resolutions of the Security Council and the General Assembly which concern certain significant matters regarding international negotiations.

The principle of *pacta sunt servanda* specifically promotes the understanding of international obligations with good faith, good action, and good deeds. However, what 'good faith' refers to, and its legal, moral and political interpretation depends on the context of the given case. The scope of the definition of the principle should not be violated deliberately through aggression. In other words, the chief merit of this principle is to grant rights to the right people and to establish an arbitration method that relies upon appropriate legal and moral strength. Such moral and legal grounding results

---

14, pp.9–27; Jacob Haas De, *History Of Palestine - The Last Two Thousand Years* (USA: Macmillan, 1934).

in something positive--a democratic foundation for our decisions, which prevents us from making any unjustified, immoral, or unfair judgements. In addition, use of the term 'good faith' increases the basic understanding of decisions and their eventual results. This means that with the use of the term 'good faith' we are not only seeking to find legal support, but also moral support for our decisions. In other words, the term 'good faith' relates to the love for justice, and not only for the truth, but the naked truth.

This principle of *pacta sunt servanda* also implies that a person or an authority who makes a decision has, more or less, met their obligations in a given situation. Moreover, the term 'good faith' serves as the basis for most decisions, and without this, the value of decisions decreases and becomes invalid. When we refer to the decision of a judge or the judgement of a tribunal, we automatically assume that the decision or the judgement was written with honest intentions, and that all circumstances surrounding the case had been examined using the principles of good faith and fairness,[59] which constitute some of the significant sources of international law. The question therefore is, how could the states which ratified the Convention on Genocide then turn a blind eye to the serious issues and human rights violations in places such as Palestine, Afghanistan, Libya, Iraq, Sudan, North Korea, and even now in Yemen?

Therefore, the decision of any government to vote against the membership of the Palestinian population in UNESCO violated the principles of proportionality, fairness, objectivity, neutrality, humanity, *pacta sunt servanda*, and democracy, as well as the principle of universal morality. This is the morality which limits all decisions, conducts, and acts which violate the essence of the existing rights of man-- the fundamental natural rights. According to this principle, one has to make good decisions which propel the international community in the right direction. The principle therefore openly criticizes certain unlawful and immoral monopolisations in the international community.[60] In addition, we also have

---

[59] Farhad Malekian, 'The Principle of Good Faith within the Sources of International Criminal Law', *Retfaerd, Nordisk Juridisk Tidsskrift,* 131, nr.4 – årgang 33 (2010) pp. 41-65.

[60] Consult Farhad Malekian, *The Monopolization of International Criminal Law in the United Nations, A Jurisprudential Approach* (Almqvist & Wiksell International, 2nd ed., 1995).

the principle of self-determination which consists of several elements: *opposition, denunciation, support, mediation, liberation, and freedom*.

For instance, the Swedish Prime Minister Palme strongly opposed the European communist regimes by calling them the "diktaturenskreatur" or the "cattle of dictatorship" in 1975. He positioned himself against the Franco Regime in Spain and denounced the regime as "satansmördare," meaning "devilish murderers," following the executions of Euskadi Ta Askatasuna (Basque Homeland and Freedom) and Frente Revolucionario Antifascista y Patriota (Revolutionary Antifascist Patriotic Front) in 1975. Furthermore, Palme demanded economic sanctions against South Africa in response to their prolong apartheid system, calling it "*a particularly horrific system,*" as well as also politically and financially supporting the African National Congress.

Palme also politically and financially supported the Frente Farabundo Martípara la Liberación Nacional (Farabundo Martí National Liberation Front) in El Salvador, and the *Frente Sandinista de Liberación Nacional* (Sandinista National Liberation Front) in Nicaragua in the 1980s, and opposed the dictatorial Pinochet regime in Chile. In addition to all this, he also denounced Fulgencio Batista's government and supported Cuban and Cambodian revolutionaries. Palme's policy also criticised the Soviet Union's actions against the Prague Spring liberalization movements in Czechoslovakia in 1968 and the United States' prolonged genocide activities during the Vietnam War from 1955 to 1975. He also protested the proliferation of nuclear weapons around the globe, and became a mediator for the Iran-Iraq War. Once again, Palme politically and financially supported the Palestine Liberation Organization (PLO). These conducts and decisions from Swedish Prime Minister required *difficult* political and economic decisions, which cannot be denied by any realistic political party.[61] It is of the utmost importance to remember that the Prime Minister of the United Kingdom, Margaret Thatcher, called the ANC and PLO

[61] It could not have been an accident when the Swedish government decided to establish a professorship in honour of its Prime Minister, Olof Palme, which is awarded each year to those who are working towards peaceful solutions.

terrorists organisations, which demonstrated her complicity in the criminal conducts of South African and Israeli governments.

7. Violation of Chief Principles

Any decision of UN members which rejects the membership of Palestine certainly violates the principles of the United Nations regarding the maintenance of justice. This may also be called the principle of *Ubuntu* which comes from the African traditional moral belief implying justice for all, humanity for all, humanness for all nations, including respect in our quest for spiritual transcendence. Moreover, we cannot separate the rights of nations from membership. As a matter of fact, the notion of membership of all nations in the United Nations is a necessary condition for the development of the organisation. This means that the well-being of the United Nations organisation is profoundly tied to the well-being of all nations of the world. One of these nations is the Palestinian population.

The membership of states in the United Nations is based on respect of the rights of other nations, the politicians of a state, governments of states, and the representative of states, which must, although free to make independent political decisions, adhere to certain rules and principles. These are rules which are tied to the basic structure of the organisation, the respect of which are essential for maintaining the legal and political personality of the organisation. These principles include membership of new states, peaceful settlement of international disputes, justice for all states, and the respect of the provisions of International Covenant on Civil and Political Rights. No decision should violate these provisions or the following rights:

i. All peoples have the right to self-determination
ii. Each party is responsible for ensuring that all individuals have access to all rights in the Covenant
iii. Equal civil and political rights for men and women
iv. No derogation from essential natural rights of man

v. Protection of customary rights and freedoms
vi. Every human being has the inherent right to life
vii. The right to not be subjected to torture or to cruel, inhumane, or degrading treatment or punishment
viii. The right not to be forced into slavery
ix. Everyone has the right to liberty and to security of person
x. *1x)* The right to be treated humanely and with full integrity
xi. The right not to be imprisoned for contractual obligations
xii. The right to freedom of movement and choice of residence
xiii. The right to not be arbitrary expelled
xiv. The right to a fair and public hearing
xv. Guarantee for the non-application of retroactive law
xvi. The right to recognition as a person before the law
xvii. The right to privacy, honour, and reputation
xviii. The right to freedom of thought, conscience, and religion
xix. The right to liberty of opinion and freedom of expression
xx. The prohibition of propaganda for war and hatred constituting incitement
xxi. The right to peacefully assemble
xxii. The right to freedom of association
xxiii. The right to marry and found a family
xxiv. The rights of the child
xxv. Political rights
xxvi. The right to equality before the law
xxvii. The rights of ethnic, religious or linguistic minorities
xxviii. The rights to access Human Rights Committee[62]

8. Powerless Prosecutors

The point here is that the majority of governments were silent during the Gaza War, and while observing other inhumane actions committed against

[62] Article 1-28.

the Palestinians, they still did not actively support the rights of the children in the Gaza Strip. All these grave criminal acts were carried out by two respected governments, both of which are the members of the United Nations. How can the children of Palestine be attacked with unlawful weapons without protest, but when attacks are carried out against certain European cities and a few innocent people are killed, we take many measures and condemn every Arab or Muslim person for the crimes of one person. Do the children of European states have a higher value than the children of Palestine? Many prosecutors are certainly responsible for the killing of children in Palestine. However, many of them deny the fact that they have the power to initiate criminal proceedings against the criminal conducts which have been systematically committed against Palestine. For instance, the international Office of the Prosecutor intentionally denied a request for investigation into international crimes in the Gaza Strip. Similarly, the vice Chief Prosecutor of the International Prosecutor's Office in Stockholm, Katarina Johansson Welin clarified tactfully and very cautiously, that the political position of the case and the control of national and international criminal law by the Swedish government did not allow them to initiate a case against actions taken in the Gaza Strip. The nature of her words is illustrated with the following:

> ... Application orients itself against representatives of the Israeli state. The application is thus addressed against persons who have committed crimes while acting in an office or appointment that includes their position in another state. In such a situation, the legislature believes that prosecution appointment is a right for the (Swedish) government, as formulated in Chapter 2, para.7 a of the Penal Code. It is a question of difficult assessments of both international law and foreign political nature.
>
> A prosecution appointment applies though formally only the issue of appointment on-going investigation. The issue of prosecution appointment is of paramount importance in determining whether preliminary investigation to begin, because the investigation is not something initiated or conducted unless the conditions for prosecution exist. In my opinion, it is not likely that the prosecution appointment will be submitted. On that basis, nor shall commence investigation.

> In view of the above, I summarize the following:
>
> Preliminary investigation should not be led. There are formal barriers to the prosecution of the notified offense. Indictment Appointment of government cannot be counted upon.[63]

The purpose of the Swedish International Prosecutor's Office is not clear to us. If the Swedish Prosecutor is not responsible for the investigation of various international cases brought before them, then what is the purpose of international criminal justice? If the principles of justice have received a different interpretation of their basic values in Sweden or in any other country, which does not correspond to the international standard, then the question arises, what is the purpose behind ratifying international human rights law conventions in the first place? I am specifically speaking about governments which are proud to be one of the permanent members of the European Union or who are active members of the European Union and supposedly support the advancement of human rights law.

9. Ignoring the UN's Report

As mentioned in the above sub-section, the Swedish policy, along with the policies of many other states, were undoubtedly in opposition to the findings of the Report of the United Nations Fact Finding Mission on the Gaza Conflict from 2009. The United Nations report vividly emphasised that, "the actions of the Government of Israel might justify a competent court finding that crimes against humanity have been committed."[64] In the *Drazen Erdemovic* case, the Trial Chamber of the ICTY described crimes against humanity as 'very grave crimes' or as violations of the collective consciousness of the human community as a whole. This means that any

---

[63] Angående anmälan om brott på Gaza (0300-K 2557-09), Åklagarmyndigheten, Internationella åklagarkammaren Stockholm, Katarina Johansson Welin (2009-01-28). Katarina Johansson Welin Prosecution Authority, International Public Prosecution Office Stockholm, 2009-01-28. (Addressed to the Institute of International Criminal Law, Uppsala, Sweden).

[64] Report of the United Nations Fact Finding Mission on the Gaza Conflict, A/HRC/12/48, 15 September 2009, paras.75 and 1329.

nation of the world, including Sweden, should understand that certain serious crimes, which have been committed by the Israeli government during the occupation of Palestine, require, at the very least, sympathy and empathy as demonstrated by supporting Palestine's membership in UNESCO. How the Chamber of the ICTY could understand what is meant by crimes against humanity, but the Swedish government and its experts in international law, and human rights law could not, is indeed a very demanding question.[65]

The Trial Chamber of the ICTY demonstrated that crimes against humanity "transcend the individual because when the individual is assaulted, humanity comes under attack and is negated. It is therefore the concept of humanity as victim which essentially characterises crimes against humanity."[66] It may not be far off to interpret this statement of the Chamber as a guideline to appreciate the principles of humanity, and as a call to not violate the rights of others through assault, negotiation, or unilateral decisions. The reason behind this is that all these conducts go beyond normal decisions when certain vital questions of justice and humanity are in play.

Thus, the Chamber sought to draw attention to the fact that the integrity of people is able to be violated by legal and political authorities. This means that the Chamber compels all legal persons and government authorities to understand that war crimes and crimes against humanity are very serious crimes which should be prevented at all costs. In other words, governments should not make decisions which in the end permit the occurrence of crimes against humanity.

10. Violation of Litigations

A considerable number of international criminal courts such as the International Criminal Tribunal in Nuremberg, the ICTY, the ICTR, the ICCSL, the ICC and many others, for instance, the Extraordinary Chambers in the Courts of Cambodia known also as Khmer Rouge Tribunal were and

---

[65] *Drazen Erdemovic*, Sentencing and Judgement, 29 November 1996, paras.27-28.
[66] *Id.*

are created in order to protect human beings and their civilizations. Furthermore, the provisions of modern international courts do not encourage the non-protection of victims or protection of the offenders, as any non-protection of victims is simultaneously accompanied by serious infringements of their rights. One of the main reasons for the quick destruction of the Gaza Strip in 2008, was that the government of the United States, under President George W. Bush, did not condemn the attack for the first two weeks, and remained silent. It was as a result of this policy of silence that over 550 children were killed. Elizabeth Wilmshurst, the Deputy Legal Adviser at the Foreign and Commonwealth Office of the United Kingdom asserted that:

> resolution had introduced an enhanced inspection regime to give Iraq a final opportunity to comply with its obligations; it stated that reports of non-compliance by Iraq would be referred to the Security Council for assessment. 'Assessment' did not mean merely an inconclusive discussion in the Council. The decision that Iraq had failed to take its final opportunity was to be one for the Council and not simply for individual governments."[67]

She went further and elucidated the task of the norms of the body of international law by stating:

> I regarded the invasion of Iraq as illegal, and I therefore did not feel able to continue in my post. I would have been required to support and maintain the Government's position in international fora. The rules of international law on the use of force by States are at the heart of international law. Collective security, as opposed to unilateral military action, is a central purpose of the Charter of the United Nations. Acting contrary to the Charter, as I perceived the Government to be doing, would have the consequence of *damaging the United Kingdom's reputation as a*

[67] Italics mine. Her work with the British government started on the eve of invasion of Iraq in 2003. Available online at www.iraqinquiry.org.uk/media/43474/wilmshurst-statement.pdf.

State committed to the rule of law in international relations and to the United Nations.[68]

According to an official examination by an Italian laboratory, the chemical weapons which were used in the Gaza Strip were similar to those which were used during the Iraq War by the United States armed forces.[69] Of course, of the fact that the United States violated international law, and in particular the principles of the United Nations Charter with due regard to their responsibility in the Security Council for the maintenance of peace and justice, was, and is nothing new. The United States has demonstrated through various international actions and decisions that they always have, and will continue to support the Israeli military and political policy regarding the occupied territories.

Although one cannot deny the fact that the United States has often played the role of mediator in the Arab-Israeli conflict, they have done so in order to support Israeli political interests, without due regard for the rights of the occupied Palestinian population. The actions of the United States in the General Assembly and in the Security Council have been identified as a misuse of power by the "big nations."[70] Similar sentiment can be expressed concerning the policy of the US in the Security Council, and particularly in the General Assembly, regarding the resolutions condemning *apartheid* in South Africa in the early decades of the Organization. It is also true that three of the major powers which continually hindered and vetoed economic sanctions against the South African *apartheid* regime were the United States, the United Kingdom, and Israel. These countries called the ANC and the PLO terrorist organisations, while they were themselves supporting and implementing state terrorism.

---

[68] *Id.* See aslo Malekian, *Condemning the Use of Force in the Gulf Crisis,* note 28.
[69] Andrew J. Bacevich, *America's War for the Greater Middle East* (Random House, 2017).
[70] See Georg Schwarzenberger, *The Frontiers of International Law* (Stevens & Sons, Ltd, 1962).

11. Legalising the Illegal

If a few members of the United Nations have decided to side with the United States and not recognise Palestine or its international legal personality, this does not mean that other states should also follow suit and block the Palestinian's inalienable right to self-determination.[71] One should remember that according to the provisions of the United Nations Charter, that all members of the organization have certain conventional duties for the establishment of peace, justice, equality, and security. Therefore, the violation of international rules by some offending states does not grant the right to complicity for other states. The concept of international legal personality and statehood do not disappear during an occupation.[72]

The following principles of the United Nations are obviously very important and should not be violated by any state. These include: saving successive generations from the scourge of war, and reaffirming faith in fundamental human rights, in the dignity and the worth of people, and in the equal rights of men and women and of nations both large and small. This list is also accompanied by other core principles such as those which establish conditions under which justice and respect for the obligations arising from treaties and other sources of international law can be maintained, and which promote social progress and better standards of life in larger freedom. Therefore, the governments of the world should be aware of the fact that by supporting PLO membership to UNESCO, they both directly and indirectly cooperate with providing justice for the Palestinian population. Therefore, states should avoid voting against the principle of equal rights and the self-determination of peoples.[73]

It is therefore very problematic to assert that the decisions or policies of governments to maintain close relations with the Israeli government are not

---

[71] But see *also* Alain Pellet, 'The Palestinian Declaration and the Jurisdiction of the International Criminal Court,' *Journal of International Criminal Justice* 2010, 8 (4), 981-999; John Quigley, 'The Palestine Declaration to the International Criminal Court: The Statehood Issue,' in: *Rutgers Law Record*, 35 (2009).

[72] Consult James Crawford, *The Creation of States in International Law* (Oxford University Press, 2006).

[73] Article 1.

harmful to the process of ending of occupation. We are morally forced to analyse what is behind the mask of injustice, if our intention is to achieve justice. Overall, the issue of Palestine's UNESCO membership concerns the very significant principle of the Charter governing the subject of self-determination. This implies the fact that the occupation is unjust and violates the Jewish principle of respect.

In fact,

> Kavod habriot is the Jewish principle that requires we accord every one of God's creatures a level of dignity. Traditionally, this principle has been applied to all human beings although some have extended it to the animal kingdom as well. Long before western society embraced the concept of universal human rights, Judaism taught that every person – Jew and gentile, male and female, rich and poor – deserves to be treated with respect.

The prophet Jeremiah stated that the House of the Lord and the land of Israel is reserved for people who follow a certain ethical course of action in their lives and: "If you execute justice between one person and another, if you do not oppress the stranger, the orphan and the widow, if you do not shed the blood of the innocent, if you do not follow other Gods...then will I let you dwell in the land which I gave to your fathers for all time."[74]

Moreover, the very significant principle of the Charter governing the matter of self-determination is an integral part of positive cooperation, mutual understanding, and multilateral necessity in the system of international law. We should not put aside the fact that the modern system of international law is based on eliminating colonialism, neocolonialism, and all forms of racial discrimination, as well as on supporting the right to be released from foreign occupation, and the recognition of the dignity of peoples and their right to self-determination. Certainly, it is an established duty of governments to know about this modern philosophy for achieving international peace. They should therefore severely condemn the occupation

---

[74] (Jeremiah 7:5-8). See Rabbi Sid Schwarz, Judaism and Social Justice: Five Core Values from the Rabbinic Tradition, http://www.qscience.com/doi/pdf/10.5339/rels.2012.justice.10.

of Palestinian territories as being a threat to world peace, security, and human morality.

12. MISLEADING *JUS COGENS*

What is significant here is not the negative vote of governments against the independence of Palestine, but the way in which they ignored their international obligations. For instance, a Swedish minister of foreign affairs who was also a Prime Minster from 1991 to 1994, expressed that Sweden would still vote 'no' again if Palestine sought permanent membership in the United Nations as an independent state.[75] He explained that the basic reason for this was that the peace process had not yet been settled in the region. The situation however would have been different if it were the Israeli population asking for full statehood under the provisions of international law. A quick glance at the historical background of Israel's creation speaks for this conclusion.[76] While nothing was official, the statehood of Israel was settled before the paint could even dry on the walls of the newly established UN. It is a historical fact that the state of Israel was created through the use of force with direct assistance from the United States and the United Kingdom, and not through peace processes and negotiations.[77]

The question is how the Swedish government could not realise that working for justice and working to preserve peace, equality, humanity, and security in the world (in particular to release human beings from suffering as a result of armed occupation), constitutes an integral part of *jus cogens* norms today, and therefore is obligatory. *Jus cogens* norms are norms of international law that have achieved a high level of recognition in international relations, and are therefore obligatory for all states to comply with, regardless of their military, political, or economic strength. *Jus cogens* norms are significant for the safeguarding of international peace. They are

---

[75] Carl Bild. Dala-Demokraten, Låt Palestina bli FN-Medlem, 2012, 08, 30.

[76] Farhad Malekian, 'Judging International Criminal Justice in the Occupied Territories,' 12 *International Criminal Law Review* (2012), 827–869.

[77] *Id*. Malekian, *Condemning the Use of Force in the Gulf Crisis*, note 28.

peremptory norms which are vital for the peaceful settlement of international disputes.

Any violation of these norms therefore constitutes a serious violation of international law and calls for the international responsibility of the violating state. In addition, *jus cogens* norms are also accompanied by the principle of *obligatory erga omnes*, which creates an obligation upon states to fulfil the provisions of *jus cogens* law.[78,79]

However, it is possible that a number of governments and their experts in international law and human rights law did not accept that the 2011 decision of their governments to vote against Palestinian membership violated *jus cogens* law. They may argue that a state is not under any obligation to give a positive vote to the position of Palestine, and thus to the creation of its international legal and political personality in the United Nations. This argument is invalid based on the fact that while expressing or not expressing consent under national and international law is a matter of state choice, under jus *cogens* norms, which play a significant role in the establishment of peace and justice, especially when it comes to the question of self-determination, it is not.[80] Therefore, why the governments did not react to violations of international human rights law, the international humanitarian law of armed conflict, or to the recent wars is a question that creates a conundrum for humanity.[81]

13. Impeachable Duties

Without a doubt the 'no' decision of certain governments in 2011 concerning the membership of Palestine in UNESCO was a serious mistake. It went against international political diplomacy, which ought to soon be redressed. The decision also went against a considerable number of

---

[78] *Barcelona Traction*, Light and Power CO. Ltd. (Belg.v.Spain), 1970 I.C.J. 3, 32-33 (Feb. 5).

[79] *Id.*

[80] See Report of the United Nations Fact Finding Mission on the Gaza Conflict, A/HRC/12/48, 15 September 2009.

[81] Jonathan Power, *Conundrums of Humanity: The Quest for Global Justice* (Brill, 2007).

principles of legality and morality. It was an obvious violation of the resolutions of the General Assembly and the resolutions of the Security Council which had attempted to create the state of Israel as well. For instance, one of the states which voted against the membership of the Palestine, was Sweden. There were few other states who had the same attitude and diplomatic policies which violated their international obligations. In other words, states are obliged to fulfil their given international obligations under the Charter of the United Nations with good faith, and to distance themselves from the actions of any state which violate the rights of other nations of the world.

It is the duty of all states to bring international violators under procedure of justice, and to fight against any lawful or unlawful humiliation, discrimination, occupation, apartheid, enslavement, and armed conflicts. It is very important for all states to adopt international policy that does not take the side of states whose language of international diplomacy is the use of force, occupation, injustice, and war.[82] It should be entirely clear to the governments of the world that Israel has engaged in a campaign of ethnic cleansing in Jerusalem by bulldozing Palestinian homes, and also by intentionally destroying and preventing the building of different necessary civilian structures. The Israeli authorities have also continuously built houses and expanded a number of settlements throughout the West Bank.

However, we should remember that it is one of the chief duties of all states to refrain from resorting to the use of force, although this has not been respected. In addition, the Draft Declaration on Rights and Duties of States clearly recognises certain duties for all states that must be respected at all times. The Draft recognises the duty of all states to participate in the peaceful settlement of international disputes. According to Article 1 of the Declaration, "Every State has the right to independence and hence to exercise freely, without dictation by any other State, all its legal powers, including the choice of its own form of government." Article 4 continues, "Every State has the duty to refrain from fomenting civil strife in the territory of another State, and to prevent the organization within its territory of

---

[82] Malekian, *Condemning the Use of Force in the Gulf Crisis*, note 28, pp. 1-10.

activities calculated to foment such civil strife." Additionally, Article 5 of the Draft maintains that every State has the right to equality before the law. These intentions of the Draft are particularly emphasised in the provisions of Articles 9 and 11. The articles read respectively, "Every State has the duty to refrain from resorting to war as an instrument of national policy, and to refrain from the threat or use of force against the territorial integrity or political independence of another State, or in any other manner inconsistent with international law and order," and, "Every State has the duty to refrain from recognizing any territorial acquisition by another State acting in violation of article 9."

The Draft therefore clearly mentions the duties of states in the international community and that they should not engage in intrigues against other states. Moreover, according to the Draft Declaration, which constitutes an integral part of customary international law, each state has the duty to conduct its relations with other states in accordance with the system and principles of international law. It is also the duty of states to respect the core principle of international law. The principle states that sovereignties are subject to the supremacy of the principles, norms, and provisions of the system of international law. It is therefore on these basic grounds that the Palestinian's right to their own territory and sovereignty should not be violated by states, nor by any resolution of the UN Security Council.

14. Injustice by Superior States

On 27 September 2012, Palestine asked for non-Member State status in the General Assembly.[83] This was in response to the rejection of its application for membership in 2011.[84]It was unclear from the beginning whether or not the same governments would again attempt to vote against this proposal, due to the political climate. In November 2012, governments voted in favour of Palestine, and on 30 October 2014 recognised its

---

[83] See the United Nations News Centre, www.un.org/apps/news/story.asp?NewsID=43083&Cr....
[84] *Id.*

statehood. However, the U.N. Security Council rejected a Palestinian resolution calling for an Israeli withdrawal from the occupied West Bank and East Jerusalem and the establishment of a Palestinian state by late 2017. In 2015, 2016 and again in 2018, the policy of the United States towards Palestine was drastically modified.

Regardless of all this, the Palestinian State must be established as a state in order to prevent more injustice, inhumanity, and suffering.[85] Without a doubt, the international legal personality of the state of Palestine is an established historical phenomenon, and this has to be recognised by all states which stand in the way of their legitimate rights. The hope is that states will discover a passion for justice, peace, equality, humanity, and multilateral understanding of the world with the pure theory of bare love for the truth. However, certain states have not understood this, and continue to follow the policies of big political powers. Two states have even unfortunately moved their embassies to occupied Jerusalem, calling it the capital of the state of Israel. Hanan Ashrawi, a senior Palestinian official correctly illustrates that:

> Israeli voters have chosen their representatives. Regrettably, Israelis overwhelmingly voted for candidates that are unequivocally committed to entrenching the status quo of oppression, occupation, annexation and dispossession in Palestine and escalating the assault on Palestinian national and human rights. They have chosen an overwhelmingly rightwing, Xenophobic and anti-Palestinian parliament to represent them. Israelis chose to entrench and expand apartheid.
>
> The extremist and militaristic agenda, led by Benjamin Netanyahu, has been emboldened by the Trump administration's reckless policies and blind support. This cynical alliance against Palestinian rights and the standing of the rules-based international order remains unchallenged by the rest of the international community, thereby reinforcing the rightist and populist agendas.

---

[85] As Ban Ki-moon, the General Secretary of the United Nations demands in the General Assembly: "The two-state solution is the only sustainable option. Yet the door may be closing, for good. The continued growth of Israeli settlements in the occupied Palestinian territory seriously undermines efforts toward peace."

> The Palestinian people will overcome this dark and highly dangerous chapter and remain deeply rooted in our homeland. We are a resilient people and we will persist and forge alliances with like-minded and responsible international actors to create a counterbalance to the dangerous and reckless agenda and its adherence among other racist and fundamentalist governments, particularly in Israel.[86]

Furthermore, "the deal of the century" is another act of humiliation for the Palestinians which supports the continued occupation of Palestine. The deal has been imposed upon the entire nation of Palestine and their territory. It is clear that the deal is not truly a deal, since the term "deal" implies that all parties have expressed clear consent. Thus, these acts which result from the 'deal' should be recognised as creating "*the funeral of the century*" for hope and for the struggle for rights. It should also be called the "*slaughtering of human rights*" as the rights of Palestinians have been decimated. The "*deal of the century*" has rightly been called the "*bluff of the millennium,*"[87] "*the joke of the century,*"[88] and "*the biggest dead deal of the century.*"[89] In reality this deal is a fraud and the world keeps watching the cinema of international criminal justice in silence to protect their own interests, as usual. In addition, the permanent members of the United Nations and their allies such as Israel, Saudi Arabia, the United Arab Emirates, Egypt, Jordan, and Bahrain have been humiliating the provisions of Chapter VII of the UN Charter through their actions/inaction.

The other four permanent members of the Security Council are essentially deadweight, as they have failed to stand up against the monopolisation of rights in the Security Council. The United States has closed the PLO office in Washington, D.C., cut all funding for Palestinian refugees, and moved their Embassy from Tel Aviv to Jerusalem. This action is a crime of crimes, much more brutal than any unlawful use of force.

---

[86] https://www.theguardian.com/world/live/2019/apr/09/israel-election-2019-exit-polls-winner-netanyahu-benny-gantz-latest-live-news-vote-results-today.

[87] https://www.aljazeera.com/indepth/opinion/deal-century-bluff-millennium-200131181206622.html.

[88] https://www.haaretz.com/israel-news/.premium-how-trump-s-deal-of-the-century-became-the-joke-of-the-century-1.8472956.

[89] https://www.youtube.com/watch?v=V6yB8abzaUk.

15. Crucifying Self-Determination

The actions taken by the US concerning Jerusalem marked the end of international criminal law, international criminal justice, international human rights law, and of the political policy of all those who are struggling for the rights of self-determination and equality of arms. Their actions are a disgrace to the system of international criminal justice, and are not welcome within the provisions of international human rights law. Additionally, policies under the Obama administration which led to violations of international criminal justice in Libya and Afghanistan were gross violations of international law. This means that the idiom the devil is in the details is not correct, as it is more accurate to say that *the devil is in the silence of the UN member states.*

A US Senator asserted, "The United States can bring unequalled leadership to resolving the Israeli-Palestinian conflict, but we must use that leadership to promote a just and durable agreement. Any acceptable peace deal must be consistent with international law and multiple UN resolutions."[90] In addition, antecedent "must end the Israeli occupation and enable Palestinian self-determination in an independent state of their own alongside a secure Israel. Trump's so-called 'peace deal' does not come close, and will only perpetuate the conflict. It is unacceptable."[91]

A further complicating factor in this situation is that most Arab states do not have democratic forms of government, and this fact is often exploited to the benefit of the United States and Israel. Although the United Nations has stated that Israeli settlements in Bethlehem and other parts of the occupied West Bank violate the rule of the law, and has called them a "flagrant violation" of international law, Israel and its allies continue to reject the all resolutions of the General Assembly and the Security Council concerning the status of the international legal personality of Palestine.[92] One must not

---

[90] Bernie Sanders.

[91] *Id.*

[92] Zogby recently wrote: "Suffering under Israeli military occupation since 1967, Bethlehem has slowly been strangled. It has lost most of its land to settlement construction. It is hemmed in by a 30-foot-high concrete wall, stripped of its resources, and denied access to external markets. "James J. Zogby, The importance of knowing Bethlehem' *The Jordan Times* (Dec

put aside the fact that regime changes in the Arab world during the Arab Spring were the result of conspiracies carried out by Western intelligence agencies. US intelligence agencies, with compliance from allied states, manipulated fanatic Islamic groups in order to take control of Arab states, ensure the supremacy of Israel over Palestine, and to gain direct access to oil. In addition, a large number of companies around the world are wilfully and knowingly operating their businesses in violation of the system of international criminal law and justice. Article 49 of the Fourth Geneva Convention was adopted to protect civilian populations in war-torn countries. It emphasizes that occupying powers shall not transfer their population to occupied territories. The recently issued UN Human Rights Office's report on business activities related to settlements in the Occupied Palestinian Territory identified such violations. It reads:

> GENEVA (12 February) – The UN Human Rights Office on Wednesday issued a report on business enterprises involved in certain activities relating to settlements in the Occupied Palestinian Territory, in response to a specific request by the UN Human Rights Council, contained in a March 2016 resolution, that mandated the Office to produce a database of business enterprises involved in such activities.[93]
>
> In an interim report (A/HRC/37/39) presented to the Human Rights Council in March 2018 by the then High Commissioner, Zeid Ra'ad Al Hussein, the UN Human Rights Office noted it had reviewed information that was publicly available, or had been received from a variety of sources, about an initial 307 companies. After further research, the total number reviewed increased to 321. Of these, a total of 206 companies were considered for further assessment.

31, 2019), available online at https://www.jordantimes.com/opinion/james-j-zogby/importance-knowing-bethlehem.

[93] Human Rights Council resolution 31/36, adopted on 24 March 2016, requested the Office of the UN High Commissioner for Human Rights to produce a report to follow up on the 2013 report of the Independent International Fact-Finding Mission to investigate the implications of the Israeli settlements on the civil, political, economic, social and cultural rights of the Palestinian people throughout the Occupied Palestinian Territory, including East Jerusalem (A/HRC/22/63). The resolution defined the parameters of the current report by reference to ten specific activities listed in Paragraph 96 of the Fact-Finding Mission's report. Human Rights Council resolution 31/36 was adopted with 32 States in favour, none against and 15 abstentions.

> The report released on Wednesday sets out conclusions following further communications with business entities, as well as a thorough review and assessment of all information available. It identifies 112 business entities which the UN Human Rights Office, on the basis of the information it has gathered, has reasonable grounds to conclude have been involved in one or more of the specific activities referenced in Human Rights Council resolution 31/36.
>
> Of the 112 business entities identified in the report, 94 are domiciled in Israel and 18 in six other States. During the complex process of drawing up the database, the Office consulted the UN Working Group on Business and Human Rights, and held widespread discussions with numerous States, civil society organizations, think tanks, academics and others, as well as having extensive interactions with the companies themselves.
>
> The report makes clear that the reference to these business entities is not, and does not purport to be, a judicial or quasi-judicial process. While the settlements as such are regarded as illegal under international law,[94] this report does not provide a legal characterization of the activities in question, or of business enterprises' involvement in them. Any further steps with respect to the continuation of this mandate will be a matter for the Member States of the Human Rights Council, which will consider the report during the Council's next session, beginning on 24 February.
>
> "I am conscious this issue has been, and will continue to be, highly contentious," said Michelle Bachelet, the current High Commissioner for Human Rights. "However, after an extensive and meticulous review process, we are satisfied this fact-based report reflects the serious consideration that has been given to this unprecedented and highly complex mandate, and that it responds appropriately to the Human Rights Council's request contained in resolution 31/36," Bachelet said.

The Western States constantly lie about the reality of occupations, revolutions, and wars in Arab states in order to maintain their political, economic, and legal advantages in the region. This leads to a game of politics beyond politics without end. Professor Kennedy correctly summarised:

---

[94] Human Rights Council resolution 31/36 recalls reports of the UN Secretary-General, resolutions of the UN General Assembly and Security Council, an advisory opinion of the International Court of Justice and the opinions of several human rights bodies reaffirming the illegality of the Israeli settlements in the Occupied Palestinian Territory, including in East Jerusalem.

In part because my father was murdered by an Arab, I've made an effort to understand the impact of U.S. policy in the Mideast and particularly the factors that sometimes motivate bloodthirsty responses from the Islamic world against our country.

… During the 1950s, President Eisenhower and the Dulles brothers — CIA Director Allen Dulles and Secretary of State John Foster Dulles — rebuffed Soviet treaty proposals to leave the Middle East a neutral zone in the Cold War and let Arabs rule Arabia. Instead, they mounted a clandestine war against Arab nationalism … particularly when Arab self-rule threatened oil concessions. …

The CIA began its active meddling in Syria in 1949. …Syrian patriots had declared war on the Nazis, expelled their Vichy French colonial rulers and crafted a fragile secularist democracy based on the American model. But in March 1949, Syria's democratically elected president, Shukri-al-Quwatli, hesitated to approve the Trans-Arabian Pipeline, an American project … [I]n retaliation … the CIA engineered a coup replacing al-Quwatli with the CIA's handpicked dictator, a convicted swindler named Husni al-Za'im. …

…The Syrian people again tried democracy in 1955, re-electing al-Quwatli and his National Party. Al-Quwatli was still a Cold War neutralist, but, stung by American involvement in his ouster, he now leaned toward the Soviet camp. That posture caused CIA Director Dulles to send his two coup wizards, Kim Roosevelt and Rocky Stone, to Damascus. …

But … CIA money failed to corrupt the Syrian military officers. The soldiers reported the CIA's bribery attempts to the Ba'athist regime. In response, the Syrian army invaded the American Embassy, taking Stone prisoner. After harsh interrogation, Stone made a televised confession of his roles in the Iranian coup and the CIA's aborted attempt to overthrow Syria's legitimate government. The Eisenhower White House hollowly dismissed Stone's confession as "fabrications" and "slanders," a denial swallowed whole by the American press, led by the New York Times and believed by the American people. …

Of course, the Russians, who sell 70 percent of their gas exports to Europe, viewed the Qatar/Turkey pipeline as an existential threat. … In 2009, Assad announced that he would refuse to sign the agreement to allow the pipeline to run through Syria "to protect the interests of our Russian ally."

… Soon after [that] … the CIA began funding opposition groups in Syria. It is important to note that this was well before the Arab Spring-engendered uprising against Assad.

Bashar Assad's family is Alawite, a Muslim sect widely perceived as aligned with the Shiite camp. … Before the war started, according to [journalist Seymour] Hersh, Assad was moving to liberalize the country. … Assad's regime was deliberately secular and Syria was impressively diverse. The Syrian government and military, for example, were 80 percent Sunni. Assad maintained peace among his diverse peoples by a strong, disciplined army loyal to the Assad family, an allegiance secured by a nationally esteemed and highly paid officer corps, a coldly efficient intelligence apparatus and a penchant for brutality that, prior to the war, was rather moderate compared to those of other Mideast leaders, including our current allies. According to Hersh, "He certainly wasn't beheading people every Wednesday like the Saudis do in Mecca."

… By the spring of 2011, there were small, peaceful demonstrations in Damascus against repression by Assad's regime. … However, WikiLeaks cables indicate that the CIA was already on the ground in Syria. …

The idea of fomenting a Sunni-Shiite civil war to weaken the Syrian and Iranian regimes [and thus] to maintain control of the region's petrochemical supplies was not a novel notion. … A damning 2008 Pentagon-funded Rand report … recommended using "covert action, information operations, unconventional warfare" to enforce a "divide and rule" strategy. …

… Two years before ISIL throat cutters stepped on the world stage, a seven-page August 12, 2012, study by the U.S. Defense Intelligence Agency, obtained by the right-wing group Judicial Watch, warned that … "the Salafist, the Muslim Brotherhood and AQI ([Al-Qaeda Iraq,] now ISIS), are the major forces driving the insurgency in Syria."

Using U.S. and Gulf state funding, these groups had turned the peaceful protests against Bashar Assad toward "a clear sectarian (Shiite vs. Sunni) direction." …

Not coincidentally, the regions of Syria occupied by the Islamic State exactly encompass the proposed route of the Qatari pipeline.

… Beginning in 2011, our allies funded the invasion by AQI [Al-Qaeda Iraq] fighters into Syria. In April 2013, having entered Syria, AQI

> changed its name to ISIL. According to Dexter Filkins of the New Yorker, "ISIS is run by a council of former Iraqi generals. ... Many are members of Saddam Hussein's secular Ba'ath Party who converted to radical Islam in American prisons." ...
>
> But then, in 2014, our Sunni proxies horrified the American people by severing heads and driving a million refugees toward Europe. ...[95]

Therefore, the powerful political parties should not demand the virginity of the powerless nations when themselves violate the virginity of justice and humanity through their own international conducts. The court asked the fox: Are there any witnesses who can attest that you did not eat the chicken? Yes, the fox replied. The Court said what the name of the witness was. Very arrogantly, the fox responded: My tail while looking at the members of the jury. If the permanent members of the Security Council or any other member state of the UN wishes to keep the pure philosophy of justice virginal, and demand untainted policy from all members of the organisations, they then need to first establish a virgin policy themselves. If we wish our justice to be virgin, then the judges of the system must be morally pure. With regards to the ICC, it is the prosecutor duty who has to be virgin and not cultivate impunity. In order to determine if international criminal law and international human rights law are pure, one has to examine the virginity of lawyers and the opponents of these legal disciplines. In order to obtain the purity we seek for the system, the big political parties have to stop looting the essence of the law. We are obliged to be watchful; otherwise, we impose tribulation and anguish upon every victim because of the impure virginity of the big political parties, whose actions lead to lawlessness upon lawlessness. Virginity and love should not fall prey to the evil conducts of powerful nations, rather they should be granted to the victims without any bias. Here,

---

[95] Emphasis mine. Robert F. Kennedy, Jr, 'Why the Arabs don't want us in Syria', (March 1, 2016). Available online at website https://www.politico.eu/article/why-the-arabs-dont-want-us-in-syria-mideast-conflict-oil-intervention/. See also Robert Roth, 'What's Really Happening in Syria: Who Started the War, Who Can You Trust to Tell the Truth?', available online at https://www.globalresearch.ca/whats-really-happening-in-syria-who-started-the-war-who-can-you-trust-to-tell-the-truth/5570297.

we are without any hesitation referring to the Palestinian population which is the serious victims of last and the contemporary century.

Chapter 3

The Notion of International Legal Personality

1. The Notion of Personality

The concept of international legal personality (ILP) is both one of the most controversial aspects of public international law, as well as one of the most significant subjects of legal, political, and economic disciplines of the law. Lord McNair compared the treaty-making power of international organizations by asserting that "if fully sovereign States possess a treaty-making power, when acting alone, it is not surprising to find the same power attributed to an international organization which they have created and the members of which are usually sovereign States."

The concept of ILP does not necessarily refer to a certain legal framework, but to the fact that the relationships between certain subjects of public international law have achieved the standard of internationally acceptable legal and political conformity.[96] This is also true concerning the

[96] Farhad Malekian, 'Judging International Criminal Justice in the Occupied Territories,' 12 *International Criminal Law Review* (2012) 827–869; Malekian, 'Emasculating the Philosophy of International Criminal Justice in the Iraqi Special Tribunal,' note 1, pp.673-723, 368; Farhad Malekian, 'Consolidating the International Criminal Law of Children,' 26 (3) *Criminal Law Forum* (2015), 569-593, 592-3; Farhad Malekian, 'The International

international legal personality of certain international organisations. Still, the concept of ILP and its recognition or rejection varies depending upon the legal aspects of different subjects of the law, and depending on the power of constitutions of relevant subject; although the entire concept of a constitution may be more of a *political* consideration than a legal one.[97] For instance, the International Court of Justice, in its advisory opinion regarding its legal capacity in the *Reparations* Case announced:

> In the opinion of the Court, the Organization was intended to exercise and enjoy, and is in fact exercising and enjoying, functions and rights which can only be explained on the basis of the possession of a large measure of international personality and the capacity to operate upon an international plane. It is at present the supreme type of international organization, and it could not carry out the intentions of its founders if it was devoid of international personality. It must be acknowledged that its Members by entrusting certain functions to it with the attendant duties and responsibilities, have clothed it with the competence required to enable those functions to be effectively discharged. Accordingly, the Court has come to the conclusion that the Organization is an international person.[98]

The concept of international legal personality becomes more significant when it comes to the rights of populations which have been the victims of occupation, humiliation, and which have been targeted for eradication by another state.[99] This will be further examined in the following sections.

Criminal Law of Children on War Crimes,' Vol. 13, No. 25 *Prawa Dziecka i Ich Ochrona, Horyzonty Wychowania* (2014), 31-69, 49, 60 and 67; Zaha Hassan, 'The Palestinian Constitution and the Geneva Accord: The Prospects for Palestinian Constitutionalism,' 16 *Florida Journal of International Law*, (2004), 897-924.

[97] Winston P. Nagan & Alitza M. Haddad, 'Recognition of Palestinian Statehood: A Clarification of the Interests of the Concerned Parties', 40 *Georgia Journal of International and Comparative Law*, p.341 (2012), at 344. Available online at http://scholarship.law.ufl.edu/facultypub/590.

[98] Exchange of Greek and Turkish Population Case, PCUI, Series B No.10; Reparation for Injuries Suffered in the Service of the U.N., [1949] I.CJ. Rep. 178.

[99] https://www.facebook.com/QudsN/videos/2097536333656590/; https://www.facebook.com/PsyCoM.M1/videos/vb.198411123523029/1994226047274852/?type=2&theater; https://www.facebook.com/PsyCoM.M1/videos/vb.198411123523029/1926208574076600/?type=2&theater; https://www.facebook.com/ajaquds/videos/vb.203705396659830/788940878103596/?type=2&theater.

2. Subjects of Personality

There are two subjects of public international law which strongly demand the proof of certain ILPs, i.e., states and organisations. Achieving the status of ILP for the latter is much easier than for the former, based on the fact that the ILP of organisations is conventional/constitutional and depends on their provisions in most cases. A clear example of the ILP of an organisation is the permanent International Criminal Court (ICC), which was created by state parties through the adoption of the Statute of the Court. The ICC has a recognised international legal right to conclude international treaties with any state. However, the question of the ILP of states is not conventional, but instead political decisions, and attaining such a level of political relations is primarily a question of give and take.[100] For these reasons, the ILP of a state may be recognised as valid for certain groups of states, but it may not have any legal validity for another group of states.[101] Thus, the recognition of a state's ILP is more of a political decision than a legal one in the end.

3. Criteria of Personality

There are certain criteria in the system of public international law dealing with the question of ILP, and which further strengthen the position of ILP of the relevant state. These are the existence of a territory, historical evidence of a population, a constitution, a political government, and, occasionally, a military force. However, these criteria are subject to litigious judgements from the majority of writers, and the situation depends on along which political lines with the state falls. The intention of this book is not to be a political treatise, rather solely legal one, yet I am also aware of the fact

---

[100] *Id.*, pp. 334-345.

[101] Philip Marshall Brown, 'Editorial Comment: 'The Legal Effects of Recognition', 44 *American Journal of International Law*, 617 (1950), 617.

that the questions of international legal personality in international criminal law are basically the consequence of political assessments.

4. Legal Personality of Palestine

The situation concerning international legal personality becomes much more contentious when it relates to one of the most important ancient subjects of public international law dating from the time of Herodotus, namely the region and the state of Palestine.[102] However, it has been rightly clarified that:

> ... just as a king owes his sovereignty and majesty to no one outside his realm, so he need not obtain the consent and approval of other kings or states, before he may carry himself like a king and be regarded as such.... It would be an injury to the sovereignty of such a king to be called in question by a foreigner.[103]

This means that, through the examination of the question in this book, we are (as usual) insulting the long-established rights of a nation, by merely suggesting that their validity is up for debate.[104]

The question is whether the relevant subject of international law has or has not satisfied the conditions for ILP in agreement with the necessary conditions of the legal discipline. The intention is thus twofold, to assess the matter, and to re-establish the legitimate legal rights of the Palestinian state which have been deliberately humiliated and ignored in international legal and political relations by certain members of the United Nations. In particular, the United States' and the United Kingdom's very close political

---

[102] For an examination of the legal monopolisation of the territories of Palestine, see Farhad Malekian, 'Judging International Criminal Justice in the Occupied Territories,' 12 *International Criminal Law Review* (2012), 827–869.

[103] De Jure Naturae et Gentium Libri Octo (1672) (trans. C. H. and W. A. Old father, 1934), Bk. VII, Ch., 3, para. 690. Cited in James Crawford, 'The Criteria for Statehood in International Law', *British Yearbook of International Law* (1977), 93-182, 96.

[104] Farhad Malekian, 'Judging International Criminal Justice in the Occupied Territories,' 12 *International Criminal Law Review* (2012), 827–869.

and economic ties with Israel have played a very large diplomatic role against the Palestinian population. In this book, we will prove that the Palestinian status constitutes a basic norm of the international law of *jus cogens*, under which the rights are peremptory and should not be denied by any state of the world--including Israel or any international organisation.[105] This book will argue that self-determination, self-implementation, and statehood are the basic rights of the relevant state, and that any other interpretation of the situation amounts to an abuse of the rules of basic human rights law.

5. Establishing Legal Personality

The concept of international legal personality can be traced back to a time in the history of several 'laws of nations', in which there was no concept of public international law. These were the European law of nations, the Indian law of nations, the Persian law of nations, the Egyptian law of nations, and the Islamic law of nations.[106]

It is true that these laws had certain criteria for the interpretation of the legal and political sovereignty of states. However, while there was no discussion of such terminology as the "international legal personality" of a state, the primary subjects of all these laws were states. This meant there were existed essential criteria for the recognition of states. Those being that the state must have a population, a territory, a constitution, military power, and a government, and each of these conditions was strongly connected with the others. Still, it was possible that a state had full sovereign power without necessarily having to have strong military force. A state could secure its territorial independence through acquiring assistance from the military of another state. This also meant that the concept of ILP relied on particular sources of the law.

---

[105] See *infra* section on *Jus Cogens*.

[106] Farhad Malekian, *International Criminal Responsibility of States* (Almqvist & Wiksell International, 1985).

6. Membership in International Organisations

Looking comprehensively at the long history of the wars in Europe from the conclusion of the 1648 Peace of Westphalia up until the Second World War, the sources of ILP were not very complex.[107] Until the beginning of the 18th century, sovereign states alone were recognised as having ILP and consequently, were the only international entities which fulfilled the criteria for ILP. This created rights and obligations for them under the European Law of Nations. This position was not changed until the formation of the League of Nations. Before then, there was not much discussion concerning the *capacity* of individuals, international organisations, and non-state actors. They were of no concern to international law, and the only subject of international law were states which were recognised as having traditional statehood.

However, not all states of the world were eligible to be members of the League of Nations, and the process of membership was very controversial due to several factors including that the League of Nations was an assembly of the big political parties, most other states were not independent, and ultimately their membership was not welcome. Above all, most prerequisite conditions, i.e., elements of human rights, were missing. Due to colonisation, many states of the world had not yet gained their full independence, and therefore had no *capacity* to enter into free international relations, or to conclude treaties for the development of their political positions.[108]

---

[107] Amos S. Hershey, 'History of International Law since the Peace of Westphalia,' *The American Journal of International Law*, Vol. 6, No. 1 (Jan., 1912), pp. 30-69.

[108] League of Nations, 12 August 1922, C. 529. M. 314. 1922. VI., Communiqué au Conseil et aux Membres de la Société, Genève, le 12 août 1922. Mandate for Palestine; Nele Matz, 'Civilization and the Mandate System under the League of Nations as Origin of Trusteeship,' 9 *Max Planck Year Book of United Nations Law*, 47-95 (2005).

7. Breach of Personality

As a rule, European powers had a monopoly on international law, international legal personality, and even on deciding how 'civilised' other nations were Therefore, Oppenheim, the most authoritative European international lawyer of his time, was given the authority to divide states into civilised and uncivilised in his book published just before the Second World War. It might be upon the conclusions drawn by Lutherpath that the United States later requested that there be a certain degree of civilisation required for the recognition of a state. Such a request obviously violates the basic provisions of international human rights law.

Accordingly, "the inhabitants of the territory must have attained a degree of civilization such as to enable them to observe with respect to the outside world those principles of law which are deemed to govern the members of the international society in their relations with each other."[109] *This meant that European states were seen as civilised, and most other states as uncivilised. In other words, states which were engaged in the slave trade, the manufacturing of weapons, the occupation of other territories, the killing of indigenous people, and the monopolisation of other nations were civilised, and nations which did not engage in any of the aforementioned inhumane and unjust conducts were designated as uncivilised.* Thus, civilised states included the likes of the Netherlands, Spain, the United States, the United Kingdom, France, Belgium, Denmark, and many other colonial and imperial powers.

8. Monopolisation of Legal Personality

Throughout the history of international law, there have been different conceptualizations of state-forms, including the full sovereign state, the half-

---

[109] C C. Hyde, *International Law: Chiefly as interpreted and applied by the United States* (Boston, *1947*), Vol. I, p. 23; cf. pp, 127-30; cited in relation to *Indonesia, Whiteman, Digest*, Vol. I, pp, 223-224.

sovereign state, the suzerain state (which exercises political control over another state), and the colony state. The question of the disappearance of the sovereignty of a state was never raised in any of these instances. The legal personality of a state could not be vanquished. It was solely a matter of time, and the monopolization of colonised states by the military power of the strong states. This meant a state could regain its territory through political manoeuvres inside or outside of its territory. In 1948, the United States Military Tribunal in Nuremberg stated the following: "In belligerent occupation this occupying power does not hold enemy territory by virtue of any legal right. On the contrary, it merely exercises a precarious and temporary actual control." This can be seen in Article 42 of the Hague Regulations which grants certain limited rights to a military occupant in enemy territory which is 'actually placed' under their control.[110]

The history of the African continent indicates that a majority of the contemporary African states have recovered their territories from the unlawful occupations by European states. In other words, their ILPs were not eliminated through the act of occupation. This is because an act of occupation is an illegal act and does not create any rights for the occupying power. For example, Palestine has been a sovereign state ever since the end of the Ottoman Mandate, as demonstrated by the British Mandate for Palestine. The Treaty of Versailles states the following:

> Certain communities formerly belonging to the Turkish Empire have reached a stage of development where their existence as independent nations can be provisionally recognised subject to the rendering of administrative advice and assistance by a Mandatory until such time as they are able to stand alone. The wishes of these communities must be a principal consideration in the selection of the Mandatory.[111]

The provisions of the Treaty of Versailles were not respected due to many political considerations including the hunger of the British colonial

---

110 Available online at http://www.nizkor.org/hweb/orgs/german/einsatzgruppen/esg/trials/partisans.html.

111 Article 22.

power. "The fact that statehood was not achieved for the Palestinians could be found in Great Britain's commitment to the Balfour Declaration for the creation of a homeland for the Jewish Diasporas which would occupy the boundaries of the ancient state of Israel."[112] In retrospect, this can be seen in the provisions of the secret Sykes-Picot Agreement of 1916 vis-à-vis the division of the territory between two colonial powers, the UK and France after the collapse of the Ottoman Empire[113] in the Middle East.[114]

9. VIOLATION OF PERSONALITY

The Sykes-Picot Agreement between the United Kingdom and France clearly delineated their respective spheres of control and influence in the Middle East.[115] In traditional international law, the term "the spheres of influence" refers to the special, extraordinary power of one or several states to exercise military, political, juridical, and economic power in a certain region.[116] In addition, the British Balfour Declaration proved that the British diplomatic language was clearly in violation of the provisions of Article 22 of the League of Nations. Balfour,[117] one of the main British destroyers of traditional Palestinian land, confessed that "the weak point of their mutually

[112] Nagan and Haddad, Recognition of Palestinian Statehood: A Clarification of the Interests of the Concerned Parties' note 97, p.349.

[113] Mim Kemal Oke, 'The Ottoman Empire, Zionism and the Question of Palestine,' 14 *International Journal of Middle East Studies*, (1982), 329, at 330.

[114] David Fromkin, *A Peace to End All Peace: The Fall of the Ottoman Empire and the Creation of the Modern Middle East* (Owl Books, United States, 1989), pp. 286, 288.

[115] The agreement stated, "It is agreed that measures to control the importation of arms into the Arab territories will be considered by the two Governments."

[116] Fromkin, note 114.

[117] Mahmoud Abbas, the president of Palestine has announced his intention to sue the government of the United Kingdom over the 1917 Balfour Declaration, which immigrated people to the land of Palestine who had no right to Palestinian territories. Available online at http://gulfnews.com/news/mena/palestine/palestine-to-sue-britain-for-israel-s-creation-1.1868703 and http://ilawyerblog.com/palestine-plans-lawsuit-uk-1917-balfour-declaration/.

agreed position was that in Palestine we deliberately and rightly declined to accept the principal of self-determination."[118] He further asserted that:

> The contradiction between the letters of the Covenant and the policy of the Allies is even more flagrant in the case of the 'independent nation' of Palestine than in that of 'independent nation' of Syria. For in Palestine we do not propose even to go through the form of consulting the wishes of the present inhabitants of the country... [119]

All this was negotiated by the big powers in London and Petrograd, with little value or thought given to the wishes of the economically weak Palestinian population, as more attention and value was given to Jewish interests. In addition, the extermination of the Jews during the Second World War ultimately helped to pave the way for the establishment of a Jewish state.[120] Thus, the Palestinians' right to international legal personality was disregarded as a result of the control of strong colonial forces who were pursuing following their own interests.

It is crucial to mention that the present British authorities and lawyers do not take responsibility for the destruction, humiliation, and killing of thousands of Palestinians which falls on their nation's shoulders. In the history of Palestine, immorality in the present situation is much stronger than the facts and reality. One may draw a similar conclusion about the British complicity in the destruction of Iraq,[121] as well as the United States and the United Kingdom accusing Muslims groups for the orchestrated 11 September attacks.[122]

---

[118] This is a statement between Prime Minister Lloyd and Balfour. A.P. Thornton, *Imperialism in the Twentieth Century* (U of Minnesota Press, *United State,* 1977), p.123.

[119] *John Quigley, The Statehood of Palestine*: *International Law in the Middle East Conflict* (Cambridge University Press, New York, 2010), p.107.

[120] Walter Laqueur, *A History of Zionism: From the French Revolution to the Establishment of the State of Israel* (Schocken Books, United States, 2009); Walter Laqueur, *The History of Zionism* (Schocken Books, United States, 2003).

[121] : Malekian, 'Emasculating the Philosophy of International Criminal Justice in the Iraqi Special Tribunal', note 1, pp.673-723. Search *also* Google relating to the recent confessions by the British Prime Minister concerning his complicity in Iraq.

[122] See the excellent article by Kennedy, Robert F. "*Why the Arabs don't want us in Syria: They don't hate 'our freedoms.' They hate that we've betrayed our ideals in their own countries — for oil.*" Available online at https://www.politico.com/magazine/story/2016/02/rfk-jr-why-

10. Legal Capacity in International Legal Personality

In international law, a sovereign state is a political state entity with an authorised government and a supreme independent power over certain territories. In other words, ILP refers to the legal *capacity* of a state to establish international relations with other states. The concept not only creates rights for the state in question but also duties. This is because the whole system of public international law deals with questions of the legal duties of states towards one another, and towards the international legal and political community as a whole. ILP authorises a state to be a direct member of different international organisations and, consequently, to have voting rights. Thus, when a state wants to become a member of the United Nations or a member of the ICC, it has to apply for membership, and its application may be accepted or rejected, depending on the political situation at the time.

11. Right to Jurisdiction

Eventually, by participating in international legal activities, a state binds itself to certain obligations, thus creating for itself certain rights and duties. Based on this development, Article 1 of the Draft Declaration on Rights and Duties of States formulated by the International Law Commission, with reference to a considerable number of provisions of the Panamanian draft, clarifies the nature of the independent power of the state. It reads, "Every State has the right to independence and hence to exercise freely, without dictation by any other State, all its legal powers, including the choice of its own form of government." This independence means that "Every State has the right to exercise jurisdiction over its territory and over all persons and things therein, subject to the immunities recognized by international law."[123]

arabs-dont-trust-america-213601; Ahmed Al-http://www.politico.eu/article/why-the-arabs-dont-want-us-in-syria-mideast-conflict-oil-intervention/.

[123] Article 7.

The concluding phrase concerns the safeguarding of immunities, such as those for diplomatic officers, including the officials of international entities. These provisions were also derived from the provisions of Article 105 of the Charter of the United Nations.

12. CONSENSUS *FACIT LEGEM*

According to the provisions of the UN Charter, the organisation should not reject an application for membership as any rejection of an application may be regarded as a violation of the UN system, and therefore raises serious moral and legal questions. This is because the system of international law is obliged to make certain serious decisions of essential importance for the immunity of a state, and to not violate its own basic principles. The UN also has similar obligations.[124]

The UN is obliged to respect all member and non-member states, and is also responsible for not violating certain provisions, rules, principles, and norms of international law.[125] This means that since the general body of *jus cogens* law condemns racial discrimination, slavery, colonisation, and occupation, and regards the concept of self-determination as an integral part of peremptory norms, the UN is also obliged to follow suit.[126] More significantly, the permanent members of the United Nations are obliged by the principle of *consensus facit legem* to follow majority decisions made by the body.[127] Otherwise, they would be assisting governments which are committing international crimes, including in occupied territories. The

---

[124] Farhad Malekian, *The Monopolization of International Criminal Law in the United Nations, A Jurisprudential Approach* (Almqvist & Wiksell International, Stockholm, 2nd ed, 1995).

[125] For instance, see H.P. Gasser, 'Ensuring respect for the Geneva Conventions and Protocols: The Role of Third States and the United Nations,' in H. Fox. & M.A. Meyer (eds.), *Armed Conflict and the New Law*, Vol. II, *Effecting Compliance* (The British Institute of International and Comparative Law, London, 1993), pp.15-49.

[126] *Application of the Convention on the Prevention and Punishment of the Crime of Genocide*, (Bosnia-Herzegovina *v.* Yugoslavia) (Preliminary objections), ICJ Reports (1996), 616, para. 31.

[127] The UN is even obliged to respect the judgments of the ICJ, which constitutes one of its organs. *Reservations to the Convention on the Prevention and Punishment of the Crime of Genocide, Advisory Opinion*, ICJ Reports (1951).

International Criminal Court recognizes such omission as active attacks. In the *Akayesu* case, the ICTR clarified that

> the concept of attack may be defined as an unlawful act of the kind enumerated in Article 3(a) to (I) of the Statute, like murder, extermination, enslavement etc. An attack may also be nonviolent in nature, like imposing a system of apartheid, which is declared a crime against humanity in Article 1 of the Apartheid Convention of 1973, or exerting pressure on the population to act in a particular manner, may come under the purview of an attack, if orchestrated on a massive scale or in a systematic manner.[128]

The decisions of the majority not only imply the need for the implementation of the principle of democracy, but also indicate the legal obligation of the permanent members to accept and follow the majority decisions. Were that not the case, then it would be reasonable to imagine that the most powerful states would disregard votes which do not align with their interests. The function of the principle of *consensus facit legem* is to indicate that the consent of the majority effects the final decision of the law, and that the permanent members are obliged to respect only the majority views. However, the practices of the UN since its establishment prove the contrary, and there have always been serious enemies of democratic decisions of the Charter among the United Nations Security Council permanent members.

13. Customary Right

The system of international law is based on rules formulated by states which are found in the content of international treaties or in customary international law. This implies the fact that the states of the world, due to their ILP and sovereign power, are on equal footing in their international relations, and can enter into international treaties with other states. However, this independence of states is not unlimited, therefore states cannot conclude treaties which violate established norms of international law, or *jus cogens*

---

[128] *ICTR-96-4-T,* para. 581.

norms, which prevents certain acts of peremptory nature. The concept of ILP indicates the capacity of states, which is established within a certain framework of public international law and which has been consolidated overtime through international conventions, customary international law, and the general principles of law recognised within, and beyond the civilisation of mankind. Given all this, it logically follows that the rights and duties which international entities have towards the Palestinian state have always existed.

Chapter 4

TRADITIONAL RECOGNITION OF PALESTINE

1. CONSENT TO RECOGNITION

The concept of the international legal personality of a state comes into political consideration and consolidation through acts of recognition.[129] The concept of recognition creates a new political and legal status for a state. Therefore, a state may express its consent concerning the official existence of a new state in the international legal and political community through various acts of recognition. This does not necessarily mean that a new state has been formed, but rather that their position in the international arena and in relations with other states has been confirmed. Many revolutionary governments which have seized power from the previous government are given legitimacy through acts of recognition by other governments.[130] Some states may immediately recognise a new government after it has taken power, others before their power is made official, and still others may not for years after, if ever. This recognition, or lack thereof, of the government does not affect the legal existence of the state in question. The new

---

[129] Nagan and Haddad, *Recognition of Palestinian Statehood: A Clarification of the Interests of the Concerned Parties*, note 97, pp.2, 356, and 357.

[130] See, for instance, *Peru: A Milestone in the Struggle for Justice, Crimes against Humanity*. Fujimori was sentenced to 25 years in prison.

government continues to exist politically and legally regardless of the status of recognition.

In addition, recognition of a state by other states does not necessarily mean that all states recognize each other. All states of the world should, by one means or another, express their own respective consent regarding the recognition of the new government. Recognition can, however, be confirmed or rejected in different ways including[131] through initiating diplomatic relations or sending diplomats, and by writing and initiating cooperation in certain matters or in a voting process in the General Assembly. One of the most recent decisions of the GA Resolution A/67/L.28 declared the political and legal status of Palestine, as per the United Nations Charter.[132]

2. Resolution Confirming Personality

Concerning international legal personality of Palestine, Resolution A/67/l.28 passed with 138 votes in favour (73% of those present and voting), 9 votes against, and 41 abstentions. By voting in favour of the resolution, these 138 states gave their implied recognition of the state of Palestine, not only within the UN system but in the arena of public international law as well. Consequently, the vote upgraded the Palestinian entity's status at the UN from "permanent observer entity" to "non-member observer state." This shows the tendency of the majority of voting states to legally recognise Palestine as a permanent member of the international legal community, and their full willingness to accept Palestine as a permanent member of the United Nations. This vote was very controversial for those nations fighting

[131] For instance, in 1990, President GHW Bush rejected Palestine's recognition before UNESCO and the WHO. He declared that any United Nations agency, which recognises the PLO, might lose United States funding. Barry Carter and Phillip R. Trimble, International Law (1991), 450. However, on 10 November, 1993, the PLO and Israel exchanged letters of mutual recognition. This was the reason why the United States modified its policy of recognition concerning the PLO. Clyde R. Mark, Cong. Research Serv., 1B82008, Israeli-United States Relations (2004), Available online at http://www.fas.org/man/crs/IB82008.pdf.

[132] The resolution was adopted on 29 November, 2012 by a vote of 138 in favour, nine against, and forty-one abstentions.

against full political and legal rights for Palestine, namely the US and Israel. [133]

The General Assembly Resolution A/67/1.28 governing the international legal personality or the Status of Palestine in the United Nations provides:

> The General Assembly, [134]
>
> Guided by the purposes and principles of the Charter of the United Nations, and stressing in this regard the principle of equal rights and self-determination of peoples,
>
> Recalling its resolution 2625 (XXV) of 24 October 1970,[135] by which it affirmed, inter alia, the duty of every State to promote, through joint and separate action, realization of the principle of equal rights and self-determination of peoples,
>
> Stressing the importance of maintaining and strengthening international peace founded upon freedom, equality, justice and respect for fundamental human rights,
>
> Recalling its resolution 181 (II) of 29 November 1947,
>
> Reaffirming the principle, set out in the Charter, of the inadmissibility of the acquisition of territory by force,
>
> Reaffirming also relevant Security Council resolutions, including resolutions 242 (1967) of 22 November 1967, 338 (1973) of 22 October 1973, 446 (1979) of 22 March 1979, 478 (1980) of 20 August 1980, 1397 (2002) of 12 March 2002, 1515 (2003) of 19 November 2003 and 1850 (2008) of 16 December 2008,
>
> Reaffirming further the applicability of the Geneva Convention relative to the Protection of Civilian Persons in Time of War, of 12 August 1949,[136] to the Occupied Palestinian Territory, including East Jerusalem, including with regard to the matter of prisoners,
>
> Reaffirming its resolution 3236 (XXIX) of 22 November 1974 and all relevant resolutions, including resolution 66/146 of 19 December 2011,

---

[133] See the veto of the United States against a resolution condemning all Israeli settlements since 1967 as illegal. The resolution was voted against on 18 February 2011. UN News Centre: www.un.org/apps/news/story.asp?NewsID=37572&Cr… Cr1

[134] Resolution adopted by the General Assembly [*without reference to a Main Committee (A/67/L.28 and Add.1)*] 67/19. Status of Palestine in the United Nations.

[135] [1]Declaration on Principles of International Law concerning Friendly Relations and Cooperation among States in accordance with the Charter of the United Nations.

[136] United Nations, *Treaty Series*, vol. 75, No. 973.

reaffirming the right of the Palestinian people to self-determination, including the right to their independent State of Palestine,

Reaffirming also its resolutions 43/176 of 15 December 1988 and 66/17 of 30 November 2011 and all relevant resolutions regarding the peaceful settlement of the question of Palestine, which, inter alia, stress the need for the withdrawal of Israel from the Palestinian territory occupied since 1967, including East Jerusalem, the realization of the inalienable rights of the Palestinian people, primarily the right to self-determination and the right to their independent State, a just resolution of the problem of the Palestine refugees in conformity with resolution 194 (III) of 11 December 1948 and the complete cessation of all Israeli settlement activities in the Occupied Palestinian Territory, including East Jerusalem,

Reaffirming further its resolution 66/18 of 30 November 2011 and all relevant resolutions regarding the status of Jerusalem, bearing in mind that the annexation of East Jerusalem is not recognized by the international community, and emphasizing the need for a way to be found through negotiations to resolve the status of Jerusalem as the capital of two States,

Recalling the advisory opinion of the International Court of Justice of 9 July 2004,[137]

Reaffirming its resolution 58/292 of 6 May 2004 affirming, inter alia, that the status of the Palestinian territory occupied since 1967, including East Jerusalem, remains one of military occupation and that, in accordance with international law and relevant United Nations resolutions, the Palestinian people have the right to self-determination and to sovereignty over their territory,

Recalling its resolutions 3210 (XXIX) of 14 October 1974 and 3237 (XXIX) of 22 November 1974, by which, respectively, the Palestine Liberation Organization was invited to participate in the deliberations of the General Assembly as the representative of the Palestinian people and was granted observer status,

Recalling also its resolution 43/177 of 15 December 1988, by which it, inter alia, acknowledged the proclamation of the State of Palestine by the Palestine National Council on 15 November 1988 and decided that the designation "Palestine" should be used in place of the designation "Palestine Liberation Organization" in the United Nations system, without

---

[137] See A/ES-10/273 and Corr.1.

prejudice to the observer status and functions of the Palestine Liberation Organization within the United Nations system,

Taking into consideration that the Executive Committee of the Palestine Liberation Organization, in accordance with a decision by the Palestine National Council, is entrusted with the powers and responsibilities of the Provisional Government of the State of Palestine,[138]

Recalling its resolution 52/250 of 7 July 1998, by which additional rights and privileges were accorded to Palestine in its capacity as observer,

Recalling also the Arab Peace Initiative adopted in March 2002 by the Council of the League of Arab States,[139] Reaffirming its commitment, in accordance with international law, to the two-State solution of an independent, sovereign, democratic, viable and contiguous State of Palestine living side by side with Israel in peace and security on the basis of the pre-1967 borders,

Bearing in mind the mutual recognition of 9 September 1993 between the Government of the State of Israel and the Palestine Liberation Organization, the representative of the Palestinian people,

Affirming the right of all States in the region to live in peace within secure and internationally recognized borders,

Commending the Palestinian National Authority's 2009 plan for constructing the institutions of an independent Palestinian State within a two-year period, and welcoming the positive assessments in this regard about readiness for statehood by the World Bank, the United Nations and the International Monetary Fund and as reflected in the Ad Hoc Liaison Committee Chair conclusions of April 2011 and subsequent Chair conclusions, which determined that the Palestinian Authority is above the threshold for a functioning State in key sectors studied,

Recognizing that full membership is enjoyed by Palestine in the United Nations Educational, Scientific and Cultural Organization, the Economic and Social Commission for Western Asia and the Group of Asia-Pacific States and that Palestine is also a full member of the League of Arab States, the Movement of Non-Aligned Countries, the Organization of Islamic Cooperation and the Group of 77 and China,

Recognizing also that, to date, 132 States Members of the United Nations have accorded recognition to the State of Palestine,

---

[138] See A/43/928, annex.

[139] A/56/1026-S/2002/932, annex II, resolution 14/221.

Taking note of the 11 November 2011 report of the Security Council Committee on the Admission of New Members,[140]

Stressing the permanent responsibility of the United Nations towards the question of Palestine until it is satisfactorily resolved in all its aspects,

Reaffirming the principle of universality of membership of the United Nations,

1. Reaffirms the right of the Palestinian people to self-determination and to independence in their State of Palestine on the Palestinian territory occupied since 1967;

2. Decides to accord to Palestine non-member observer State status in the United Nations, without prejudice to the acquired rights, privileges and role of the Palestine Liberation Organization in the United Nations as the representative of the Palestinian people, in accordance with the relevant resolutions and practice;

3. Expresses the hope that the Security Council will consider favourably the application submitted on 23 September 2011 by the State of Palestine for admission to full membership in the United Nations;[141]

4. Affirms its determination to contribute to the achievement of the inalienable rights of the Palestinian people and the attainment of a peaceful settlement in the Middle East that ends the occupation that began in 1967 and fulfils the vision of two States: an independent, sovereign, democratic, contiguous and viable State of Palestine living side by side in peace and security with Israel on the basis of the pre-1967 borders;

5. Expresses the urgent need for the resumption and acceleration of negotiations within the Middle East peace process based on the relevant United Nations resolutions, the terms of reference of the Madrid Conference, including the principle of land for peace, the Arab Peace Initiative[5] and the Quartet road map to a permanent two-State solution to the Israeli-Palestinian conflict[142] for the achievement of a just, lasting and comprehensive peace settlement between the Palestinian and Israeli sides that resolves all outstanding core issues, namely the Palestine refugees, Jerusalem, settlements, borders, security and water;

6. Urges all States and the specialized agencies and organizations of the United Nations system to continue to support and assist the Palestinian

---

[140] S/2011/705.

[141] A/66/371-S/2011/592, annex I.

[142] S/2003/529, annex.

people in the early realization of their right to self-determination, independence and freedom;

7. Requests the Secretary-General to take the necessary measures to implement the present resolution and to report to the General Assembly within three months on progress made in this regard.[143]

This clear movement of Palestine towards its full independence as a state of the international legal community created a much stronger ILP for them under the Charter. However, its traditional concept of ILP was just as strong before. By this we mean that the customary legal statute of Palestine cannot be diminished through any political debates by the big political powers under the Charter, or outsides its boundaries. The Resolution both explicitly and implicitly conferred statehood on Palestine and created rights and duties for the relevant state. This was not just the granting of statehood, but, as I will discuss below, Resolution A/67/L.28, in combination with customary and conventional international human rights law, confirmed the full position of Palestine as a state as per the Charter. In addition, one has to read the words of the resolution in conjunction with the notion of state immunity and its relevant protections. A recent example of such a case is the decision of the International Court of Justice concerning *Jurisdictional Immunities of the State* (*Germany v. Italy: Greece Intervening*), in which the concept of state immunity was protected.[144]

3. Recognition through Resolutions

Some resolutions of the General Assembly, which without a doubt refer to certain natural rights of all people, constitute a strong source of international law, and are therefore enforceable. Although the validity of GA resolutions may be discussed from different perspectives, they definitely

[143] *44th plenary meeting 29 November 2012.*

[144] International Court of Justice, Jurisdictional Immunities of the State (Germany *v.* Italy: Greece intervening), Judgment of 3 February 2012, para. 64, Available online at http://www.icj-cij.org/docket/files/143/16883.pdf. See also *infra.*

contribute to the creation of customary international law. A clear example is the Universal Declaration of Human Rights, which was adopted in the content of a GA resolution.

The resolution or the Declaration constitutes not only an integral part of customary international law today, but also an integral part of the international law of *jus cogens*, thus making its provisions non-derogable. In addition, the Declaration is an integral part of the EU's human rights law and served as the basic framework for its development. One should also add that the Declaration is an integral part of the national legislations of many states in the world. In addition to these factors, nearly every word of the Declaration has been developed into their own separate international convention on different aspects of human rights law.[145]

Resolutions of the General Assembly are a means through which states express their opinions concerning certain very significant questions of international law. One may also argue that the resolutions and declarations of established international organizations such as the Red Cross, the ICC, and the ICJ, whose international legal personalities are widely recognised in international law, may constitute *opinio juris.* [146] *Opinio juris* denotes a subsidiary source of international law following the provisions of Article 38 of the permanent International Court of Justice and relates to the legal validity of Palestine's statehood. Similarly, it is occasionally possible that a judgment of ICJ is not only an opinion, but possess a declaratory nature as well. A clear example of such a judgment is the 2004 International Court of Justice Advisory Opinion governing the *Legal Consequences of the Construction of a Wall in the Occupied Palestinian Territory*.[147]

---

[145] Consult Farhad Malekian, *Documents on the Principles of International Human Rights* (Norstedts Juridik Student, 2007).

[146] H. Lauterpacht, *The Development of International Law by the International Court* (Cambridge University Press, 1958), 6-22 and 61-71; M. Mendelson, 'The International Court of Justice and the sources of international law,' in V. Lowe V. & M. Fitzmaurice (eds.), *Fifty Years of the International Court of Justice: Essays in Honour of Sir Robert Jennings* (Grotius Publications, 1996), 63-89.

[147] Legal Consequences of the Construction of a Wall in the Occupied Palestinian Territory, International Court of Justice Advisory Opinion, 9 July 2004, para. 163. See also the section on *Jus Cogens*.

4. Constitutive Recognition

The concept of recognition in the system of international law is dominated by two competing legal philosophies, the declarative and the constitutive theories. The difference between these two theories is that one clearly approves the position of the new state through direct declaration, while the other examines the question only under certain conditions. Consequently, the constitutive theory points to the fact that the recognition of a state entity is not automatic. While the declarative theory is the customary method for the recognition of state sovereignty, the constitutive theory is the modern approach to certain questions of international law in the General Assembly.

The declarative concept is actually favoured in state practice. Ian Brownlie states the position succinctly: "Recognition, as a public act of state, is an optional and political act and there is no legal duty in this regard. However, in a deeper sense, if an entity bears the marks of statehood, other states put themselves at risk legally, if they ignore the basic obligations of state relations."[148]

According to the declarative theory, a state has achieved its ILP when it meets several objective criteria for statehood. Article 1 of the 1933 Montevideo Convention of the Rights and Duties of States lists the following criteria for statehood: *i)* permanent population; *ii)* defined territory; *iii)* effective government; and *iv)* capacity to enter into relations with other states. It is clear that the provisions of the article do not put any value on the traditional concept of international law relating to needing military power as a prerequisite for statehood.[149]

One may assert that all these conditions exist in the case of Palestine and that no condition is missing. However, there are several disputes about the legal territory of Palestine from those who are opposed to an independent Palestinian state. Even though there are arguments about the territory of the

---

[148] Ian Brownlie, *Principles of Public International Law* (Oxford University Press, 1973), 94.

[149] It is also asserted that the criteria in the Convention constitute a minimum standard for statehood. See Anonymous, 'China and the Principle of Self-Determination of Peoples,' 6 *St. Antony's International Law Review* (2010), 79-82.

West Bank and Gaza Strip, and even all of what is the modern state of Israel, these disputes do not in any way lessen the principle of the territorial boundaries of the state of Palestine. The reason being that the question of territorial disputes has always existed in the international relations of states, and has never had any effect on the value of statehood. [150] For instance, territorial disputes have long existed between the Iranian, Russian, and Afghan governments and many other Arian countries, but all states have continuously maintained their international legal personality despite this territorial arguments.

5. Arguments Facing Recognition

One cannot deny the fact that the question of a "defined territory" is subject to disagreement between Israel, Hamas, and Palestine. It is a fact that the Palestinian government has no exclusive authority over any of the aforementioned territories, however this does not necessarily speak against its ILP or its customary international rights. In reality, the Israeli government organizes much of the West Bank through the use of force, and Hamas administers the Gaza Strip. This does not diminish at any level the territorial integrity of Palestine, and also does not affect the Palestinian state capital in East Jerusalem.

There is also another objection to the existence of a Palestinian government, as in order to be qualified as an independent state, the relevant state should have an established government with powerful control over its territories. This argument is rather vague and non-sensical. The history of international relations implies the fact that many governments have been forced to leave their country, or did have not had full control over their territories, without it affecting the position of their statehood. For instance, "an autonomous Finland which ... on the 6th December 1917, proclaimed her full and entire independence of Russia, detached herself from the latter

---

[150] In the history of civilisation, the territorial integrity of Palestine was referred to in 5th century B.C.

by *an act of her own free will*, and became thereafter herself a sovereign State instead of a dependent State."[151] In reference to the existence of the new state of Poland, the German-Polish Mixed Arbitral Tribunal stated "... the recognition of a State is not constitutive but merely *declaratory*. The State exists by itself and the recognition is nothing else than a declaration of this existence, recognized by the States from which it emanates."[152] In both cases, their governments or representative authorities were not more powerful than the present cases under consideration at the UN.

International law does not preclude a government from existing if said government does not yet have control over its territories. Historically, many governments have been forced to move out from their territories and have subsequently regained them. Thus, it is not a necessary condition of statehood that a government be present in order for the state to have an effective control over its territories.[153] Moreover, the term "government" is not qualified by the term "effective" in the Montevideo Convention, rather, it indicates a new state practice where territorial units can be substituted for statehood. This is regardless of whether or not a government exercises complete substantive authority over its territories. There are many examples that fit this description including Bosnia and Herzegovina, the Democratic Republic of Congo, East Timor, Guinea-Bissau, and Kosovo.

6. Criteria for Recognition

There are different criteria for the recognition of a new state through both constitutive and declarative means:

a) According to the provisions of Article 2 (1) of the UN, the equality of states constitutes a legal fact. The principle of equality of states

---

[151] League of Nations, Council Doc. B7: 21/68/106 (1921), p. 22.

[152] *Deutsche Continental Gas Gesellschaft v. Polish State* (1929), Annual Digest, 5 (1929-30), NO·5·

[153] However, see also Sean D. Murphy, 'Self-Defense and the Israeli Wall Advisory Opinion: An Ipse Dixit from the ICI?' 99 *American Journal of International Law* (2005), 62.

is a formal principle and has nothing to do with political, economic, military, or moral principles.

b) A state may also be recognised as a new subject of international law through the act of concluding treaties with other states. This is one of the general meanings of the term "sovereign" as applied to states. Illustrative examples are agreements concluded between Palestine and several other states.[154]

c) A state may receive support, including political, military, and financial aid for its creation. A clear example is the assistance given by certain permanent members during the creation of Israel.

d) The competence of a state is not based upon its foreign relations, but rather upon its internal situation. This means that a state should have control over its internal territories. This position is clearly manifested in Article 2 (7) of the Charter and implies that the jurisdiction of a new state is *prima facie* not subject to the recognition by other states.

e) No state of the international legal community can force another state to establish international relations with other states, as that would be illegal and unjust. In principle, no state is obliged to have relations with another state, but as a matter of international cooperation, all states need to have international relations in order to achieve political and economic goals. Again, the establishment or non-establishment of international relations does not increase, nor decrease, the legitimacy of the state in question, rather it serves to demonstrate the manifestation of how states react concerning the existence of a relevant power in force. In practice, however, it is meaningless if states, for example, argue for the human rights of the indigenous population of Australia, while ignoring the plight of the Palestinians.[155]

---

[154] See *infra*.

[155] For instance, see *Recognizing the Palestinian State on the 1967 Border & Admission of Palestine as a Full Member of the United Nations, PLO Negotiations Office*, http://www.nad-plo.org (2011).

f) Any derogation from the above principles has to be confirmed by international courts, and such a judgment would never be written on paper as it violates *jus cogens* law. [156]

g) Recognition may also be indirectly affirmed by the acceptance of cases brought before jurisdiction of the ICC by a new state against another state such as the case brought by Palestine against Israel.

7. Owning Statehood Conditions

As we have analysed in different interpretations, there are four paths to statehood. These are:

a) The sovereign state has achieved its internal power and other states may or may not accept its political and legal position. This can be called the *traditional theory of statehood*, and is based mostly on military strength.

b) The *constitutive theory* requires that other countries recognise the statehood of a state through various acts, such as through the establishment of customary or conventional relations with the state in question. This has a mostly political nature and may be called *conclusive statehood*.

c) The *declarative theory* is the concept of recognition of statehood of a territorial entity arising from the provisions of the Montevideo Convention. This has a mostly *normative nature of statehood*.

---

[156] On *jus cogens*, see A. Verdross, 'Jus dispositivum and jus cogens in international law,' 60 *American Journal of International Law* (1966), 55-63; E. Suy, 'The concept of jus cogens in public international law,' in *Lagonissi Conference on International Law* (1967), 17-77; A. Gomez Robledo, "Le ius cogens international: sa genèse, sa nature, ses fonctions," *III RCADI* (1981), 9-217; R. St. J. Macdonald, 'Fundamental norms in contemporary international law,' 25 *Canadian Yearbook of International Law* (1987), 115-149; L. Alexidze, "Legal nature of jus cogens in contemporary international law," *III RACADI* (1981), 223-268; G. Gaja "Jus cogens beyond the Vienna Convention," III RACADI (1981), 271-31; G.A. Christenson, 'Jus cogens: Guarding interests fundamental to international society,' 28 *Virginia Journal of International Law* (1988), 585-628; G.M. Danilenko, 'International jus cogens: Issues of law-making,' 2 *European Journal of International Law* (1991), 42-65.

d) There is also the fourth concept of statehood. This may be deemed a *mixed theory of statehood,* which is a combination of (*b*) and (*c*) or of all three concepts, i.e., (*a*), (*b*), and (*c*). Looking at this systematically, the consolidation of Palestine's statehood fulfils the conditions of all four theories. Article 3 of the 1933 Montevideo Convention on the Rights and Duties of States[157] points out that:

> The political existence of the state is independent of recognition by the other states. Even before recognition the state has the right to defend its integrity and independence, to provide for its conservation and prosperity, and consequently to organize itself as it sees fit, to legislate upon its interests, administer its services, and to define the jurisdiction and competence of its courts.
>
> The exercise of these rights has no other limitation than the exercise of the rights of other states according to international law.

8. Permanent Population

Concerning the population requirement for statehood, the Palestinian territories have obviously had a permanent population since ancient times, and said population has been governed by various governments since the end of the Second World War. The condition of having a defined territory is also clear in the case of Palestinian statehood. The Palestinian territories consist of the West Bank, the Gaza Strip, and East Jerusalem, as well as of the border between the Palestinian territories and Israel. The aforementioned description also includes the territories that are occupied through unlawful force.[158]

---

[157] The convention *was signed at the International Conference of American States in Montevideo, Uruguay on December 26, 1933. It entered into force on 26 December, 1934.*

[158] However, see also Adam G. Yoffie, 'Comment, The Palestine Problem: The Search for Statehood and the Benefits of International Law,' 36 Yale Journal of International Law (2011), p.497.

The integrity of the territories of Palestine has been recognised and confirmed in several ways[159] including through UN Security Council resolutions, a large number of General Assembly resolutions, the International Court of Justice's judgment, and the strong political propensity of a majority of states to support the territories. Any limited level of control over Palestinian territories would violate the integrity of their statehood. This is because the system of international law recognises all relevant illegal occupations. Therefore, different divisions of the territories, and any question concerning a lack of defined borders are certainly weak arguments against the many positivist or naturalist reasonings arising from customary or conventional international law. If the question of undefined territory is important, in that case such argumentation also could call into question the Israeli territories.

Concerning the necessary condition of having the capacity to enter into relations with other states, the Palestinians have signed a number of international treaties such as the Arab Charter on Human Rights and the UNESCO Cultural Heritage Charter.[160] Further evidence for this is the General Assembly Declaration of Independence by the Palestinian National Council of November 15, 1988 in Resolution 43/177. Remarkably, only the United States and Israel voted against recognition thereof, and Germany abstained. This abstention must be regarded as wholly political and observant, based on the genocide during the Second World War committed against innocent Jews by the German government.

---

[159] Ron Wilkinson, Resolution 181: A state for some, occupation for others (Al-Jazeerah, BADIL, November 27, 2004) Available online at http://www.aljazeerah.info/Documents/Resolution%20181%20A%20state%20for%20some,%20occupation%20for%20others%20By%20Ron%20Wilkinson.htm.

[160] However, see also Zaha Hassan, 'The Palestinian Constitution and the Geneva Accord: The Prospects for Palestinian Constitutionalism,' 16 *Florida Journal of International Law*, (2004), 897-924.

9. Legitimacy of Statehood

In the old system of the law of nations, recognition was not a necessary condition of statehood,[161] and as such the early scholars of international law rarely dealt with the question of recognition. The concept of recognition had no place in the law of nations before the mid-eighteenth century. When a new sovereign came into existence, it was accepted without question, and its recognition came from its territory and its people, not from outsiders. The concept of statehood therefore did not traditionally require recognition by outside states. Moreover, one could also interpret modern recognition as an intervention into the political affairs of another state. Therefore, "… in order to consider the sovereignty of a State as complete in the Law of Nations, there is no need for its recognition by foreign powers; though the latter may appear useful, the *de facto* existence of sovereignty is sufficient."[162]

In fact, in the system of international law, no one theory has emerged which deals with questions of recognition in cases of questions of statehood. None of the works of classical scholars of international law, deal with the question of state recognition as a condition for statehood for example. These include both naturalist and positivist writings. According to early positivist scholars of international law, the obligation to comply with the provisions of the system of international law is derived from the consent of each individual state. When a new state was formed, then new obligations would arise, and new international relations could commence. The positivist premise consequently demanded either consent for the establishment of the new state, or depended upon its being subject to the system of international law with regard to the states affected by its creation. The shift in the idea of creation and recognition of a new state which occurred at the beginning of the twentieth century was gradual and did not have any effect on the pre-existing rules of statehood.

---

[161] For different concepts of statehood, consult Thomas D. Grant, 'Defining Statehood: The Montevideo Convention and its Discontents,' 37 *Columbia Journal of Transnational Law*, (1999), p.403.

[162] Saalfeld, Handbuch das positiven Volkerrechts (1833), p. 26; cited in James Crawford, 'The Criteria for Statehood in International Law', *British Yearbook of International Law* (1977), pp.93-182, 96.

10. Territorial Acquisition

The concept of statehood plays a key role in the body of international law. The so-called "divided states" in southern Africa since 1945 were clear examples of the concept and development of statehood. Although it is sometimes suggested that the concept of statehood has no separate place in international law, such a view is hard to deny given the extensive reliance on the concept in international "constitutional" documents such as the UN Charter, and in the practice of states. Notwithstanding this practice, there has been a surprising lack of detailed examination into the criteria for statehood in international law.[163]

We should remember that the formation of a new state, as I have previously stated, is a matter of fact and not of the law. The birth of a new state's statehood comes, however, through recognition, which means it becomes a matter of law and politics, as was the case of Israel in 1948. This implies that the new state becomes the new subject of international law and obligations. Here, according to certain scholars, recognition brings the territory of the new state into the realm of international law, and therefore it is of no interest how the territory was acquired. However, this argument is very weak and cannot be accepted in the modern system of international law, otherwise, it would validate states which seize territory by force, and the concept of self-determination would become a nonsensical theory.

One may assert that there are five methods of territorial acquisition by a sovereign power, namely: occupation, conquest, prescription, cession, and accretion. Even if a territory has been acquired during war, if certain conditions are not present, the acquisition cannot be regarded as valid in the modern system of international law, and cannot impact the question of statehood. This also includes acquisition through occupation.[164] Otherwise, most provisions of international law would merely represent an imperfect

---

[163] Examine Santiago Gonzalez Vallejo, *Recognition of the State of Palestine and the Hypocrisy, Committee in Solidarity with the Arab Cause* (2011).

[164] "The authorities on International Law now combine in laying it down with one consent that discovery in itself gives no title, and even temporary occupation will suffice to create a title merely inchoate, that occupation to be valid must be (a) effective." Thomas A. Walker, *The Science of International Law* (C.J. Clay and Sons, London, 1893), p.160.

communication between states, and all provisions of the system would be subject to reservation. In addition, this would mean that we would accept that any acquisition of territories through occupation would serve as a new method of establishing statehood, which could lead to states seizing new territories and integrating them into their own legal systems.

11. Conditions of Defined Territories

The existence of a defined territory is not an essential condition of statehood. The establishment of the state of Israel bears clear witness to this principle. In one way or another, the General Assembly Resolution 181 (II) of 29 November 1947 specified the territory of the newly created Israel, albeit not very clearly. The case was simply one of new, undefined frontiers. Nonetheless, Israel was admitted to the United Nations on 11 May 1949. The United States representative, Philip Jessup argued for the admission of Israel in the UN with the following argument:

> One does not find in the general classic treatment of this subject any insistence that the territory of a State must be exactly fixed by definite frontiers ... The formulae in the classic treatises somewhat vary, ... but both reason and history demonstrate that the concept of territory does not necessarily include precise delimitation of the boundaries of that territory. The reason for the rule that one of the necessary attributes of a State is that it shall possess territory is that one cannot contemplate a State as a kind of disembodied spirit ... [T]here must be some portion of the earth's surface which its people inhabit and over which its Government exercises authority. No one can deny that the State of Israel responds to this requirement...[165]

Furthermore, the practice of the UN and its members demonstrates the fact that claims concerning the disputed territories of a new state do not in principle affect the concept of statehood in the modern system of

[165] *Security Council, Official Records*, 383rd Meeting, 2 December 1948, p.41.

international law, or even in its traditional forms. In 1929, a German-Polish Mixed Arbitral Tribunal clarified the rule concisely:

> Whatever may be the importance of the delimitation of boundaries, one cannot go so far as to maintain that as long as this delimitation has not been legally effected the State in question cannot be considered as having any territory whatever ... In order to say that a State exists ... it is enough that this territory has a sufficient consistency, even though its boundaries have not yet been accurately delimited, and that the State actually exercises independent public authority over that territory.[166]

The concept of the existence of sovereignty or statehood without the consideration of the question of settled boundaries, was also confirmed in the ICJ during the North Sea Continental Shelf cases. The *en passant* situation clarified the following:

> The appurtenance of a given area, considered as an entity, in no way governs the precise delimitation of its boundaries, any more than uncertainty as to boundaries can affect territorial rights. There is for instance no rule that the land frontiers of a State must be fully delimited and defined, and often in various places and for long periods they are not, as is shown by the case of the entry of Albania into the League of Nations.[167]

We should remember that at the present stage of the development of the system of international law, the concepts of sovereignty and statehood exist as legal rights. Therefore, we speak about the existence of the principle of sovereignty, because the notion of a right presupposes the recognition of the subject of the right, and that recognition is the reason for the existence of the principle of sovereignty. It may even be the case, that territories can be regarded as "sovereign," due to the political consideration of a majority of states, without necessarily achieving legal recognition in the UN. Thus, all-

---

[166] *Deutsche Continental Gas-Gesellschaft v. Polish State* (1929), Annual Digest, (1929-30), NO. 5, at pp.14-15.

[167] ICJ Reports, 1969, p.3, at p.32.

legal consequences of recognition are originally based on political consideration.

12. STATEHOOD THROUGH SELF-DETERMINATION

The relationship between statehood and self-determination is an important aspect of the right to statehood.[168] In other words, self-determination is the means through which one gains the right to enter into statehood. The General Assembly has attempted to more precisely define self-determination in a considerable number of resolutions.[169] Accordingly, "all peoples have the right to self-determination; by virtue of that right they freely determine their political status and freely pursue their economic, social and cultural development."[170]

The Security Council has also reaffirmed the principle of self-determination, for example in Resolution 183 of 2 December 1963, by a vote of 10:0:1. The concept of self-determination as a "fundamental obligation" is also further mentioned because of its association to the "prohibition of the threat or use of force in international relations." Resolution 2160 (XXI) reaffirmed that:

> (b) Any forcible action, direct or indirect, which deprives peoples under foreign domination of their right to self-determination and freedom and independence and of their right to determine freely their political status and pursue their economic, social and cultural development constitutes a violation of the Charter of the United Nations. Accordingly, the use of force to deprive peoples of their national identity, as prohibited by the Declaration on the Inadmissibility of Intervention in the Domestic Affairs

---

168 See Edward W. Said, *The Politics of Dispossession: The Struggle for Palestinian Self-Determination 1969-1994*, (Vintage Books, 1995).

169 Eugene V. Rostow, 'Palestinian Self-Determination: Possible Futures for the Unallocated Territories of the Palestine Mandate,' 5 *Yale Studies of World Public Order* (1978), 147-149.

170 G.A. Res. ISI4 (XV), 14 December 1960 (89-0: 9), 'Declaration on the Granting of Independence to Colonial Countries and Peoples.' For the status of the "Colonial Declaration," see Obed Y. Asamoah, The Legal Significance of the Declarations of the General Assembly (ebook, 1966), pp. 164-173. See also G.A. Resns. 1541 (XV); 2105 (XX); 2200A (XXI); 2625 (XXV), Annex.

of States and the Protection of Their Independence and Sovereignty contained in General Assembly Resolution 2131 (XX), constitutes a violation of their inalienable rights and of the principle of non-intervention,"

In the provisions of the Declaration on Principles of International Law concerning Friendly Relations and Co-operation among States in accordance with the Charter of the United Nations annexed to Resolution 2625 (XXV), the General Assembly dealt with the concept of self-determination. It clearly confirmed the principle of equal rights and the self-determination of peoples:

> By virtue of the principle of equal rights and self-determination of peoples enshrined in the Charter . . . all peoples have the right freely to determine, without external interference, their political status and to pursue their economic, social and cultural development, and every State has the duty to respect this right in accordance with the provisions of the Charter. . . The territory of a colony or other non-self-governing territory has, under the 'Charter, a status separate and distinct from the territory of the State administering it; and such separate and distinct status under the Charter shall exist until the people of the colony or non-self-governing territory have exercised their right of self-determination in accordance with the Charter.... Every State shall refrain from any action aimed at the partial or total disruption of the national unity or territorial integrity of any other State or country.[171]

13. Inalienable Right of Self-Determination

The World Conference on Human Rights adopted the Vienna Declaration and Programme of Action in 1993. The Declaration encourages the inalienable right of self-determination of the people. The Helsinki Final

---

[171] 24 November 1970 (adopted without vote); see Edward McWhinney, The 'New Countries and the 'New International Law," *American Journal of International Law*, 60 (1966), pp.1-33.

Act also has similar provisions regarding rights of self-determination.[172] In addition, the principle of self-determination also constitutes a principle of customary international law, because when the General Assembly accepts a resolution based on the views of the majority of states, it implies the existence of a customary norm, which is of significant importance for the international community as a whole. This also indicates that there was reasonable consensus at the time of the adoption of a resolution. The assessment of the subject of the resolution may be based on several criteria, *inter alia* whether there was any reason for the determination of territories to which a "right of self-determination" should be accorded, and whether the concept of self-determination can appropriately be recognised as a legitimate legal right in its application to relevant territories. The right to self-determination is an inalienable right granted to the Palestinians in a number of UN resolutions.

The existence of the PLO has strengthened the Palestinian's right to self-determination. The Arab League has recognised the PLO almost since the organization's founding. Over 100 states have given their full recognition to the PLO in its legitimate struggles for the independence of the Palestinian territories and for Palestinian statehood.[173] Similarly, over sixty states have established diplomatic relations with the PLO, and fifty other states have recognised its legitimate struggles. However, the PLO has not established embassies under their jurisdictions. In addition, the PLO offices function under the Arab League. Yet, the PLO exists as the sole official representative

---

[172] Article VIII of the Act governing *equal rights and self-determination of peoples* provides that "The participating States will respect the equal rights of peoples and their right to self-determination, acting at all times in conformity with the purposes and principles of the Charter of the United Nations and with the relevant norms of international law, including those relating to territorial integrity of States. By virtue of the principle of equal rights and self-determination of peoples, all peoples always have the right, in full freedom, to determine, when and as they wish, their internal and external political status, without external interference, and to pursue as they wish their political, economic, social and cultural development. The participating States reaffirm the universal significance of respect for and effective exercise of equal rights and self-determination of peoples for the development of friendly relations among themselves as among all States; they also recall the importance of the elimination of any form of violation of this principle."

[173] See also Longobardo, Marco, 'The Palestinian Right to Exploit the Dead Sea Coastline for Tourism (21 January, 2016)' 58 *German Yearbook of International Law* (2015), Available online at SSRN: http://ssrn.com/abstract=2719593.

of Palestine in its struggle for self-determination. Additionally, the PLO also represents Palestine's statehood and population at all conferences organized under the authority of the General Assembly and the Security Council.

14. Full Statehood of Palestine

In international law, there is a clear, yet seldomly expressed distinction between the identification of territories from which the legal concept of sovereignty arises, and the theory of legal application of rights to territories which have already been occupied through the use of force by a third state. Thus, a population could be in its own territory and require statehood, or be outside of its territory and require territory, or any combination thereof, which would mean that part of its territory, where a portion of its population resides, is occupied by a third state.

In 2012, a historic resolution promoted the position of Palestine at the UN from "permanent observer" to "non-member observer state,"[174] a status also held by the Holy See (the Vatican). The General Assembly adopted this resolution by 138 votes to 9, with 41 abstentions, including from Great Britain. Few nations did not cast a vote: Canada, the Czech Republic, Israel, Micronesia, the Marshall Islands, Nauru, Palau, Panama, and the US.

The situation of Palestine can be easily compared with Kosovo's unilateral claim of statehood and independence in accordance with the provisions of international law. Kosovo was an independent region after the 1974 Constitution of Yugoslavia was ratified. However, because of political shifts, Serbia carried out serious acts of discrimination against the Kosovar population. Serbia's position of influence led to massive ethnic cleansing programmes against the population of Kosovo. In order to prevent these crimes, the legal authorities of Kosovo drafted a declaration which established a provisional form of governance under the UN. The illegal

[174] *United Nations* General Assembly *Resolution* 67/19 (29 November, 2012). This is the date of the International Day of Solidarity with the Palestinian People and the 65th anniversary of the adoption by the General Assembly of Resolution 181(II) on the Future Government of Palestine.

actions taken against the Kosovar population are similar to the discriminative policy practised against the Palestinians by the Israelis. The situations in Kosovo and in the occupied territories therefore resemble *one another, because* in both cases, the purpose was/is to come to a final settlement concerning statehood using the authority of UN Security Council resolutions.

In the case of Kosovo, a Security Council resolution created an interim government, and in the case of the occupied territories of Palestine this was accomplished through the Oslo Accords. The latter fell under the broad authority of UN Security Council resolutions, and in combination with these provisions, created the Palestinian National Authority as an interim institution of governance. The International Court of Justice in The Hague (ICJ) maintained that the authorities representing Kosovo were not limited by the provisions of the UN Security Council resolutions in their residual claim to governing independence and sovereignty.[175]

15. Judgments of Courts

The UN General Assembly resolutions in conjunction with many principles of international law, including the framework of *jus cogens,* have obviously strengthened the competence of the Palestinians to declare their sovereign independence. This means that the Israeli government has no power to claim a sovereign title over the territories which it has occupied through the unlawful use of force. Therefore, the statement of the ICJ is completely in support of Palestinian rights of sovereign independence. However, there is a large difference between the Kosovo case and the Palestine case.[176] In the former, the claim by Serbia concerned territorial authority, while the latter deals with occupied territories. One addresses the

---

[175] However, Kosovo had to fulfil several other conditions. See Ilriana Islami, 'The Insufficiency of International Legal Personality of Kosovo as Attained through the European Court of Human Rights: A Call for Statehood,' 80 *Chicago-Kent Law Review*. (2005), 83, 88.

[176] Zohar Nevo & Tamar Megiddo, 'Lessons from Kosovo: The Law of Statehood and Palestinian Unilateral Independence,' 5 *Journal of International Law & International Relations* (2009), p.89.

right to territory, while the other an unlawful act of occupation. In addition, a territorial claim in international law is a question of substance, not procedure. This means that the illegal Israeli occupation of Palestinian territories is solely a question of an illegal conduct of war, and not of rights. The ICJ was aware of the fact that Kosovar territory was an integral part of Serbia and, through analogy, Israel's unlawful claims over Palestinian territories relate to the occupation of the territories of a neighbouring country. This means that the case before the ICJ strongly protects the legitimate right of the Palestinian people to sovereign national independent statehood.

A parallel example to the Palestinian right for sovereign independence can also be found in the decision of the Supreme Court of Canada in the case *Reference re Secessions of Quebec*. The Court, after the examination of different matters concerning the question of the right to self-determination, concluded that the province of *Quebec* had the right to self-determination. The Court, in its answers to various questions of the legislature, ruled that the right to self-determination constituted an integral right of the population of the relevant province, and was therefore an inalienable right. The judgment of the Court clarified that the right did not arise from the present situation of the population of the relevant province, since they were not under attack by any means, but rather from the fact that the relevant population was forced to follow the order of former colonial powers.[177]

---

[177] *Reference re Secession of Quebec*, [1998] 2 S.C.R. 217 (Can.).

Chapter 5

VIOLATIONS OF INTERNATIONAL PEREMPTORY CRIMINAL LAW

1. PROBLEM OF LAW-MAKING TREATIES

One of the most controversial questions concerning the statehood of Palestine arose when Palestine entered into the conclusion of a number of treaties in 2014. In fact, becoming a party to the treaties was based on a unanimous decision by the Palestinian leadership, including the PLO Executive Committee under President Mahmoud Abbas, who signed letters of accession to 15 multilateral treaties. He did so in accordance with the rights that Palestine gained after the UN General Assembly upgraded its international legal personality to observer state status in November of 2012. The ratification of these treaties however, spurred a considerable number of arguments concerning the legal validity of said treaties. There were many arguments in response to the issue. Nevertheless, the Palestine Liberation Organization believed that the ratification of multilateral conventions was an integral part of their change of status in the United Nations.[178]

---

[178] State of Palestine, available online at "Q & A: Palestine's Accession to International Treaties" (2 April, 2014) http:// nad-plo.org/userfiles/file/fact%20sheets/Q&A%20Accession.pdf.

These controversies intensified when the State of Palestine formally submitted letters of accession to the Dutch and Swiss representatives, to the Palestinian Authority, and to the Special Coordinator of the Middle East Peace Process and Personal Representative of the Secretary-General. The content of the letters specified the intention of the state of Palestine to accede to a significant number of law-making treaties. In addition, the PLO clarified that formulations in the treaties were planned in 2013, but had had to be postponed because of the political situation arising from a peace plan arranged by the United States Secretary of State John Kerry which led to the release of 104 Palestinian prisoners who had been detained by Israel prior to the conclusion of the Oslo Accords in mid-1993.[179] However, as we will see, the United States' plan for peace had a hidden plan for the occupation of Jerusalem within it, and therefore could not be trusted. Similarly, the peace plan for 2019 is "…really a lie." "Everybody is working on this fictitious concept. The United States became partners with Israel and they are implementing Israeli policies. All we see are unilateral measures by the US and by Israel…The reality on the ground is now being engineered."[180]

The purpose of the international treaties is simply to assist and protect the basic rights of the Palestinian people, as well as to enable the state of Palestine to be a responsible actor on the international stage. The international treaties in question include:

1) The Four Geneva Conventions of 12 August 1949 and the First Additional Protocol.
2) The Vienna Convention on Diplomatic Relations.
3) The Vienna Convention on Consular Relations.
4) The Convention on the Rights of the Child and the Optional Protocol to the Convention on the Rights of the Child on the involvement of children in armed conflict.
5) The Convention on the Elimination of All Forms of Discrimination against Women.

---

[179] *Id.*

[180] The statement of Hanan Ashrawi, the senior Palestinian politician.

6) The Hague Convention (IV) respecting the Laws and Customs of War on Land and its annex: Regulations Concerning the Laws and Customs of War on Land.
7) The Convention on the Rights of Persons with Disabilities.
8) The Vienna Convention on the Law of Treaties.
9) The International Convention on the Elimination of All Forms of Racial Discrimination.
10) The Convention against Torture and Other Cruel, Inhuman or Degrading Treatment or Punishment.
11) The United Nations Convention against Corruption.
12) The Convention on the Prevention and Punishment of the Crime of Genocide.
13) The International Convention on the Suppression and Punishment of the Crime of Apartheid.
14) The International Covenant on Civil and Political Rights.
15) The International Covenant on Economic, Social and Cultural Rights.[181]

The intention of this series of resolutions is to end the over 50-year-long-occupation of the Palestinian Territories by Israel. Consequently, the UN General Assembly adopted a non-binding resolution, against the Israeli occupation of the Occupied Palestinian Territories (OPT) in 2014. The resolution therefore concerned the permanent sovereignty of the Palestinian people in the Occupied Palestinian Territory, including East Jerusalem, and that of the Arab population in the Syrian Golan, which was occupied for its natural resources.[182] Similarly, and in the same year, Jordan submitted a draft resolution to the UN Security Council recommending an end to the Israeli

181 Palestine's Accession to International Treaties Q&A, available online at https://www.nad.ps/en/publication-resources/faqs/palestine%E2%80%99s-accession-international-treaties-qa.

182 *A/RES/69/241*.

occupation of the OPT within a 12-month period, suggesting a withdrawal of Israeli troops by 2017.[183]

2. Mishandling of the Concept

As usual, the content of the aforementioned resolution was not effective in resolving this situation. Several states abstained from the voting process, e.g., the United Kingdom, Nigeria, the Republic of Korea, Rwanda, and Lithuania, and the United States and Australia voted against the resolution.[184] Since the resolution was the reason that the state of Palestine signed letters of accession to 18 additional international law-making treaties the PLO therefore declared that:

> Although the majority of the Security Council voted in favour of the resolution, certain countries continue to actively block steps towards ending Israel's belligerent occupation and its systematic violations of international law. We signed the treaties, and particularly the Rome Statute of the International Criminal Court, in order to ensure the protection and advance the rights of our people. There must be accountability and those who are concerned about courts, should stop committing crimes. This does not constitute a unilateral step. On the contrary, this is a step towards the internationalization of the solution. Palestine has, and will continue to use, all legitimate tools within its means, in order to defend itself against Israeli colonization and other violations of international law.[185]

---

183 "Text of Draft Palestinian Resolution," New York Times, 30 December, 2014, available online at http://www.nytimes.com/interactive/2014/12/30/world/middleeast/United-Nations-Resolution-for-Palestinian-State-Fails.html?_i=0.

184 Security Council 7354th Meeting, "Resolution in Security Council to Impose 12-Month Deadline on Negotiated Solution to Israeli-Palestinian Conflict Unable to Secure Nine Votes Needed for Adoption," (30 December, 2014). Available online at http://www.un.org/press/en/2014/scl 1722.doc.htm.

185 Statement by PLO Executive Committee Member Dr. Saeb Erekat on Palestine's Accession to International Treaties (31 December, 2014), available online at http://unispal.un.0rg/UNISPAL.NSF/O/ 6AC3115500C569E985257DC 100552B95.

The statement above and the ratification of a number of international treaties by different states were sharply rejected by the United States, who has been against the establishment of a Palestinian state since the start. The US clarified their position saying:

> As we have said previously, we have made clear our opposition to Palestinian action in seeking to join the Rome Statute of the International Criminal Court. This step is counter-productive, will damage the atmosphere with the very people with whom Palestinians ultimately need to make peace, and will do nothing to further the aspirations of the Palestinian people for a sovereign and independent state.[186]

Thus, in the international legal and political community most discussions have concentrated on the question of whether the treaties which were ratified by the PLO as the official representative of the state of Palestine have conventional legal validity. The answer to this question is very clear, since international treaties are formulated between states and states, organisations and organisations, or states and organisations, the PLO or the state of Palestine, as a matter of fact, possesses all of these legal identities. They have been the sole representative of the Palestinians since 1974, and since that time, they have held observer status in the UNGA. The resolution, along with other legal precedents, granted the PLO a considerable amount of observer functions, which also included the right to participate in the sessions and meetings of the General Assembly.[187]

3. Validity of Treaties Ratified by Palestinians

Another argument put forward concerning the validity of the treaties ratified by the PLO under the authority of the state of Palestine are the

---

[186] U.S. Department of State, "Regarding Palestinian Efforts to Accede to the Rome Statute of the International Criminal Court," Diplomacy in Action (8 January, 2015), available online at http://www.state.gov/r/pa/prs/ps/2015/01/235695.htm.

[187] Observer Status for the Palestine Liberation Organization, A/RES/3237 (XXIX) (22 November, 1974).

requirements found in Article 81 of the Vienna Convention on the Law of Treaties. The article reads that the Convention "shall be open for signature by all Member States of the United Nations or of any of the specialized agencies or Parties to the Statute of the International Court of Justice, and by any other State invited by the General Assembly of the United Nations to become a Party to the Convention."

Despite this, in 1989 the Swiss Federal Council unfairly and unethically rejected Palestinian statehood, and its accession to the four Geneva Conventions and Additional Protocols was not welcomed. Although the representatives of the PLO attended all working groups and relevant conference meetings during the formulation of the Convention on the Elimination of All Forms of Discrimination against Women, the PLO had no legal capacity to become a party to the Convention, as this capacity was reserved solely for nation states. A majority of the world's nations ratified the CEDAW agreement, save for three states which did not ratify the convention due to political reasons, thus placing their own political and economic interests above humanitarian ones. These states were: Canada,[188] Israel,[189] and the United States.[190]

4. Palestine Constituting *Jus Cogens* Norms

The term "*jus cogens*" came into existence in accordance with the provisions of the 1969 Vienna Convention, despite not being explicitly referenced in the convention. For instance, many established rules of international law did not need the expression of consent to exist, but were solely based on the existence of facts, such as the right of a population to its homeland. Moreover, the traditional principle of a full sovereign state and the rights which come with that designation, are strongly subject to the principles of human rights law. The provisions of the Vienna Declaration

[188] https://treaties.un.org/doc/Publication/CN/2015/CN.62.2015-Eng.pdf.
[189] https://treaties.un.org/doc/Publication/CN/2014/CN.300.2014-Eng.pdf.
[190] https://treaties.un.org/doc/Publication/CN/2015/CN.64.2015-Eng.pdf.

and Programme of Action adopted through consensus at the World Conference on Human Rights in 1993 also reflect the universal normative peremptory standards of human rights principles, which are indivisible, interdependent, and interconnected. This implies the fact that certain high standards of peremptory norms cannot be denied by the principle of state sovereignty or through acts of occupation. The Vienna Convention on the law of treaties specifies in Article 53 that:

> A treaty is void if, at the time of its conclusion, it conflicts with a peremptory norm of general international law. For the purposes of the present Convention, a peremptory norm of general international law is a norm accepted and recognized by the international community of States as a whole as a norm from which no derogation is permitted and which can be modified only by a subsequent norm of general international law having the same character.

Here the term "treaty" refers not only to multilateral and bilateral treaties, but also to unilateral treaties. The term "treaty" also covers *inter alia* conventions, agreements, protocols, arrangements, covenants, declarations, and unilateral annexations. When we say that *jus cogens* norms encompass the notion of peremptory norms of international law, we mean that states are permanently obliged to respect those norms, e.g., norms concerning the prohibition of commission of genocide, the prohibition of application of torture, and the right to self-determination.[191]

Acts of genocide are of concern not only to the jurisdiction within which they occurred, but to the international community as well.[192] Similarly, the prohibitions relating to crimes of torture and slavery have the nature of *jus cogens* norms.[193] The principle of self-determination, which implies the right of nations to be released from the unlawful activities of an occupying or colonial power, merits the same value. This has been made particularly

---

[191] See Erika de Wet, The Prohibition of Torture as an International Norm of Jus Cogens and its Implications for National and Customary Law, European Journal of International Law, 15 (1) (2004), 111.

[192] *Id.*, 111 and 117.

[193] *Id.*, 97-121.

evident concerning the territories of Palestine, which have long been occupied through force by big powerful states. In other words, they have occupied *jus cogens* norms.

These *jus cogens* rights of the Palestinian population to its homelands and the rejection of any form of occupation or annexation can also be examined in light of the provisions of the United Nations Security Council Resolution 478,40 (14:1).[194] This resolution officially denied the claim of the Israeli government concerning the legitimacy of the annexation of East Jerusalem from the West Bank in 1980, thus recognising Palestine's international legal personality, which needed to then be respected by the occupying power. We should remember that certain resolutions of the United Nations Security Council concerning certain important issues are so imperative, that no state can reject their legal validity, including resolutions which relate to rules of law or rules of customary international law regarding the formation of states.

5. Palestine in the International Court of Justice

In addition to what we have already said above, Resolution 478 the International Court of Justice Advisory Opinion governing the *Legal Consequences of the Construction of a Wall in the Occupied Palestinian Territory* declared that all members of the international community were under an internationally recognized obligation to reject the unlawful situation in and around East Jerusalem. The Court also supported its opinion by referring to the racial segregation wall. The advisory view of the ICJ clarified that the Israeli authorities had violated the basic principles of human rights law. The Court declared, "All States are under an obligation not to recognize the illegal situation resulting from the construction of the

[194] The United States abstention.

wall and not to render aid or assistance in maintaining the situation created by such construction."[195] They went further, stating:

> Given the character and the importance of the rights and obligations involved, the Court is of the view that all States are under an obligation not to recognize the illegal situation resulting from the construction of the wall in the Occupied Palestinian Territory, including in and around East Jerusalem. They are also under an obligation not to render aid or assistance in maintaining the situation created by such construction. It is also *for all States*, while respecting the United Nations Charter and international law, to see to it that any impediment, resulting from the construction of the wall, to the *exercise by the Palestinian people of its right to self-determination* is brought to an end. In addition, all the States parties to the Geneva Convention relative to the Protection of Civilian Persons in Time of War of 12 August 1949 are under an obligation, while respecting the United Nations Charter and international law, to ensure compliance by Israel with international humanitarian law as embodied in that Convention.[196]

The Advisory Opinion of the Court also clarified that the illegal actions in the occupied territories were just that, illegal and invalid. This meant that the Israeli authorities had seriously and extensively hindered the fulfilment of many fundamental rights of the Palestinians, including their right to self-determination. According to the Court, the issue of the wall built by the Israeli authorities was of concern to all states. The example of the ICJ demonstrates that any violation of the ILP of Palestine creates accountability for the Israeli government.[197] For instance, the violation of the right to self-determination of the Palestinian population by means of building a wall or

---

[195] *The Legal Consequences of the Construction of a Wall in the Occupied Palestinian Territory* (I.C.J. Reports 2004), para. 159.

[196] *Id.* See also Christian Tomuschat and Jean-Marc Thouvenin (eds.), *The Fundamental Rules of the International Legal Order: Jus Cogens and Obligations Erga Omnes* (Brill, Leiden, 2006). See also the Advisory Opinion of the ICJ concerning the Namibia case in 1971. The Court ruled that the presence of South Africa in Namibia was illegal and that the State Members of the United Nations should not carry out any act implying recognition of the legality of South Africa's presence.

[197] Farhad Malekian, 'International Criminal Responsibility: International Criminal Responsibility of Individuals' in Bassiouni, M. Cherif. *International Criminal Law*. 2nd ed. Crimes. (Transnational Publishers, Inc. Ardsley. 1999), pp.153-192.

other harmful acts, undoubtedly calls for civil and criminal accountability for the occupying power.

6. Accountability

Accountability should not only mean that the Palestinians are able to return to their homelands, but they should also receive a form of financially redress for their suffering over the decades. The financial restoration here is associated with the gravity associated with the infringement upon the right to self-determination. A similar example is the Chinese occupation of Tibet which has been ongoing since 1950. The General Assembly of the United Nations in Resolution 1723 called for a "cessation of practices which deprive Tibetan peoples of their fundamental human rights and freedoms, including the right to self-determination."[198] The content of the resolution, together with several other resolutions, called for the accountability of the occupied power through restitution.[199]

Obviously, the General Assembly, through the provisions of several resolutions, wanted to underline the fact that the right to self-determination was an integral right of the Tibetan people, and that the Chinese government had to be held responsible for their criminal conduct, including the occupation. Similarly, in the *East Timor Case*, the ICJ asserted that "the rights of self-determination and permanent sovereignty over natural resources are rights *erga omnes* belonging to the people of East Timor, and therefore generate a corresponding duty upon all States, including the Respondent, to recognize and respect those rights."[200]

The ICJ, in its Advisory Opinion concerning the *Legality of the Threat or Use of Nuclear Weapons,* and considering the major value of humanitarian principles, suggested that the rules of humanitarian law

---

[198] General Assembly Resolution 1723 (1961) 'Question of Tibet'.

[199] Reference to earlier Resolutions that date to the time China occupied Tibet show that, while political considerations may have dissuaded the General Assembly from expressly mentioning China, the "practices" referred to stem from its occupation. General Assembly Resolution 1723 (1961) 'Question of Tibet'.

[200] *The ICJ Case Concerning East Timor (Portugal v. Australia), Judgment (30 June 1995).*

pertinent to armed conflict are fundamental to the respect of human natural personality or "elementary considerations of humanity."[201] The Court went further and clarified that "these fundamental rules are to be observed by all States whether or not they have ratified the conventions that contain them, because *they constitute intransgressible principles of international customary law*."[202] Taking these three cases and the conclusions of the General Assembly resolutions concerning the occupying power in Palestinian territories into consideration, one should have to admit that the Israeli legal authorities should be held accountable before both the ICC and the ICJ for the various violations of international human rights law and international criminal law that have occurred over several decades.[203]

7. Expansion of Settlements

The United Nations Security Council identified the construction and expansion of settlements, the transfer of Israeli settlers, the confiscation of land, and the demolition of homes and displacement of Palestinian civilians, as being in violation of international peremptory criminal law in a 2016 resolution. This means that the Israeli settlements are illegal, immoral, and violate the basic principles of justice and international law. The resolution reads:

> The Security Council,
>
> Reaffirming its relevant resolutions, including resolutions 242 (1967), 338 (1973), 446 (1979), 452 (1979), 465 (1980), 476 (1980), 478 (1980), 1397 (2002), 1515 (2003), and 1850 (2008),
>
> Guided by the purposes and principles of the Charter of the United Nations, and reaffirming, inter alia, the inadmissibility of the acquisition of territory by force,

---

201 *Legality of the Threat or Use of Nuclear Weapons, Advisory Opinion, I.C.J. Reports* 1996, para.79.

202 *Id.*

203 Farhad Malekian, 'Judging International Criminal Justice in the Occupied Territories,' 12 *International Criminal Law Review* (2012), pp.827–869.

Reaffirming the obligation of Israel, the occupying Power, to abide scrupulously by its legal obligations and responsibilities under the Fourth Geneva Convention relative to the Protection of Civilian Persons in Time of War, of 12 August 1949, and recalling the advisory opinion rendered on 9 July 2004 by the International Court of Justice,

Condemning all measures aimed at altering the demographic composition, character and status of the Palestinian Territory occupied since 1967, including East Jerusalem, including, inter alia, the construction and expansion of settlements, transfer of Israeli settlers, confiscation of land, demolition of homes and displacement of Palestinian civilians, in violation of international humanitarian law and relevant resolutions,

Expressing grave concern that continuing Israeli settlement activities are dangerously imperilling the viability of the two-State solution based on the 1967 lines,

Recalling the obligation under the Quartet Roadmap, endorsed by its resolution 1515 (2003), for a freeze by Israel of all settlement activity, including "natural growth," and the dismantlement of all settlement outposts erected since March 2001,

Recalling also the obligation under the Quartet roadmap for the Palestinian Authority Security Forces to maintain effective operations aimed at confronting all those engaged in terror and dismantling terrorist capabilities, including the confiscation of illegal weapons,

Condemning all acts of violence against civilians, including acts of terror, as well as all acts of provocation, incitement and destruction,

Reiterating its vision of a region where two democratic States, Israel and Palestine, live side by side in peace within secure and recognized borders,

Stressing that the status quo is not sustainable and that significant steps, consistent with the transition contemplated by prior agreements, are urgently needed in order to (i) stabilize the situation and to reverse negative trends on the ground, which are steadily eroding the two-State solution and entrenching a one-State reality, and (ii) to create the conditions for successful final status negotiations and for advancing the two-State solution through those negotiations and on the ground,

1. Reaffirms that the establishment by Israel of settlements in the Palestinian territory occupied since 1967, including East Jerusalem, has no legal validity and constitutes a flagrant violation under international law

and a major obstacle to the achievement of the two-State solution and a just, lasting and comprehensive peace;

2. Reiterates its demand that Israel immediately and completely cease all settlement activities in the occupied Palestinian territory, including East Jerusalem, and that it fully respect all of its legal obligations in this regard;

3. Underlines that it will not recognize any changes to the 4 June 1967 lines, including with regard to Jerusalem, other than those agreed by the parties through negotiations;

4. Stresses that the cessation of all Israeli settlement activities is essential for salvaging the two-State solution, and calls for affirmative steps to be taken immediately to reverse the negative trends on the ground that are imperilling the two-State solution;

5. Calls upon all States, bearing in mind paragraph 1 of this resolution, to distinguish, in their relevant dealings, between the territory of the State of Israel and the territories occupied since 1967;

6. Calls for immediate steps to prevent all acts of violence against civilians, including acts of terror, as well as all acts of provocation and destruction, calls for accountability in this regard, and calls for compliance with obligations under international law for the strengthening of ongoing efforts to combat terrorism, including through existing security coordination, and to clearly condemn all acts of terrorism;

7. Calls upon both parties to act on the basis of international law, including international humanitarian law, and their previous agreements and obligations, to observe calm and restraint, and to refrain from provocative actions, incitement and inflammatory rhetoric, with the aim, inter alia, of de-escalating the situation on the ground, rebuilding trust and confidence, demonstrating through policies and actions a genuine commitment to the two-State solution, and creating the conditions necessary for promoting peace;

8. Calls upon all parties to continue, in the interest of the promotion of peace and security, to exert collective efforts to launch credible negotiations on all final status issues in the Middle East peace process and within the time frame specified by the Quartet in its statement of 21 September 2010;

9. Urges in this regard the intensification and acceleration of international and regional diplomatic efforts and support aimed at achieving, without delay a comprehensive, just and lasting peace in the

Middle East on the basis of the relevant United Nations resolutions, the Madrid terms of reference, including the principle of land for peace, the Arab Peace Initiative and the Quartet Roadmap and an end to the Israeli occupation that began in 1967; and underscores in this regard the importance of the ongoing efforts to advance the Arab Peace Initiative, the initiative of France for the convening of an international peace conference, the recent efforts of the Quartet, as well as the efforts of Egypt and the Russian Federation;

10. Confirms its determination to support the parties throughout the negotiations and in the implementation of an agreement;

11. Reaffirms its determination to examine practical ways and means to secure the full implementation of its relevant resolutions;

12. Requests the Secretary-General to report to the Council every three months on the implementation of the provisions of the present resolution;

13. Decides to remain seized of the matter.

8. Settlements against Peremptory Norms

Let us begin with the following:

> from the outset, it will be obvious that I differ from other writers of international criminal law and international human rights law who speak about positive law, who do not share the idea of moral law, who express amusement and criticise the idea of judgments of love in criminal justice. However, I am positively convinced, and I am exceptionally sure that the principles of love and morality are the basic factors of positive law. They are to be the real positive law. If positive law does not contain the principles of morality and love, it is no longer law but a dictatorial or barbarous imposition of law. This means protection of inequality of man.[204]

How can we say that crimes against humanity, war crimes, genocide, and violations of the international humanitarian law of armed conflicts

[204] Farhad Malekian, *Classical Morality in International Peremptory Criminal Law* (Cambridge Scholars Publishing, 2018), p.23.

violate basic principles of international peremptory criminal law, but occupation and illegal settlement through the use of force do not? According to Amnesty International USA's advocacy director for the Middle East and North Africa, Philippe Nassif, "expansion of settlements in Occupied Territory is illegal under international law." Therefore, "a peaceful two-state solution is being threatened, and those United Nations member states who believe in peace and security should now lead the way in recognising the State of Palestine." The director further asserted that:

> Today the United States government announced to the rest of the world that it believes the US and Israel are above the law: that Israel can continue to violate international law and Palestinians' human rights and the US will firmly support it in doing so. Today's announcement does not and will not change the law which is crystal clear: the construction and maintenance of settlements in the Occupied West Bank, including East Jerusalem, breaches international law and amounts to war crimes. It does however place the Palestinians in the occupied West Bank, including East Jerusalem, at increased risk by giving Israel the green light to continue with its settlement building and expansion policy which sit at the heart of human rights crisis in the area. The US announcement not only goes against the international consensus on the illegality of Israeli settlements but also goes against the US's legal obligation to respect and ensure respect for the Geneva Conventions.[205]

How can we say that the decisions and judgements of the international court are correct and authoritative, when its decisions concerning the legality of settlements in the Palestinian territory are invalid? If the decisions of the court of the international legal and the political community are correct, then their decisions concerning the legality of settlements are also correct. If the theory is contrary, then the position is also contrary. This means that the system of the international court of justice is invalid, as are its decisions. Thus, the system of international law, the body of international human rights

---

[205] Jack Quann, 'Palestine Ambassador 'welcomes' Irelands Commitment after US Decision on Israel', available online at https://www.newstalk.com/news/palestine-ambassador-welcomes-irelands-commitment-us-decision-israel-926825.

law, and the system of international criminal law cannot be valid if the validity of certain decisions of the international court of justice at The Hague is invalid.

Let us look at another example:

> the fact that Nazi law was positive law, that the Zionist law in Israel is positive law and that communist law was positive law, too. Similarly, the Islamic Republic of Iran also claims to impose positive law. If positive law means the just mentioned laws or other laws, if the positive law and international peremptory criminal law means killing our nations as well as children in the name of the law, if positive law means the killing of Afghans, Iraqis, Yazidis, Yemeni, Kurdish, Lebanese, Libyan, Palestinian, Rwandan, Sudani, Syrian, Tibetan peoples and any other people in our cruel civilisations, including the children of innocent Jews during the Second World War, then that is no longer positive law but humiliating human morality and mentality.[206]

We should remember that *jus cogens* norms are the peremptory obligations which must be valued by all states and should never be violated. If there are *jus cogens* norms involved in a case, then there are also obligations of an indispensable character. If the obligations of indispensable character are violable, then we would have to acquiesce that the crimes of the Nazis against the Jews, and the violation of their *jus cogens* rights were therefore not illegal nor criminal in nature. However, for any realistic writer, it is evident that the Third Reich not only committed crimes against the Jewish population, but that their crimes violated universal peremptory norms.

The *Prosecutor v. Mitar Vasiljević* case made clear the motivation of tribunals relating to the permissible character of *jus cogens*. It becomes obvious that existing law should not hinder the improvement of the international legal discipline in tackling serious international crimes such as occupation and evacuation through military force. The principle of *nullum crimen sine lege* encourages the recognition of new offenses in order to

---

[206] *Id.*

prevent illegal and *ex post facto* law. The International Criminal Tribunal for the former Yugoslavia clarified that if we suppose that the crimes enumerated in its Statute were not identified as part of customary international law, it should have been obvious to the perpetrator that such conduct or criminal behaviour violated moral law. Further, the Court clarified that it did not create a novel theory of international criminal responsibility of individuals in the system of international criminal law, rather they sought to create a method of punishing criminality which could bring criminals under the appropriate criminal jurisdiction for prosecution and punishment. Therefore, the ICTY went further and clarified that:

> 196. The principle of *nullum crimen sine lege* "does not prevent a court from interpreting and clarifying the elements of a particular crime." Nor does it preclude the progressive development of the law by the court. But under no circumstances may the court create new criminal offences after the act charged against an accused either by giving a definition to a crime which had none so far, thereby rendering it prosecutable and punishable, or by criminalizing an act which had not until the present time been regarded as criminal.
>
> 197. The scope of the Tribunal's jurisdiction *ratione materiae* is determined by customary international law as it existed at the time when the acts charged in the indictment were allegedly committed. This limitation placed upon the jurisdiction of the Tribunal is justified by concerns for the principle of legality. …
>
> 198. Accordingly, the Tribunal's Statute was not intended to create new criminal offences. Instead, as stated by the Appeals Chamber, in establishing the Tribunal, the Security Council 'simply created an international mechanism for the prosecution of crimes which were already the subject of individual criminal responsibility.' The fact that an offence is listed in the Statute, or comes within Article 3 of the Statute through common article 3 of the Geneva Conventions, does not therefore create new law, and the Tribunal only has jurisdiction over any listed crime if it was recognised as such by customary international law at the time the crime is alleged to have been committed. Each Trial Chamber is thus

obliged to ensure that the law which it applies to a given criminal offence is indeed customary. The Trial Chamber must further be satisfied that this offence was defined with sufficient clarity for it to have been foreseeable and accessible, taking into account the specificity of customary international law.

199. The Trial Chamber must be satisfied that a given act is criminal under customary international law, because, for instance, a vast number of national jurisdictions have criminalized it or a treaty provision which provides for its criminal punishment has come to represent customary international law. On the other hand, as stated by the *Delalić* Appeals Chamber, 'a finding of individual criminal responsibility is not barred by the absence of treaty provision on punishment of breaches.' The Trial Chamber may also, as suggested by the Appeals Chamber, be satisfied that, in the language of the ICCPR, those acts were 'criminal according to the general principles of law recognized by the community of nations'. For criminal liability to attach, it is not sufficient, however, merely to establish that the act in question was *illegal* under international law, in the sense of being liable to engage the responsibility of a State which breaches that prohibition, nor is it enough to establish that the act in question was a crime under the domestic law of the person who committed the act.[207]

9. VIOLATIONS OF *JUS COGENS* NORMS

It would be a big surprise and humiliating for the legal and political disciplines if it were expressed that the settlements in, and the occupation of Palestinian land did not violate the sovereignty of the peremptory international criminal law and *jus cogens* norms. Such an expression would also violate the moral standards of the international legal community. Bearing these principles in mind, the nature of *jus cogens* norms should give a strong signal to all states of the world that certain norms are related to the nature of man, and should be respected in all contexts of their political, legal, military, and economic relations.

[207] Trial Chamber Judgement, IT-98-32-T, 29 November 2002, paras.196-99.

The significant norms of *jus cogens* or peremptory norms, however, are unfortunately violated by the provisions of Chapter VII of the United Nations Charter, which gives full priority to the abolished principle of inequality. We are referring here to the position of certain members of the United Nations. The Chapter is the most unjustifiable part of our international legal system, which should be based on the voice of political powers, and should not allow violations of international peremptory criminal law through military might.

We should keep in mind that the term "*jus cogens*" primarily arises from the provisions of the law of international treaties.[208] Besides, certain provisions and policies arising from the 1969 Vienna Convention have become an integral part of international human rights law, international criminal law, international criminal justice, and the international humanitarian law of armed conflicts. This means that their provisions must be respected, which is impossible under occupation. We should not, and cannot violate the sovereignty of a population, a group, or indigenous people in order to plunder their lands, as this obviously violates international criminal law and criminal justice. Moreover, it is a fact that the system of

---

[208] Consult Czaplinski, Wladyslaw 'Concepts of Jus cogens and Obligations Erga Omnes in International Law in the Light of Recent Developments' 23 *Polish Yearbook of International Law* (1997–1998), p.87; G Danilenko, 'International Jus cogens: Issues of Law-Making' 2 (1) *European Journal of International Law* (1991), p.42; A. D'Amato, 'It's a Bird, It's a Plane, It's Jus cogens' 6 *Connecticut Journal of International Law* (1990), p.1 AJJ de Hoog, 'The Relationship between Jus cogens, Obligations Erga Omnes and International Crimes: Peremptory Norms in Perspective' 42 *Österreichische Zeitschrift für öffentliches Recht und Völkerrecht* (1991), p.183; E de Wet, 'Jus cogens and Obligations Erga Omnes' in de Wet, E and J. Vidmar (eds.), *Hierarchy in International Law: The Place of Human Rights* (2012); P Dupuy, 'Some Reflections on Contemporary International Law and the Appeal to Universal Values: a Response to Marti Koskenniemi' 16 *European Journal of International Law* (2005), p.131; C. Focarelli, 'Promotional Jus cogens: A Critical Appraisal of Jus cogens' Legal Effects' 77 *Nordic Journal of International Law* (2008), p.429; Glennon, MJ 'De l'Absurdité du Droit Impératif (Jus cogens)' 110 *Revue Générale de Droit International Public* (2006), p.529; Robledo Gómez, A El Ius Cogens Internacional (Estudio Histórico Crítico) (1982); Robledo Gómez, A 'Le Jus cogens International: Sa Genése, sa Nature, ses Fonctions' 9 *Recueil des Cours de l'Académie de Droit International de la Haye* (1982), p.172; L Hannikainen, *Peremptory Norms (Jus Cogens) in International Law: Historical Development, Criteria, Present Status* (1988); Janis, MW 'The Nature of Jus cogens' 3 *Connecticut Journal of International Law* (1988), p.359; Kawasaki, A 'A Brief Note on the Legal Effects of Jus cogens in International Law in International Law' 34 *Hitotsubashi Journal of Law and Politics* (2006), p.27.

customary international (criminal) law and justice does not condone the annexation of the territories of an occupied land.

It is therefore not without reason that we can conclude that:

> 2. Since the opening of the preliminary examination of the Situation in Palestine, Israel has continued unabated to commit crimes within the jurisdiction of the Court. It has done so brazenly in order to advance its settlement regime to an unprecedented level with the aim of pursuing its policy of displacement and replacement of the Palestinian people. This settlement policy has been carried out through the commission of multiple crimes within the Court's jurisdiction. It has been executed in the face of international condemnation of Israel's actions by the Secretary-General of the United Nations, the Security Council, and a wide range of other international fora.
>
> 3. The Israeli settlement regime represents much more than the physical structures that make up the actual housing units in a specific settlement. The physical structures are part of an entire settlement policy which is enacted, maintained, and expanded by top Israeli officials, governmental and military, and which encompasses a range of sub-policies and practices that allow for the planning, construction, expansion, maintenance, security and development of settlements. The unlawful occupation of the territory of the State of Palestine and the establishment and maintenance of settlements by Israel in Occupied Palestinian Territory ("OPT"), including East Jerusalem, has involved the enactment and maintenance of a multi-layered system of violence and intimidation against the Palestinian population, the destruction and unlawful appropriation of their properties, the severe violation of their fundamental rights on discriminatory grounds and the institutionalization of a separate structure of life and dual system of law and other measures deliberately intended to change the demographic composition of the OPT, including in particular in East Jerusalem. It has also involved the widespread and systematic attack on the Palestinian civilian population, through the commission of

crimes, to create and perpetuate such a regime. These acts qualify under the Rome Statute as both war crimes and crimes against humanity.[209]

10. Recurrence of Serious Crimes

The Human Rights Committee of the Latin American region, expressed the concept of legitimate or illegitimate conduct concerning the death penalty, stating:

> The right enshrined in Article (6) is the supreme right of the human being. It follows that the deprivation of life by the authorities of the State is a matter of the utmost gravity. This follows from the article as a whole and in particular is the reason why paragraph 2 of the article lays down that the death penalty may be imposed only for the most serious crimes. The requirements that the right shall be protected law and that no one shall be arbitrarily deprived of his life mean that the law must strictly control and limit the circumstances in which a person may be deprived of his life by the authorities of a State.

The Human Rights Committee is obviously referring to the immorality and criminality of the death penalty. Immorality is most often accompanied by the notion of criminality. This implies the fact that there are certain connections between immoral conducts and criminal conducts, and since both have wrongful intentions, their consequences or results cannot be correct or lawful.

The question that arises therefore is, how we can violate the established principles of *jus cogens* norms, and/or the right to one's own territory, the right to sovereignty, the right to international personality, and the right to be an official member of the United Nations, but avoid recognising these rights as being indispensable? No state or government should violate these rights.

---

[209] The State of Palestine, Referral by the State of Palestine Pursuant to Articles 13(a) and 14 of the Rome Statute (15 May 2018), 18 pp, at 2-3. https://www.icc-cpi.int/items Documents/2018-05-22_ref-palestine.pdf.

In other words, the right to be released from the forceful power of an occupied power is a significant customary, conventional, and consolidated right which must be respected by all states and political powers.[210]

It is today a fact and a settled principle that *jus cogens* norms are the 'concern of all states', and cannot be derogated to the contrary effect. What is really meant by 'concern of all states', is that the international legal and political community is responsible for ensuring certain rights are indispensable and cannot be infringed upon through policies of aggression, or through allowing crimes against humanity to occur, such as war crimes, genocide, or torture.

With the term 'concern of all states', we are making clear that the character of a norm, a principle, an element, and finally, a pillar, in the systems of international criminal law and justice and international human rights, is the most consolidated element of humanity to have achieved international recognition. Such an element may have roots in international conventional law, customary international law, and/or in the system of universal morality. With the system of universal morality, we refer to the system which is not influenced by the thoughts of human beings or by the legislation of big political authorities. Also precluded is the manipulated legislation of the Security Council.

We refer rather to a system which is free from all political influences, and which is concentrated on human integrity, human essence, and human substance. If the system of universal human rights does not support the substantial rights of all human beings, then such law not only does not exist, but then all laws are but the result of the political policy of a military power. How can we agree that the Jews living in Germany before and during the Second World War were treated inhumanely, but we cannot see that something similar has been occurring with the Palestinians for decades? If

---

[210] AJJ de Hoog, 'The Relationship between *Jus cogens*, Obligations *Erga Omnes* and International Crimes: Peremptory Norms in Perspective' 42 *Österreichische Zeitschrift für öffentliches Recht und Völkerrecht* (1991), p.18; M Byers, 'Conceptualising the Relationship Between *Jus cogens* and *Erga Omnes Rules*' 66 *Nordic Journal of International Law* (1997), p.211; A Cassese, 'For an Enhanced Role of *Jus cogens*' in Cassese, A (ed.), *Realizing Utopia* (2012); C Chinkin, '*Jus cogens*, Article 103 of the UN Charter and other Hierarchical Techniques of Conflict Solution' *Finnish Yearbook of International Law* (2008), p.63.

humanity implies the existence of certain rights, if humanity means the respect of those rights, and if the intention of the UN Security Council is the maintenance of international rights for all states, then we are surely going in the wrong direction.

Similarly, if the United Nations was established in order to maintain, and fight for the right to self-determination for all people, then we must understand that the present conducts of the Israeli government violates the rights of the Palestinians, similar to how the rights of the Jews were violated through acts of genocide during WWII. If the Israeli government does not understand this very simple logic, then they are dishonouring the *memory of the Holocaust* by carrying out criminal conducts against the Palestinians. We are not speaking here about a national identity, but about the philosophy of justice and the philosophy of understanding the rights of man, regardless of religion. In other words, suffering is suffering no matter what it may be called. The dignity of man, the integrity of human beings, and the established rights of certain groups, populations, and nations exist whether the people are Jewish or Palestinian.

Wrongful conduct is wrongful conduct regardless of whether it is carried out against the population of the US, China, Russia, or Italy. In the end, it all comes down to the same questions of rights, ethics, and the consolidation of all rights for human beings, regardless of their identity. If this is not the purpose of human rights law, if this is not the intention of the Security Council, if this is not the purpose of the International Court of Justice, then it is the question of military power and the question of use of force, as is occurring in the traditional territories of the Palestinians. Therefore, the following statement is not only correct, but also authoritative regarding both the current situation of the Palestinians, and that of the Jews who suffered under the Third Reich:

> 4. As reflected in communications and twenty-five successive monthly reports submitted by the State of Palestine to the OTP, war crimes and crimes against humanity have continued to be committed on an aggravated basis throughout the period of the preliminary examination. The impunity of Israeli officials and Israeli nationals responsible for the commission of

these crimes has contributed to the continuation, intensification and recurrence of these crimes.

5. The gravity and ongoing nature of this criminality, as well as the fact that State officials are involved in the commission of these crimes, calls for the Prosecution to conduct and finalise its investigation without delay, and with a view to bringing those responsible to justice.

6. It is thus necessary, on behalf of the citizens of the State of Palestine who have suffered for generations the consequences of crimes committed with impunity by Israeli officials and citizens, and who continue to suffer from ongoing, widespread and systematic crimes, for the State of Palestine to hereby exercise its right as a State Party to the Rome Statute to refer the Situation of Palestine for immediate investigation so that those most responsible for these crimes may be held accountable for their actions without further delay.

7. The State of Palestine stresses the importance of achieving justice for the victims of crimes, reaffirms its commitment to cooperate fully with the Court and maintains that ensuring justice and accountability is crucial to achieving peace, to deterring the commission of crimes, and to the integrity and credibility of the ICC itself. A failure to punish, let alone investigate, crimes associated with the unlawful occupation of Palestine has only emboldened perpetrators to carry on with their criminal deeds.

8. The present referral is without prejudice to the Prosecutor's ongoing duty and responsibility to continue and finalise her preliminary examination without delay in accordance with Article 53 of the Rome Statute regarding crimes currently the subject of her preliminary examination in the Situation of Palestine. However, given the acceleration of settlement-related crimes and their irreversible impact on the lives of Palestinians and on the prospects for a lasting peace, it is imperative that the OTP immediately commence an investigation into the crimes herein referred as its highest priority.[211]

[211] The State of Palestine, Referral by the State of Palestine Pursuant to Articlesl3(a) and 14 of the Rome Statute (15 May 2018), 18 pp, at 3-5. https://www.icc-cpi.int/itemsDocuments/2018-05-22_ref-palestine.pdf.

11. Crimes within the ICC Authority

The Referral by the State of Palestine Pursuant to Articles 13 (a) and 14 of the Rome Statute (15 May 2018) is one of the actions taken by the state of Palestine to defend its rights under the jurisdiction of the International Criminal Court. The Referral identifies where and how the provisions of the system of international criminal justice have been violated by the legal, political, and military actions of the Israeli government. It lists a number of criminal acts which have been committed through the use of force, or by the imposition of power over the innocent, and essentially defenceless population of Palestine. The Referral identifies crimes which fall within the jurisdiction of the court. Accordingly:

> 11. Pursuant to Article 14(2) of the Rome Statute, the State of Palestine specifies that the circumstances relevant to the present referral include but are not limited to, all matters related to the Israeli settlement regime outlined in earlier communications, monthly reports and submissions by the Government of Palestine, confidentially filed with or conveyed to the Office of the Prosecutor. 6 In particular, the present referral incorporates as matters to be subject to investigation, any conduct, policies, laws, official decisions and practices that underlie, promote, encourage or otherwise make a contribution to the commission of these crimes in accordance with the terms of the Statute, including but not limited to those coming within the terms of the following Articles of the Statute: Articles 7(l)(a), (d), (e), (f), (h), (j) and (k), 8(2)(a)(i), (ii), (iii), (iv), (vi),' (vii), (b)(i), (ii), (iii), (iv), (viii), (ix), (xiii), (xvi) and (xxi) of the Rome Statute.
>
> 12. The Referral highlights certain categories of war crimes and crimes against humanity of particular seriousness and concern to the Palestinian people and the international community (as expressed in repeated Security Council Resolutions, including most recently Resolution 2334), to ensure that they form an integral part of the OTP's investigation. However, the crimes set forth below are not the only crimes committed within the jurisdiction of the ICC and are not intended to limit the scope of the OTP's investigation. For current purposes, and given the urgent need for an investigation to be opened without further delay, the State of Palestine

hereby specifically identifies the following categories of crimes as being core to the *present* referral:

i. Crimes involving the unlawful appropriation and destruction of private and public properties, including land, houses and buildings, as well as natural resources;

ii. Crimes involving the forcible transfer of Palestinians, including by means of violence, compulsion, duress and the creation of inhumane living conditions;

iii. Crimes involving the unlawful transfer of the Israeli Occupying Power's population into Occupied Palestinian Territory;

iv. Crimes involving murders and unlawful attacks on civilians, including through excessive use of force and unlawful killings of Palestinians, including demonstrators exercising their right to protest;

v. Crimes involving the torture, cruel and inhumane treatment of Palestinians;

vi. Crimes involving persecution, including the grave, widespread and systematic denial or violation of basic human rights on discriminatory grounds against Palestinians, including those resulting in or intended to achieve the deportation or forcible transfer, directly or indirectly, of the Palestinian population, the re-populating of "cleansed" territories with Israeli settlers and the unlawful appropriation of Palestinian land and properties; and,

vii. Crimes involving the establishment of a system of apartheid based in particular on the adoption of discriminatory laws, policies and practices as well as the commission of inhumane acts intended to establish an institutionalized regime of separation and advancement of Israeli settlements accompanied by the systematic oppression and domination by Israeli settlers over Palestinians.

13. The present referral pertains to all categories of criminal participation in the commission of the crimes described above, as provided for under the Statute of the Court, pursuant to Articles 25 - 28 of the Statute. This includes, but is not limited to, those who plan, prepare and implement policies linked to the settlements regime as well as those who enable it, whether through financial, military, or logistical support or otherwise aid and abet or encourage the commission of crimes connected to that regime. The referral includes, in particular, those civilian and military leaders who are in a position of command or authority towards those committing the

underlying crimes and who, through their acts or omission, contribute to the commission of these crimes or fail to prevent, stop or punish them.[212]

12. Reasonable Basis for Investigation

We know without hesitation that the occupation of a country is wrong when it is carried out through the use force. It does not matter whether this occupation was carried out with Israeli military power or with the military power of the United States. Similarly, it is not a valid justification to claim that the occupation of Palestine is legitimate because the land taken is considered ancestral or traditional homeland. These are not legitimate excuses for occupation as if they were, then many countries would have to change their borders in order to align with historical claims. We are not here to defend the Palestinian people, but the philosophy of legal development and the philosophy behind which the United Nations stands. The UN was not founded to create war, but justice. The UN was not founded to create rights for some at the expense of others, but to create equality between all nations of the world. Thus, the UN should facilitate the restoration of rights to those affected by occupation or colonization at the hands of the great powers.

There are reasonable grounds for investigation when the population of a country is being forced from their territory and attacked by the arms of the world's strongest nations, such as is the case with Palestine and the attacks from Israel and the US. Palestinians have not only been left homeless from attacks, but many have been brutally killed. If we accept this as justice, then justice will not survive, as it will be replaced by instability. Obviously, the killing and occupation of Palestinian territory is wrong, and is barbaric behaviour. Certainly, killing the children of one nation not only constitutes a crime against humanity, but also a crime against a generation. Thus, there is logical support and facts to justify investigating the crimes committed

---

[212] The State of Palestine, Referral by the State of Palestine Pursuant to Articles 13 (a) and 14 of the Rome Statute (15 May 2018), 18 pp, at 5-8. Available at https://www.icc-cpi.int/itemsDocuments/2018-05-22_ref-palestine.pdf.

against the Palestinian people. The problem here is obvious. The law promotes violations of the law, and it is allowing the resort to the unlawful use of force.

> In other words, if the use of force is prohibited by all means, it cannot be permitted by any means. If the application of capital punishment is abolished, it cannot be justified in any situation, as is the case in Article 6 of the Covenant. If the norms of legality are correctly divided into primary and secondary rules, then we cannot deprive them of their high human values. Likewise, if Islamic law is a permanent brotherhood, then it cannot be removed from this significant principle. If the communist idea is to share greater common interests of humanity, then it cannot be isolated from other theories. The norm of love is built on the strength of justice and our ability to understand that if every human being has the inherent right to life, freedom of speech and marriage, this is a collective inheritance, and therefore no human being should be isolated from this right by any means. Particularly, the above rights are an integral part of peremptory norms of international law. According to one view, "The risk of political abuse would nonetheless exist in the sense that proceedings of this nature will most likely only be instituted against less powerful states. For example, it is not very likely that a permanent member of the Security Council would face civil claims in foreign courts for damages resulting from the violation of *jus cogens* norms.[213]

It seems that the State of Palestine Referral by the State of Palestine Pursuant to Articles l3 (a) and 14 of the Rome Statute correctly identifies the "*Rationale*" for the crimes committed against the population of Palestine. It states:

> 14. This referral aims at securing justice for millions of Palestinian victims who look upon the ICC to provide justice and to help bring an end to, and prevent the recurrence of, such crimes against them. These crimes are among the most widely documented in contemporary history. In line

[213] Erika de Wet, 'The Prohibition of Torture as an International Norm of *jus cogens* and Its Implications for National and Customary Law', 15 (1) *European Journal of International Law* (2004), pp.97-121, at 110.

with the *raison d'etre* of the ICC, they must be investigated and their perpetrators held to account without further delay.

15. The crimes committed by Israeli officials, including officials at the highest levels of the State, are entrenched as a matter of State policy, planned and perpetrated pervasively, systematically and on a widespread basis, attract no accountability, and have continued with impunity despite the OTP's preliminary examination. This state of affairs imposes unimaginable and long-lasting harm to victims and risks undermining the legitimacy of international law and international judicial institutions, including the ICC.

16. During the current preliminary examination, there has been an alarming intensification of Israeli crimes with an attendant and compounding impact on the Palestinian population and, in particular, on children. Such intensification is further evidenced, *inter alia,* by the following:

a. There was a 70% surge in Israeli settlement construction starts on Occupied Palestinian Territory between April 2016 and March 2017, as compared to the same period in 2015-2016.7 In 2017 alone, the Israeli government advanced plans for over 6,742 additional Israeli settler housing units. "Israel's illegal settlement activities ... continued at a high rate, a consistent pattern" throughout the year.

b. Israeli occupation forces and settlers killed or injured, with impunity, over 1,100 Palestinian children in 2017, worsening a child protection crisis in the territory of the Occupied Palestinian State. In total, members of Israeli forces murdered, unlawfully killed or injured over 7,300 Palestinian civilians throughout the course of the year.

c. On 14 May 2018 alone, during peaceful demonstrations in the Gaza Strip, the Israeli Occupation Forces killed over 60 Palestinians, and injured thousands more, including with live ammunition and artillery fire. The casualties included 6 children, a double amputee, and a paramedic. Hundreds were also injured, including 11 journalists. Since 30 March 2018, Israeli Occupation Forces killed over 110 peaceful demonstrators and other protected persons, including 2 journalists, children, and 1 paramedic. During this period, the Israeli Occupation Forces repeatedly stated their knowledge of where every bullet fired on protestors landed12, while top Israeli officials congratulated the snipers on a job well done, including the Prime Minister13 and Defense Minister, who declared that "there are no innocent people in the Gaza Strip."[214]

d. In 2017, Israeli occupation forces demolished or unlawfully appropriated 424 Palestinian homes and structures necessary to Palestinian livelihood. In 2016, at least 1,054 Palestinian structures were demolished, marking the highest number of unlawful demolitions and appropriations of Palestinian homes and livelihood structures in the Occupied Palestinian Territory, including East Jerusalem, since 2009. e. Within the context of this deliberate pattern of destruction and appropriation of civilian property, Israeli occupation forces forcibly displaced 3,861 Palestinians, including 1,960 children, since 13 June 2014, the date from which the ICC's temporal jurisdiction over the matter began. They also impacted the livelihood and access to services of a further 19,555 Palestinians. f. There was a record level of ratifications of "state land" declarations on Occupied Palestinian Territory by the Israeli government in 2016, which qualifies, *inter alia,* as pillage, unlawful appropriation of property and persecution; g. By the end of 2016, 7,000 Palestinians were being arbitrarily detained in Israeli jails, including 700 held under "administrative detention" (indefinitely renewable, without charge or trial or basic legal protections and on the basis of 'secret evidence' kept from both detainee and attorney), the highest level since 2008.20 With a bi-weekly average of 79 raids into the West Bank per week and 67 in total into the Gaza Strip in 2017,21 the policy of mass arbitrary arrest and unlawful imprisonment by Israeli occupation forces continued.

17. In parallel, the Israeli government has guaranteed almost complete impunity to its leadership, occupying forces, settlers and other citizens responsible for crimes committed against the Palestinian population in the Occupied Palestinian Territory, demonstrating the discriminatory nature of the dual justice system applied there and the fact that it forms part of a State-sponsored policy of promoting, encouraging and authorizing the commission of such crimes.

18. Based on information already made available to the OTP, the State of Palestine submits that, in accordance with articles 14(1) and 53(1) of the Statute, there is clearly a "reasonable basis to proceed with an

[214] See, The Middle East Eye, 'No innocent people in Gaza' says Israeli defense minister, 8 April 2018, available online at: http://www.middleeasteye.net/news/no-innocent-people-gaza-says-israeli-defence-minister-1 155018849.

investigation" in relation to each and all of the above-mentioned crimes. The existence of a reasonable basis to conduct an investigation is also established by the following: a. Over the last 50 years, the United Nations Security Council, the United Nations General Assembly23 and the Human Rights Council have passed numerous resolutions recognizing that Israeli settlements in the Occupied Palestinian Territory are in violation of international law, including the right of the Palestinian people to self-determination, and calling on Israel, the occupying power, to abide by its obligations under international law; b. On 8 December 2003, the General Assembly requested an advisory opinion from the International Court of Justice ("ICJ") on the legality of Israel's construction of a wall on and through the Occupied Palestinian Territory.27 On 9 July 2004, after full deliberations, the ICJ ruled that Israel's building of a wall on occupied Palestinian territory is "contrary to international law." In its Opinion the ICJ unanimously held that "Israeli settlements in the Occupied Palestinian Territory (including East Jerusalem) have been established in breach of international law." In this opinion, the Court, after noting the illegality of settlements and fears that Israel may integrate these settlements and their means of access, stated "that the construction of the wall and its associated regime create *a fait accompli* on the ground that could well become permanent, in which case, and notwithstanding the formal characterization of the wall by Israel, it would be tantamount to *d* annexation." The concluded that the establishment of Israeli settlements in the Occupied Palestinian Territory breached the prohibition under international law, whereby "the Occupying Power shall not deport or transfer parts of its own civilian population into the territory it occupies." c. On 23 December 2016, the United Nations Security Council adopted Resolution 2334 (2016) which, in line with the longstanding positions of the United Nations Security Council, condemned "all measures aimed at altering the demographic composition, character and status of the Palestinian Territory occupied since 1967, including East Jerusalem, including *inter alia,* the construction and expansion of settlements, transfer of Israeli settlers, confiscation of land, demolition of homes and displacement of Palestinian civilians, in violation of international humanitarian law and relevant resolutions'7, and reaffirmed that the "establishment by Israel of settlements in the Palestinian territory occupied since 1967, including East Jerusalem, has no legal validity and constitutes a flagrant violation under international law and a major obstacle to the achievement of the two-State solution and a just, lasting and comprehensive peace." It also reiterated "its demand that Israel immediately and completely, cease all settlement activities in the occupied Palestinian territory, including East Jerusalem, and that it fully respect all of its legal obligations in this regard." This and previous resolutions, by addressing Israel, acknowledge the Israeli State and officials' role in the planning, implementation, expansion and maintenance of the settlement regime and their responsibility in the ongoing criminality linked to this regime. d. Several United Nations fact-finding and inquiry commissions have found credible and reliable evidence establishing reasonable grounds to believe international crimes have been committed by Israeli forces and officials on the territory of the State of Palestine. e. On 14 September 1967, shortly after the Six-Day War, Judge Theodor Meron, then Legal Adviser of the Israel Ministry of Foreign Affairs, issued a legal opinion "that the establishment of civilian settlements in the occupied West Bank and other conquered territories violates the Fourth Geneva Convention related to the protection of victims of war and, specifically, its prohibition on settlements (Article *49(6)*)." 36 Judge Meron reaffirmed this opinion on the fiftieth anniversary of the occupation: But if the continuation of the settlement project on the West Bank has met with practically universal rejection by the international community, it is not just because of its illegality under the Fourth Geneva Convention or under international humanitarian law more generally. Nor is it only because, by preventing the establishment of a contiguous and viable Palestinian territory, the settlement project frustrates any prospect of serious negotiations aimed at a two state solution, and thus of reconciliation between the Israelis and the Palestinians. It is also because of the growing perception that individual Palestinians' human rights, as well as their rights under the Fourth Geneva Convention, are being violated and that the colonization of territories populated by other peoples can no longer be accepted in our time.[215]

---

[215] The State of Palestine, Referral by the State of Palestine Pursuant to Articles 13 (a) and 14 of the Rome Statute (15 May 2018), 18 pp, available at 8-17. https://www.icc-cpi.int/itemsDocuments/2018-05-22_ref-palestine.pdf.

Chapter 6

THE *MENS REA* OF POLITICAL LAUNDERING CRUCIFYING *AL-QUDS/JERUSALEM*

1. INTRODUCTION

القُدس/*Al-Quds* is the historical Arabic name for the city of Jerusalem, which serves as a holy city for three world religions: Judaism, Christianity, and Islam. All three cultures have certain similarities that could not be disputed by any wise man. Their goals and strengths have been misinterpreted, as in reality, friendly relations between them is indispensable for the *corpus juris* of peace, justice, and humanity. This chapter deals with serious violations of the provisions of the system of international criminal law with the complete awareness on the part of perpetrator, i.e., the United States government. The malicious declaration/statement about *Al-Quds* by the United States President is the clearest indicator of the presence of the *mens rea* and an *actus reus,* of a violation. The major powers are brutally engaged, not only in economic laundering, but also in political laundering--which constitutes the basis of the former. Nevertheless, *Al-Quds/Jerusalem* has its own legal discipline, as was vividly stated in Resolution 181 of the Security Council and as imposed on the Palestinian population through the use of force.

2. Civilization on Palestinian Soil

The system of international criminal law is not a private system, rather it is public, as is UN law, the provisions of the UNSC, the ICJ, the ICC, and many other international organisations.[216] The core intention of all these organisations is to stand firmly against the use of force in any form, and to promote the fact that such acts are contrary to the equal application of international laws. As a result, a unilateral decision is unacceptable in international forums. Likewise, the *corpus juris* of international criminal law does not belong to one particular regime or authority, but to the entire international community. The system of international criminal law intends to bring criminals under the legal sovereignty of the law and to punish the perpetrators of international crimes.[217] This not only includes the weak

---

[216] See Vespasian V. Pella, *Plan d'un Code Répressif Mondial, 6 Rewe International de Droit Pénal* 1948 (1955); United Nations War Crimes Commission, History of the United Nations War Commission and the Development of the Laws of War. 445-450 (1949); Vespasian V. Pella, Towards an International Criminal Court, 44 *American Journal of International Law* 57 (1950); Sowilet A, *The Problem of the Creation of a Permanent International Criminal Court* (Nendeln, Liechtenstein : Kraus reprint, 1951); Yeun-Li Liang, 'The Establishment of an International Criminal Jurisdiction: The First Phase', 46 *American Journal of International Law* (1952); Quincy Wright, Proposal for an International Criminal Court, 46 *American Journal of International Law* 60 (1952); Bienvenido C. Ambion, '*Organization of a Court of International Criminal Jurisdiction'*, 29 *Philippine Law Journal* 545 (1954); Fannie Klein & Daniel Wilkes, 'United Nations Draft Statute for an International Criminal Court: An American Evaluation', in *International Criminal Law* 526 (Gerhard O.W. Mueller & Edward M. Wise, eds, 1965); Stone Julius and Robert Woetzel, *Toward a Feasible International Criminal Court* (1970). William A. Schabas, The International Criminal Court: A Commentary on the Rome Statute (Oxford University Press, 2016); Farhad Malekian, *Jurisprudence of International Criminal Justice* (Introduction by Professor Benjamin B. Ferencz, the former Prosecutor of the Nuremberg Tribunal (Cambridge: Cambridge Scholars Publishing, 2014); Carsten Stahn, *The Law and Practice of the International Criminal Court* (Oxford University Press, 2015).

[217] Consult John E Ackerman and Eugène O'Sullivan, *Practice and Procedure of the International Criminal Tribunal for the Former Yugoslavia with selected material from the International Criminal Tribunal for Rwanda* (2000); Michael Akehurst, *Jurisdiction in International Law*, 1972-1973 BYIL 145; Allmand Warren, 'The International Criminal Court and the Human Rights Revolution', 46 (1) *McGill Law Journal* (2000); Ambion Bienvenido C, 'Organization of a Court of International Criminal Jurisdiction', 29 *Philippine Law Journal* 345 (1954); Amann D.M. and M.N.S. Sellers, 'The United States of America and the International Criminal Court', *American Journal of Comparative Law* 381-404 (2002); Kofi Annan, 'Advocating for an International Criminal Court', 21 *Fordham International Law Journal* 363 (1997); J. Holmes Armstead, 'The International Criminal Court: History, Development and Status', 38 *Santa Clara Law Review* 745-835 (1998).

individuals or powerless states, but also the leading political parties which consistently violate the system of international criminal justice through their political, military, and illegal activities.[218]

Gudmundur Alfredsson the Director of the Raoul Wallenberg Institute for Human Rights and Humanitarian Law at Lund University, Sweden writes in a foreword of a book entitled *Conundrums of Humanity* "It is a pleasure and a privilege to invite Jonathan Power to publish this book in the Human Rights Library (blue series) of the ... Institute... The author's forward-looking, realistic and ultimately optimistic assessment is an encouragement to us all." Power formulates in his book that:

> The Christians for their part were rarely tolerant, always angling to recapture Jerusalem which they considered part of their heritage and unable to come terms with Islamic and Jewish minorities in the midst. *Indeed, the long persecution of the Jews which culminated in Hitler's gas chambers was always pursued by Christians not Muslims. Today we are seized by the clash between Jew and Arab over the ancient land of Palestine.* It has produced a poisonous, deadly relationship between Islam and Judaism. But this is a comparatively new phenomenon unlike what went on for most of their centuries of co-existence. If it hadn't been for the Christian sentimentality of the British government of the Lloyd George that led to the Balfour Declaration and the creation of a Jewish homeland on British-occupied Palestinians territory, and if it hadn't been for Nazi Holocaust which drove so many of Europe's Jews away from their almost equally ancient homelands, there would not be today's Islamic/Jewish clash of civilization on Palestinian soil.

3. International Criminal Law Regarding Brutality

The basic pillars of international criminal law are very clear: prohibition, prevention, rehabilitation, elimination, extradition, jurisdiction, prosecution,

[218] However, the application of international criminal law is not so easy.

and imputation of proper criminal sanctions against individuals, superiors, and political leaders who deliberately violate the provisions of the system with utter cruelty such as Al-Bashir, George W. Bush, Tony Blair, Benjamin Netanyahu, and Barack Obama. Here, I aim to examine page by page the records of the one-sided-policy of the United States government and Israel, who jointly, systematically, and knowingly, have ignored the principles of international criminal law in their political actions and military strategies. Without any hesitation, the policy of the three governments i.e., the United States, the United Kingdom, and Israel has even violated the provisions of the Atlantic Charter of 1941. The Charter reads:

> The President of the United States of America and the Prime Minister, Mr. Churchill, representing His Majesty's Government in the United Kingdom, being met together, deem it right to make known certain common principles in the national policies of their respective countries on which they base their hopes for a better future for the world.
>
> First, their countries seek no aggrandizement, territorial or other;
>
> Second, they desire to see no territorial changes that do not accord with the freely expressed wishes of the peoples concerned;
>
> Third, they respect the right of all peoples to choose the form of government under which they will live; and they wish to see sovereign rights and self-government restored to those who have been forcibly deprived of them;
>
> Fourth, they will endeavour, with due respect for their existing obligations, to further the enjoyment by all States, great or small, victor or vanquished, of access, on equal terms, to the trade and to the raw materials of the world which are needed for their economic prosperity;
>
> Fifth, they desire to bring about the fullest collaboration between all nations in the economic field with the object of securing, for all, improved labour standards, economic advancement and social security;
>
> Sixth, after the final destruction of the Nazi tyranny, they hope to see established a peace which will afford to all nations the means of dwelling in safety within their own boundaries, and which will afford assurance that all the men in all lands may live out their lives in freedom from fear and want;

Seventh, such a peace should enable all men to traverse the high seas and oceans without hindrance;

Eighth, they believe that all of the nations of the world, for realistic as well as spiritual reasons must come to the abandonment of the use of force. Since no future peace can be maintained if land, sea or air armaments continue to be employed by nations which threaten, or may threaten, aggression outside of their frontiers, they believe, pending the establishment of a wider and permanent system of general security, that the disarmament of such nations is essential. They will likewise aid and encourage all other practicable measure which will lighten for peace-loving peoples the crushing burden of armaments.[219]

4. Ignominy by *Crucifixion*

It is plain to see that from its inception, that the purpose of Balfour Declaration of 1917 of establishing a Jewish state was fundamentally wrong, unfair, and signified a move against the long-established civilization of Palestine. Although the Palestinian President decided to sue Britain over the 1917 Balfour Declaration and their support for "Israeli crimes," the road to accomplishing this has not been very smooth.[220] One hundred years have passed since the Declaration was issued, and since then violations have occurred not only in the traditional and historical territories of the Palestinian nation, but also in Syria, Egypt, Iraq, Libya, and Afghanistan – not to mention the dishonourable crucifixion of Muslims in the Abu-Ghraib prison, where the majority of the illegal inhumane offences have occurred.

The crucifixions have insulted and humiliated Islamic, Christian, and Jewish believers. This method of execution was utilised in ancient times and involves nailing and binding the victim to an erect cross and leaving them there until they died. In fact, several US soldiers tortured prisoners while they were being crucified naked, by scaring them with their dogs and

[219] Franklin Roosevelt and Winston Churchill (14 August 1941).

[220] http://www.independent.co.uk/news/world/middle-east/palestinian-President-plans-to-sue-britain-over-1917-balfour-Declaration-and-support-for-israeli-a7157726.html.

taunting them. The United States actually published a book introducing the method of torturing and crucifying Muslims in Iraq. For instance, there was one case which

> represents the most emblematic image of the torture scandal: the hooded man standing on a box with wires attached to his hands, who was told by Specialist Sabrina Harmon that he would be electrocuted if he fell off the box. According to the testimony of the victim, *Abdou Husain Saad Faleh*, the wires were not only attached to his fingers but also his toes and penis. Known as the 'Vietnam,' the image resonates with allusions to the crucifixion, robed monks, the Statue of Liberty, the Klan, the executioner, the mask of death. But most of all, like the mortified Christ.[221]

Many photos taken in Abu-Ghraib were banned from being released at the beginning of Barack Obama's presidency. According to an article entitled *A Nation Crucified*, Obama "did not want the world to see pictures of Iraqi kids being raped by US military personnel in front of their mothers or kids sodomized. He definitely did not want the world to see pictures of detainees' hair shaved to resemble a Christian cross."[222]

The torture at Abu-Ghraib intentionally violated Islamic rules and customs as it was designed to exploit religious taboos. The manual given to the United States troops during a week-long course on Iraqi culture appears to have served as a guide to torturing Muslim prisoners. It reads: "Shame is given by placing hoods over a detainee's head. Avoid this practice. Placing a detainee on the ground or putting a foot on him implies that you are God. This is one of the worst things we can do."

---

[221] Torture Culture: Lynching Photographs and the Images of Abu Ghraib, Art Journal, Vol. 64, No. 2 (Summer, 2005), pp. 88-100, available online at http://www.sjsu.edu/people/ruma.chopra/courses/H170_MW9am_S12/s1/Abu_Ghraib.pdf.

[222] http://voicesfromiraq.blogspot.de/2009/05/normal-0-false-false-false-en-us-x-none.html.

5. THE LEADING MASTERS OF INTERNATIONAL CRIMINAL JUSTICE

Violations of the system of international criminal law are not just violations of the legal body of our criminal law, but are obvious violations of the law of humanity, which is regrettably known as the system of international human rights law. It is like a mirage, you can see something beautiful just out of reach, but you can never reach it.[223] This is because when human rights law is needed the most, it loses its capacity, such as with the cases of the massacre of Palestinian children in Gaza and the children in Rwanda.[224] The International Criminal Tribunal for Rwanda correctly asserted that:

> The rape of Tutsi women was systematic and was perpetrated against all Tutsi women and solely against them. A Tutsi woman, married to a Hutu, testified before the Chamber that she was not raped because her ethnic background was unknown. As part of the propaganda campaign geared to mobilizing the Hutu against the Tutsi, the Tutsi women were presented as sexual objects. Indeed, the Chamber was told, for example, that before being raped and killed, Alexia, who was the wife of the Professor, Ntereye, and her two nieces, were forced by the Interahamwe to undress and ordered to run and do exercises "in order to display the thighs of Tutsi women." The Interahamwe who raped Alexia said, as he threw her on the ground and got on top of her, "let us now see what the vagina of a Tutsi woman takes [sic] like." As stated above, Akayesu himself, speaking to the Interahamwe who were committing the rapes, said to them: "don't ever ask against [sic] what a Tutsi woman tastes like." This sexualized representation of ethnic identity graphically illustrates that Tutsi women were subjected to sexual violence because they were Tutsi. Sexual violence

---

[223] Malekian, *The Mirage of International Criminal Law*, note 9.

[224] Farhad Malekian, 'Judging International Criminal Justice in the Occupied Territories,' 12 *International Criminal Law Review* (2012), 827–869; see also Farhad Malekian, 'Mutilating the Philosophy of Justice in the Time of Armed Conflicts', *Contemporary Journal of International Criminal Law* (2007); see *also* Malekian, *International Criminal Law of Children*, note 6.

was a step in the process of destruction of the tutsi group-destruction of the spirit, the will to live, and of life itself.[225]

In reality, the system of international criminal law violates its own legal humanitarian mechanisms,[226] and consequently the entire discipline of international criminal law is under serious duress concerning the legality, morality, and love for justice within the framework of its own codification system. The degree of these violations can be examined under the system of the International Criminal Court (ICC), which is severely paralysed concerning the matter of jurisdiction over and prosecution of the major political parties.[227] The serious criminal offences in Afghanistan, including the widespread killing of men, women, and innocent children, demonstrate the brutal superiority of these powers, and the exploitation of the inequality of the victims. Correspondingly, crimes against humanity, war crimes,

---

[225] *Akayesu Judgment,* Prosecutor v Akayesu, Case No. ICTR-96-4-T (Judgment, September 2, 1998) ch. 6.3.1, 496, available online at ICTR website, http://www.ictr.org; See also http://unictr.irmct.org/sites/unictr.org/files/case-documents/ictr-96-4/appeals-chamber-judgements/en/010601.pdf; http://unictr.irmct.org/en/cases/ictr-96-4.

[226] On international criminal law, see Georg Schwarzenberger, 'The Problem of an International Criminal Law,' 5 *Current Legal Problems* (1950) 265; Edward M. Wise, 'Prolegomenon to the Principles of International Criminal Law,' 16 *New York University Law Review* (1970) 562; Farhad Malekian, *International Criminal Law: The Legal and Critical Analysis of International Crimes* (2 vols. 1991); Farhad Malekian, *Principles of Islamic International Criminal Law: A Comparative Search* (2011); Farhad Malekian, *The Monopolization of International Criminal Law in the United Nations: A Jurisprudential Approach* (2nd ed., 1995); M. Cherif Bassiouni (ed.), *International Criminal Law* (5 vols., 1999); Farhad Malekian, *International Criminal Responsibility,* in M. Cherif Bassiouni (ed.), *International Criminal Law*, (1999), p.155.

[227] Jean Dautricourt, 'The Concept of International Criminal Court Jurisdiction – Definition and Limitations of the Subject', in vol.I, *A Treatise on International Criminal Law* 656 (M.C. Bassiouni & V.P. Nanda, eds, 1975); 'La Création d'une Juridiction Pénale Internationale et la Coopération Internationale en Matière Pénale', 45 *Revue Internationale de Droit Penale* 455 (1974); Louis Kos-Rabcewicz-Zubrowski, 'The Creation of an International Criminal Court', in *International Terrorism and Political Crimes* 519 (M. Cherif Bassiouni, ed, 1975); Ferencz Benjamin, *International Criminal Court* (2 vols. 1980); M. Cherif Bassiouni & Daniel Derby, 'Final Report on the Establishment of an International Criminal Court for the Implementation of the Apartheid Convention and Other Relevant Instruments', 7 *Hofstra Law Review* 525 (1981); Benjamin N. Schiff, *Building the International Criminal Court* (Cambridge; Cambridge University Press, 2008); William A. Schabas, *An Introduction to the International Criminal Court* (Cambridge University Press, 2011).

aggression, and acts of genocide in Gaza have always been seen as an inferior, insignificant question.[228]

6. The Weakness of the ICC

The system of justice has to deal with the impunity of leaders of the strongest military powers, and the indictment of militarily weak states, thus the court does not levy complete justice, rather only selective justice and unilateral punishments. Therefore, the International Criminal Court in The Hague is a very strong and powerful legislative force when it comes to weaker nations. To date, the tribunal has succeeded in prosecuting and punishing the leaders of African states.[229] Thus, it demonstrates the political instrumentality of the court, and how it encourages impunity, as if it were its task and duty. Regrettably, this impunity is so strong, powerful, and painful that it has become an established principle within the international legal personality of the Court. Hanan Ashrawi, a Palestinian political authority rightly asserted that "the Israeli concept that security is its exclusive right somehow generates the U.S.-enforced notion that the Palestinians are obligated to deliver security to the Israelis while Israel delivers death and destruction with impunity to the Palestinians."

The above policy of the United States government was confirmed in a recent statement made by US foreign minister John Bolton who sharply

---

[228] Consult Farhad Malekian, 'Judging International Criminal Justice in the Occupied Territories,' 12 *International Criminal Law Review* (2012), pp.827–869.

[229] For the concept of justice, see Malekian, note 1; Farhad Malekian, 'Mutilating the Philosophy of Justice in the Time of Armed Conflicts', *Contemporary Journal of International Criminal Law* (2007); Farhad Malekian, *The Concept of Islamic International Criminal Law, A Comparative Study* (1994); Farhad Malekian, 'The Miserable Wedding of Naturalism into Positivism,' 2 *ID EST Journal* (2009). Immanuel Kant, *Religion within the Limits of Bare Reason* (1795), p. 87. Launched by Jonathan Bennett, Available online at http://www.earlymoderntexts.com/pdfs/kant1795part4.pdf; Alf Ross, *On Law and Justice* (London: Stevens & Sons Limited, 1958); Vagn Greve, 'Sheep or Wolves' 4 *European Journal of Crime, Criminal Law and Criminal Justice* (2005), 515-552; Kelsen Hans, 'What is Justice?' *Justice, Law and Politics in the Mirror of Science* (1957); Farhad Malekian, 'The Functions of International Criminal Law and the Problem of Positivism and Neutralism Philosophy', *Contemporary Journal of International Criminal Law* (2007).

rejected the entire system of international criminal law, international criminal justice, and international human rights law. For him, the rule of law is the rule of power, the rule of power is the rule of weapons, and the rule of weapons seeks to kill arrogantly and with impunity. He stated that:

> I am here to make a major announcement on US policy toward the International Criminal Court, or ICC. After years of effort by self-styled "global governance" advocates, the ICC, a supranational tribunal that could supersede national sovereignties and directly prosecute individuals for alleged war crimes, was agreed to in 1998. For ICC proponents, this supranational, independent institution has always been critical to their efforts to overcome the perceived failures of nation-states, even those with strong constitutions, representative government, and the rule of law. In theory, the ICC holds perpetrators of the most egregious atrocities accountable for their crimes, provides justice to the victims, and deters future abuses. In practice, however, the court has been ineffective, unaccountable, and indeed, outright dangerous. Moreover, the largely unspoken, but always central, aim of its most vigorous supporters was to constrain the United States. The objective was not limited to targeting individual US service members, but rather America's senior political leadership, and its relentless determination to keep our country secure. The ICC was formally established in July 2002, following the entry into force of the Rome Statute. In May 2002, however, President George W Bush authorised the United States to "un-sign" the Rome Statute because it was fundamentally illegitimate. The ICC and its prosecutor had been granted potentially enormous, essentially unaccountable powers, and alongside numerous other glaring and significant flaws, the International Criminal Court constituted an assault on the constitutional rights of the American people and the sovereignty of the United States. In no uncertain terms, the ICC was created as a free-wheeling global organisation claiming jurisdiction over individuals without their consent. According to the Rome Statute, the ICC has authority to prosecute genocide, war crimes, crimes against humanity, and crimes of aggression. It claims "automatic jurisdiction," meaning that it can prosecute individuals even if their own governments have not recognised, signed, or ratified the treaty. Thus, American soldiers, politicians, civil servants, private citizens, and even all of you sitting in the room today, are purportedly subject to the court's

prosecution should a party to the Rome Statute or the chief prosecutor suspect you of committing a crime within a state or territory that has joined the treaty. To protect American service members from the ICC, in 2002 Congress passed the American Service-Members' Protection Act, or ASPA, which some have branded "The Hague Invasion Act." This law, which enjoyed broad bipartisan support, authorises the president to use all means necessary and appropriate, including force, to shield our service members and the armed forces of our allies from ICC prosecution. It also prohibits several forms of cooperation between the United States and the court. I was honoured to lead US efforts internationally to protect Americans from the court's unacceptable overreach, starting with un-signing the Rome Statute. At President Bush's direction, we next launched a global diplomatic campaign to protect Americans from being delivered into the ICC's hands. We negotiated about 100 binding, bilateral agreements to prevent other countries from delivering US personnel to the ICC. It remains one of my proudest achievements. Unfortunately, we were unable to reach agreement with every single nation in the world, particularly those in the European Union, where the global governance dogma is strong. And last fall, our worst predictions about the ICC's professed and overly broad prosecutorial powers were confirmed. In November of 2017, the ICC prosecutor requested authorisation to investigate alleged war crimes committed by US service members and intelligence professionals during the war in Afghanistan - an investigation neither Afghanistan nor any other state party to the Rome Statute requested. Any day now, the ICC may announce the start of a formal investigation against these American patriots, who voluntarily went into harm's way to protect our nation, our homes, and our families in the wake of the 9/11 attacks.[230]

He went even further and clarified vividly that:

The ICC prosecutor has requested to investigate these Americans for alleged detainee abuse, and perhaps more - an utterly unfounded, unjustifiable investigation. Today, on the eve of September 11th, I want to

---

[230] https://www.aljazeera.com/news/2018/09/full-text-john-bolton-speech-federalist-society-180910172828633.html.

deliver a clear and unambiguous message on behalf of the president of the United States. The United States will use any means necessary to protect our citizens and those of our allies from unjust prosecution by this illegitimate court. We will not cooperate with the ICC. We will provide no assistance to the ICC. We will not join the ICC. We will let the ICC die on its own. After all, for all intents and purposes, the ICC is already dead to us. The United States bases this policy on five principal concerns about the court, its purported authority, and its effectiveness. First, the International Criminal Court unacceptably threatens American sovereignty and US national security interests. The prosecutor in The Hague claims essentially unfettered discretion to investigate, charge, and prosecute individuals, regardless of whether their countries have acceded to the Rome Statute. The court in no way derives these powers from any grant of consent by non-parties to the Rome Statute. Instead, the ICC is an unprecedented effort to vest power in a supranational body without the consent of either nation-states or the individuals over which it purports to exercise jurisdiction. It certainly has no consent whatsoever from the United States. As Americans, we fully understand that consent of the governed is a prerequisite to true legal legitimacy, and we reject such a flagrant violation of our national sovereignty. To make matters worse, the court's structure is contrary to fundamental American principles, including checks and balances on authority and the separation of powers. Our founders believed that a division of authority among three separate branches of government would provide the maximum level of protection for individual liberty. The International Criminal Court, however, melds two of these branches together: the judicial and the executive. In the ICC structure, the executive branch - the Office of the Prosecutor - is an organ of the court. The framers of our constitution considered such a melding of powers unacceptable for our own government, and we should certainly not accept it in the ICC. Other governments may choose systems which reject the separation of powers, but not the United States. There are no adequate mechanisms to hold the court and its personnel accountable or curtail its unchecked powers when required. ICC proponents argue that corrupt or ineffective judges can be removed by a two-thirds vote of parties to the Rome Statute and that a prosecutor can be removed by a majority vote. However, I ask everyone in the room today: would you consign the fate of American citizens to a committee of other nations, including Venezuela and the

> Democratic Republic of the Congo, and entities that are not even states, like the Palestinian Authority? You would not. I would not. And this Administration will not. The ICC's Assembly of States Parties cannot supervise the court any more than the United Nations General Assembly can supervise the UN bureaucracy.[231]

This shameful principle of the impunity of major military powers under the provisions of international criminal law has been seriously threatening peace and justice in the Middle East; currently however, it is being done in the name of the United States Declaration. Even Saudi Arabia, the United States' political ally has "called for a political solution to resolve regional crises, foremost of which is the Palestinian issue and the restoration of the Palestinian people's legitimate rights, including the right to establish their independent state with East *Al-Quds/Jerusalem* as its capital."[232] The situation is also critical concerning the Islamic Republic of Iran and Russia's recognition of East *Al-Quds/Jerusalem* as the capital of Palestine. Egypt and Jordan are, like the rest of the world, strongly opposed to the Declaration. However, the international legal and political community is aware of the fact that the Egyptian policy and politics are in line with the interests of Israel, the United States, Saudi Arabia, and the United Arab Emirates. It is just a political game.

7. *Mens Rea* in the Unilateral Illegal Declaration

This unilateral declaration of the President of the United States was announced on 6 December 2017. Its content violates the legal voice of the world, the legacy of the history of the civilisation of criminal justice, the natural rights of man, and the rights regarding the importance of sovereign

---

[231] *Id.*

[232] http://www.aljazeera.com/news/2017/12/saudi-arabia-king-salman-skips-oic-summit-jerusalem-171213161923915.html.

immunities.[233] These are the rights of the city of *Al-Quds/Jerusalem*, which historically, and legally, has belonged to the innocent population of Palestine.[234] Although we have already stated this, we will continue to repeatedly: *Al-Quds* originally, and without any legal doubt, belonged to the Palestinian population alone, and this only changed following the conspiracies of the United Kingdom, and the *beyond barbarities committed by Hitler against the European Jews*. The Cuban government has correctly asserted that the US Declaration "constitutes a serious and flagrant violation of the Charter of the UN, of International Law and of the relevant resolutions of the United Nations…"[235] Furthermore, the declaration violates the basic intentions of the Charter of the United Nations and all other declarations on human dignity.[236]

The declaration of the President of the United States not only contained inclinations towards criminal evil, but also violated the United Nations Security Council resolutions concerning the creation of Israel. If the United States rejects one part of the imposed resolutions of the Security Council, it also simultaneously, *ipso facto,* denounces the part of the same resolution concerning the creation of the State of Israel. This is because Chapter VII of the United Nations Charter emphasises the obligations and duties of the permanent members to maintain justice, peace, and equality between members. Overall, they are responsible for preventing any violations of the system of international criminal law.

An international convention, as Kant asserted, should not have a propensity for evil. All international conventions are the result of intensive

---

[233] As de Vattel asserts "we ought to hate the crime, but love the man, since all mankind ought to love each other." M. Vattel, The law of nations or the principles of the law of nations applied to the conduct and affair of nations and sovereign (6th American Addition, A new edition by Joseph Chitty, 1844.), para. 231, p. 108. Available online at http://www.loc.gov/rr/frd/Military_Law/Lieber_Collection/pdf/DeVattel_LawOfNations.pdf.

[234] Consult Farhad Malekian, 'Judging International Criminal Justice in the Occupied Territories,' 12 *International Criminal Law Review* (2012), 827–869.

[235] *Cuba rejects US recognition of Jerusalem as the capital of Israel* http://www.juventudrebelde.cu/en/internationals/2017-12-08 /cuba-rejects-us-recognition-of-jerusalem-as-the-capital-of-israel/print. The Cuba statement was announced on 8 December.

[236] The Declaration can be put into context with a book entitled *The American Torture: From the Cold War to Abu Ghraib and Beyond* written by Michael Otterman and published by an Australian university in 2007.

international negotiations, and regardless of any political influence during negotiations of international treaties, certain principles have to be maintained. These principles are the equality of arms, equality of provisions, fairness, proportionality, and justice. In other words, when there are unequal provisions within a treaty, the concept of good faith – which is the fundamental principle in the law of treaties, in the philosophy of justice, and in the theory of judgments and any other decision – is completely violated. Promoting unequal provisions thus implies the existence of a mental element of the crime, or an intention to commit an international crime.[237]

The statement of the United States government has been strongly condemned and rejected by a General Assembly resolution entitled, *Illegal Israeli actions in Occupied East Jerusalem and the rest of the Occupied Palestinian Territory*. Through this resolution, it is therefore quite clear that the declaration violates all principles of justice. The resolution reads:

> The General Assembly,
>
> Reaffirming its relevant resolutions, including resolution 72/15 of 30 November 2017 on Jerusalem,
>
> Reaffirming also the relevant resolutions of the Security Council, including resolutions 242 (1967) of 22 November 1967, 252 (1968) of 21 May 1968, 267 (1969) of 3 July 1969, 298 (1971) of 25 September 1971, 338 (1973) of 22 October 1973, 446 (1979) of 22 March 1979, 465 (1980) of 1 March 1980, 476 (1980) of 30 June 1980, 478 (1980) of 20 August 1980 and 2334 (2016) of 23 December 2016,
>
> *Guided* by the purposes and principles of the Charter of the United Nations, and reaffirming, inter alia, the inadmissibility of the acquisition of territory by force,
>
> *Bearing* in mind the specific status of the Holy City of Jerusalem and, in particular, the need for the protection and preservation of the unique spiritual, religious and cultural dimensions of the city, as foreseen in relevant United Nations resolutions, Stressing that Jerusalem is a final status issue to be resolved through negotiations in line with relevant United Nations resolutions,

---

[237] Malekian, *The Mirage of International Criminal Law,* note 9 p. 59.

Expressing, in this regard, its deep regret at recent decisions concerning the status of Jerusalem,

1. *Affirms* that any decisions and actions which purport to have altered the character, status or demographic composition of the Holy City of Jerusalem have no legal effect, are null and void and must be rescinded in compliance with relevant resolutions of the Security Council, and in this regard calls upon all States to refrain from the establishment of diplomatic missions in the Holy City of Jerusalem, pursuant to Security Council resolution 478 (1980);

2. *Demands* that all States comply with Security Council resolutions regarding the Holy City of Jerusalem, and not recognize any actions or measures contrary to those resolutions; A/ES-10/L.22 2/2 17-22856

3. *Reiterates* its call for the reversal of the negative trends on the ground that are imperilling the two-State solution and for the intensification and acceleration of international and regional efforts and support aimed at achieving, without delay, a comprehensive, just and lasting peace in the Middle East on the basis of the relevant United Nations resolutions, the Madrid terms of reference, including the principle of land for peace, the Arab Peace Initiative 1 and the Quartet road map,2 and an end to the Israeli occupation that began in 1967;

4. *Decides* to adjourn the tenth emergency special session temporarily and to authorize the President of the General Assembly at its most recent session to resume its meeting upon request from Member States.[238]

---

[238] Tenth emergency special session Agenda item 5, Illegal Israeli actions in Occupied East Jerusalem and the rest of the Occupied Palestinian Territory. The resolution drafted by Turkey and Yemen governing the Status of Jerusalem. A/ES-10/L.22 (19 December 2017). States which voted for the resolution were Afghanistan, Albania, Algeria, Andorra, Angola, Armenia, Austria, Azerbaijan, Bahrain, Bangladesh, Barbados, Belarus, Belgium, Belize, Bolivia, Botswana, Brazil, Brunei, Bulgaria, Burkina Faso, Burundi, Cape Verde, Cambodia, Chad, Chile, China, Comoros, Republic of the Congo, Costa Rica, Cuba, Cyprus, Democratic People's Republic of (North) Korea, Denmark, Djibouti, Dominica, Ecuador, Egypt, Eritrea, Estonia, Ethiopia, Finland, France, Gabon, Gambia, Germany, Ghana, Greece, Grenada, Guinea, Guyana, Iceland, India, Indonesia, Iran, Iraq, Ireland, Italy, Ivory Coast, Japan, Jordan, Kazakhstan, Kuwait, Kyrgyzstan, Laos, Lebanon, Liberia, Libya, Liechtenstein, Lithuania, Luxembourg, Macedonia, Madagascar, Malaysia, Maldives, Mali, Malta, Mauritania, Mauritius, Monaco, Montenegro, Morocco, Mozambique, Namibia, Nepal, Netherlands, New Zealand, Nicaragua, Niger, Nigeria, Norway, Oman, Pakistan, Papua New Guinea, Peru, Portugal, Qatar, Republic of (South) Korea, Russia, Saint Vincent and the Grenadines, Saudi Arabia, Senegal, Serbia, Seychelles, Singapore, Slovakia, Slovenia, Somalia, South Africa, Spain, Sri Lanka, Sudan, Suriname, Sweden, Switzerland, Syria, Tajikistan, Thailand, Tanzania, Tunisia, Turkey, United Arab Emirates, United Kingdom, Uruguay, Uzbekistan, Venezuela, Vietnam, Yemen and Zimbabwe. List of states which

8. Negation of International Criminal Law

There are a considerable number of significant legal arguments against the United States' declaration concerning the city of *Al-Quds/Jerusalem.* Here are few examples:

a) Resolution 181: Recommending a partition of Mandated Palestine into Arab and Jewish states, and international status for the City of *Al-Quds/Jerusalem*.

i) The legal status of the State of Israel is based on the provisions of the aforementioned resolution. If the US denounces one part of the resolution, they automatically denounce the other parts as well. This means the State of Israel ceases to exist as an international person. The State of "Israel" is thereby *ipso facto* terminated and rendered *non est* and *ab initio null* and *void*.

b) The Security Council resolutions do not permit it.

c) The resolutions of the General Assembly are against it:

i) If the contents of the resolutions of the GA and UNSC concerning Palestine are not valid, then they are also not valid concerning the Israeli state. The Israelis would have to move back to their former homes in Europe or other parts of the world, and all borders would revert to pre-Balfour Declaration lines. Israelis should bring claims against those who are perpetuating the legacy of Hitler's government and need their homes back. The Second World War ended only 70 years ago, and if the Israeli government is of the opinion that they can occupy the lands some Jews inhabited over 2,500 years ago, they could just as easily, or even more

---

abstained, are Antigua and Barbuda, Argentina, Australia, Bahamas, Benin, Bhutan, Bosnia and Herzegovina, Cameroon, Canada, Colombia, Croatia, Czech Republic, Dominican Republic, Equatorial Guinea, Fiji, Haiti, Hungary, Jamaica, Kiribati, Latvia, Lesotho, Malawi, Mexico, Panama, Paraguay, Philippines, Poland, Romania, Rwanda, Solomon Islands, South Sudan, Trinidad and Tobago, Tuvalu, Uganda and Vanuatu. List of states which were absent are Central African Republic, Democratic Republic of the Congo, East Timor (Timor Leste), El Salvador, Georgia, Guinea-Bissau, Kenya, Mongolia, Myanmar, Moldova, Saint Kitts and Nevis, Saint Lucia, Samoa, San Marino, São Tomé and Príncipe, Sierra Leone, Swaziland, Tonga, Turkmenistan, Ukraine and Zambia. List of states which rejected the resolution were Central African Republic, Democratic Republic of the Congo, East Timor (Timor Leste), El Salvador, Georgia, Guinea-Bissau, Kenya, Mongolia, Myanmar, Moldova, Saint Kitts and Nevis, Saint Lucia, Samoa, San Marino, São Tomé and Príncipe, Sierra Leone, Swaziland, Tonga, Turkmenistan, Ukraine and Zambia.

easily claim land in Germany where many of them, or their grandparents had citizenship of. The provisions of the system of international law, international criminal law, and of human rights law have much more precedent for this than the hypothetical case.

d) International customary law does not accept annexation by means of occupation:

i) Otherwise, we would violate customary law, and even the claims of Israeli authorities would become null and void.

e) The majority of international doctrines do not accept occupation as annexation.

f) The international law-making treaties do not accept the annexation of occupied territories.

g) The International Court of Justice is opposed to annexation by occupation and simultaneously also against the Wall.

h) A majority of states support East *Al-Quds/Jerusalem* as being an integral part of Palestine.

i) The actual practice of states is against annexation.

k) Security Council Resolutions 242 and 478 condemn the declaration of the United States government (and promoted by Israel). Thus, the Declaration flagrantly violates the provisions of those resolutions.

m) The practice of the International Criminal Court is clearly against the occupation.

n) The practices of *ad hoc* international criminal tribunals clearly demonstrate that occupation is not accepted.

o) Just cogens norms are against occupation.

p) Annexation violates the principle of *erga omnes.*

q) The "general principles of law," one of the main sources of international law, are against occupation.

r) National, regional, and international case law also do not permit annexation.

s) Annexation violates natural law.

t) Annexation violates the Declaration of Human Rights of 1948.

u) Annexation violates the basic principles of international human rights law.

v) No elements of positive law accept annexation.

w) Annexation violates the international legal personality of Palestine.

x) Annexation violates the principle of self-determination.

y) Annexation seriously endangers the principle of peace in the Middle East and permits defence against the unlawful use of force, which may be seen a positive response against state terrorism.

z) Annexation violates the principle of proportionality and *de lege lata*. It is an act of aggression against the will of the occupied state.

9. The Immoral Force of the Declaration

The state authorities have a duty to know international law and to know which actions or omissions constitute violations thereof. In other words, International Court of Justice should not support or accept any plea of ignorance of the rules, ignorance of the law, or ignorance of violations in the political agendas of the major political parties. We are also supposed to have strong motivation, sound politics, and strength of mind, as well as an understanding of how the provisions of the criminal law of neighbouring states can violate the system of international criminal law. This duty politically falls squarely on the five permanent members of the UN Security Council. Likewise, due to the provisions of the United Nations, the Council members have a greater responsibility than others in preventing any action that may result in a threat to peace, justice, or which could lead to acts of aggression.[239]

The concept of *mens rea* in the legal writing of doctrines of the term is not confined to a personal spite against a particular individual, but exists in any conscious violation of the law as a result of prejudice.[240] Regardless of the various possible interpretations and criteria for the recognition of *mens rea* in a criminal investigation, the presumption of knowledge of the law and its understanding is not only necessary for us as civilians, but also for major

[239] Chapter VII of the United Nations Charter deals with action with respect of threats to the peace, breaches of the peace, and acts of aggression. In particular, Articles 39 to 51 imply the duties of the permanent members for the maintenance of security, peace, and prevention of aggression.

[240] For different aspects of *mens rea* and its scope of application, examine Malekian, *Trading Virginity of International Criminal Justice*, note 16, pp.37, 51, 52 and 54. Mohamed Elewa Badar, *The Concept of Mens Rea* (Hart Publishing, 2013). For a fresh study of new aspects of *mens rea,* examine Malekian, *The Mirage of International Criminal Law,* note 9.

political parties of any nation, including the leading authorities of our nations, those leading the peace negotiations, and who occupy the UN. This is where the concept of *mens rea* against the innocent victim or victims shapes, and therefore fulfils, the conditions of violations of the system of international criminal law and justice. The Declaration of the United States is evidently part of a clear plan to commit criminal acts against the positive and natural rules of criminal law.[241]

The declaration has an obvious criminal propensity against the territorial integrity of Palestine, and the ancient population of the territory, i.e., the Palestinians. It intends, with full *mens rea,* to encourage crimes against humanity, war crimes, genocide, rape, torture, the murder of children/infanticide, and other grave violations of the international humanitarian law of armed conflict as regulated in the contents of the 1949 Geneva Conventions and their additional Protocols of 1977. This is because when taken together, the immorality of the Declaration, the illegality of its recognition, and the aggressive scope of its application, permit the violation of the rights of the victims.[242]

10. *Mens Rea* of a Magic Show

Within the body of criminal law, there is no doctrine which is more significant, than that of the concept of *mens rea*. In certain obvious criminal cases, however, it is not essential to establish *mens rea*. This implies the fact that, although it is important to establish *mens rea*, in certain situations the act or omission may have occurred as a result of the defendant's conscious exercise of free will. Otherwise, the contrary would have to be proven.

---

[241] Malekian, The Miserable Wedding of Naturalism into Positivism, note 229.

[242] The Cuba statement rejecting the Declaration of the United States government clarifies that "Cuba calls on the Security Council to fulfil the responsibility given to it by the UN Charter in the maintenance of international peace and security, to adopt the necessary decisions and to demand from Israel an immediate end to the occupation of the Palestinian territories and of aggressive policies and colonizing practices, as well as compliance with the resolutions adopted by that body on the situation in the Middle East, including the Palestinian issue." *Cuba rejects US recognition of Jerusalem as the capital of Israel* http://www.juventudrebelde.cu/en/ internationals/2017-12-08 /cuba-rejects-us-recognition-of-jerusalem-as-the-capital-of-israel/print.

By this, we mean that in a number of specific situations arising from supreme prohibitions, the peremptory international legal norms, and the superiority of the rights of oppressed people, the concept of *mens rea* does not necessarily have to be explicitly proven. The criminal act itself provides the proof of criminal intent to harm the international public. This includes the fact that, if the wording of certain provisions of international criminal law, international law, and international human rights law is of concern, or if the fully recognized strategy of the law is to prevent certain acts such as genocide, rape, torture, crimes against humanity, discrimination, and apartheid, then proving *mens rea* certainly loses its legitimate value. All this means that committing certain acts against a population may constitute genocide when the acts are carried out with a specific intention. It is rightly concluded that:

> Rape, although committed in internal and international armed conflicts throughout history, is not explicitly enumerated as a "grave breach" or a war crime in the conventional law of armed conflict. Recently, however, rape has been defined as a crime against humanity. The Genocide Convention does not include rape as one of the listed acts of genocide. However, as evidenced by the events in Bosnia and Rwanda, rape and other acts of sexual violence can be used to commit genocide. A debate arose around "genocidal rape" in which scholars took opposing positions. One side argued in effect that rape as an act of genocide should not receive special treatment and that it should not be specially denominated. The other side contended that genocidal rape is different from rape that occurs outside of a genocide and that the international community should acknowledge a woman's gender identity along with her identity as a member of a particular national, ethnic, racial or religious group. Although the Rwandan genocide had occurred at the time that most of the legal scholarship about the debate on genocidal rape had been written, it was not until the *Akayesu Judgment* that there was analysis and discussion of how the mass rapes committed in Rwanda constituted acts of genocide or genocidal rapes. By so analyzing and discussing genocidal rape in the *Akayesu Judgment,* the International Tribunal for Rwanda provides some clarity to the debate about genocidal rape. For example, in finding and defining genocidal rape, the Tribunal recognized how rape and sexual

> violence worked to destroy the Tutsis. Second, it recognized the intersectionality of genocidal rape. And, lastly, the International Tribunal for Rwanda acknowledged that, although the group is a focal concern of the crime of genocide, genocidal rape is one of the worst ways of inflicting harm and injury on an individual member of that group, here, Tutsi women.[243]

This means, regardless of knowledge and state of mind at the time of the commission of the crime, no proof of *mens rea* is necessary. The central issue is that neither deficiencies in knowledge nor a genuine confidence therein can constitute a defence for Trump or any other leader. Thus, any act, policy, or decision made with the aim of achieving their own interests, regardless of the value of their intention, is wrong and provocative, and may, in certain circumstances, constitute the commission of genocide.

Under a system of criminal law, whether a common law or a civil law system, a statute creates criminal liability for the omission or commission of a particular behaviour, performance, or utterance without designating *mens rea*. Here, we are referring to strict liability statutes. While we are aware of the fact that one of the basic elements of criminal law is that a crime contains both a mental and a physical element, this does not necessarily mean that we need to necessarily prove the existence of both elements simultaneously, for example in a case of political laundering with the clear intent of money laundering. The mental element implies the superior's awareness of the fact that their action, such as making a declaration, is criminal in nature, and presents the concept of *actus reus*, thus comprising the physical element of the crime.

11. Legitimising Illegality

In fact, the legal method of alleging the presence of *mens rea* in political policy is very simple and clear: an illegal claim in our international relations

---

[243] Sherrie L. Russell-Brown, *Rape as an Act of Genocide*, 21 Berkeley J. Int'l Law. 350 (2003), pp.550-374, at 373-4.

is obviously illegal and violates the fundamental natural and positive rights of man.[244] In addition, when a state initiates relations with a state whose policy is criminal (such as with the US, the United Kingdom, Saudi Arabia, or Israel to name but a few), they are then responsible under international human rights law for any harm that comes to innocent populations at the hands of the state with which they have entered into relations with. Having relations with a state implies complicity in their crimes, and even in part, a form of assistance and support therefore. Such relations imply intended cooperation in the commission of crimes against humanity, war crimes, and genocide, as well as co-conspiracy in their execution.

What is the true definition of *mens rea* in the Statute of the ICC? Does the ICC have a concept of political *mens rea* and a concept of legal *mens rea?* Do we also have arbitrary and discriminatory factors which influence the deliberations of *judicial* matters and judges regarding international criminal charges? If so, what is the difference between the two concepts of mens rea? One must refer to the *intent* or knowledge that the conduct would lead to killing and the destruction of a nation-- this is the traditional concept. The other must signify the political mental *intent,* or the political state of mind of the defendant at the time the statement is made, which implies the genocide of the cultural, historical, legal, and political rights of a nation, as the declaration of the US achieved.

Likewise, the international legal system is very concerned about the hidden diplomacy that is being conducted by the Russian government. It seems that the political laundering between both Israel and Russia has already occurred, and satisfaction on both sides has been guaranteed by the Russian's politically sub-divided ethic. Although Russia voted in favour of the recent resolution of the Security Council condemning the declaration, (which was vetoed by the United States), the situation must be more complicated than it appears. Similarly, Australia and Canada abstained from political diplomacy, which obviously violates the system of international human rights law and justice, when the immunity and international legal

[244] Consult Malekian, Emasculating the Philosophy of International Criminal Justice in the Iraqi Special Tribunal, note 1, pp. 675-725; examine also Malekian, *The Miserable Wedding of Naturalism into Positivism*, note 229.

personality of a state is considered an integral norm of *erga omnes*. Any abstention against peremptory norms of international law is null and void and the fact is that Australia and Canada are those states which claim to support the basic principles of international human rights law.

> *Jus cogens* norms are not only based by law, but also by morality. on "considerations of morals and of international good order."[245] This theory implies that *jus cogens* norms have an ethical basis that is unquestionable and part of the universal order. The theory of *jus cogens* may also go back to the distinction made in Roman law between *jus strictum* and *jus dispositivum* and to Grotius' references to *jus strictum.* Beyond these explanations, however, any law or theory that creates unequal treatment of the integrity of one man in comparison with another certainly has a tendency to violate *jus cogens* law. When we refer to the law of *jus cogens*, we are at the same time referring to the *existing field of morality*. This includes the morality of man in all aspects of universal life in which justice has to prevail if wrongs are not going to be served as rights, and rights are not going to violate rights.[246] ....These rights are not legislated by governments and international organisations, but by the perpetual protection of the rights of man stemming from our shared values as inalienable classical rights independent from manmade laws. These rights ascend to the echelon of *jus cogens and therefore encompass the character of obligatio erga omnes*, which is inderogable. Thus, the terms "*jus cogens*," "peremptory," and "*erga omnes*" all represent the modern version of the *universal rights of man*, love for justice, love of civilisation, and love for the health of our natural environment which are unchangeable. My purpose here is not to convince international lawyers or the judges of the national and international courts that there is a powerful norm in law which is called love, but I definitely fear, and I am concerned about the truth that law which does not build its basic *raison d'eˆtre* on love for human beings cannot survive properly.14 As a result, the construction of the law is at all times in very serious threat. When we speak about the genocide law and its relevant regulations in the system of international law of *jus cogens*, we

[245] Third Report by G.G. Fitzmaurice, Special Rapporteur (UN Doc. A/CN.4/115), *in* II *Yearbook of the International Law Commission* (1958), 20, 41, para.76.

[246] Malekian, *Classical Morality in International Peremptory Criminal Law*, note 201, p.7.

are trying to assert that its elements are based on love for human nature and humanity as a whole.15 The intention of the relevant law is clearly to prevent certain acts against human beings as a whole and is thus vital for justice.[247]

12. The Codex of Prejudice Covering *Mens Rea*

The question is: *how can we bring claims against those carrying out violations of human rights law and European law, while at the same time violating the rights of other states ourselves, without justification? Similarly, how can we say that we have a system of criminal justice and talk about the American Declaration of Human Rights and Independence while ignoring the same fundamental rights in the territories of other nations?*[248] The U.N. Human Rights Council (HRC) voted overwhelmingly to endorse the recommendations of the Goldstone Report of 2009. The report was written by Goldstone, the former South African judge who was responsible for finding out the truth about the situation in Israel. He concluded that Israeli authorities seriously violated the system of international criminal law during their 2008-2009 military campaign against those who were defending the Palestinian international legal personality.

Although the report was criticised by supporters of the Israeli government, the words of the report and its finding cannot be objected to given the actions, conducts, policies, and politics of Israel today. Therefore, the statement of Professor Christine Chinkin,[249] one of the four mission members for the report was any hesitation fairly authentic when declaring that the criminal actions committed by Israel "amount to aggression, not self-defense" and that "the manner and scale of its operations in Gaza amount to an act of aggression and is contrary to international law."[250] The

---

[247] *Id.*, pp.9-10.

[248] Consult Farhad Malekian, 'Judging International Criminal Justice in the Occupied Territories,' 12 *International Criminal Law Review* (2012), pp.827–869.

[249] She was a member of the four-person United Nations Fact Finding Mission on the Gaza Conflict established by the United Nations Human Rights Council.

[250] https://wikimili.com/en/Palestine_and_the_United_Nations#cite_note-75.

conclusions of the report are certainly true regarding the illegal occupation which continues to be carried out by the Israeli government. The report to the Human Rights Council recommended the following:

> (a) The Mission recommends that the United Nations Human Rights Council should endorse the recommendations contained in this report, take appropriate action to implement them as recommended by the Mission and through other means as it may deem appropriate, and continue to review their implementation in future sessions;
>
> (b) In view of the gravity of the violations of international human rights and humanitarian law and possible war crimes and crimes against humanity that it has reported, the Mission recommends that the United Nations Human Rights Council should request the United Nations Secretary-General to bring this report to the attention of the United Nations Security Council under Article 99 of the Charter of the United Nations so that the Security Council may consider action according to the Mission's relevant recommendations below;
>
> (c) The Mission further recommends that the United Nations Human Rights Council should formally submit this report to the Prosecutor of the International Criminal Court;
>
> (d) The Mission recommends that the Human Rights Council should submit this report to the General Assembly with a request that it should be considered;
>
> (e) The Mission recommends that the Human Rights Council should bring the Mission's recommendations to the attention of the relevant United Nations human rights treaty bodies so that they may include review of progress in their implementation, as may be relevant to their mandate and procedures, in their periodic review of compliance by Israel with its human rights obligations. The Mission further recommends that the Human Rights Council should consider review of progress as part of its universal periodic review process.
>
> To the United Nations Security Council,
>
> (a) The Mission recommends that the Security Council should require the Government of Israel, under Article 40 of the Charter of the United Nations:

(i) To take all appropriate steps, within a period of three months, to launch appropriate investigations that are independent and in conformity with international standards, into the serious violations of international humanitarian and international human rights law reported by the Mission and any other serious allegations that might come to its attention;

(ii) To inform the Security Council, within a further period of three months, of actions taken, or in process of being taken, by the Government of Israel to inquire into, investigate and prosecute such serious violations;

(b) The Mission further recommends that the Security Council should at the same time establish an independent committee of experts in international humanitarian and human rights law to monitor and report on any domestic legal or other proceedings undertaken by the Government of Israel in relation to the aforesaid investigations. Such committee of experts should report at the end of the six-month period to the Security Council on its assessment of relevant domestic proceedings initiated by the Government of Israel, including their progress, effectiveness and genuineness, so that the Security Council may assess whether appropriate action to ensure justice for victims and accountability for perpetrators has been or is being taken at the domestic level. The Security Council should request the committee to report to it at determined intervals, as may be necessary. The committee should be appropriately supported by the Office of the United Nations High Commissioner for Human Rights;

(c) The Mission recommends that, upon receipt of the committee's report, the Security Council should consider the situation and, in the absence of good-faith investigations that are independent and in conformity with international standards having been undertaken or being under way within six months of the date of its resolution under Article 40 by the appropriate authorities of the State of Israel, again acting under Chapter VII of the Charter of the United Nations, refer the situation in Gaza to the Prosecutor of the International Criminal Court pursuant to article 13 (b) of the Rome Statute;

(d) The Mission recommends that the Security Council should require the independent committee of experts referred to in subparagraph (b) to monitor and report on any domestic legal or other proceedings undertaken by the relevant authorities in the Gaza Strip in relation to the aforesaid investigations. The committee should report at the end of the six-month period to the Security Council on its assessment of relevant domestic

> proceedings initiated by the relevant authorities in Gaza, including their progress, effectiveness and genuineness, so that the Security Council may assess whether appropriate action to ensure justice for victims and accountability for perpetrators has been taken or is being taken at the domestic level. The Security Council should request the committee to report to it at determined intervals, as may be necessary;
>
> (e) The Mission recommends that, upon receipt of the committee's report, the Security Council should consider the situation and, in the absence of good-faith investigations that are independent and in conformity with international standards having been undertaken or being under way within six months of the date of its resolution under Article 40 by the appropriate authorities in Gaza, acting under Chapter VII of the Charter of the United Nations, refer the situation in Gaza to the Prosecutor of the International Criminal Court pursuant to article 13 (b) of the Rome Statute;
>
> (f) The Mission recommends that lack of cooperation by the Government of Israel or the Gaza authorities with the work of the committee should be regarded by the Security Council to be obstruction of the work of the committee.
>
> *To the Prosecutor of the International Criminal Court*, with reference to the declaration under article 12 (3) received by the Office of the Prosecutor of the International Criminal Court from the Government of Palestine, the Mission considers that accountability for victims and the interests of peace and justice in the region require that the Prosecutor should make the required legal determination as expeditiously as possible.[251]

Here, I am certainly directing my thoughts toward the United States and Israel, who have constantly resorted to the use of force, terrorism through their intelligence agencies (including the attacks of 11 September which resulted in the death of 3,500 individuals), and the creation of antagonism via the Islamic State of Daesh between Muslim nations.[252] These are just a few examples of their criminality. When we speak of terror, we are speaking about both physical and mental terror, both of which imply a guilty mind

---

[251] Goldstone's Report, p.424.

[252] Examine Malekian, *The Mirage of International Criminal Law*, note 9.

and double morality on the part of the perpetrators. There is no doubt that we must plan for the natural consequences of our behaviour, and we must surely be responsible for the manifestations of this behaviour. This is the meaning of *mens rea* in international criminal law.

13. *Mens Rea* with Intent

Another assumption of *mens rea* or even *actus reus* is that when we are carelessly, tactlessly, and even deliberately indifferent to the plausible and possible effects of our international responsibilities, we ignore the rights of people of other states. The reverse is also true: when we intend to carry out international relations, even simple ones, and commit a greater crime against the essence of humanity as a whole, we do not respect the rights of others. An example of this are the provisions of the United States Declaration, which are not only dictatorial, but constitute serious violations of the system of international humanitarian law. This is because the intention of the Declaration is malicious, and the development of malice in this context shows a clear inclination to commit crimes against the established rights of others, or the *mens rea* of the criminal conduct.[253] The Goldstone Report was certainly correct, although many tried to diminish its value, with some even attempting to bully the author into announcing that his statements were not wholly true. The Report ordered the General Assembly to take the following actions:

> (a) The Mission recommends that the General Assembly should request the Security Council to report to it on measures taken with regard to ensuring accountability for serious violations of international humanitarian law and human rights in relation to the facts in this report and any other relevant facts in the context of the military operations in Gaza, including the implementation of the Mission's recommendations. The General Assembly may remain appraised of the matter until it is satisfied

---

[253] For deep discussions on *mens rea* and intent see the knowledgeable work Badar, *The Concept of Mens Rea, note* 240.

> that appropriate action is taken at the domestic or international level in order to ensure justice for victims and accountability for perpetrators. The General Assembly may consider whether additional action within its powers is required in the interests of justice, including under its resolution 377 (V) on uniting for peace;
>
> (b) The Mission recommends that the General Assembly should establish an escrow fund to be used to pay adequate compensation to Palestinians who have suffered loss and damage as a result of unlawful acts attributable to Israel during the December-January military operation and actions in connection with it, and that the Government of Israel should pay the required amounts into such fund. The Mission further recommends that the General Assembly should ask the Office of the United Nations High Commissioner for Human Rights to provide expert advice on the appropriate modalities to establish the escrow fund;
>
> (c) The Mission recommends that the General Assembly should ask the Government of Switzerland to convene a conference of the high contracting parties to the Fourth Geneva Convention of 1949 on measures to enforce the Convention in the Occupied Palestinian Territory and to ensure its respect in accordance with its article 1;
>
> (d) The Mission recommends that the General Assembly should promote an urgent discussion on the future legality of the use of certain munitions referred to in this report, and in particular white phosphorous, flechettes and heavy metal such as tungsten. In such discussion the General Assembly should draw inter alia on the expertise of the International Committee of the Red Cross (ICRC). The Mission further recommends that the Government of Israel should undertake a moratorium on the use of such weapons in the light of the human suffering and damage they have caused in the Gaza Strip.[254]

The report went further and demanded that the government of Israel take the following measures:

> (a) The Mission recommends that Israel should immediately cease the border closures and restrictions on passage through border crossings with the Gaza Strip and allow the passage of goods necessary and sufficient to

---

[254] A/HRC/12/48 page 425.

meet the needs of the population, for the recovery and reconstruction of housing and essential services, and for the resumption of meaningful economic activity in the Gaza Strip;

(b) The Mission recommends that Israel should cease the restrictions on access to the sea for fishing purposes imposed on the Gaza Strip and allow such fishing activities within the 20 nautical miles as provided for in the Oslo Accords. It further recommends that Israel should allow the resumption of agricultural activity within the Gaza Strip, including within areas in the vicinity of the borders with Israel;

(c) Israel should initiate a review of the rules of engagement, standard operating procedures, open fire regulations and other guidance for military and security personnel. The Mission recommends that Israel should avail itself of the expertise of the International Committee of the Red Cross, the Office of the United Nations High Commissioner for Human Rights and other relevant bodies, and Israeli experts, civil society organizations with the relevant expertise and specialization, in order to ensure compliance in this respect with international humanitarian law and international human rights law. In particular such rules of engagement should ensure that the principles of proportionality, distinction, precaution and non-discrimination are effectively integrated in all such guidance and in any oral briefings provided to officers, soldiers and security forces, so as to avoid the recurrence of Palestinian civilian deaths, destruction and affronts on human dignity in violation of international law;

(d) The Mission recommends that Israel should allow freedom of movement for Palestinians within the Occupied Palestinian Territory - within the West Bank, including East Jerusalem, between the Gaza Strip and the West Bank, and between the Occupied Palestinian Territory and the outside world - in accordance with international human rights standards and international commitments entered into by Israel and the representatives of the Palestinian people. The Mission further recommends that Israel should forthwith lift travel bans currently placed on Palestinians by reason of their human rights or political activities;

(e) The Mission recommends that Israel should release Palestinians who are detained in Israeli prisons in connection with the occupation. The release of children should be an utmost priority. The Mission further recommends that Israel should cease the discriminatory treatment of Palestinian detainees. Family visits for prisoners from Gaza should resume;

(f) The Mission recommends that Israel should forthwith cease interference with national political processes in the Occupied Palestinian Territory, and as a first step release all members of the Palestinian Legislative Council currently in detention and allow all members of the Council to move between Gaza and the West Bank so that it may resume functioning;

(g) The Mission recommends that the Government of Israel should cease actions aimed at limiting the expression of criticism by civil society and members of the public concerning Israel's policies and conduct during the military operations in the Gaza Strip. The Mission also recommends that Israel should set up an independent inquiry to assess whether the treatment by Israeli judicial authorities of Palestinian and Jewish Israelis expressing dissent in connection with the offensive was discriminatory, in terms of both charges and detention pending trial. The results of the inquiry should be made public and, subject to the findings, appropriate remedial action should be taken;

(h) The Mission recommends that the Government of Israel should refrain from any action of reprisal against Palestinian and Israeli individuals and organizations that have cooperated with the United Nations Fact Finding Mission on the Gaza Conflict, in particular individuals who have appeared at the public hearings held by the Mission in Gaza and Geneva and expressed criticism of actions by Israel;[255]

(i) The Mission recommends that Israel should reiterate its commitment to respecting the inviolability of United Nations premises and personnel and that it should undertake all appropriate measures to ensure that there is no repetition of violations in the future. It further recommends that reparation to the United Nations should be provided fully and without further delay by Israel, and that the General Assembly should consider this matter.

Furthermore, if our decision is taken hastily, paying no mind to the possible consequences, and if these are the natural consequences of that decision, and a large number of people suffer due to not receiving their historical and indispensable rights, we surely have a flawed policy regarding the fundamental rights of man. Such policy certainly violates the entire

---

[255] A/HRC/12/48, pp.425-7.

codex of international criminal law. This also means there is *mens rea* and *actus reus* with obvious malicious intent, the perpetrators of which are the major political powers.

Here, I question the structure of our policy, the reason for the increase in human rights violations, and the reason for deprivation and cowardice in the system of international criminal law and justice, despite the establishment of permanent or *ad hoc* tribunals, and the empowerment of states or courts through the principle of complementarity.

Chapter 7

ACTUS REUS OF THE DECLARATION IMPLYING THE GUILTY MIND

1. INTERNATIONAL CRIMINAL LAWS CONDEMNING *MENS REA*

It is important to highlight that the entire system of Islamic international criminal law and justice deals with the previously discussed concepts, focusing on the questions of *mens rea* by guiding human beings toward peace and away from evil in their thoughts and actions.[256] These are also, as we have told elsewhere, the basic provisions of international criminal law

---

[256] For the concept of Islamic jurisdiction and Islamic criminal jurisdiction, see, Farhad Malekian, *Corpus Juris of Islamic International Criminal Justice* (Cambridge Scholars Publishing, 2017), p.17; M Abdel Haleem (ed.), *Criminal Justice in Islam: Judicial Procedure in the Sharīah* (2000); Abdelkader, Deina, *Social Justice in Islam* (Herndon, VA: IIIT, 2000); Mohamed Elewa Badar, 'Islamic Criminal Justice in the 21st Century', *International Criminal Law Review*, Vol. 9, Number 4, 2009, pp. 591-595; M. Cherif Bassiouni, *The Islamic Criminal Justice System* (London: Oceana Publications, 1982); M. Cherif Bassiouni, 'Protection of Diplomats under Islamic Law', *74 American Journal of International Law* (1980), pp. 609-655;, M. Cherif Bassiouni, '*Islam: Concept, Law and Word Habeas Corpus*', 2 *Rutgers Camden Law Journal* (1970); M. Cherif Bassiouni, *Sources of Islamic Law, and the Protection of Human Rights in the Islamic Criminal Justice System*, see Bassiouni, pp. 5-55;, M. Cherif Bassiouni, *Studies in Early Hadith Literature* (Indianapolis, 1978); Richard Bell, *Introduction to the Quran,* (Edinburgh University Press, 1955).

and international justice. That is why both international criminal laws declare any act related to planning, collaborating, instigating, inciting, helping, aiding, facilitating, supporting, assisting, depriving, or encouraging aggression and creating inequality between nations, unlawful.[257]

In order to prevent crime and human suffering, both legal disciplines condemn any conspiracy against individuals, groups, or nations.[258] Additionally, a series of articles of the *Qur'an*, the main source of Islamic international criminal law, prohibits Muslims from taking any action that involves cooperation in, aiding of, support of, or collaboration in, making or enforcing decisions that prevent, deny, or deprive certain individuals, groups, or nations of their historical, cultural, or territorial rights.[259] Similar legal philosophy is assembled in the body of international criminal law and international criminal justice of the international political and legal community. The method of reasoning and prohibition is included in both legal systems, which are fundamentally directed against all types of *mens rea*, even those carried out with the intent of gaining power.[260] Political, economic, and legal affairs in both legal systems should be settled face-to-face due to the principles of the equality of arms, the equality of views, and the equality in the application of the principle of proportionality. Still, Islamic international criminal law prohibits any victory which comes from intrigues, e.g., from using poisonous arrows, poisoning water resources, or poisoning diplomacy with the *mens rea* of annihilation of the rights of others.[261]

---

[257] Farhad Malekian, 'The Canon of Love against the Use of Force in Islamic and Public International Law: Part I: The Chamber of Love within Legal Discipline,' 15 *International Criminal Law Review*, 2015), pp. 591-628; Farhad Malekian, 'The Canon of Love against the Use of Force in Islamic and Public International Law: Part II: The Anatomy of Love Against Violations,' 15 *International Criminal Law Review*, 2015), pp. 861-895; consult *also* Badar, *The Concept of Mens Rea, note* 240. See also Malekian, *Condemning the Use of Force in the Gulf Crisis*, note 28.

[258] *Id.*

[259] *Id.*

[260] Badar, *The Concept of Mens Rea, note* 239; Farhad Malekian, 'The Heaven of Justice with Love,' The *Journal of the Henry Martyn Institute* (2017), pp. 5-29; Farhad Malekian, 'The Homogeneity of the International Criminal Court with Islamic Jurisprudence,' 9 (4) *International Criminal Law Review* (2009), pp. 595-621.

[261] Here, we are not however dealing with the criminal activities of many Islamic authorities in the Islamic countries against their own population.

The Goldstone report further clarified that:

1973. To Palestinian armed groups,

(a) The Mission recommends that Palestinian armed groups should undertake forthwith to respect international humanitarian law, in particular by renouncing attacks on Israeli civilians and civilian objects, and take all feasible precautionary measures to avoid harm to Palestinian civilians during hostilities;

(b) The Mission recommends that Palestinian armed groups who hold Israeli soldier Gilad Shalit in detention should release him on humanitarian grounds. Pending such release they should recognize his status as prisoner of war, treat him as such, and allow him ICRC visits.

1974. To responsible Palestinian authorities,

(a) The Mission recommends that the Palestinian Authority should issue clear instructions to security forces under its command to abide by human rights norms as enshrined in the Palestinian Basic Law and international instruments, ensure prompt and independent investigation of all allegations of serious human rights violations by security forces under its control, and end resort to military justice to deal with cases involving civilians;

(b) The Mission recommends that the Palestinian Authority and the Gaza authorities should release without delay all political detainees currently in their power and refrain from further arrests on political grounds and in violation of international human rights law;

(c) The Mission recommends that the Palestinian Authority and the Gaza authorities should continue to enable the free and independent operation of Palestinian non-governmental organizations, including human rights organizations, and of the Independent Commission for Human Rights.

1975. To the international community,

(a) The Mission recommends that the States parties to the Geneva Conventions of 1949 should start criminal investigations in national courts, using universal jurisdiction, where there is sufficient evidence of the commission of grave breaches of the Geneva Conventions of 1949. Where so warranted following investigation, alleged perpetrators should be arrested and prosecuted in accordance with internationally recognized standards of justice;

(b) International aid providers should step up financial and technical assistance for organizations providing psychological support and mental health services to the Palestinian population;

(c) In view of their crucial function, the Mission recommends that donor countries/assistance providers should continue to support the work of Palestinian and Israeli human rights organizations in documenting and publicly reporting on violations of human rights and international humanitarian law, and advising relevant authorities on their compliance with international law;

(d) The Mission recommends that States involved in peace negotiations between Israel and representatives of the Palestinian people, especially the Quartet, should ensure that respect for the rule of law, international law and human rights assumes a central role in internationally sponsored peace initiatives;

(e) In view of the allegations and reports about long-term environmental damage that may have been created by certain munitions or debris from munitions, the Mission recommends that a programme of environmental monitoring should take place under the auspices of the United Nations, for as long as deemed necessary. The programme should include the Gaza Strip and areas within southern Israel close to impact sites. The environmental monitoring programme should be in accordance with the recommendations of an independent body, and samples and analyses should be analysed by one or more independent expert institutions. Such recommendations, at least at the outset, should include measurement mechanisms which address the fears of the population of Gaza and southern Israel at this time and should at a minimum be in a position to determine the presences of heavy metals of all varieties, white phosphorous, tungsten micro-shrapnel and granules and such other chemicals as may be revealed by the investigation.

1976. To the international community and responsible Palestinian authorities,

(a) The Mission recommends that appropriate mechanisms should be established to ensure that the funds pledged by international donors for reconstruction activities in the Gaza Strip are smoothly and efficiently disbursed, and urgently put to use for the benefit of the population of Gaza;

(b) In view of the consequences of the military operations, the Mission recommends that responsible Palestinian authorities as well as international aid providers should pay special attention to the needs of persons with disabilities. In addition, the Mission recommends that medical follow-up should be ensured by relevant international and Palestinian structures with regard to patients who suffered amputations or were otherwise injured by munitions, the nature of which has not been clarified, in order to monitor any possible long-term impact on their health. Financial and technical assistance should be provided to ensure adequate medical follow-up to Palestinian patients.

1977. To the international community, Israel and Palestinian authorities,

(a) The Mission recommends that Israel and representatives of the Palestinian people, and international actors involved in the peace process, should involve Israeli and Palestinian civil society in devising sustainable peace agreements based on respect for international law. The participation of women should be ensured in accordance with Security Council resolution 1325 (2000);

(b) The Mission recommends that attention should be given to the position of women and steps be taken to ensure their access to compensation, legal assistance and economic security.

1978. To the United Nations Secretary-General, the Mission recommends that the Secretary- General should develop a policy to integrate human rights in peace initiatives in which the United Nations is involved, especially the Quartet, and request the United Nations High Commissioner for Human Rights to provide the expertise required to implement this recommendation.

1979. To the Office of the United Nations High Commissioner for Human Rights,

(a) The Mission recommends that the Office of the United Nations High Commissioner for Human Rights should monitor the situation of persons who have cooperated with the United Nations Fact Finding Mission on the Gaza Conflict and periodically update the Human Rights Council through its public reports and in other ways as it may deem appropriate;

(b) The Mission recommends that the Office of the High Commissioner for Human Rights should give attention to the Mission's recommendations in its periodic reporting on the Occupied Palestinian Territory to the Human Rights Council.[262]

2. Equal Seats in Courtrooms

For the same reasons as mentioned in the sub-sections above, both international legal systems i.e., the system of international criminal law and the body of Islamic international criminal law and justice in both, affirm that the first step in solving any political or criminal issue is to facilitate negotiation between all parties involved. This is, however, predicated on the parties being equal in arms, whether around the negotiation table or in the forum of a courtroom.

Still, Islamic law, in essence, prohibits the seats of judges or prosecutors from even being physically higher than those of the accused, witnesses, and the victims. The philosophy behind this is very straightforward: none of those involved in the proceedings takes priority over another, and all are equal in the eyes of Lady Justice until guilt is proven. This means that a certain theory of *mens rea* exists, and such a theory is not valid unless the parties are following the principle of *de lege lata* or the law in force. Consequently, in a proper Islamic legal system, the official entity, such as a

[262] A/HRC/12/48, pp.427-29. https://ia800305.us.archive.org/20/items/TheGoldstoneReport-ReportOfTheUnitedNationsFactFindingMissionOnThe/GoldstoneReport_djvu.txt.

court, decides on the matter. In our case, it is the duty of the parties to comply with, and accept, the provisions of the resolutions of the General Assembly and the Security Council, and furthermore, the permanent members of the United Nations have certain obligations to respect the law and enforce it through peaceful means.[263]

How can the United States government fabricate news and adopt resolutions in the Security Council concerning the terrorist attacks of 11 September in order to allow them to enrich their oil reserves, but they cannot accept and implement the provisions of the resolutions of the General Assembly or the Security Council governing the established rights of the Palestinians? This hypocrisy demonstrates that the US has double standards and engages in political laundering for economic gain.

As Kant says, "the propensity to evil in human nature, in the nature of an international organisation, and in the nature of a resolution develops a bad maxim, and the evilness of our actions continues the entire time." Furthermore "we should realise that the system of human rights law, international criminal law, humanitarian law of armed conflict, and permanent international criminal justice are all mirages and do not effectively exist."[264] This is what the systems of international human rights law and international justice are facing today.

3. The Position of *Actus Reus* in Law

The growing use of the terms "intentionally," "wilfully," "knowingly," "recklessly," and "maliciously" to denote *mens rea* can not only be seen in international criminal law and Islamic international criminal law, but also in the legal literature of most nations. The Prophet of Islam "makes us aware of the original source of criminal liability, the concept of *mens rea*, and of conduct that is a constituent element in all crimes, the nature of *actus reus,*

[263] Malekian, *Trading Virginity of International Criminal Juystice*, note 16.
[264] Malekian, *Mirage of International Criminal Law*, note 7, p.152.

as opposed to the mental state of the accused. Even in the case of *mens rea*, he encourages pardon with full guiding principles."[265]

Considering the complexity of *mens rea*, the more commonly-used phrase in the modern philosophy of law is 'the guilty mind', a phrase which can also be found in most system of criminal justice. Then there is 'the guilty act', which must be proven beyond any reasonable doubt. The term 'guilty act' is also known as *actus reus* and implies another crucial facet of criminal liability. It can be asserted that "*mens rea* by itself is not enough to constitute a crime: there must also be an act *actus reus*. Even in the case of attempts to commit crimes where the criminal intent is the dominant factor, the prosecution must prove the commission of an *actus reus* sufficient to amount to an attempt."

4. Violations of the Basic Principles of Criminal Laws

The system of Islamic international criminal law and the system of international criminal law have certain shared values that should never be violated. These shared fundamental principles of criminal justice can also be found in the Nuremberg Principles, in the Statute of the International Criminal Court, the Statute of the International Criminal Tribunal for the former Yugoslavia, the Statute of the International Criminal Tribunal for Rwanda, and the statutes of a number of other ad hoc courts/tribunals. A deep analysis of the statement of the president of the United States demonstrates clearly that his declaration violated the following principles of transnational criminal law including:

a) the prohibition of *ex post facto* law (retroactive law)
b) *de lege ferenda* (the law for future)

---

[265] Farhad Malekian, *Corpus Juris of Islamic International Criminal Justice* (Cambridge Scholars Publishing, 2017), p. 17.

c) *de lege lata* (the law in force)
d) *nullum crimen sine lege* (a conduct cannot be treated as criminal unless some rule of law has already declared it to be criminal and punishable as such)
e) *nulla poena sine lege* (no punishment without law)
f) the principle of inviolability of the rights of individuals
g) *nullum crimen nulla poena sine stricta* (prohibition of inhumane sanctions);
h) *nullum crimen nulla poena sine lege scripta* (care in the application of punishment for violations of unwritten law)
i) conformity (opportunity to follow the law)
j) humanity (punishment should be humane whenever possible)
k) equivalence (similar conduct should have similar punishment)
l) the application of the principle of proportionality.[266]

5. Predominantly Oblivious Declaration

Obviously, the declaration of the United States government fulfils all necessary conditions for proving the guilty mind of the accused. The declaration stands in particular opposition to the system of international law and its significant provisions, which have also long been violated by the Israeli government. If the United States government does not understand this simple philosophy of law, it would be the most self-righteous, self-interested, unconscious, oblivious, and irresponsible government in the world. However, this cannot be true as many distinguished philosophers of international legal discipline come from the United States. Thus, there must be other hidden sources and interests behind the words of the evil declaration and the poorly utilized machinery of international criminal law.

---

[266] Farhad Malekian 'Comparative Substantive International Criminal Justice', in Ronald Slye (ed.),*The Nuremberg Principles in Non-western Societies: A Reflection on their Universality, Legitimacy and Application (*2017), pp.10-44, at 23.

6. VIOLATIONS OF THE RIGHTS OF OCCUPIED COUNTRIES

The ill-defined declaration of the United States government not only demonstrates an inclination to evil in the nature of the government, but is also against the will of international legal and political community. In particular, states engaged in various international relations rejected the Israeli government's military actions following the Six-Day War of June 1967 through which Israel occupied most of Palestine, including the West Bank and the Gaza Strip by resorting to the use of force and aggression.

The armed forces of the same state also occupied the eastern half of *Al-Quds/Jerusalem*, the capital of Palestine. This eastern part has a considerable number of historical buildings. The United Nations Security Council did not accept the occupation and opposed the aggressive use of force according to the provisions of Resolution 242. The Council clearly pointed out that "the inadmissibility of the acquisition of territory by war and the need to work for a just and lasting peace in which every State in the area can live in security." The resolution called for the complete withdrawal of the troops of the occupying power from the occupied state.

In 1980, the Israeli government aggressively snubbed the provisions of the resolutions of the Security Council and the statement by the majority of the states of the United Nations. It annexed East *Al-Quds/Jerusalem* from the West Bank. Most members of the United Nations objected to the annexation. United Nations Security Council Resolution 478[267] – with

---

[267] Resolution 478 was adopted on 20 August 1980. The text of the resolution provides that:

The Security Council,

Recalling its resolution 476 (1980),

Reaffirming again that the acquisition of territory by force is inadmissible,

Deeply concerned over the enactment of a "basic law" in the Israeli Knesset proclaiming a change in the character and status of the Holy City of Jerusalem, with its implications for peace and security,

Noting that Israel has not complied with resolution 476 (1980),

Reaffirming its determination to examine practical ways and means, in accordance with the relevant provisions of the Charter of the United Nations, to secure the full implementation of its resolution 476 (1980), in the event of non-compliance by Israel,

1. *Censures* in the strongest terms the enactment by Israel of the "basic law" on Jerusalem and the refusal to comply with relevant Security Council resolutions;

2. *Affirms* that the enactment of the "basic law" by Israel constitutes a violation of international law and does not affect the continued application of the Geneva Convention

fourteen votes to and none against (with the abstention of the United States) – recognized the annexation as null and void. Consequently, the Council has officially rejected any illogical and immoral demands made by the Israeli government which violated the sources of international law, including law-making treaties.[268] Resolution 478 was the motivating factor for states that had embassies in *Al-Quds/Jerusalem* to relocate their embassies to other cities.[269]

---

relative to the Protection of Civilian Persons in Time of War, of 12 August 1949, in the Palestinian and other Arab territories occupied since June 1967, including Jerusalem;
3. *Determines* that all legislative and administrative measures and actions taken by Israel, the occupying Power, which have altered or purport to alter the character and status of the Holy City of Jerusalem, and in particular the recent "basic law" on Jerusalem, are null and void and must be rescinded forthwith;
4. *Affirms also* that this action constitutes a serious obstruction to achieving a comprehensive, just and lasting peace in the Middle East;
5. *Decides* not to recognize the "basic law" and such other actions by Israel that, as a result of this law, seek to alter the character and status of Jerusalem and calls upon:
(a) All Member States to accept this decision; (b) Those States that have established diplomatic missions at Jerusalem to withdraw such missions from the Holy City;
6. *Requests* the Secretary-General to report to the Security Council on the implementation of the present resolution before 15 November 1980;
7. *Decides* to remain seized of this serious situation.
Adopted at the 2245th meeting by 14 votes to none, with 1 abstention (United States of America).

[268] Legal Consequences of the Construction of a Wall in the Occupied Palestinian Territory, International Court of Justice Advisory Opinion, 9 July 2004, para.163.

[269] *Recalling* its Resolution 476 (1980),
Reaffirming again that the acquisition of territory by force is inadmissible,
Deeply concerned over the enactment of a "basic law" in the Israeli Knesset proclaiming a change in the character and status of the Holy City of Jerusalem, with its implications for peace and security,
Noting that Israel has not complied with resolution 476 (1980),
Reaffirming its determination to examine practical ways and means, in accordance with the relevant provisions of the Charter of the United Nations, to secure the full implementation of its resolution 476 (1980), in the event of non-compliance by Israel,
1. *Censures* in the strongest terms the enactment by Israel of the "basic law" on Jerusalem and the refusal to comply with relevant Security Council resolutions; 2. *Affirms* that the enactment of the "basic law" by Israel constitutes a violation of international law and does not affect the continued application of the Geneva Convention relative to the Protection of Civilian Persons in Time of War, of 12 August 1949, in the Palestinian and other Arab territories occupied since June 1967, including Jerusalem; 3. *Determines* that all legislative and administrative measures and actions taken by Israel, the occupying Power, which have altered or purport to alter the character and status of the Holy City of Jerusalem, and in particular the recent "basic law" on Jerusalem, are null and void and must be rescinded forthwith; 4. *Affirms also* that this action constitutes a serious obstruction to achieving a comprehensive, just and lasting peace in the Middle East; 5. *Decides* not to recognize the "basic law" and such other actions by Israel that, as a result of this law, seek to alter the

7. The Advisory Opinion of the International Court of Justice

The advisory opinion of the International Court of Justice delivered the judgment that all states were under an internationally recognized obligation to reject the unjust and illegal situation in and around East *Al-Quds/Jerusalem*. This opinion was delivered following the creation of the apartheid or racial segregation wall. The advisory view of the International Court of Justice stated that the Israeli authorities had violated the system of human rights law, including the instruments of international humanitarian law.[270] The Court stated:

> The construction of the wall being built by Israel, the occupying Power, in the Occupied Palestinian Territory, including in and around East Jerusalem, and its associated régime, are contrary to international law;… Israel is under an obligation to terminate its breaches of international law; it is under an obligation to cease forthwith the works of construction of the wall being built in the Occupied Palestinian Territory, including in and around East Jerusalem, to dismantle forthwith the structure therein situated, and to repeal or render ineffective forthwith all legislative and regulatory acts relating thereto, in accordance with paragraph 151 of this Opinion; … Israel is under an obligation to make reparation for all damage caused by the construction of the wall in the Occupied Palestinian Territory, including in and around East Jerusalem; … All States are under an obligation not to recognize the illegal situation resulting from the construction of the wall and not to render aid or assistance in maintaining the situation created by such construction; all States parties to the Fourth Geneva Convention relative to the Protection of Civilian Persons in Time

---

character and status of Jerusalem and calls upon: (a) All Member States to accept this decision; (b) Those States that have established diplomatic missions at Jerusalem to withdraw such missions from the Holy City; 6. *Requests* the Secretary-General to report to the Security Council on the implementation of the present resolution before 15 November 1980; 7. *Decides* to remain seized of this serious situation. *Adopted at the 2245th meeting by 14 votes to none, with 1 abstention (United States of America).*

270 Farhad Malekian, 'Judging International Criminal Justice in the Occupied Territories,' 12 *International Criminal Law Review* (2012), p.838.

of War of 12 August 1949 have, in addition, the obligation, while respecting the United Nations Charter and international law, to ensure compliance by Israel with international humanitarian law as embodied in that Convention.[271]

Regrettably, over the last fifty years, Israel has forced 208,000 settlers into East *Al-Quds/Jerusalem* by resorting to military force and, as a result, the Palestinians have been deprived of their own territory, lost their houses, and have been forced to continue to live in inhumane conditions under militant and aggressive Israeli occupation. Based on the above description, the criminal laws of the majority of nations assign guilt to those who initiated or prepared certain acts through political laundering or economic laundering. A clear example is the significant December 2017 declaration of the United States government which recognized *Al-Quds/Jerusalem* as the capital of Israel, which is the historical meeting place of people from the three monotheistic religions of the world—Christianity, Judaism, and Islam.

8. Inclination in Political *Mens Rea*

Justice must be served, even if only a single Palestinian remains on the earth. The Declaration of the US President is in and of itself a declaration of war against Muslims, as well as against non-Muslim states. It violates not only the rights of the Palestinian people, but also the integrity of the Islamic world, which firmly believes *Al-Quds/Jerusalem* should enjoy religious, cultural, and political validity. It also empowers the system of international criminal law, as well as the system of Islamic international criminal law and justice to mobilise towards the self-defence of their peaceful boundaries. It can therefore be asserted that:

this intention of the United States Government to modify the historic status of Jerusalem violates the legitimate interests of the Palestinian

[271] Legal Consequences of the Construction of a Wall in the Occupied Palestinian Territory, International Court of Justice Advisory Opinion, 9 July 2004, para.163.

> people and the Arab and Islamic nations, will have serious consequences for stability and security in the Middle East, will further increase tensions in this region and will impede any effort aimed at resuming peace talks between Israelis and Palestinians.[272]

The declaration also constitutes a breach of UN law. This is because the statement is *neither* a product of an international contact group *nor* a recommendation by the unanimous consensus of the General Assembly. It also is legally and logically invalid because the case has been on table of the international legal and political community for the last 100 years and is clearly unsettled. That the President of the United States believed that he has the authority to solve it, shows how invalid the act is. It is a simple question of political *mens rea* carried out with full knowledge that such a declaration breaches the international legal personality of all states of the world. The Declaration also denounces the existence of Israel as a legitimate state of international law, based on the resolution of the Security Council and the members of the United Nations. This is based on the fact/theory that the Declaration invalidates and nullifies the provisions of Security Council Resolution 181 under which the state of Israel was founded. The object of the Declaration also cannot be supported under the principle of self-defence, which is essential in moderating the concept of *mens rea*.

On 19 December 2017, the United States vetoed the resolution of the Security Council which condemned their declaration, although it received 14 votes in its favour. However, the recent General Assembly Resolution ES-10/L.22 received 128[273] votes in favour, 9 against[274] and 35 abstentions.[275] It put forth the following significant norms:

---

[272] Cuba rejects the USA's recognition of Jerusalem as the capital of Israel, available online at http://www.juventudrebelde.cu/en/ internationals/2017-12-08/cuba-rejects-us-recognition-of-jerusalem-as-the-capital-of-israel/print.

[273] The resolution was adopted at the 37th plenary meeting of the tenth emergency special session of the United Nations General Assembly during the tenure of the seventy-second session of the United Nations General Assembly on 21 December 2017.

[274] Guatemala, Honduras, Israel, Marshall Islands, Micronesia, Nauru, Palau, Togo, and the United States.

[275] Antigua-Barbuda, Argentina, Australia, Bahamas, Benin, Bhutan, Bosnia-Herzegovina, Cameroon, Canada, Colombia, Croatia, Czech Republic, Dominican Republic, Equatorial Guinea, Fiji, Haiti, Hungary, Jamaica, Kiribati, Latvia, Lesotho, Malawi, Mexico, Panama,

> Bearing in mind the specific status of the Holy City of Jerusalem and, in particular, the need for the protection and preservation of the unique spiritual, religious and cultural dimensions of the City, as foreseen in the relevant United Nations resolutions,
>
> Stressing that Jerusalem is a final status issue to be resolved through negotiations in line with relevant United Nations resolutions,
>
> Expressing in this regard its deep regret at recent decisions concerning the status of Jerusalem,
>
> Affirms that any decisions and actions which purport to have altered, the character, status or demographic composition of the Holy City of Jerusalem have no legal effect, are null and void and must be rescinded in compliance with relevant resolutions of the Security Council, and in this regard, calls upon all States to refrain from the establishment of diplomatic missions in the Holy City of Jerusalem, pursuant to resolution 478 (1980) of the Security Council;
>
> Demands that all States comply with Security Council resolutions regarding the Holy City of Jerusalem, and not to recognize any actions or measures contrary to those resolutions;
>
> Reiterates its call for the reversal of the negative trends on the ground that are imperilling the two-State solution and for the intensification and acceleration of international and regional efforts and support aimed at achieving, without delay, a comprehensive, just and lasting peace in the Middle East on the basis of the relevant United Nations resolutions, the Madrid terms of reference, including the principle of land for peace, the Arab Peace Initiative and the Quartet Roadmap and an end to the Israeli occupation that began in 1967.

The concept of *mens rea,* or guilty intent, does not necessarily refer to the intent to perform acts which are not permitted by law. The notion of intent may be expressed in various juxtaposing forms. It may apply to acts that are legally wrong, but only if they are truly carried out. We should raise

---

Paraguay, Philippines, Poland, Romania, Rwanda, Solomon Islands, South Sudan, Trinidad-Tobago, Tuvalu, Uganda, and Vanuatu.

similar concerns about the illegal and illegitimate scope of the declaration made by Trump. Accordingly, there are many acts not prohibited by any statute of international law or international criminal law, such as trading various forms of weapons and basing our arguments on the freedom of the trade, which no wise man would hesitate to call morally wrong.[276] This means that not only is the object of the declaration legally wrong, but the act of even drafting such a theory is morally and practically criminal.

9. THE HIDDEN *MENS REA*

The declaration contains a *hidden mens rea* against the rights of occupied nations, which are recognized by numerous international treaties and resolutions of the General Assembly. The declaration violates the right to self-determination for groups or nations, which are entitled to struggle for their inalienable and indisputable rights. A parallel argument can be found in the words of the Declaration of Independence of the United States, which reads "We hold these truths to be self-evident, that all men are created equal and endowed by their creator with certain unalienable rights including life, liberty, and the pursuit of happiness."

The city of *Al-Quds/Jerusalem* is an integral part of the Palestinian heritage of truthfulness, Jewish integrity, and the Christian history. It also represents a central love for all three faiths in communicating and achieving more in terms of unity, transparency, mutual advantages, and preservation, including the safeguarding of peace, justice, and cultural morality. The United States government has, unfortunately, once again led the people of the United States into a political storm, which is neither productive nor advisable given the current state of the world. The United Sates government should have guided its population towards creating a peaceful reputation with love for bare justice, instead of perpetuating evil injustice.

---

[276] Malekian, *Trading Virginity of International Criminal Justice,* note 16, pp. pp.2, 4, 31 and 34.

10. A One-Eyed Justice

One cannot deny the fact that the voice of *Al-Quds/Jerusalem* is crucial, essential, and indispensable to the maintenance of peace for all parties. We should keep in mind that as a result of the unlawful occupation of Palestinian territorial sovereignty by the British colonial power, and the subsequent establishment of the Israeli state, millions of people have had to seek asylum in other states, and even in the desert.[277] It is therefore imperative that the

---

[277] Of particular is the General Assembly Resolution of 212 (III) of 19 November 1948. The resolution reads that: WHEREAS the problem of the relief of Palestine refugees of all communities in one of immediate urgency and the United Nations Mediator on Palestine in his progress report of 18 September 1948, part Three, states that "action must be taken to determine the necessary measures (of relief) and to provide for their implementation" and that "the choice is between saving the lives of many thousands of people now or permitting them to die", WHEREAS the Acting Mediator, in his supplemental report of 18 October 1948, declares that "the situation of the refugees is now critical" and that "aid must not only be continued but very greatly increased if disaster in to be averted," WHEREAS the alleviation of conditions of starvation and distress among the Palestine refugees is one of the minimum conditions for the success of the efforts of the United Nations to bring peace to that land, THE GENERAL ASSEMBLY 1. EXPRESSES its thanks to the Governments and organizations which, and the individual persons who, have given assistance directly or in response to the Mediator's appeal: 2. CONSIDERS, on the basis of the Acting Mediator's recommendation, that a sum of approximately $29,500,000 will be required to provide relief for 500,000 refugees for a period of nine months from 1 December 1948 to 31 August 1949, and that an additional amount of approximately $2,500,000 will be required for administrative and local operational expenses; 3. AUTHORIZES the Secretary-General, in consultation with the Advisory Committee on Administrative and Budgetary Questions, to advance immediately a sum of up to $5,000,000 from the Working Capital Fund of the United Nations, the said sum to be repaid before the end of the period specified in paragraph 2, from the voluntary governmental contributions requested under paragraph 4; 4. URGES all State Members of the United Nations to make as soon an possible voluntary contributions in kind or in funds sufficient to ensure that the amount of supplies and funds required is obtained, and states that, to this end, voluntary contributions of non-member States would also be accepted, contributions in funds may be made in currencies other than the United States dollar, in so far as the operations of the relief organization can be carried out in such currencies; 5. AUTHORIZES the Secretary-General to establish a Special Fund into which contributions shall be paid, which will be administered as a separate account; 6. AUTHORIZES the Secretary-General to expend the funds received under paragraphs 3 and 4 of this resolution; 7. INSTRUCTS the Secretary-General, in consultation with the Advisory Committee on ADMINISTRATIVE and BUDGETARY QUESTIONS, to establish regulations for the administration and supervision of the Fund; 8. REQUESTS the Secretary-General to take all necessary steps to extend aid to Palestine refugees and to establish such administrative organization as may be required for this purpose, inviting the assistance of the appropriate agencies of the several Governments, the specialized agencies of the United Nations, the United Nations International Children's Emergency Fund, the International Committee of the Red Cross, the League of Red Cross Societies and other voluntary agencies it being

international community realises this significant fact. The demand for justice and its high priority and urgency cannot come through acts with *mens rea* concerning the full knowledge/intent of violating the Islamic rights of Islamic nations, Islamic international law, Islamic international criminal law, and Islamic international criminal justice, including Islamic international human rights law and its relevant Declaration on Human Rights.

Certainly, a wise man would not violate the cultural and legislative principles of other nations. In addition, the system of international law constantly reconsiders the rules of law, and therefore it continuously re-codifies the body of customary principles that have become controversial.[278] The establishment of the United Nations, however, abolished many principles of international law which were based on a one-sided justice and which had led to serious conflicts between different states.[279] This is why most significant questions of international law must be recognised by the General Assembly, and the most contentious issues must be resolved before

---

recognized that the participation of voluntary organizations in the relief plan would in no way derogate from the principle of impartiality on the basis of which the assistance of these organizations is being solicited; 9. REQUESTS the Secretary-General to appoint a Director of United Nations Relief for Palestine Refugees, to whom he may delegate such responsibility and he may consider appropriate for the overall planning and implementation of the relief programme; 10. AGREES to the convoking, at the discretion of the Secretary- General of an ad hoc advisory committee of Seven members to be selected by the President of the General Assembly to which the Secretary-General may submit any matter of principle or policy upon which he would like the benefit of the committee's advice; 11. REQUESTS the Secretary-General to continue and to extend the implementation of the present relief programmer until the machinery provided for by the present resolution is set up; 12. URGES the World Health Organization, the Food and Agriculture Organisation the International Refugee Organization, the United Nations International Children's Emergency Fund, and other appropriate organizations and agencies, acting within the framework of the relief programme herein established, promptly to contribute supplies, specialized personnel and other services permitted by their constitutions and their financial resources, to relieve the desperate plight of Palestine refugees of all communities; 13. REQUESTS the Secretary-General to report to the General Assembly, at the next regular session, on the action taken as a result of this resolution.

[278] Farhad Malekian 'Comparative Substantive International Criminal Justice', in Ronald Slye (ed.), *The Nuremberg Principles in Non-western Societies: A Reflection on their Universality, Legitimacy and Application (*2017), pp.10-44, at 27-30.

[279] *Year Book of the International Law Commission: 1963 Vol. II*, UN Doc. A/CN.4/SER.A/1963/ADD.1, at 187, 198.

the International Court of Justice.[280] The codification of international law by the International Law Commission is one of the clearest examples.

In other words, unilateral declarations have no legal validity in international relations, especially those which deprive people of their inalienable rights. If the contrary were true, we would no longer need the United Nations, and would revert to the old, abolished international legal system. The judgments of the ICJ and the resolutions of the General Assembly and the Security Council are contrary to the declaration of the President of the United States.

This implies the existence of a body of conventional and customary international law which contradicts the words of the evil *mens rea* in the declaration of the United States. If the words of the declaration are authentic and legitimate, then the US government should return the traditional territory of the Native Americans to its rightful occupants, as the Native Americans have a greater claim to that land than the Jews do to Palestinian territory, as Europeans only reached North America in the 16th century, whereas the Jews left Palestine over 2,500 years ago.

One should also add that international problems cannot be resolved through one-sided justice and by killing innocent Palestinians, or any other population. The declaration is an act of force or aggression under Chapter VII of the United Nations Charter. In other words, it violates the entire system of international law. An individual, a group, an entity, or a state, which resorts to the use of force, is strongly condemned – even the principle of proportionality cannot save any evil declarations or military arguments.

When the philosophy or substance of our existence and human morality are harmed, we can no longer heal it with aspiration. This is what is happening to the nation of Palestine – a nation which is *humbled* by its situation, which is a result of our silence, and our need to keep our jobs, various titles, and private bank accounts.[281]

---

[280] See the Statutes of the Court and the United Nations Charter.

[281] Examine R. Pearce., Model Rule 1.0: lawyers are morally –accountable, Fordham Law Review (2002), 70, 1805. Also Malekian, *Judgments of Love in Criminal Justice*, note 17.

11. The *Actus Reus* of the Declaration

Mens rea is *mens rea*, no matter who the victims or actors are. The *actus reus* of the declaration implies the guilty mind or *mens rea* of the President. The term *mens rea* in criminal law comes from the maxim: *actus non facit reum, nisi mens sit rea*, which implies that the occurrence of an act does not in and of itself make a defendant guilty unless there is also a guilty intent – as is present in the United States' declaration, with the intent of this *mens rea* being to stamp out a considerable number of rights.[282]

Actus reus and *mens rea* on the part of a defendant are required in order to establish criminal responsibility. The Trial Chamber in the *Kordic* and *Cerkez* cases shed light on the relationship between a guilty mind and a guilty act as a mode of attribution of individual criminal responsibility to all individuals no matter their standing:[283]

> Article 7(1) is concerned with persons directly responsible for planning, instigating, ordering, committing, or aiding and abetting in the planning, preparation or execution of a crime. Thus, both the individual who himself carries out the unlawful conduct and his superior who is involved in the conduct not by physical participation, but for example by ordering or instigating it, are covered by Article 7(1). For instance, a superior who orders the killing of a civilian may be held responsible under Article 7(1), as might a political leader who plans that certain civilians or groups of civilians should be executed, and passes these instructions on to a military commander. [284]

The Chamber continued and clarified:

> The criminal responsibility of such superiors, either military or civilian, in these circumstances is personal or direct, as a result of their

---

[282] Consult Malekian, *Mirage of International Criminal Law*, note 7.

[283] Consult Giulia Majori, 'Joint Criminal Enterprise in the Jurisprudence of the International Criminal Tribunal for the Former Yugoslavia and the Prosecution of Senior Political and Military Leaders: The Krajišnik Case' 14 *Max Planck United Nations Yearbook* (2010), pp. 51-83, in particular p. 54 and pp.75-170.

[284] *Kordic and Cerkez,* (Trial Chamber), February 26, 2001, para.367.

direct link to the physical commission of the crime. The criminal responsibility of a superior for such positive acts, except where the superior orders the crime in which case he may be more appropriately referred to as primarily responsible for its commission, may be regarded as 'follow(ing) from general principles of accomplice liability.[285]

The declaration is not aimed at the annihilation of one or several persons, but of a nation. This means that the declaration constitutes an act of genocide. While not directly carrying out mass killings, as is typical of genocides, the Declaration deprives a nation of the indispensable rights that constitute a part of its identity.[286] The crime of genocide does not necessarily only involve physical killing, but also the deprivation of rights, mutilation of integrity of mind, maiming of personal integrity, elimination of culture, eradication of peace, and the aggression towards, and annihilation of, another civilisation.[287]

---

[285] *Id.* "The theory of the criminal responsibility of individuals is essentially based on the principle of *actus reus* which implies the objective element of a crime giving rise to the notion of the criminal responsibility of individuals. The principle should also be examined in conjunction with the principle of *mens rea* dealing with the guilty mind of perpetrators of the Gaza crimes. This means that the concept of the criminal responsibility of the perpetrators in this case must be read in connection with their obvious aims to attack homeless Palestinians. Although we are aware that the Security Council of the United Nations, especially the United States government because of military, political and highly economic ties will not let the Gaza crimes be submitted to the jurisdiction of the ICC, this criminal prevention and indirect participation and affirmation of the criminal activities of the Israeli armed forces do not hinder the Court from applying international criminal justice in the future." Farhad Malekian, 'Judging International Criminal Justice in the Occupied Territories,' 12 *International Criminal Law Review* (2012), 827–869.

[286] Report to the Council on the 17th Extraordinary Session of the PMC, Doc. No. C.355 (1) M.147 (1), 1930, VI, Geneva, 1930, p. 140.

[287] Mark J Osiel, *Obeying orders: Atrocity, Military Discipline, and the Law of War* (Transaction Publishers, 1999); Timothy L. H McCormack, *The Law of War Crimes: National and International Approaches* (Brill, 1997); Rene Provost, *International Human Rights and Humanitarian Law* (2002); William A. Schabas, *War Crimes and Human Rights: Essays on the Death Penalty, Justice and Accountability* (Cameron May, 2008); Steven R. Ratner, Jason S. Abrams, and James L. Bischoff, *Accountability for Human Rights Atrocities in International Law: Beyond the Nuremberg Legacy*, (3rd ed., Oxford Press, 2009); Eric Stover, *My Neighbour, My Enemy: Justice and Community in the Aftermath of Mass Atrocity* (Cambridge University Press, 2004); Benjamin B. Ferencz, *New Legal Foundations for Global Survival: Security Through the Security Council* (Oceana Publications,1994).

12. Preliminary Sanctions in Resolution 181

The international legal and political community adopted the United Nations Partition Plan 70 years ago. Its purpose was to protect Jews in the territories of Palestine whose rights were being ignored in most European states. Therefore, international efforts suggested a two-state solution. As we have stated elsewhere, the provisions of the Balfour Declaration were the reason for the genocide against the Palestinians, the genocide of their cultural heritage, the genocide of their population, and the genocide of their children.

Needless to say, the Palestinians have not accepted the situation. Particularly since the occupation of the West Bank and East Jerusalem, they have strongly protested Israeli aggression by resorting to the Intifada method. This means that they have demonstrated that the Israeli authorities should not settle in the Palestinian homelands and thereby negate the historic rights of the owners, and this resistance against occupation has been very powerful.

However, no peaceful solutions have been found thus far, due to the fact that the governments of the United States and Israel always use certain hidden tricks in their international policies. This is especially true when it comes to matters relating to Palestine. Usually, they pretend they are ratifying a peace agreement, but as they come closer to signing an agreement, the hidden trick reveals itself and brings humiliation to the Palestinians.

13. Solving the Dilemma Created by Great Britain

As long as the problem of Palestine and Palestinian heritage is not resolved, the following actions can be taken against the Israeli authorities to consolidate the relevant provisions of the Security Council:

1) The European Union members must pass certain political and economic sanctions against Israel.
2) The distribution of public funds to Israel must be severely restricted for the purpose of peace.
3) Any businesses with any entity or subsidiary located in settlements must be considered invalid. No cargo should be purchased or be transported to Israeli settlers.
4) Business should not extend into East Jerusalem for as long as the East is under occupation.
5) The EU members should support Palestinian companies.
6) Palestinian politicians should be given honorary seats in EU committees, courts, and so forth as this would help foster their political experience/education and their acceptance in Europe.
7) Financial assistance for justice, not war, and the development of transparency should be granted to official Palestinian organisations.
8) A two-state solution should be recognized as being the proper interpretation of the customary provisions of the Security Council resolutions and the General Assembly.
9) States of the world, including European states, should declare and refer to East *Al-Quds/Jerusalem* as the capital of Palestine in their governmental sessions and official documents.
10) The members of the European Union and other countries of the world should refer to East *Al-Quds/Jerusalem* as the capital of Palestine in their official papers and speeches.
11) All regional and international organizations should refer, if necessary, to the capital of Palestine – East *Al Quds/Jerusalem* in their international relations.
12) All violations by Israeli authorities should be condemned internationally.
13) The authorities of Israel, who have violated the system of international criminal law, should not be granted entry to the territories of European states or other states of the world.

14) The political authorities of Israel should be called upon to accept the reality of the international legal personality of Palestine, and to respect the sources of international law, including the resolutions of the Security Council and the General Assembly.
15) The European Union and the world should respect and support all Jews who recognize East *Al-Quds/Jerusalem* as the capital of Palestine.
16) *Israeli authorities should urge Palestinian authorities to sell the Israeli territory as delineated in Resolution 181, for one dinar, as a symbol of peace and to mark the end of hostilities, and this dinar should forever sit at the top of the Security Council's door. The deal is to be conducted in a ceremony in the presence of the members of the United Nations General Assembly.*
17) The principal organs of the United Nations, namely the General Assembly, the Security Council, the Economic and Social Council, the Secretary-General, the International Court of Justice, and the Trusteeship Council, should be vigilant and ensure the restoration of the provisions of Resolution 181.[288]
18) The rule of love for true equality, peace, and justice should be given priority by all Jews of the world.
19) The United Nations should provide intensive programs in which Jews and Muslims develop peaceful relations in various social fields.

[288] Resolution 181 was approved by a vote of 333 to 13 with 10 abstentions on 29 November, 1947.

Chapter 8

CHARACTERISING DIGNITY THROUGH THE EXPLOITATION OF LEGAL PERSONALITY

1. LIMITING THE RECOGNITION OF THE DIGNITY OF EUROPEANS

The fact is that the notion of equality and the provisions of a number of articles of the UN Charter are indeed ambiguous, and thus the notion of dignity is subject to interpretation by the five permanent members, a certain tactic seems to be helpful in understanding the reality of justice presented by the permanent members of the United Nations.

Nevertheless, these conclusions are incontrovertibly constructive based on the fact that we are referring to the already existing Charter of the United Nations and its very violative principles of the monopolisation of the notion of integrity the provisions of Chapter VII.[289] In fact, the diversity in the dignity and the validity of the international legal personality of states and their membership, are in part structured in the United Nations Charter, and

[289] Consult Malekian, *Trading Virginity of International Criminal Justice,* note 16, pp.44, 47, and 48.

even in its practice.[290] However, this is not because the Charter requires the notion of unequal dignity, but because the application of this unequal notion of dignity seems to be the principle in its Chapter VII.[291] This means that the situation makes it impossible to define the notion of dignity because of its inconsistent application by the permanent members of the UNSC.[292]

Many books have been written concerning the questions of the dignity of man and the principles of human rights law. These questions have also been discussed in a variety of legal disciplines, and have been the subject of a large number of lectures at European institutions. European politicians have constantly spoken about the rights of man, the rights of human beings, the rights of groups, and the rights of nations. They have criticised the manner of application of human rights law in non-European countries. Their reasoning has not only been strong, but has also criticised other nations for their gross violations of international human rights law, international criminal law, and international criminal justice.

If these claims or accusations are really valid concerning the true nature of justice, reasoning behind justice, and the colour of genuine justice, then why are they targeted at others? Is it true that European states are the most innocent states of the world and the purest humanists as well? It was European states, politicians, and governments which reduced the population of the world to slavery. If European states are authentically objective in their judgments, statements, and orations, why are the results of these judgements

---

[290] "Clear examples of this phenomenon include certain sanctions passed in the Security Council of the United Nations which sought to destroy nations to reach oil, such as with those levied against the Iraqi regime. All those states who voted in support of those resolutions should have realised the true intent hidden in their words. The killing of children, of civilians, and the destruction of Babylonian civilisation could not be hidden, the states had to have known. Thus, a soldier who engages in the commission of genocide on a massive scale, cannot claim that they carried out the crime only because of orders from their superior, nor can the superior legitimately claim that he gave the order without intending to commit genocide on a massive scale. This means we cannot trade the guilty mind with *actus reus*, although the perpetrators try to. We can make similar conclusions concerning the brutal criminal conducts committed by Blackwater under the command of its chief, or a number of other criminal groups working under the orders of the Chinese government." *Id.*, p.53.

[291] *Id.*, p.54.

[292] *Id.*, pp.55, 68, 99, 276, 272 and 263.

and such so varied? If they are bona fide humanists and sympathetic to the understanding of the nature and values of rights, why can the same nations, states, politicians, judges, and prosecutors not see the reality which has been created for the homeless Palestinians who are treated as less than slaves and beasts?

2. Instrumentality of Human Rights Law

Why can they not see that the children of the innocent victims of the Second World War have themselves become the destroyers of one of the oldest nations of the world, and committers of genocide?[293] If justice is the way in which the Europeans understand the principles of human rights law, if justice is a question of the priority of common basic principles and not personal ones, why do these superior European states, whose understanding is broad and powerful, not protest against the violations of human rights law? Why do these European states, whose manner of application of human rights law is logical and righteous, not protest against the big permanent members of the United Nations Security Council and their allies? Why does the German government have good political relations with those governments? Here, we refer to those who are destroying the Palestinian's homeland using the most powerful weapons in the history of humankind.[294]

My arrow is pointed at states such as the Netherlands which possesses various institutions of human rights law, legislations, judgments, and governments' policy, which are constantly speaking about counterterrorism movements, and organising various support for human rights. My arrow is also pointed toward states such as Sweden, Denmark, Germany, Norway, Finland, and the United Kingdom, which are constantly speaking about justice and human rights law in Europe, and supporting their own world behind the philosophy of *democratic integrity*. I am also pointing my weapon of love to all states of Europe and their system of international

[293] *Id.*, pp.251, 257, 264 and 260.
[294] *Id.*, pp.46, 47, 48, 209, 212, 251,275, 286 and 288.

criminal law, their methods of international criminal justice, and their principles of international human rights law, which are blind to the organised criminal conducts carried out against the Palestinian population. Socrates correctly stated that it is to your advantage to be just and to your disadvantage to be unjust. Are we really just? Do we really understand the merit of Socrates' principle within our cannon of justice?

The real problem is that the European states have placed a great value on their integrity, on their own priorities, and on their own knowledge of human rights law. They respect the value of their interpretation of criminal justice, and the privilege of their political policy, even though this policy is the policy of silence and the policy of turning a blind eye to the crimes committed against the Palestinians by the Israelis. What is the true value of man, the merit of the word 'dignity', and the value of moral philosophy? Are we fairly fulfilling and applying this united concept of dignity to all when we witness that millions of Palestinians are the subjects of trade by the big political parties? Or when we see that the United Nations Charter is being violated and we stand by silently?

Based on the examination of laws, opinions from various national bodies governing the ethics of human rights law, and court rulings, we are respecting the value of the basic principles of human rights law in European courts, while simultaneously disrespecting the same principles when it comes to the Palestinian population.[295] The fact is that the notion of dignity, perceived by Europeans as an important and universal concept, becomes vague and entirely meaningless regarding the integrity of the Palestinian population. Here, integrity is measured upon political power, sovereign power, and membership in European organisations.[296]

Thus, integrity designates the way in which European states understand and practice norms by trading their weapons to the Middle East or other parts of the world.[297]

> How can we assert that our criminal justice is true when the political system of the same country is engaged in trading weapons? Was the trade

[295] *Id.*, p.109.

[296] *Id.*, p. 95 and 115.

[297] Malekian, *Trading Virginity of International Criminal Justice,* note 16, pp. pp.2, 4, 31, 34,

> of weapons between the United States and Saudi Arabia morally, or even legally permissible when it was already known that said weapons would be used against the Yemeni population? Did the Yemeni or Syrian population commit any crimes against the United States government through military attacks on American soil? Not one single state of human animals protested against the trade. Is this not complicity to the criminal actions of big political parties? Are most states of the world not the traders of criminal justice? According to what morality, if any, can the legal standard of international conventions which concern the trade of weapons, be correct? This philosophy is only acceptable in the civilisation of human animals and not animals human. The former have rules permitting the trade of weapons, and even the trade of human beings, as well as rules which have permitted the killing of both human beings and animals human. This points to the fact that animals human are much more civilised than we human beings are.[298]

Although we do not reject the fact that European politicians and governments do not officially violate the integrity of the population of Palestine, they do so through their policy of neutrality and apathy.[299] What remains for the Palestinian population is only themselves and their inferior political and military powers. Where are the hidden true integrity of man, the genuine integrity of the world's politicians, the authentic concept of a democratic government, and the notion of humanity expressed by thousands of symbolic provisions contained in human rights covenants?

Additionally, most European states remain silent concerning violations of international law by the United States, the United Kingdom, and Israel and above all, through this policy of silence, release themselves from any responsibility by convincing themselves that every matter was planned by those superior powers alone. Thus, they ignore the fact that each member of the United Nations not only has the duty, but also the responsibility, to protest against unjust actions, conducts, and decisions. Moreover, since the European states do not protest by in any way, they are contributing to the system of injustice, and therefore are responsible for the serious violations of the system of international law against the Palestinian population and their

---

[298] Id., p.35.
[299] *Id.*, p.134.

integrity by the superior military powers.[300] This notion of responsibility is based on the united essence of man which is ought to and not selective.

3. Impunity Constituting the Principle of Unity

The United Nations Charter speaks about the prevention of impunity and the application of the basic principle of non-impunity. Certainly, the system of international law not only includes individualistic rules, but also united rules, united responsibility, and the united identification of international crimes. The European states cannot escape from their own responsibility concerning Palestine by acting against criminal violations in some cases--such as in Iran, China, and Russia and then avoiding taking action in others-- such as in Palestine, Yemen, and Egypt.

Beyond all, the borderlines of responsibility under the provisions of Chapter VII of the UN Charter, do not mean that the other members have no duty to protect the rights of other members, as we saw in the case of apartheid in South Africa. By all this I mean that even though the United States government is behind all these criminal movements against Palestinians, and many other nations in the world, the European states with their silent policy are complicit in it, and hence participate in the commission of those crimes, and without doubt thus violate international human rights law. This in its own terms is a serious violation of the system of *jus cogens* and *erga omnes,* and obviously of the system of international criminal justice.

Plato gave an imperative description of the notion of justice. He used the Greek word "Dikaisyne" in order define justice, morality, and

[300] "Not only Hitler, his inner circle, his officers, and the government identified Jews as the cause of economic depression, - - but almost all members of German society held that view. Crimes against innocent Jews were crimes of the state, the government, and the parliaments; they were offences of the legislation, crimes of the jurisdiction of the courts, of police—they were crimes of crimes more savage than previously imaginable. Obviously, they were the crimes of the people of Germany, of German families, crimes of commonality, of cities, and of all generations. The same conclusion can be easily drawn about the situation of the Palestinians under the Israeli government's criminal military forces." *Id.*, p.128.

'righteousness'. Justice relates to certain duties that one has both to themselves and to others. Plato believed that the notion of justice deals with the equality of the essence of man, which prevents irrational desire and malicious acts. *How could the European states and their lawyers who carry the slogan of justice and particularly certain powers fight against German Nazism and protected the innocent Jews from grave criminal acts against their personal and group dignity, but then remain silent after almost seventy-five years concerning the criminal acts of the great powers against the Palestinian population?* Plato, through his philosophy, intended to vanquish self-interested satisfaction from politics, and to create justice with the notion of united benefit for the essence of humankind. However, the fact is that European states have multiple definitions of justice-- one for themselves and one for the Palestinians, Yemenis, Syrians, Iraqis, Afghanis, and for Myanmar's humiliated Muslim population.

The fact is that there is zero hope for humanity, as justice today is just a game played through the provisions of international human rights law. Similarly, the notion of integrity and the respect thereof is another game, as is the concept of equality of states under the dictatorship provisions of international law concerning the international legal personality of states. If there exists a true international legal personality for each state which makes them all equal, then why we are inconsistent in our practices, policies, values, and even in the monopolised system of the United Nations Charter? The fact is *also* that the entire system of international human rights law is monopolised through interpretation, and is dominated by big political parties and their allies in Europe, and filled with meaningless words and provisions which are used as tools in political games.

Even if certain phases may not be obvious in the evolution of differentiated dignity for states, there has definitely been an observable impact on the evolution of the notion of dignity between members, which is dependent upon a state's relation with the permanent members. Consequently, the principle of dignity is itself largely insignificant when it is not effective in its political and juridical reality. Consequently, the necessary knowledge of how the notion of dignity may apply and how it is valued, depends broadly on the will of the permanent members and their private interests, as for instance, in the case of Palestine or the criminal activities of the authorities of Saudi Arabia.[301]

4. Membership Paralyzing Justice

Politically and even legally the notion of dignity, which has a strong connection to the theory of justice, is applied under different criteria with regard to the monopolised provisions of the Charter of the United Nations and thereby creates impunity where it should not. In addition, terms such as 'dignity' and 'justice' have not been seen as part of one legal and political concept in the provisions of Chapter VII of the Security Council. This is because the permanent members provide different definitions to the concepts of justice and dignity. Basically, there are different ideas concerning the respect of the integrity of members of the United Nations. Without any hesitation, the Charter itself has different definitions of the concept of justice and dignity when it comes to its powerful and non-powerful members.

In addition, most Asian and African nations have less dignity than most European members do in practice, which of course although not written in the Charter, the seventy-five-year practice of the Charter implies this fact. With this we do not mean to reduce the integrity of these states, but to reveal the fact that all matters in the Charter are not based on the same idea of respect, although they superficially appear to be. The same is true concerning the notion of justice which is linked to the limits of power. The long practice of apartheid by the white supremacist government in South Africa was not only not seen as an injustice, but as the consequence of justice. Thus, the concept of equal justice may be excluded in some situations which denote the rights of powerful states to decide, take measures, attack, kill, or destroy as an integral part of the presentation of the forum of justice, as it is carried out in many countries such as Palestine.

---

301 In 1980, the president of the United States stated clearly that "the Persian Gulf [is] a vital US national security interest." Jimmy Carter (January, 1980).

Consequently, suffering an indignity or an injustice does not necessary mean that one's rights have been violated, since in the eyes of the Charter, there is no such thing as victims. The fact is that all states are considered equal by the very provisions of unequal character. All states are identified as the best members of the organisation under the very insulting provisions of Chapter VII. Similarly, all states are the subject of the peaceful settlement of international disputes by the heavily monopolised idea of veto rights. Thus, the questions of dignity, justice, and equality expressed by the Charter of the United Nations should be evaluated by the inequality of votes and the unequal position of the General Assembly as compared to the Security Council. This implies the fact that the notion of impunity remains much stronger than the notion of non-impunity is the fact.

Both organs i.e., the Security Council and the General Assembly are internal gathering points for the organisation, however the power of the UN is concentrated within the Security Council, and justice, dignity, and peace are monopolised by its strongest members. Dignity, justice, peace, and the settlement of international disputes all relate to the very unfortunate fact of the system of international law i.e., which state can kill more, which state can terrorise more, which state can commit more genocide. This means that the United Nation Charter empowers the commission of genocide by the most powerful states of the world. This is regardless of the political position of other states or members. This is because the biggest permanent members can interpret the provisions of the Security Council as they wish, and have constantly violated the most basic principles of the charter relating to peace, security, and the use of force. They have also employed international machinery for the promotion of their own economic and social advancement.

5. Big Powers Institutionalising the Decision Makers

Big powers are able to make decisions without the approval of the UN, such as with 'the deal of century' made regarding the territory of Palestinian population. The deal has in fact proven that the United Nations is powerless and entirely paralysed. Consequently, terms like 'human dignity', 'the dignity of all the members', 'the dignity of international legal personality', 'personal dignity', and 'the dignity of an international organisation', are employed only metaphorically and without any impact. Such terms do not have any legal power as long as the big permanent members have not given their practical consent. Thus, consent appears to be more unilateral than multilateral in nature. This denotes the fact that there are no morally right decisions in the practices of the big political parties of the United Nations.

As a result, human and state dignity serve to support the ideal of equality, without granting any power of enforceability. Examples of depriving human beings from their dignity are indeed ample. This is particularly evident by the fact that millions of human beings have been denied their dignity since the establishment of the Charter, simply based on their nationality, ethnicity etc. However, it is completely taboo to speak about Western criminality, big power criminality, or the grave criminality of the members of the Security Council. However, it is fully permitted to speak about criminality of non-Western states, their terrorist conducts, their terrorist groups, and their terrorist organisations.

But if one were to raise such questions about European states then out they would be condemned and ignored. The big powers of the UN and their allies do not consider themselves criminals, regardless of the fact that they are the only countries in the world with advance militaries. They are the only countries in the world that kill in the millions. They are also the only countries in the world which have created international panic, international terror, and which support the evacuation of the Palestinians from their homeland-- and yet they still consider the criminal activities of their military forces as legal and just and non-Western governments mostly criminals or conspirators.

That is why the terms 'justice' and 'integrity' have both been employed as tools of monopolisation, degradation, destruction, and humiliation. If this is not true then why does the most well-established organisation in the world not respect these terms to any degree, and ignores the existence of inequality between its members? That is why the principles of the Universal

Declaration of Human Rights are seriously harmful to the true nature of dignity, the true nature of humanity, to the foundation of justice and peace in the world. This freedom, this dignity, and this justice are considered very significant for the universal rights of man, and yet are the principles which are most often violated through monopolisation.

Although one cannot reject the high value of the Declaration, the fact is that its words, and the words of other similar instruments of justice, have no value in practice. This has been proven time and again through wars waged by the big political powers in Iraq, Syria, Afghanistan, Palestine, and Vietnam -- to name but a few. If the provisions, principles, and terms of the Universal Declaration of Human Rights had any practical value in reality, the United States, the United Kingdom, Israel, Bahrain, Egypt, and many others would not have ignored the rights of the Palestinians over the last seventy-five years. We should keep in mind that when the rights of one nation takes precedence over another in any convention, such as the Charter of the United Nations, then all rights become invalid and hobby.

In other words, the Charter of the United Nations has been violating the entire system of international law since its conception. This means also that the policy of the Charter violates the universal dignity inherent to humankind which is linked to the united essence of mankind. The fact is that the Charter does not recognise that its provisions create the absence of legal recognition for the dignity of man. The intention of human rights conventions is to prevent the tyranny of one nation over other nations, however this intention becomes moot because of the veto power granted in the UN charter to the five permanent members.

6. Security Council Imposing Justice

The theory of the big political nations in the Security Council is similar to the theory of Thrasymachus in Plato's *The Republic*. According to Thrasymachus regarding the definition of justice and injustice "An unjust is superior to a just in character and intelligence. Injustice is a source of strength. Injustice brings happiness." This definition of justice is indeed what the permanent members of the United Nations and their allies are imposing upon the traditional Palestinian sovereign state. This is what one of the most well-known philosophers of human civilisation, Socrates, rejected entirely. For him,

> Justice implies superior character and intelligence while injustice means deficiency in both respects. Therefore, just men are superior in character and intelligence and are more effective in action. Injustice implies ignorance, stupidity and badness. It cannot be superior in character and intelligence. A just man is wiser because he acknowledges the principle of limit…Unlimited self-assertion is not a source of strength for any group organized for common purpose. Unlimited desire and claims lead to conflicts…Life of just man is better and happier. There is always some specific virtue in everything, which enables it to work well. If it is deprived of that virtue, it works badly. The soul has specific functions to perform. When it performs its specific functions, it has specific excellence or virtue. If, it is deprived of its peculiar virtue, it cannot possibly do its work well. It is agreed that the virtue of the soul is justice. The soul which is more virtuous or in other words more just is also the happier soul. Therefore, a just man lives happy. A just soul, in other words a just man, lives well; an unjust cannot.

This humiliation of Palestinian rights, integrity, personality, and existence through various immoral rules and decisions of militarily powerful states means that the world is facing a situation in which injustice has become superior. Plato described this in *The Republic,* saying that "The heaviest penalty for declining to rule is to be ruled by someone inferior to yourself." Plato has proven that justice is not dependent on trade deals or on military force or on the commission of genocide, crimes against humanity, war crimes, or aggression. According to him, justice has to come from the human spirit, strength, and soul, and it must have good intentions for all. Justice is therefore a natural phenomenon of wisdom, and not an artificial justification for the occupation of the territory of other nations. It is in this way that Plato's philosophy of justice condemns the theory of the United

State, Israel, Saudi Arabia, Egypt, United Arab Emirates, and Bahrain regarding the 'century deal' which intends to destroy Palestine.

Are all these immoral actions acts of justice? Have we really understood the virtue of justice and how it should be implemented? We should realise the fact that justice is not promoted through our universities, or faculties of law, or through our politics. While justice may be discussed *ad nauseum* in our universities, when it comes to the reality of justice, one can observe that there is no justice at all in practice, and only the theatrical misunderstanding of it and its boundaries. In other words, we are content to believe that the notion of justice is what it has been provided by governments or tutors, despite this being an illusion.

Many faculties of law lecture intensively on the questions of justice, the elements of international human rights law, and most significantly, on Kant's theories of enlightenment, good habit, and evil. Are these faculties of law and politics the barriers to true justice? Or, do they support the theory of Thrasymachus? A number of faculties of laws in Europe lecture about justice, but not mentioning even a single word about the production of weapons and the trade of weapons by their own governments to the states in war. Without any hesitation, production of weapons for war is or should be recognised criminal conduct.

This theory is also true in the international arena where justice is not a question of righteousness, where justice is not a matter of principle, but is rather a means of political survival and way through which to pursue group interests. This means that justice is measured on a scale against interests and politics. For instance, membership in the European Union is not about being in a regional organisation to promote justice, but instead is about preserving international personality and political strength.

Many governments of the EU have worked to ensure that faculties of law and politics tell a certain truth about their actions, in order to preserve their political image. This policy is not a new tactic, however, and has also been employed in other countries such as China and Russia. Thus, the questions of justice, the questions of its developments, and the questions of the definition of what is right and wrong, are all monopolised questions, and do not truly produce answers about correct definitions and conducts. This monopolisation of justice and its principles is so great and powerful that agents of intelligence agencies and diplomats have become the indirect decision-makers of international human rights law and organisations.

This means that the definition of the basic principles of justice varies from country to country, and even from regime to regime. In other words, governments always have a hidden hand in universities in order to propagate their versions of disputes, theories, and interests. Even though we have learned that we cannot allow injustice to be carried out by our governments, we still allow it. This implies the fact that a more rational basis for the definition of justice or for the prevention of justice falls in the hands of our governments, regardless of the fact that the definition may be wrong and harmful. Here, we do not mean that governments are not aware of their evil decisions or actions of injustice against the Palestinians, but that they ignore the question entirely and are complicit in the commission of crimes through their inaction.

7. Dealing the Principles of Justice

The big permanent members of the United Nations have seriously insulted and violated the very basic principles of international law which are formulated in the Charter. Here, I am speaking about those principles which should not only not be violated by the permanent members of the Council, but which should also be protected under all circumstances. For instance, the United States government, which is considered to be one of the most important members of the organisation, has been one of the most serious violators of the Charter since its establishment around the world through its actions in places such as Afghanistan, Vietnam, Latin America, Japan, the Persian Gulf, Africa, and the Middle East—including in Jerusalem.

Contrary to the above criminal policy, we read in the Charter of the United Nations the most significant principles authorising peace, humanity, and social progress including better standards of life in larger freedom. The Charter clearly intends to reaffirm faith in fundamental human rights, in the dignity and worth of the individual, and to support the equal rights of men and women and of nations large and small. It also vividly states that it is the duty of member states, especially permanent members, to support justice and respect the obligations which arise from treaties and other sources of international law.

The above principles imply the fact that the reasons behind our judgments must be clear and not violate the basic principles of international law, international human rights law, international criminal law, or international criminal justice. Yet, in taking certain vital decisions, such as in the Palestinian case, we must understand that we cannot make unilateral decisions and call it the implementation of international law. An annexation announcement about Jerusalem which violated international treaties and UN resolutions, cannot and will not be considered to be a deal, but rather as a violation of international criminal justice and the principles of *erga omens*. Although we understand that Palestinians are powerless against the strong military powers, their country is still theirs, even if it is occupied by foreign armed forces.

If justice is occupation by force, if justice is the result of political trading and deals, then we are talking about the justice of the strong.[302] That is the justice of guns, the justice of the President of the United States, the justice of the Prime Minister of Israel, and the justice of barbarous decisions. Thomas Hobbes in *Leviathan* properly put forward that a system based on inequality is one of punishment, imprisonment, and torture, as in such a system, the stronger parties force the weaker to obey through force.[303] This is referred to as *bellum omnium contra omnes* or the war of all against all.

> Hereby it is manifest that during the time men live without a common Power to keep them all in awe, they are in that condition which is called War; and such a war as is of every man against every man... In such condition there is no place for Industry, because the fruit thereof is uncertain: and consequently no Culture of the Earth; no Navigation, nor use of the commodities that may be imported by Sea; no commodious

---

302 Malekian, *Trading Virginity of International Criminal Justice,* note 16.
303 Thomas Hobbes, *Leviathan* (1651).

> Building; no Instruments of moving and removing such things as require much force; no Knowledge of the face of the Earth; no account of Time; no Arts; no Letters; no Society; and which is worst of all, continual Fear, and danger of violent death; And the life of man solitary, poor, nasty, brutish, and short.

The situation of the Palestinian population and their homeland, its occupation, and the brutal influence of the United States and Israeli governments show the existing anarchy in the world. The fact is that anarchists believe that the big political parties over-exploit their monopolies on aggression, hostility, and brutality by various methods, including by unreasonably punishing protesters. They believe that a supreme society, such as the United Nations, should operate on the basis of voluntary cooperation between its members and does not need any authoritarian sanctions to function. [304]

8. The Powerful Game of Justice

In the world of super political parties and UNSC permanent members, there is no aspect of law, or conduct, or decision which could be called moral. In fact, the justice of the big powers is a justice which does not follow the rule of law, the rule of morality, the rule of humanity, the rule of mutual understanding of one another's needs, nor the rule of respect and love. The notion of justice which has been described by many philosophers and lawyers does not have room when it comes to economic interests, even at the price of killing millions of people in other countries, and destroying the oldest civilisation of Hammurabi in Iraq, for example.

For some of the American presidents, the system of law and the system of international human rights law did/do not exist, and thus telling them that

---

[304] Stephen Nicolae Pinkstaff, Structure Violence and the United Nations: How the Security Council Shifts Attitudes, Expectations and Presuppositions in the International Community About the Gulf Conflict (1990-2003), available online at http://mars.gmu.edu/jspui/bitstream/handle/1920/7489/Pinkstaff_thesis_2011.pdf;jsessionid=B5E8C9CF6E3217BDC6158AFDDC81BEE2?sequence=1.

they violated international law is futile.[305] This is also true in the case of the chiefs of US intelligence agencies, such as Gina Haspel, who was responsible for running a secret "black site" prison in Thailand where suspects were tortured with waterboarding. Haspel was also later involved in attempting to destroy the evidence of said torture. For Bush, waterboarding did not constitute international crimes of torture, because it was used by American forces and thus could not be a crime. Similar views exist about crimes committed in Afghanistan and Abu Ghraib.

The fact is that the systems of international law, international criminal law, international human rights law, international criminal justice, and international humanitarian law are indeed meaningless under the machinery of big political parties. These systems, and particularly the system of international criminal justice in The Hague, are at the disposal of the political parties for their games of cat and mouse. *The jurisdiction of the International Criminal Court was established to mostly hunt African criminals and to address conflicts between clans, tribes, and ethnic groups. It is on this account that the entire mechanism of international justice becomes a game of cat and mouse, but the mechanism is incapable of bringing the big criminals under its jurisdiction, which leads to impunity for the real criminals.*

9. Instrumentality of the Principles of Legality

The system of international criminal justice is very weak and international criminal law is much weaker than its juridical mechanism. This is because the big criminals are its architects, the regulators of conventions, the implementers and destroyers. These big criminals have forced others to accept their conditions and designated them as terrorists and prosecuted those who have suffered as a result of their crimes. The US has the ability to prevent certain countries from coming to meetings of the General Assembly

---

[305] For instance, George W. Bush.

by not granting them diplomatic visas, which is against the basic fundamental provisions of the United Nations Charter.

Here, we are speaking about those criminals who are the chief regulators of international law and international criminal justice. My arrow is pointed at those who violate laws and who kill people and expel them from their homelands. This is in fact the real definition of international democracy. The weak do not have a choice, they must either accept the situation, or face the consequences. In other words, the notion of voting in any organ of the United Nations is indeed a preposterous one. The United States and the United Kingdom have waged war against Iraq, Afghanistan, Yemen, Libya, and Palestine according to their own concepts of democracy and law. Here, the weak nations have to satisfy the big criminals, and give up their land and resources, and accept the interference in their national interests by the big criminals.[306]

Furthermore, if the weak protest, then they have to suffer from sanctions and the potential blockage of their economic activities. This means that the democracy of the Security Council which is based on the veto power, is the most decisive factor for the future of the weak groups, populations, and nations. The idiom *the road to hell is paved with good intentions* has an alternative form, *hell is full of good meanings, but heaven is full of good works*.[307] In other words, the United Nations Charter contains good provisions, but the Security Council represents injustice and protects the permanent members and their interests at a cost to others. In any event, it is the satisfaction of the strongest criminal which brings peace and happiness, not the satisfaction of the weak.

> In other words, the priorities of the United Nations do not have as much to do with membership of states and entities, nor with the questions of regulations and law, as with the categorisation of members as strong/big and weak/small. This is clear from the intention and purpose behind Chapter VII of the UN Charter, which states that the organisation is not

---

[306] Malekian, *International Criminal Law: The of Somebodiness, The Law of Nobodiness*, note 1; Farhad Malekian, *International Criminal Law of Children* (New York: Nova Sciences Publishers, 2021); Malekian, *Trading Virginity of International Criminal Justice*, note 16.

[307] *Id.*

> based on equality between members, despite its appearances. Chapter VII speaks about how the power and authorities within the organisation are controlled by whichever state has the strongest human being international legal personality at a given time. *As a result, it is true that the notion of any equality of international legal personality is only a joke under the legal framework of the United Nations, and exists only in the abstract. Otherwise, we would not have the Security Council, only the General Assembly. In other words, the entire concept of the United Nations is based on the inequality between the international legal personality of states. This is the naked truth and not an interpretation of the law.*[308]

For instance, European states committed genocide against innocent Jews, and then they sent the remaining generation to Palestine, occupied almost the entire country, and today, call it the 'deal of the century'. This has nothing to do with the Jews or Muslims, it is theory of the democracy and justice of the big permanent members of the United Nations including certain Europeans. The weak have to accept the force of gun, the power of the use of force, and the provisions of brutal unilateral sanctions. Several hundred European criminal court justice systems have witnessed the killing of millions of our brothers and sisters, seen their homes occupied by force, their children killed en masse, thousands of families burned together, and millions subjected to medical experimentation. However, the European nations were silent concerning the result of their unjust peace agreements written after the end of the First World War and their negotiations of treaties. All these movements, negotiations, gatherings, formulations, signatures, ratifications, and conventions were carried out to give a true definition to justice and to prevent the unlawful use of force. The intention was to prevent injustice, irregularity, immorality, irrationality, and the undermining of the dignity of one nation by another.

It may not be without reason that Jeremy Bentham, a utilitarianist, deemed natural law which supports human rights as "nonsense stilts." Certainly, his theory is true concerning the current situation concerning the violation of the fundamental principles of justice in Palestine by the big

[308] Malekian, *Trading Virginity of International Criminal Justice*, note 16, pp.116-117.

politically and military powerful state – the United States.[309] Thus, here with the notion of justice offered up by the big political parties is really only the justice of big criminals.[310] In 2006, the then-president of Venezuela, Hugo Chávez stated before the General Assembly in reference to the United States:

> The devil is himself home. Yesterday, the devil came here. Yesterday, the devil was here, in this very place. It still smells of sulphur, here, at this podium, where I am to speak. Yesterday, ladies and gentlemen, from this very podium, Mr. President of the United States who I call the devil, came here and spoke as though, he was the owner of the world, a psychiatrist would not be too much to analyse the president's speech yesterday. As the mouthpiece of Imperialism, he came here to give us his recipes to try to maintain the current shame of domination, exploitation, and looting of the people of the world. It would be perfect for an Alfred Hitchcock movie. In fact, it would give it the title 'The Devil's Recipe'. In other words, North American imperialism, and Chomsky says it, here with profound clarity is in a desperate push to consolidate its hegemonic system of domination. We can't allow this happen. We can't allow the installation of the world dictatorship. We can't allow to consolidate itself.[311]

A justice which is one-sided- is not justice at all but the enforcement of the brutal use of force by big political parties. The big political parties enforced such justice upon Germany after the First World War. Similar justice was enforced during the Second World War against the European Jews by Germany and other states; and is currently enforced by the United States, the United Kingdom, Israel, Saudi Arabia, United Arab Emirates, Egypt, and Bahrain upon the Palestinian population, with the silent support of European states with interests in the region for the trade of their weapons. Criminal policies here are not directed at European states but against the innocent Palestinians and the basic provisions of international human rights law, international criminal law and international criminal justice.

---

[309] W. Bush. Hugo Chávez, the President of Venezuela continued "He came here talking as if he was the owner of the world."

[310] Consult also Noam Chomsky, Hegemony or Survival: America's Quest for Global Dominance (2004).

[311] The General Assembly, 20 September 2006.

10. OPPRESSOR OF INJUSTICE IN PALESTINE

How can we say that the system of international criminal law, the body of international criminal justice, and the provisions of international human rights law (including the European Convention on Human Rights law) should be respected when it comes to British nationals, but not concerning nationals of Palestine, Iraq, Syria, etc.? By this I mean that how could the British political, economic, military, and social power be used and employed to support American power to kill and destroy, and yet all these criminal conducts do not lead to the British being held accountable in the procedures of international criminal justice? How could the Palestinian population and its properties be taken by force and be given to a population comprised of people from other nations and be called Israel, and these criminal actions and decisions not lead to any consequences or accountability of the British government before the permanent International Criminal Court?

If a British national was killed or attacked by a national of another state, it would immediately be identified as an act of terror, which implies the existence of injustice in the system of international human rights law. If the system of international criminal law is objective, if the structure of international human rights law is really pure and based on humanity, if the body of international criminal justice is impartial in the application of its provisions, norms, principles, and regulations, if the system of the United Nations is truly equal, and if the governments of the United States and the United Kingdom are fair in their politics, then why do our politics and laws only punish the victims and not criminals?

My goal here is not to find which countries are guilty or not according to international criminal justice or international human rights law, but rather to say that our decisions and our actions are subject to serious controversy and require greater impartiality. It is normally this lack of impartiality which creates serious problems for the victims and perpetuates military conflicts, thus creating an unsolvable conflict which benefits the strong at the expense of the weak. This situation is certainly dangerous for the health of international peace, security, and justice in the world. This is what the big political powers are now organising against the existence of Palestine. The situation also helps the Israeli government to take any action or pass any legislation against the native of population of Palestine. This is also formulated into the Israeli national law which was recently adopted:

1) It states that "the right to exercise national self-determination" in Israel is "unique to the Jewish people."
2) It establishes Hebrew as Israel's official language, and downgrades Arabic — a language widely spoken by Arab-Israelis — to a "special status."
3) It establishes "Jewish settlement as a national value" and mandates that the state "will labor to encourage and promote its establishment and development."[312]

The given law is indeed proof of the commission of genocide by the children of those who were the victims of genocide in Europe, because these provisions give priority to one group (Israelis) over another (Palestinians/Arabs). If genocide is wrong, if genocide was committed by Germans, if genocide constituted a holocaust, if genocide is the crimes of crimes, why are the same actions not considered genocide now? The new regulation means that the Israeli state law creates and cultivates *the law of nobodiness* and banishes *the law of somebodiness,* which is an integral principle in all documents of international human rights law. This is not only the fault of the Israeli government but of the United States and the United Kingdom governments, to name but a few supporters, whose silence constitutes complicity in the genocide of the Palestinians.

We all see and understand what is happening, and yet choose to be silent, although we realise that the system of international human rights law is being grossly violated by the relevant states. We are silent, not because we do not understand what is happening or because the offending nations have the right to carry out such acts, but because we are obsessed with our own

---

312 https://www.vox.com/world/2018/7/31/17623978/israel-jewish-nation-state-law-bill-explained-apartheid-netanyahu-democracy.

economic interests, and thus give them priority over all other matters, including over international human rights law.[313] Martin Luther King aptly stated “there comes a time when one must take a position that is neither safe, nor politic, nor popular, but he must take it because his conscience tells him it is right.” However, this conscience has yet to take form in Europe. Malcolm X summarised this situation by asserting that “Time is on the side of the oppressed today, it’s against the oppressor. Truth is on the side of the oppressed today, it’s against the oppressor. You don’t need anything else.”

---

313 Consult Malekian, *International Criminal Law: the Law of Somebodiness, the Law of Nobodiness*, note 1.

Chapter 9

CONCLUSION

The key and simple question at the end of this short book is why did I not write about the actions of the Netherlands, Germany, France, Russia, Sweden, Denmark, Norway, Pakistan, Afghanistan, India, China, Iraq, or any state in Latin America, but rather decided to focus on the declaration of the United States government? The answer is very clear. None of the states listed above or any other states have issued such an immature declaration, which was in blatant violation of the systems of international criminal law and human rights law, and of the natural rights of man.

There is no difference between Jews, Muslims, Christians, Buddhists, Baha'i, and the people of any other religion in the world. Everyone is equal regarding their heritage and entry into the heaven of God, and in terms of justice and love. The disappearance of love in theory would surely kill the entire goodness of God's philosophy. *Ergo*, if the love of God means killing, let us arrest the God of all Gods and bring him before the ICC for the crimes he has committed with full *mens rea* in the name of Gods. If this does not work, then we – in the name of justice, in the name of peace, and on behalf of the United Nations Security Council – should announce that God is condemned to die by crucifixion for all the atrocities and brutalities committed in his name with the intent of carrying out his cruel theory.

The murder of God would certainly bring peace, and take away the need for the ICC and, ultimately, vanquish our cruel Declaration to commit genocide against the Palestinians. Then God himself would have committed genocide against all members of the group, no one would live, and the United States and the government of Israel would have reached the greatest extent of their inhumanity, justice, and peace. Is this the heaven promised to us by Jesus and Mohammed, achieved through the Security Council and the instruments of human rights law?

Here, I have certainly wrestled with my faith, with my heart, with the rights of indigenous people, with the rights of Palestinians, and with the rights of our Gods. I am certain that if there is one God, He is the same for all people, and does not approve of violations of the system of international criminal law and justice. This is independent of the name and provisions of the judiciary, whether Islamic or non-Islamic, whether European or non-European. No doubt, if God exists, it will not help us to kiss the Holy Quran at international conferences and keep it in our pockets. The same applies to Judaism. The swaying of believers at the Wailing Wall also brings no peace, if transparency between religions is at war with God.

The notion of heaven is coupled with an entrance to enlightenment through a garden of love, justice, generosity, happiness, awareness, wisdom, of the attainment, of non-punishment, of the existence of solely one decree, and the proportionality between means and end. In the heaven of divine law, there no longer exists a propensity for evil deeds in the nature of man. The soul is free from positive law. Thus, if we can correctly imagine the meaning of heaven, we can also understand the connotation of justice with love. The term "heaven" is the complete concept of humanity with justice, however such a heaven may not exist in reality.[314]

Al-Quds/Jerusalem cannot be the object of force and occupation by the state of Israel.[315] The fact is that *Al-Quds/Jerusalem* is the capital of love, as long as the unity between different religions is preserved. If we violate the rights of a nation through violence and aggressive military power, and march

---

[314] Malekian, *The Heaven of Justice with Love*, note 260, p.5.

[315] https://www.aljazeera.com/news/2018/09/paraguay-returns-embassy-israel-tel-aviv-180905171257155.html.

forward with our Declaration, love cannot remain. Such a city can no longer function with its peaceful religious intentions. Nor can it be the capital of a state due to the inequality and injustice there. It would, however, become the capital of devils, and the base for the evil military power. The city would become the forum through which aggressive wars were waged and it would be defended through acts of genocide.

In addition, there is no doubt that the sovereign integrity or international legal personality of *Al-Quds/Jerusalem* is one of the integral subjects of the international law of *jus cogens*. The International Court of Justice in The Hague has also confirmed this. One main characteristic of a *jus cogens* norm is that it restricts the freedom of states to formulate certain international treaties, conventions, pacts, or unilateral statements whose subjects are in conflict with the norms of *jus cogens,* or with the peremptory norms of international law. Such agreements have no binding or legal force within the jurisdiction of international courts, and indicate the criminal responsibility of the perpetrators, thus if even only one Palestinian is killed, such an act can be seen as a sign of the genocide of the entire population.

One cannot deny the fact that the concept of international legal personality has a major function in the international relations of states. This body of law indicates the legal and political power of a state and the bounds of its national and international responsibility. This also means that states are, in practice, responsible for not violating the international personality of any other state. Any violation of the international legal personality of another state may amount to serious restitutions on the part of the offending state. The reason for this is that the concept of ILP not only confers rights to states, but also duties towards each other within the international political community as a whole.

In fact, the theories of prosecution and restitution are two of the basic principles of the normative characters of *jus cogens* and *obligatio erga omnes*. The Inter-American Court of Human Rights in the *La Cantuta, Fujimori* case clarified that "access to justice constitutes a peremptory norm of International Law and, as such, it gives rise to the States' *erga omnes* obligation to adopt all such measures as are necessary to prevent such violations from going unpunished."[316] Undoubtedly, this judgment is also useful in understanding the grave violations of the ILP of the Palestinian population by the big powerful nations. Moreover, the concept of ILP implies the very substance of the jurisdictional integrity of a state. Therefore, the entire system of international law demonstrates its legal ability and credibility in the genuine framework of statehood. In other words, both of the terms, "ILP" and "statehood," are integral parts of the same legal discipline.

Considering all the arguments addressed throughout, this book has driven home the fact that the ILP of Palestine is an unavoidable phenomenon of the history of human civilisation in the Middle East, which needs to be understood by all states. In addition, UN members, and in particular permanent members, have a political and legal responsibility to follow the majority view concerning any case brought before the General Assembly. With this, we do not necessarily mean that they should only protect Palestine-- instead, we mean that the United Nations' core policy should orient itself towards the will of its democratic vote. This means that if the majority votes for the interests of Israel and the continuation of the occupation of Palestine, this has to be respected by all members, including the state of Palestine itself, but also *vice versa*. I wonder very much, however, whether the majority of United Nations members are willing to violate the system of international morality, legality, and the framework of peremptory norms of international law. It is a reality that the international legal and political community has to be wise if does not wish to violate the statehood of Palestine. The questions are for how long, and how many nations are intending to kill another nation over their own inevitable right to independence?[317]

> A clear example of prolonged antagonism is the useless conflict between the two neighbours in the Middle East, namely Israel and

---

[316] *IACHR, Case La Cantuta v. Peru, judgment of 29 November 2006, Ser. C.* No.160.

[317] Marco Longobardo Some Developments in the Prosecution of International Crimes Committed in Palestine: Any Real News? 35 *Polish Year Book of International Law* (2015), doi: 10.7420/pyoil2015d, pp. 109–138.

Palestine. The Israeli-Palestinian crisis can be solved solely by a proper understanding of the term “strength of love” and not just of “law”. Grotius clearly indicates, “The debt of love and forbearance to our enemies is an obligation, which it is honourable to discharge.” …

The military personnel of both sides and the members of the United Nations have to learn side-by-side from the lessons of international humanitarian law of armed conflict and international human rights law that to love one another is the first cornerstone of resorting to law as well as justice. Thereby, they should avoid violence and causing unnecessary human suffering. In fact, the canon of armed use of force must be replaced with the power of love, the power of understanding of the nature of human beings, and the power of brotherhood and unity. We have to take into recognition the obvious similarities between both systems of law.

If a superior order contains a command not to kill but to love, this upholds the pure philosophy of law for the security of humanity and provides the basis for peace. It also brings the governments of both sides face-to-face in a moral or legal obligation that the killing has to be prevented, that problems have to be solved, and that both nations are of the same human race. Although we know that a superior has a responsibility to obey orders and that our obedience to the law is a necessary condition of a legal system, one should not put aside the fact that any superior order to a subordinate to kill or destroy simultaneously constitutes in itself a use of force. This means violating the entire body of international human rights law.

If war is lawful, then peace is unlawful; if justice means killing, then all killing is just; if a law that does not contain the substance of love for human beings is judged to be acceptable, then let us announce that all laws in different civil societies are identical to human rights laws. Similarly, if the pure philosophy of Islamic and public international law or European Union law do not put any emphasis on the function of love in law, i.e. authentic justice for the protection of human dignity, let us declare that these laws are laws but without the first basic sense of humanity. Consequently, the word ‘love’ here means a mutual understanding of the fundamental rights of both sides, reciprocity denoting a relationship between both nations involving the historical exchange of favours, obligations, and allowing for similar requirements of daily life.

The concept of love should naturally require of both nations—Israel and Palestine—love for justice, love for human beings, and love of peace. These are surely not only the true cornerstones of Jewish norms but also the foundations of Islamic international law, European Union Law, and also the real meaning of public international law.

The point of justice is humanity and not development of religious attitude. This norm of love is based on the understanding that human rights norms are to be applied to situations of both nations with the power of love for justice, trust in justice, and in the nature of all Palestinian and Jewish women/men.[318]

[318] Malekian, *Judgments of Love in Criminal Justice*, note 17, pp.264-266.

Appendices

Resolution 181 (II). Future Government of Palestine

A. The General Assembly,

Having met in special session at the request of the mandatory Power to constitute and instruct a special committee to prepare for the consideration of the question of the future government of Palestine at the second regular session;

Having constituted a Special Committee and instructed it to investigate all questions and issues relevant to the problem of Palestine, and to prepare proposals for the solution of the problem, and *Having received and examined* the report of the Special Committee (document A/364) [1/] including a number of unanimous recommendations and a plan of partition with economic union approved by the majority of the Special Committee,

Considers that the present situation in Palestine is one which is likely to impair the general welfare and friendly relations among nations;

Takes note of the declaration by the mandatory Power that it plans to complete its evacuation of Palestine by 1 August 1948;

Recommends to the United Kingdom, as the mandatory Power for Palestine, and to all other Members of the United Nations the adoption and implementation, with regard to the future government of Palestine, of the Plan of Partition with Economic Union set out below;

Requests that

(a) The Security Council take the necessary measures as provided for in the plan for its implementation;

(b) The Security Council consider, if circumstances during the transitional period require such consideration, whether the situation in Palestine constitutes a threat to the peace. If it decides that such a threat exists, and in order to maintain international peace and security, the Security Council should supplement the authorization of the General Assembly by taking measures, under Articles 39 and 41 of the Charter, to empower the United Nations Commission, as provided in this resolution, to exercise in Palestine the functions which are assigned to it by this resolution;

(c) The Security Council determine as a threat to the peace, breach of the peace or act of aggression, in accordance with Article 39 of the Charter, any attempt to alter by force the settlement envisaged by this resolution;

(d) The Trusteeship Council be informed of the responsibilities envisaged for it in this plan;

Calls upon the inhabitants of Palestine to take such steps as may be necessary on their part to put this plan into effect;

Appeals to all Governments and all peoples to refrain from taking action which might hamper or delay the carrying out of these recommendations, and

Authorizes the Secretary-General to reimburse travel and subsistence expenses of the members of the Commission referred to in Part I, Section B, paragraph 1 below, on such basis and in such form as he may determine most appropriate in the circumstances, and to provide the Commission with the necessary staff to assist in carrying out the functions assigned to the Commission by the General Assembly. *The General Assembly*

Authorizes the Secretary-General to draw from the Working Capital Fund a sum not to exceed $2,000,000 for the purposes set forth in the last paragraph of the resolution on the future government of Palestine.

Hundred and twenty-eighth plenary meeting

29 November 1947

[At its hundred and twenty-eighth plenary meeting on 29 November 1947 the General Assembly, in accordance with the terms of the above resolution [181 A], elected the following members of the United Nations Commission on Palestine: Bolivia, Czechoslovakia, Denmark, Panama and Philippines.]

PLAN OF PARTITION WITH ECONOMIC UNION

Part I: Future Constitution and Government of Palestine

A. Termination of Mandate, Partition and Independence

1. The Mandate for Palestine shall terminate as soon as possible but in any case not later than 1 August 1948.

2. The armed forces of the mandatory Power shall be progressively withdrawn from Palestine, the withdrawal to be completed as soon as possible but in any case not later than 1 August 1948.

The mandatory Power shall advise the Commission, as far in advance as possible, of its intention to terminate the Mandate and to evacuate each area. The mandatory Power shall use its best endeavours to ensure than an area situated in the territory of the Jewish State, including a seaport and hinterland adequate to provide facilities for a substantial immigration, shall be evacuated at the earliest possible date and in any event not later than 1 February 1948.

3. Independent Arab and Jewish States and the Special International Regime for the City of Jerusalem, set forth in part III of this plan, shall come into existence in Palestine two months after the evacuation of the armed forces of the mandatory Power has been completed but in any case not later than 1 October 1948. The boundaries of the Arab State, the Jewish State, and the City of Jerusalem shall be as described in parts II and III below.

4. The period between the adoption by the General Assembly of its recommendation on the question of Palestine and the establishment of the independence of the Arab and Jewish States shall be a transitional period.

B. Steps Preparatory to Independence

1. A Commission shall be set up consisting of one representative of each of five Member States. The Members represented on the Commission shall be elected by the General Assembly on as broad a basis, geographically and otherwise, as possible.

2. The administration of Palestine shall, as the mandatory Power withdraws its armed forces, be progressively turned over to the Commission; which shall act in conformity with the recommendations of the General Assembly, under the guidance of the Security Council. The mandatory Power shall to the fullest possible extent co-ordinate its plans for withdrawal with the plans of the Commission to take over and administer areas which have been evacuated. In the discharge of this administrative responsibility the Commission shall have authority to issue necessary regulations and take other measures as required. The mandatory Power shall not take any action to prevent, obstruct or delay the implementation by the Commission of the measures recommended by the General Assembly.

3. On its arrival in Palestine the Commission shall proceed to carry out measures for the establishment of the frontiers of the Arab and Jewish States and the City of Jerusalem in accordance with the general lines of the recommendations of the General Assembly on the partition of Palestine. Nevertheless, the boundaries as described in part II of this plan are to be modified in such a way that village areas as a rule will not be divided by state boundaries unless pressing reasons make that necessary.

4. The Commission, after consultation with the democratic parties and other public organizations of The Arab and Jewish States, shall select and establish in each State as rapidly as possible a Provisional Council of Government. The activities of both the Arab and Jewish Provisional Councils of Government shall be carried out under the general direction of the Commission. If by 1 April 1948 a Provisional Council of Government cannot be selected for either of the States, or, if selected, cannot carry out its

functions, the Commission shall communicate that fact to the Security Council for such action with respect to that State as the Security Council may deem proper, and to the Secretary-General for communication to the Members of the United Nations.

5. Subject to the provisions of these recommendations, during the transitional period the Provisional Councils of Government, acting under the Commission, shall have full authority in the areas under their control, including authority over matters of immigration and land regulation.

6. The Provisional Council of Government of each State acting under the Commission, shall progressively receive from the Commission full responsibility for the administration of that State in the period between the termination of the Mandate and the establishment of the State's independence.

7. The Commission shall instruct the Provisional Councils of Government of both the Arab and Jewish States, after their formation, to proceed to the establishment of administrative organs of government, central and local.

8. The Provisional Council of Government of each State shall, within the shortest time possible, recruit an armed militia from the residents of that State, sufficient in number to maintain internal order and to prevent frontier clashes. This armed militia in each State shall, for operational purposes, be under the command of Jewish or Arab officers resident in that State, but general political and military control, including the choice of the militia's High Command, shall be exercised by the Commission.

9. The Provisional Council of Government of each State shall, not later than two months after the withdrawal of the armed forces of the mandatory Power, hold elections to the Constituent Assembly which shall be conducted on democratic lines. The election regulations in each State shall be drawn up by the Provisional Council of Government and approved by the Commission. Qualified voters for each State for this election shall be persons over eighteen years of age who are: (a) Palestinian citizens residing in that State and (b) Arabs and Jews residing in the State, although not Palestinian citizens, who, before voting, have signed a notice of intention to become citizens of such State. Arabs and Jews residing in the City of

Jerusalem who have signed a notice of intention to become citizens, the Arabs of the Arab State and the Jews of the Jewish State, shall be entitled to vote in the Arab and Jewish States respectively. Women may vote and be elected to the Constituent Assemblies. During the transitional period no Jew shall be permitted to establish residence in the area of the proposed Arab State, and no Arab shall be permitted to establish residence in the area of the proposed Jewish State, except by special leave of the Commission.

10. The Constituent Assembly of each State shall draft a democratic constitution for its State and choose a provisional government to succeed the Provisional Council of Government appointed by the Commission. The constitutions of the States shall embody chapters 1 and 2 of the Declaration provided for in section C below and include inter alia provisions for:

(a) Establishing in each State a legislative body elected by universal suffrage and by secret ballot on the basis of proportional representation, and an executive body responsible to the legislature;

(b) Settling all international disputes in which the State may be involved by peaceful means in such a manner that international peace and security, and justice, are not endangered;

(c) Accepting the obligation of the State to refrain in its international relations from the threat or use of force against the territorial integrity of political independence of any State, or in any other manner inconsistent with the purposes of the United Nations;

(d) Guaranteeing to all persons equal and non-discriminatory rights in civil, political, economic and religious matters and the enjoyment of human rights and fundamental freedoms, including freedom of religion, language, speech and publication, education, assembly and association;

(e) Preserving freedom of transit and visit for all residents and citizens of the other State in Palestine and the City of Jerusalem, subject to considerations of national security, provided that each State shall control residence within its borders.

11. The Commission shall appoint a preparatory economic commission of three members to make whatever arrangements are possible for economic co-operation, with a view to establishing, as soon as practicable, the Economic Union and the Joint Economic Board, as provided in section D below.

12. During the period between the adoption of the recommendations on the question of Palestine by the General Assembly and the termination of the Mandate, the mandatory Power in Palestine shall maintain full responsibility for administration in areas from which it has not withdrawn its armed forces. The Commission shall assist the mandatory Power in the carrying out of these functions. Similarly the mandatory Power shall co-operate with the Commission in the execution of its functions.

13. With a view to ensuring that there shall be continuity in the functioning of administrative services and that, on the withdrawal of the armed forces of the mandatory Power, the whole administration shall be in the charge of the Provisional Councils and the Joint Economic Board, respectively, acting under the Commission, there shall be a progressive transfer, from the mandatory Power to the Commission, of responsibility for all the functions of government, including that of maintaining law and order in the areas from which the forces of the mandatory Power have been withdrawn.

14. The Commission shall be guided in its activities by the recommendations of the General Assembly and by such instructions as the Security Council may consider necessary to issue. The measures taken by the Commission, within the recommendations of the General Assembly, shall become immediately effective unless the Commission has previously received contrary instructions from the Security Council. The Commission shall render periodic monthly progress reports, or more frequently if desirable, to the Security Council.

15. The Commission shall make its final report to the next regular session of the General Assembly and to the Security Council simultaneously.

C. Declaration

A declaration shall be made to the United Nations by the provisional government of each proposed State before independence. It shall contain inter alia the following clauses:

General Provision

The stipulations contained in the declaration are recognized as fundamental laws of the State and no law, regulation or official action shall conflict or interfere with these stipulations, nor shall any law, regulation or official action prevail over them.

Chapter 1

Holy Places, Religious Buildings and Sites

1. Existing rights in respect of Holy Places and religious buildings or sites shall not be denied or impaired.

2. In so far as Holy Places are concerned, the liberty of access, visit and transit shall be guaranteed, in conformity with existing rights, to all residents and citizens of the other State and of the City of Jerusalem, as well as to aliens, without distinction as to nationality, subject to requirements of national security, public order and decorum. Similarly, freedom of worship shall be guaranteed in conformity with existing rights, subject to the maintenance of public order and decorum.

3. Holy Places and religious buildings or sites shall be preserved. No act shall be permitted which may in any way impair their sacred character. If at any time it appears to the Government that any particular Holy Place, religious building or site is in need of urgent repair, the Government may call upon the community or communities concerned to carry out such repair. The Government may carry it out itself at the expense of the community or communities concerned if no action is taken within a reasonable time.

4. No taxation shall be levied in respect of any Holy Place, religious building or site which was exempt from taxation on the date of the creation of the State. No change in the incidence of such taxation shall be made which would either discriminate between the owners or occupiers of Holy Places, religious buildings or sites, or would place such owners or occupiers in a position less favourable in relation to the general incidence of taxation than existed at the time of the adoption of the Assembly's recommendations.

5. The Governor of the City of Jerusalem shall have the right to determine whether the provisions of the Constitution of the State in relation to Holy Places, religious buildings and sites within the borders of the State and the religious rights appertaining thereto, are being properly applied and respected, and to make decisions on the basis of existing rights in cases of disputes which may arise between the different religious communities or the rites of a religious community with respect to such places, buildings and sites. He shall receive full co-operation and such privileges and immunities as are necessary for the exercise of his functions in the State.

Chapter 2

Religious and Minority Rights

1. Freedom of conscience and the free exercise of all forms of worship, subject only to the maintenance of public order and morals, shall be ensured to all.

2. No discrimination of any kind shall be made between the inhabitants on the ground of race, religion, language or sex.

3. All persons within the jurisdiction of the State shall be entitled to equal protection of the laws.

4. The family law and personal status of the various minorities and their religious interests, including endowments, shall be respected.

5. Except as may be required for the maintenance of public order and good government, no measure shall be taken to obstruct or interfere with the enterprise of religious or charitable bodies of all faiths or to discriminate against any representative or member of these bodies on the ground of his religion or nationality.

6. The State shall ensure adequate primary and secondary education for the Arab and Jewish minority, respectively, in its own language and its cultural traditions. The right of each community to maintain its own schools for the education of its own members in its own language, while conforming to such educational requirements of a general nature as the State may impose, shall not be denied or impaired. Foreign educational establishments shall continue their activity on the basis of their existing rights.

7. No restriction shall be imposed on the free use by any citizen of the State of any language in private intercourse, in commerce, in religion, in the Press or in publications of any kind, or at public meetings.

8. No expropriation of land owned by an Arab in the Jewish State (by a Jew in the Arab State)[4/] shall be allowed except for public purposes. In all cases of expropriation full compensation as fixed by the Supreme Court shall be paid previous to dispossession.

Chapter 3

Citizenship, International Conventions and Financial Obligations

1. Citizenship. Palestinian citizens residing in Palestine outside the City of Jerusalem, as well as Arabs and Jews who, not holding Palestinian citizenship, reside in Palestine outside the City of Jerusalem shall, upon the recognition of independence, become citizens of the State in which they are resident and enjoy full civil and political rights. Persons over the age of eighteen years may opt, within one year from the date of recognition of independence of the State in which they reside, for citizenship of the other State, providing that no Arab residing in the area of the proposed Arab State shall have the right to opt for citizenship in the proposed Jewish State and no Jew residing in the proposed Jewish State shall have the right to opt for citizenship in the proposed Arab State. The exercise of this right of option will be taken to include the wives and children under eighteen years of age of persons so opting. Arabs residing in the area of the proposed Jewish State and Jews residing in the area of the proposed Arab State who have signed a notice of intention to opt for citizenship of the other State shall be eligible

to vote in the elections to the Constituent Assembly of that State, but not in the elections to the Constituent Assembly of the State in which they reside.

2. International conventions. (a) The State shall be bound by all the international agreements and conventions, both general and special, to which Palestine has become a party. Subject to any right of denunciation provided for therein, such agreements and conventions shall be respected by the State throughout the period for which they were concluded. (b) Any dispute about the applicability and continued validity of international conventions or treaties signed or adhered to by the mandatory Power on behalf of Palestine shall be referred to the International Court of Justice in accordance with the provisions of the Statute of the Court.

3. Financial obligations.

(a) The State shall respect and fulfil all financial obligations of whatever nature assumed on behalf of Palestine by the mandatory Power during the exercise of the Mandate and recognized by the State. This provision includes the right of public servants to pensions, compensation or gratuities.

(b) These obligations shall be fulfilled through participation in the Joint economic Board in respect of those obligations applicable to Palestine as a whole, and individually in respect of those applicable to, and fairly apportionable between, the States.

(c) A Court of Claims, affiliated with the Joint Economic Board, and composed of one member appointed by the United Nations, one representative of the United Kingdom and one representative of the State concerned, should be established. Any dispute between the United Kingdom and the State respecting claims not recognized by the latter should be referred to that Court.

(d) Commercial concessions granted in respect of any part of Palestine prior to the adoption of the resolution by the General Assembly shall continue to be valid according to their terms, unless modified by agreement between the concession-holder and the State.

Chapter 4

Miscellaneous Provisions

1. The provisions of chapters 1 and 2 of the declaration shall be under the guarantee of the United Nations, and no modifications shall be made in them without the assent of the General Assembly of the United nations. Any Member of the United Nations shall have the right to bring to the attention of the General Assembly any infraction or danger of infraction of any of these stipulations, and the General Assembly may thereupon make such recommendations as it may deem proper in the circumstances.
2. Any dispute relating to the application or the interpretation of this declaration shall be referred, at the request of either party, to the International Court of Justice, unless the parties agree to another mode of settlement.

D. Economic Union and Transit

1. The Provisional Council of Government of each State shall enter into an undertaking with respect to economic union and transit. This undertaking shall be drafted by the commission provided for in section B, paragraph 1, utilizing to the greatest possible extent the advice and co-operation of representative organizations and bodies from each of the proposed States. It shall contain provisions to establish the Economic Union of Palestine and provide for other matters of common interest. If by 1 April 1948 the Provisional Councils of Government have not entered into the undertaking, the undertaking shall be put into force by the Commission.

The Economic Union of Palestine

2. The objectives of the Economic Union of Palestine shall be:

(a) A customs union;

(b) A joint currency system providing for a single foreign exchange rate;

(c) Operation in the common interest on a non-discriminatory basis of railways; inter-State highways; postal, telephone and telegraphic services, and port and airports involved in international trade and commerce;

(d) Joint economic development, especially in respect of irrigation, land reclamation and soil conservation;

(e) Access for both States and for the City of Jerusalem on a non-discriminatory basis to water and power facilities.

3. There shall be established a Joint Economic Board, which shall consist of three representatives of each of the two States and three foreign members appointed by the Economic and Social Council of the United Nations. The foreign members shall be appointed in the first instance for a term of three years; they shall serve as individuals and not as representatives of States.

4. The functions of the Joint Economic Board shall be to implement either directly or by delegation the measures necessary to realize the objectives of the Economic Union. It shall have all powers of organization and administration necessary to fulfil its functions.

5. The States shall bind themselves to put into effect the decisions of the Joint Economic Board. The Board's decisions shall be taken by a majority vote.

6. In the event of failure of a State to take the necessary action the Board may, by a vote of six members, decide to withhold an appropriate portion of that part of the customs revenue to which the State in question is entitled under the Economic Union. Should the State persist in its failure to co-operate, the Board may decide by a simple majority vote upon such further sanctions, including disposition of funds which it has withheld, as it may deem appropriate.

7. In relation to economic development, the functions of the Board shall be the planning, investigation and encouragement of joint development projects, but it shall not undertake such projects except with the assent of both States and the City of Jerusalem, in the event that Jerusalem is directly involved in the development project.

8. In regard to the joint currency system the currencies circulating in the two States and the City of Jerusalem shall be issued under the authority of

the Joint Economic Board, which shall be the sole issuing authority and which shall determine the reserves to be held against such currencies.

9. So far as is consistent with paragraph 2 (b) above, each State may operate its own central bank, control its own fiscal and credit policy, its foreign exchange receipts and expenditures, the grant of import licenses, and may conduct international financial operations on its own faith and credit. During the first two years after the termination of the Mandate, the Joint Economic Board shall have the authority to take such measures as may be necessary to ensure that--to the extent that the total foreign exchange revenues of the two States from the export of goods and services permit, and provided that each State takes appropriate measures to conserve its own foreign exchange resources--each State shall have available, in any twelve months' period, foreign exchange sufficient to assure the supply of quantities of imported goods and services for consumption in its territory equivalent to the quantities of such goods and services consumed in that territory in the twelve months' period ending 31 December 1947.

10. All economic authority not specifically vested in the Joint Economic Board is reserved to each State.

11. There shall be a common customs tariff with complete freedom of trade between the States, and between the States and the City of Jerusalem.

12. The tariff schedules shall be drawn up by a Tariff Commission, consisting of representatives of each of the States in equal numbers, and shall be submitted to the Joint Economic Board for approval by a majority vote. In case of disagreement in the Tariff Commission, the Joint Economic Board shall arbitrate the points of difference. In the event that the Tariff Commission fails to draw up any schedule by a date to be fixed, the Joint Economic Board shall determine the tariff schedule.

13. The following items shall be a first charge on the customs and other common revenue of the Joint Economic Board:

(a) The expenses of the customs service and of the operation of the joint services;

(b) The administrative expenses of the Joint Economic Board;

(c) The financial obligations of the Administration of Palestine consisting of:

(i) The service of the outstanding public debt;

(ii) The cost of superannuation benefits, now being paid or falling due in the future, in accordance with the rules and to the extent established by paragraph 3 of chapter 3 above.

14. After these obligations have been met in full, the surplus revenue from the customs and other common services shall be divided in the following manner: not less than 5 per cent and not more than 10 per cent to the City of Jerusalem; the residue shall be allocated to each State by the Joint Economic Board equitably, with the objective of maintaining a sufficient and suitable level of government and social services in each State, except that the share of either State shall not exceed the amount of that State's contribution to the revenues of the Economic Union by more than approximately four million pounds in any year. The amount granted may be adjusted by the Board according to the price level in relation to the prices prevailing at the time of the establishment of the Union. After five years, the principles of the distribution of the joint revenues may be revised by the Joint Economic Board on a basis of equity.

15. All international conventions and treaties affecting customs tariff rates, and those communications services under the jurisdiction of the Joint Economic Board, shall be entered into by both States. In these matters, the two States shall be bound to act in accordance with the majority vote of the Joint Economic Board.

16. The Joint Economic Board shall endeavour to secure for Palestine's export fair and equal access to world markets.

17. All enterprises operated by the Joint Economic Board shall pay fair wages on a uniform basis.

Freedom of Transit and Visit

18. The undertaking shall contain provisions preserving freedom of transit and visit for all residents or citizens of both States and of the City of Jerusalem, subject to security considerations; provided that each state and the City shall control residence within its borders.

Termination, Modification and Interpretation of the Undertaking

19. The undertaking and any treaty issuing therefrom shall remain in force for a period of ten years. It shall continue in force until notice of termination, to take effect two years thereafter, is given by either of the parties.

20. During the initial ten-year period, the undertaking and any treaty issuing therefrom may not be modified except by consent of both parties and with the approval of the General Assembly.

21. Any dispute relating to the application or the interpretation of the undertaking and any treaty issuing therefrom shall be referred, at the request of either party, to the international Court of Justice, unless the parties agree to another mode of settlement.

E. Assets

1. The movable assets of the Administration of Palestine shall be allocated to the Arab and Jewish States and the City of Jerusalem on an equitable basis. Allocations should be made by the United Nations Commission referred to in section B, paragraph 1, above. Immovable assets shall become the property of the government of the territory in which they are situated.

2. During the period between the appointment of the United Nations Commission and the termination of the Mandate, the mandatory Power shall, except in respect of ordinary operations, consult with the Commission on any measure which it may contemplate involving the liquidation, disposal or encumbering of the assets of the Palestine Government, such as the accumulated treasury surplus, the proceeds of Government bond issues, State lands or any other asset.

F. Admission to Membership in the United Nations

When the independence of either the Arab or the Jewish State as envisaged in this plan has become effective and the declaration and undertaking, as envisaged in this plan, have been signed by either of them, sympathetic consideration should be given to its application for admission to membership in the United Nations in accordance with Article 4 of the Charter of the United Nations.

Part II. Boundaries

A. The Arab State

The area of the Arab State in Western Galilee is bounded on the west by the Mediterranean and on the north by the frontier of the Lebanon from Ras en Naqura to a point north of Saliha. From there the boundary proceeds southwards, leaving the built-up area of Saliha in the Arab State, to join the southernmost point of this village. Thence it follows the western boundary line of the villages of `Alma, Rihaniya and Teitaba, thence following the northern boundary line of Meirun village to join the Acre-Safad sub-district boundary line. It follows this line to a point west of Es Sammu'i village and joins it again at the northernmost point of Farradiya. Thence it follows the sub-district boundary line to the Acre-Safad main road. From here it follows the western boundary of Kafr I'nan village until it reaches the Tiberias-Acre sub-district boundary line, passing to the west of the junction of the Acre-Safad and Lubiya-Kafr I'nan roads. From south-west corner of Kafr I'nan village the boundary line follows the western boundary of the Tiberias sub-district to a point close to the boundary line between the villages of Maghar and Eilabun, thence bulging out to the west to include as much of the eastern part of the plain of Battuf as is necessary for the reservoir proposed by the Jewish Agency for the irrigation of lands to the south and east.

The boundary rejoins the Tiberias sub-district boundary at a point on the Nazareth-Tiberias road south-east of the built-up area of Tur'an; thence it runs southwards, at first following the sub-district boundary and then passing between the Kadoorie Agricultural School and Mount Tabor, to a point due south at the base of Mount Tabor. From here it runs due west, parallel to the horizontal grid line 230, to the north-east corner of the village lands of Tel Adashim. It then runs to the north-west corner of these lands, whence it turns south and west so as to include in the Arab State the sources of the Nazareth water supply in Yafa village. On reaching Ginneiger it follows the eastern, northern and western boundaries of the lands of this village to their south-west corner, whence it proceeds in a straight line to a point on the Haifa-Afula railway on the boundary between the villages of Sarid and El Mujeidil. This is the point of intersection.

The south-western boundary of the area of the Arab State in Galilee takes a line from this point, passing northwards along the eastern boundaries of Sarid and Gevat to the north-eastern corner of Nahalal, proceeding thence across the land of Kefar ha Horesh to a central point on the southern boundary of the village of `Ilut, thence westwards along that village boundary to the eastern boundary of Beit Lahm, thence northwards and north-eastwards along its western boundary to the north-eastern corner of Waldheim and thence north-westwards across the village lands of Shafa 'Amr to the south-eastern corner of Ramat Yohanan'. From here it runs due north-north-east to a point on the Shafa 'Amr-Haifa road, west of its junction with the road to I'Billin. From there it proceeds north-east to a point on the southern boundary of I'Billin situated to the west of the I'Billin-Birwa road. Thence along that boundary to its westernmost point, whence it turns to the north, follows across the village land of Tamra to the north-westernmost corner and along the western boundary of Julis until it reaches the Acre-Safad road. It then runs westwards along the southern side of the Safad-Acre road to the Galilee-Haifa District boundary, from which point it follows that boundary to the sea.

The boundary of the hill country of Samaria and Judea starts on the Jordan River at the Wadi Malih south-east of Beisan and runs due west to meet the Beisan-Jericho road and then follows the western side of that road in a north-westerly direction to the junction of the boundaries of the sub-districts of Beisan, Nablus, and Jenin. From that point it follows the Nablus-Jenin sub-district boundary westwards for a distance of about three kilometres and then turns north-westwards, passing to the east of the built-up areas of the villages of Jalbun and Faqqu'a, to the boundary of the sub-districts of Jenin and Beisan at a point north-east of Nuris. Thence it proceeds first north-westwards to a point due north of the built-up area of Zir'in and then westwards to the Afula-Jenin railway, thence north-westwards along the district boundary line to the point of intersection on the

Hejaz railway. From here the boundary runs south-westwards, including the built-up area and some of the land of the village of Kh.Lid in the Arab State to cross the Haifa-Jenin road at a point on the district boundary between Haifa and Samaria west of El Mansi. It follows this boundary to the southernmost point of the village of El Buteimat. From here it follows the northern and eastern boundaries of the village of Ar'ara, rejoining the Haifa-Samaria district boundary at Wadi'Ara, and thence proceeding south-south-westwards in an approximately straight line joining up with the western boundary of Qaqun to a point east of the railway line on the eastern boundary of Qaqun village. From here it runs along the railway line some distance to the east of it to a point just east of the Tulkarm railway station. Thence the boundary follows a line half-way between the railway and the Tulkarm-Qalqiliya-Jaljuliya and Ras el Ein road to a point just east of Ras el Ein station, whence it proceeds along the railway some distance to the east of it to the point on the railway line south of the junction of the Haifa-Lydda and Beit Nabala lines, whence it proceeds along the southern border of Lydda airport to its south-west corner, thence in a south-westerly direction to a point just west of the built-up area of Sarafand el'Amar, whence it turns south, passing just to the west of the built-up area of Abu el Fadil to the north-east corner of the lands of Beer Ya'Aqov. (The boundary line should be so demarcated as to allow direct access from the Arab State to the airport.) Thence the boundary line follows the western and southern boundaries of Ramle village, to the north-east corner of El Na'ana village, thence in a straight line to the southernmost point of El Barriya, along the eastern boundary of that village and the southern boundary of 'Innaba village. Thence it turns north to follow the southern side of the Jaffa-Jerusalem road until El Qubab, whence it follows the road to the boundary of Abu Shusha. It runs along the eastern boundaries of Abu Shusha, Seidun, Hulda to the southernmost point of Hulda, thence westwards in a straight line to the north-eastern corner of Umm Kalkha, thence following the northern boundaries of Umm Kalkha, Qazaza and the northern and western boundaries of Mukhezin to the Gaza District boundary and thence runs across the village lands of El Mismiya, El Kabira, and Yasur to the southern point of intersection, which is midway between the built-up areas of Yasur and Batani Sharqi.

From the southern point of intersection the boundary lines run north-westwards between the villages of Gan Yavne and Barqa to the sea at a point half way between Nabi Yunis and Minat el Qila, and south-eastwards to a point west of Qastina, whence it turns in a south-westerly direction, passing to the east of the built-up areas of Es Sawafir, Es Sharqiya and Ibdis. From the south-east corner of Ibdis village it runs to a point south-west of the built-up area of Beit 'Affa, crossing the Hebron-El Majdal road just to the west of the built-up area of Iraq Suweidan. Thence it proceeds southwards along the western village boundary of El Faluja to the Beersheba sub-district boundary. It then runs across the tribal lands of 'Arab el Jubarat to a point on the boundary between the sub-districts of Beersheba and Hebron north of Kh. Khuweilifa, whence it proceeds in a south-westerly direction to a point on the Beersheba-Gaza main road two kilometres to the north-west of the town. It then turns south-eastwards to reach Wadi Sab' at a point situated one kilometre to the west of it. From here it turns north-eastwards and proceeds along Wadi Sab' and along the Beersheba-Hebron road for a distance of one kilometre, whence it turns eastwards and runs in a straight line to Kh. Kuseifa to join the Beersheba-Hebron sub-district boundary. It then follows the Beersheba-Hebron boundary eastwards to a point north of Ras Ez Zuweira, only departing from it so as to cut across the base of the indentation between vertical grid lines 150 and 160.

About five kilometres north-east of Ras ez Zuweira it turns north, excluding from the Arab State a strip along the coast of the Dead Sea not more than seven kilometres in depth, as far as Ein Geddi, whence it turns due east to join the Transjordan frontier in the Dead Sea.

The northern boundary of the Arab section of the coastal plain runs from a point between Minat el Qila and Nabi Yunis, passing between the built-up areas of Gan Yavne and Barqa to the point of intersection. From here it turns south-westwards, running across the lands of Batani Sharqi, along the eastern boundary of the lands of Beit Daras and across the lands of Julis, leaving the built-up areas of Batani Sharqi and Julis to the westwards, as far as the north-west corner of the lands of Beit Tima. Thence it runs east of El Jiya across the village lands of El Barbara along the eastern boundaries of the villages of Beit Jirja, Deir Suneid and Dimra. From the south-east corner of Dimra the boundary passes across the lands of Beit Hanun, leaving the Jewish lands of Nir-Am to the eastwards. From the south-east corner of Dimra the boundary passes across the lands of Beit Hanun, leaving the Jewish lands of Nir-Am to the eastwards. From the south-east corner of Beit Hanun the line runs south-west to a point south of the parallel grid line 100, then turns north-west for two kilometres, turning again in a south-westerly direction and continuing in an almost straight line to the north-west corner of the village lands of Kirbet Ikhza'a. From there it follows the boundary line of this village to its southernmost point. It then runs in a southernly direction along the vertical grid line 90 to its junction with the horizontal grid line 70. It then turns south-eastwards to Kh. el Ruheiba and then proceeds in a southerly direction to a point known as El Baha, beyond which it crosses the Beersheba-El 'Auja main road to the west of Kh. el Mushrifa. From there it joins Wadi El Zaiyatin just to the west of El Subeita. From there it turns to the north-east and then to the south-east following this Wadi and passes to the east of 'Abda to join Wadi Nafkh. It then bulges to the south-west along Wadi Nafkh. It then bulges to the south-west along Wadi Nafkh, Wadi Ajrim and Wadi Lassan to the point where Wadi Lassan crosses the Egyptian frontier.

The area of the Arab enclave of Jaffa consists of that part of the town-planning area of Jaffa which lies to the west of the Jewish quarters lying south of Tel-Aviv, to the west of the continuation of Herzl street up to its junction with the Jaffa-Jerusalem road, to the south-west of the section of the Jaffa-Jerusalem road lying south-east of that junction, to the west of Miqve Israel lands, to the north-west of Holon local council area, to the north of the line linking up the north-west corner of Holon with the north-east corner of Bat Yam local council area and to the north of Bat Yam local council area. The question of Karton quarter will be decided by the Boundary Commission, bearing in mind among other considerations the desirability of including the smallest possible number of its Arab inhabitants and the largest possible number of its Jewish inhabitants in the Jewish State.

B. The Jewish State

The north-eastern sector of the Jewish State (Eastern) Galilee) is bounded on the north and west by the Lebanese frontier and on the east by the frontiers of Syria and Transjordan. It includes the whole of the Hula Basin, Lake Tiberias, the whole of the Beisan sub-district, the boundary line being extended to the crest of the Gilboa mountains and the Wadi Malih. From there the Jewish State extends north-west, following the boundary described in respect of the Arab State.

The Jewish Section of the coastal plain extends from a point between Minat et Qila and Nabi Yunis in the Gaza sub-district and includes the towns of Haifa and Tel-Aviv, leaving Jaffa as an enclave of the Arab State. The eastern frontier of the Jewish State follows the boundary described in respect of the Arab State.

The Beersheba area comprises the whole of the Beersheba sub-district, including the Negeb and the eastern part of the Gaza sub-district, but excluding the town of Beersheba and those areas described in respect of the Arab State. It includes also a strip of land along the Dead Sea stretching from the Beersheba-Hebron sub-district boundary line to Ein Geddi, as described in respect of the Arab State.

C. The City of Jerusalem

The boundaries of the City of Jerusalem are as defined in the recommendations on the City of Jerusalem. (See Part III, Section B, below).

Part III. City of Jerusalem

A. Special Regime

The City of Jerusalem shall be established as a *corpus separatum* under a special international regime and shall be administered by the United Nations. The Trusteeship Council shall be designated to discharge the responsibilities of the Administering Authority on behalf of the United Nations.

B. Boundaries of the City

The City of Jerusalem shall include the present municipality of Jerusalem plus the surrounding villages and towns, the most eastern of which shall be Abu Dis; the most southern, Bethlehem; the most western, Ein Karim (including also the built-up area of Motsa); and the most northern Shu'fat, as indicated on the attached sketch-map (annex B).

C. Statute of the City

The Trusteeship Council shall, within five months of the approval of the present plan, elaborate and approve a detailed Statute of the City which shall contain inter alia the substance of the following provisions:

1. *Government machinery; special objectives.* The Administering Authority in discharging its administrative obligations shall pursue the following special objectives:

(a) To protect and to preserve the unique spiritual and religious interests located in the city of the three great monotheistic faiths throughout the world, Christian, Jewish and Moslem; to this end to ensure that order and peace, and especially religious peace, reign in Jerusalem;

(b) To foster co-operation among all the inhabitants of the city in their own interests as well as in order to encourage and support the peaceful development of the mutual relations between the two Palestinian peoples throughout the Holy Land; to promote the security, well-being and any constructive measures of development of the residents, having regard to the special circumstances and customs of the various peoples and communities.

2. *Governor and administrative staff.* A Governor of the City of Jerusalem shall be appointed by the Trusteeship Council and shall be responsible to it. He shall be selected on the basis of special qualifications and without regard to nationality. He shall not, however, be a citizen of either State in Palestine.

The Governor shall represent the United Nations in the City and shall exercise on their behalf all powers of administration, including the conduct of external affairs. He shall be assisted by an administrative staff classed as international officers in the meaning of Article 100 of the Charter and chosen whenever practicable from the residents of the city and of the rest of Palestine on a non-discriminatory basis. A detailed plan for the organization of the administration of the city shall be submitted by the Governor to the Trusteeship Council and duly approved by it.

3. *Local autonomy.*

(a) The existing local autonomous units in the territory of the city (villages, townships and municipalities) shall enjoy wide powers of local government and administration.

(b) The Governor shall study and submit for the consideration and decision of the Trusteeship Council a plan for the establishment of a special town units consisting respectively, of the Jewish and Arab sections of new Jerusalem. The new town units shall continue to form part of the present municipality of Jerusalem.

4. *Security measures.*

(a) The City of Jerusalem shall be demilitarized; its neutrality shall be declared and preserved, and no para-military formations, exercises or activities shall be permitted within its borders.

(b) Should the administration of the City of Jerusalem be seriously obstructed or prevented by the non-co-operation or interference of one or more sections of the population, the Governor shall have authority to take such measures as may be necessary to restore the effective functioning of the administration.

(c) To assist in the maintenance of internal law and order and especially for the protection of the Holy Places and religious buildings and sites in the city, the Governor shall organize a special police force of adequate strength, the members of which shall be recruited outside of Palestine. The Governor shall be empowered to direct such budgetary provision as may be necessary for the maintenance of this force.

5. *Legislative organization.* A Legislative Council, elected by adult residents of the city irrespective of nationality on the basis of universal and secret suffrage and proportional representation, shall have powers of legislation and taxation. No legislative measures shall, however, conflict or interfere with the provisions which will be set forth in the Statute of the City, nor shall any law, regulation, or official action prevail over them. The Statute

shall grant to the Governor a right of vetoing bills inconsistent with the provisions referred to in the preceding sentence. It shall also empower him to promulgate temporary ordinances in case the council fails to adopt in time a bill deemed essential to the normal functioning of the administration.

6. *Administration of justice.* The Statute shall provide for the establishment of an independent judiciary system, including a court of appeal. All the inhabitants of the City shall be subject to it.

7. *Economic union and economic regime.* The City of Jerusalem shall be included in the Economic Union of Palestine and be bound by all stipulations of the undertaking and of any treaties issued therefrom, as well as by the decision of the Joint Economic Board. The headquarters of the Economic Board shall be established in the territory of the City.

The Statute shall provide for the regulation of economic matters not falling within the regime of the Economic Union, on the basis of equal treatment and non-discrimination for all members of the United Nations and their nationals.

8. *Freedom of transit and visit; control of residents.* Subject to considerations of security, and of economic welfare as determined by the Governor under the directions of the Trusteeship Council, freedom of entry into, and residence within, the borders of the City shall be guaranteed for the residents or citizens of the Arab and Jewish States. Immigration into, and residence within, the borders of the city for nationals of other States shall be controlled by the Governor under the directions of the Trusteeship Council.

9. *Relations with the Arab and Jewish States.* Representatives of the Arab and Jewish States shall be accredited to the Governor of the City and charged with the protection of the interests of their States and nationals in connexion with the international administration of the City.

10. *Official languages.* Arabic and Hebrew shall be the official languages of the city. This will not preclude the adoption of one or more additional working languages, as may be required.

11. *Citizenship.* All the residents shall become ipso facto citizens of the City of Jerusalem unless they opt for citizenship of the State of which they have been citizens or, if Arabs or Jews, have filed notice of intention to

become citizens of the Arab or Jewish State respectively, according to part I, section B, paragraph 9, of this plan.

The Trusteeship Council shall make arrangements for consular protection of the citizens of the City outside its territory.

12. *Freedoms of Citizens.*

(a) Subject only to the requirements of public order and morals, the inhabitants of the City shall be ensured the enjoyment of human rights and fundamental freedoms, including freedom of conscience, religion and worship, language, education, speech and press, assembly and association, and petition.

(b) No discrimination of any kind shall be made between the inhabitants on the grounds of race, religion, language or sex.

(c) All persons within the City shall be entitled to equal protection of the laws.

(d) The family law and personal status of the various persons and communities and their religious interests, including endowments, shall be respected.

(e) Except as may be required for the maintenance of public order and good government, no measure shall be taken to obstruct or interfere with the enterprise of religious or charitable bodies of all faiths or to discriminate against any representative or member of these bodies on the ground of his religion or nationality.

(f) The City shall ensure adequate primary and secondary education for the Arab and Jewish communities respectively, in their own languages and in accordance with their cultural traditions. The right of each community to maintain its own schools for the education of its own members in its own language, while conforming to such educational requirements of a general nature as the City may impose, shall not be denied or impaired. Foreign educational establishments shall continue their activity on the basis of their existing rights.

(g) No restriction shall be imposed on the free use by any inhabitant of the City of any language in private intercourse, in commerce, in religion, in the Press or in publications of any kind, or at public meetings.

13. *Holy Places.*

(a) Existing rights in respect of Holy Places and religious buildings or sites shall not be denied or impaired.

(b) Free access to the Holy Places and religious buildings or sites and the free exercise of worship shall be secured in conformity with existing rights and subject to the requirements of public order and decorum.

(c) Holy Places and religious buildings or sites shall be preserved. No act shall be permitted which may in any way impair their sacred character. If at any time it appears to the Governor that any particular Holy Place, religious building or site is in need of urgent repair, the Governor may call upon the community or communities concerned to carry out such repair. The Governor may carry it out himself at the expense of the community or communities concerned if no action is taken within a reasonable time.

(d) No taxation shall be levied in respect of any Holy Place, religious building or site which was exempt from taxation on the date of the creation of the City. No change in the incidence of such taxation shall be made which would either discriminate between the owners or occupiers of Holy Places, religious buildings or sites, or would place such owners or occupiers in a position less favourable in relation to the general incidence of taxation than existed at the time of the adoption of the Assembly's recommendations.

14. *Special powers of the Governor in respect of the Holy Places, religious buildings and sites in the City and in any part of Palestine.*

(a) The protection of the Holy Places, religious buildings and sites located in the City of Jerusalem shall be a special concern of the Governor.

(b) With relation to such places, buildings and sites in Palestine outside the city, the Governor shall determine, on the ground of powers granted to him by the Constitutions of both States, whether the provisions of the Constitutions of the Arab and Jewish States in Palestine dealing therewith and the religious rights appertaining thereto are being properly applied and respected.

(c) The Governor shall also be empowered to make decisions on the basis of existing rights in cases of disputes which may arise between the different religious communities or the rites of a religious community in respect of the Holy Places, religious buildings and sites in any part of Palestine.

In this task he may be assisted by a consultative council of representatives of different denominations acting in an advisory capacity.

D. Duration of the Special Regime

The Statute elaborated by the Trusteeship Council on the aforementioned principles shall come into force not later than 1 October 1948. It shall remain in force in the first instance for a period of ten years, unless the Trusteeship Council finds it necessary to undertake a re-examination of these provisions at an earlier date. After the expiration of this period the whole scheme shall be subject to re-examination by the Trusteeship Council in the light of the experience acquired with its functioning. The residents of the City shall be then free to express by means of a referendum their wishes as to possible modifications of the regime of the City.

Part IV. Capitulations

States whose nationals have in the past enjoyed in Palestine the privileges and immunities of foreigners, including the benefits of consular jurisdiction and protection, as formerly enjoyed by capitulation or usage in the Ottoman Empire, are invited to renounce any right pertaining to them to the re-establishment of such privileges and immunities in the proposed Arab and Jewish States and the City of Jerusalem.

Appendix: Human Rights Council Twenty-Fifth Session

Agenda Item 7: Human Rights Situation in Palestine and Other Occupied Arab Territories

Report of the Special Rapporteur on the situation of human rights in the Palestinian territories occupied since 1967, Richard Falk[319]

I. Introduction

1. In his final presentation to the Human Rights Council, the Special Rapporteur on the situation of human rights in the Palestinian territories occupied since 1967 would like to underscore the importance of this mandate as providing an independent witness to the evolving effects of the continuing occupation of Palestine by Israel. This exposure is centred upon the presentation of information received on the persistence of severe violations of international humanitarian law and international human rights law. Bearing witness provides a record of violations by Israel and its defiant attitude, and challenges the United Nations to take steps to ensure compliance. It should be remembered that the suffering of the people of Palestine is inseparably linked to the partition arrangements initially proposed by the United Nations in 1947, and which were never implemented or revised in a manner that takes full account of the rights of the Palestinian people, above all their inalienable right of self-determination.

---

[319] The present report is the final report of the current Special Rapporteur on the situation of human rights in the Palestinian territories occupied since 1967, Richard Falk, submitted in accordance with Commission on Human Rights resolution 1993/2 A and Human Rights Council decision 2/102. In the report, the Special Rapporteur addresses Israeli settlements in the West Bank, including East Jerusalem, and the wall in the context of the tenth anniversary of the advisory opinion of the International Court of Justice, and considers the policies and practices of Israel in occupied Palestine in light of the prohibition on segregation and apartheid. He also addresses concerns in relation to the deterioration of the human rights situation of Palestinians living under the Israeli blockade in the Gaza Strip. United Nations, General Assembly, A/HRC/25/67 (13 January 2014).

2. It was unfortunate that Israel refused even minimal cooperation with this mandate to the extent of allowing the Special Rapporteur to have access to occupied Palestine during the past six years or of responding to several urgent appeals addressing specific situations of immediate concern that fell within the purview of the mandate. This Special Rapporteur was expelled in December 2008 when attempting to enter Israel to carry out a mission of the mandate to visit occupied Palestine, and detained overnight in unpleasant prison conditions. Such humiliating non-cooperation represents a breach of the legal duty of States Members of the United Nations to facilitate all official undertakings of the organization. Although it has been possible to gain information needed to report on the situation confronting Palestinians living under occupation, non-cooperation deprives the mandate of direct interaction, including the receipt of testimony bearing on international law grievances from representatives of the Palestinian people. It is to be hoped that the next Special Rapporteur to be appointed will receive sufficient backing from the Human Rights Council to induce cooperation from Israel and better protection against defamatory attacks by some non-governmental organizations (NGOs) than was the experience of the current mandate holder.

3. International Law. An abiding theme of the reports of the Special Rapporteur during the past six years has been the consistent failure of Israel to comply with clear legal standards embodied in the Geneva Convention relative to the Protection of Civilian Persons in Time of War (Fourth Geneva Convention) and elsewhere in international humanitarian law and international human rights law. This pattern, as will be detailed below, is flagrant in relation to the wall, settlements, East Jerusalem, the Gaza Strip, water and land resources, and the human rights of Palestinians living under occupation. Also relevant is the failure of the United Nations to ensure implementation of the recommendations as to international law contained in two high-profile Human Rights Council reports of 2009 and 2013, respectively those of the United Nations Fact-Finding Mission on the Gaza Conflict (A/HRC/12/48) and of the fact-finding mission to investigate the human rights implications of the Israeli settlements (A/HRC/22/63). To the extent such a pattern is tolerated, it undermines respect for international law.

4. *Palestine*. In the light of the General Assembly's recognition of Palestine as a non-member observer State in Assembly resolution 67/19 of 29 November 2012, it seems appropriate to refer to territory under Israeli occupation as "Palestine" rather than as "Occupied Palestinian Territories." Such a shift in language also emphasizes the inadequacy of the international law framework available to address a condition of prolonged occupation that has now extended for more than 45 years. Special steps and procedures need to be adopted that will confer rights and establish the rule of law. To sustain indefinitely an oppressive occupation containing many punitive elements also seems designed to encourage residents to leave Palestine, which is consistent with the apparent annexationist, colonialist and ethnic-cleansing goals of Israel, especially in relation to the West Bank, including East Jerusalem.

5. *Corporate responsibility*. Recent reports have underscored the potential implications for corporations and financial institutions that engage with and profit from Israeli settlements. The establishment and continued development of settlements is in violation of article 49(6) of the Fourth Geneva Convention, an assessment reinforced by the International Court of Justice in its advisory opinion of 2004 on the wall. Such an initiative has tried at all times to proceed cooperatively with the economic actors involved, and has acknowledged instances of compliance with international law and relevant United Nations guidelines and the encouraging recent indication of governmental and European Union reinforcement of these emergent obligations. This trend also converges with and reinforces the social mobilization of civil society in a variety of initiatives, especially the growing boycott, divestment and sanctions campaign.

6. *"Legitimacy war."* In the pursuit of Palestinian rights under circumstances of prolonged occupation, there is increasing reason to believe that despite the authority of international law and the expressed will of States Members of the United Nations, the situation is essentially frozen, if not regressing. In addition, Palestinians seem increasingly disillusioned with armed resistance and with traditional intergovernmental diplomacy. Palestinian hopes for the realization of their fundamental rights have now shifted to engagement in a "legitimacy war," which involves a worldwide

struggle to gain control over the debate about legal entitlements and moral proprieties in the conflict supported by a global solidarity movement that has begun to sway public opinion. The United Nations has a crucial role to play in this process by lending support to Palestinian claims of rights and providing assessments of associated grievances resulting from the violation by Israel of international humanitarian law and international human rights principles and standards.

7. *Language*. The Special Rapporteur believes that the language used to consider Palestinian grievances relating to international humanitarian law and international human rights law in Palestine needs to reflect everyday realities, and not remain beholden to technical wording and euphemisms that mask human suffering resulting from violations. It seems therefore appropriate to describe such unlawful impositions on the people resident in the West Bank by reference to "annexation" and "colonial ambitions" rather than "occupation." Whether these impositions constitute "apartheid" is discussed in more detail below. Such clarifications at the level of language reinforce the contention that it is a matter of urgency to pursue more concerted efforts within United Nations venues to implement the rights of the Palestinian people.

8. *Emergency in Gaza*. Developments in the region, combined with an unlawful blockade maintained since mid-2007, has created a serious emergency situation in the Gaza Strip that threatens the entire population. From the perspective of international law, as argued in prior reports (A/HRC/20/32), Gaza remains "occupied," despite the implementation by Israel of its "disengagement" plan in 2005, due to the control of borders, airspace and coastal waters, and periodic military incursions. The present situation is dire, as massive infrastructural failures cause daily hardship for the population, who are also at risk of epidemics. At the time of writing, with insufficient quantities of fuel reaching Gaza, electricity is available only for short periods, making it impossible for hospitals to provide proper treatment for seriously ill patients suffering from cancer and kidney ailments. The situation is aggravated by persisting tensions between the Palestinian Authority and the governing authorities in Gaza, and by the breakdown of cooperation along the border with Egypt. Egyptian security concerns in Sinai

have led to greater restrictions at the Rafah crossing, and to the destruction of the tunnel complex in southern Gaza that had eased some of the difficulties caused by the blockade. Some countries, notably Turkey and Qatar, have responded to this situation by providing emergency relief, but much more assistance is required, including pressure upon Israel to end the unlawful blockade.

9. *Urgency*. The stark reality is that the beleaguered occupied people of Gaza, over half of whom are children, are not receiving the protection to which they are entitled under international humanitarian law, which imposes an overall duty on the occupying Power to act in such a manner as to protect the civilian population from harm. Given the failure of Israel to live up to these obligations as set forth in the Fourth Geneva Convention, the United Nations and international society generally is challenged to take urgent action. The principles embedded in the concept of the responsibility to protect would seem to have a special applicability to the emergency conditions currently existing in Gaza that are being brought to the attention of the world by graphic pictures of sewage in the streets; widespread flooding; seasonal cold, including snow; and children entrapped by these conditions.

II. The Wall and the 2004 Advisory Opinion

10. July 2014 will mark 10 years since the International Court of Justice gave its near unanimous advisory opinion on the legal consequences of the construction of a wall in the Occupied Palestinian Territory (A/ES-10/273 and Corr.1). The refusal of Israel to implement this assessment of international law by the highest judicial body in the United Nations is cause for serious concern.

11. The question put to the Court by the General Assembly bears repeating: "What are the legal consequences arising from the construction of the wall being built by Israel, the occupying Power, in the Occupied Palestinian Territory, including in and around East Jerusalem, …, considering the rules and principles of international law, including the Fourth Geneva Convention of 1949, and relevant Security Council and

General Assembly resolutions?"[320] The International Court of Justice was unequivocal in its reply. In summary, it concluded that the construction of the wall in occupied Palestine, including East Jerusalem, and its associated regime, was contrary to international law. The crucial point is that it would not have been unlawful for Israel to build a security wall on an established international border, but to encroach unilaterally on territory occupied in 1967 was a flagrant violation of international law. The Court stated that Israel had a continuing duty to comply with its international obligations in this regard. It found that Israel was obliged to end the illegal situation, cease construction and dismantle the wall in the Occupied Palestinian Territory, and to make reparations for all damage caused as a result of the wall (A/ES-10/273 and Corr.1, para. 145).

12. In addition to the conclusions addressing the obligations of Israel, the Court stated that all States are obliged not to recognize the illegal situation arising from the wall, and that States parties to the Fourth Geneva Convention were obliged to ensure compliance by Israel with that Convention. Finally, the Court suggested that the United Nations, and especially the General Assembly and the Security Council, should consider further action to overcome this illegal situation resulting from the construction of the wall and its associated regime (ibid., para. 163 (3)(D) and (E)).

13. In clear defiance of international law, Israel has continued construction of the wall and maintains on its website a map of 30 April 2006 showing its revised route.[321] At the time of the advisory opinion, the Secretary-General estimated that approximately 180 km of the wall had been completed (A/ES-10/273 and Corr.1, para. 82). Since that time, parts of the wall have been re-routed.[322] In 2013, the Secretary-General reported that approximately 62 per cent of the wall had been completed (A/68/502, para. 22). A further 10 per cent was under construction, and construction of the

---

[320] General Assembly resolution ES-10/14.

[321] See www.securityfence.mod.gov.il/Pages/ENG/route.htm.

[322] Some decisions of the Israeli High Court have reconnected communities with the West Bank. Office for the Coordination of Humanitarian Affairs office in the occupied Palestinian territory (OCHA-oPt), Barrier Update (July 2011), p.5.

remaining 28 per cent of the planned route had not yet commenced. Upon completion, the wall is expected to run approximately 708 km.

14. About 85 per cent of the planned route of the wall lies within the West Bank, and will cut off and isolate 9.4 per cent of the West Bank territory, including East Jerusalem and so-called No-Man's Land.[323] Palestinian communities affected by the wall experience varying degrees of isolation and restrictions on their freedom of movement. The seam zone's[324] associated permit regime requires Palestinians to continually apply for temporary permits to allow them to reside in their home area and carry on aspects of their lives that require entering or exiting the seam zone. In order to have access to farming land beyond Israeli-controlled access gates, leave and return for work, have access to education, health and other services, visit family and friends or arrange for visits to those communities for non-resident Palestinians, prior permission by Israeli authorities is necessary. This permit procedure imposes daily hardships on many Palestinians.[325]

15. The Ministry of Defense states that "the Security Fence does not annex territories to the State of Israel, nor will it change the status of the residents of these areas."[326] Israel maintains that the purpose of the wall is to ensure security and protect Israeli citizens from terrorist attacks. In 2011, the Israeli High Court of Justice supported this reasoning regarding security in rejecting NGO petitions which claimed that the permit regime was aimed at expropriating and annexing Palestinian land and which argued that its exclusive application to Palestinians, and not, for example, to settlers in the zone, was discriminatory and comparable to the Pass Laws of apartheid-era South Africa.[327] However, the High Court's assertion does not overcome the conclusion by the International Court of Justice that the grave infringements of the rights of Palestinians caused by the wall in the Occupied Palestinian

---

323 See www.ochaopt.org/documents/ochaopt_atlas_barrier_affecting_palestinians_december 2011.pdf.

324 A designated "closed military zone" between the wall and the Green Line.

325 See HaMoked: Center for the Defence of the Individual, "The permit regime: human rights violations in West Bank areas known as the 'seam zone' " (2013). www.hamoked.org/files/2013/1157660_eng.pdf.

326 See www.securityfence.mod.gov.il/Pages/ENG/route.htm.

327 OCHA-oPt, Barrier Update, p. 8; HaMoked, "The permit regime," pp. 14–15. See also Virginia Tilley (ed.), *Beyond Occupation* (2012), pp.151-155.

Territory were not necessary to satisfy legitimate Israeli security requirements (A/ES-10/273 and Corr.1, para. 136).

16. If protection of Israeli citizens were indeed the only reason for the wall and the associated regime, it begs the question of why Israel continues to support the expansion of illegal settlements in the West Bank, thus moving an increasing number of Israeli citizens into the very area from which it says the risk emanates. That continued settlement on West Bank land, including East Jerusalem, cut off by the wall seems to be creating a fait accompli amounting to de facto annexation, is a grave concern raised by the Human Rights Council, which has demanded that Israel comply with the advisory opinion (Council resolution 22/26).

17. For Palestinian residents isolated from the rest of the West Bank by the wall, and living under the permit regime and other restrictions, the issue is not only about status, but also about how life is made untenable, inducing more and more Palestinians to abandon their land and leave. By way of illustration, for years, the village of Nabi Samuel reportedly attempted to improve the village school. The village's location in the seam zone complicates access to outside education. The United Nations Under-Secretary-General for Humanitarian Affairs and Emergency Relief Coordinator stated on her 2011 visit to the village: "I am horrified by the way the Barrier affects Palestinians. It divides communities and inhibits the provision of services. I visited a one-room school with no windows and very few facilities, which can't be improved because the planning rules don't allow it. This is unacceptable."[328] In September 2013, the village succeeded in installing a container on the school ground to serve as an additional classroom. However, the school is now in danger of losing one of its two rooms for lack of a building permit.[329] These acutely burdensome living conditions lead to the displacement of long-term residents. In 2012, the Village Council noted that over the past decade at least 10 families have left the village, which counts some 260 residents.[330]

---

[328] OCHA, Barrier Update, p.14.

[329] Documentation collected by OHCHR.

[330] See www.unrwa.org/galleries/photos/nabi-samuel-"we-are-living-inside-prison.

18. Another case in point is the approximately 25 houses making up the village of Al-Numan. It is also encircled by the wall, with its only access through an Israeli checkpoint, and restricted from unlicensed building activity, effectively preventing families and the population of the village from growing, as housing needs cannot be met.[331] Consequently, the villagers have seen their own number fall while observing the neighbouring illegal Har Homa settlement's steady growth in occupied territory. In 2006 Al-Haq published a case study on the indirect forcible transfer taking place in Al-Numan.[332] These are but two concrete examples of the obstacles communities face daily. In 2012, the Office for the Coordination of Humanitarian Affairs estimated that approximately 7,500 Palestinians still lived in the seam zone,[333] down from an estimated 10,000 people in 2003.[334] Upon completion of the wall, an estimated 25,000 Palestinians would be located in the seam zone, a figure which does not include the Palestinian population in East Jerusalem.[335]

19. Regular demonstrations against the wall and its associated regime staged in affected villages are often violently suppressed.[336] A website for the village of Bil'in, a farming community, describes its struggle thus: "[Bil'in] is fighting to safeguard its land, its olive trees, its resources … its liberty… Supported by Israeli and international activists, Bil'in residents peacefully demonstrate every Friday in front of the 'work-site of shame'.

---

331 See www.alhaq.org/advocacy/topics/wall-and-jerusalem/594-visiting-a-ghost-town-drawing-attention-to-the-plight-of-al-numan-village.

332 Available online at www.alhaq.org/10yrs/images/stories/PDF_Files/2%20Al-Numan%20Village%20-%20a%20case%20study%20of%20indirect%20forcible%20transfer%20-%20November%202006.pdf.

333 OCHA-oPt, "The humanitarian impact of the barrier" (July 2012), p. 1. (www.ochaopt.org/documents/ocha_opt_barrier_factsheet_july_2012_english.pdf).

334 The Special Rapporteur believes that both the re-routings of sections of the wall and Palestinians leaving due to the wall and its associated regime have contributed to the decrease in numbers.

335 OCHA-oPt, Barrier Update, p. 11.

336 See Palestinian Grassroots Anti-apartheid Wall Campaign, www.stopthewall.org/2013/04/07/further-suppression-demonstrations-occupation; B'Tselem, www.btselem.org/demonstrations; and the Russell Tribunal on Palestine, *Findings of the South Africa Session* (2011).

And every Friday the Israeli army responds with both physical and psychological violence."[337]

20. The impact of the wall on people's lives is reflected in the progress report of the Board of the United Nations Register of Damage Caused by the Construction of the Wall in the Occupied Palestinian Territory (see A/ES-10/599). As at June 2013, 36,803 claim forms for registration of damage had been received and, of the almost 9,000 claims decided, all but 576 claims were found to meet the eligibility criteria for inclusion in the register. Claimants may submit claims under categories of losses including: agriculture; commercial; residential; employment; access to services; and public resources.[338]

21. In his first report to the General Assembly, the Special Rapporteur recommended seeking the assistance of the Security Council for the implementation of the advisory opinion (A/63/326, para. 51(b)). In the face of the unequivocal opinion of the International Court of Justice, and of General Assembly resolution ES-10/15, in which the Assembly called on Israel to comply with the advisory opinion, Israel has defiantly acted as if international law and international judicial authority has no bearing on its policies and behaviour. With the tenth anniversary of the advisory opinion approaching, it is time again to examine what legitimate action by the international community can be taken to achieve compliance with international law, as set out by the International Court of Justice. It is often supposed that because the legal findings of the Court were embedded in an "advisory opinion" it has no bearing on the status of the legal obligations of Israel. This is incorrect. An advisory opinion of the International Court of Justice is as determinative with respect to the authority of international law as a judgement in a dispute between two or more States, but unlike such a judgement between States that can be directly enforced by reliance on Article 94 of the Charter of the United Nations, an advisory opinion cannot be so implemented. However, this difference does not weaken the obligation

---

[337] See www.bilin-ffj.org/index.php?option=com_content&task= blogcategory&id=15&Itemid=34.

[338] Rules and Regulations Governing the Registration of Claims, art. 11, para. 1. Available online at www.unrod.org/docs/UNRoD%20Rules%20and%20Regulations.pdf.

of Israel to act in accordance with this authoritative determination of international legal obligations, and its failure to do so puts it in breach of international law and responsible for the cumulative harm inflicted on the Palestinian people. It is past time for the United Nations to take action that seeks to protect the rights of the Palestinian people bearing on the sanctity of their territory and its relation to the underlying right of self-determination.

III. Israeli Settlements and the Fragmentation of Occupied Palestine

Facts on the Ground

22. The hallmark of Israel's 46-year prolonged annexing occupation of Palestine has been the determined pursuit by Israel of settlement construction and expansion in the West Bank, including East Jerusalem, in defiance of its international law obligations (A/68/513, paras. 4–5). This was clearly reflected in the findings of the international fact-finding mission on the implications of Israeli settlements (A/HRC/22/63). Throughout the past six years, the Special Rapporteur has periodically reported on the expansion of settlements and outposts[339] in the West Bank, including East Jerusalem (in breach of Israel's own commitment to freeze settlement expansion, including natural growth under the 2003 Quartet road map), and the impact of associated policies and practices on the human rights of Palestinians living in the occupied territory.[340] While the pro-settlement camp claims that "settlements aren't the problem,"[341] this view stands in sharp contrast to the facts on the ground.

23. Increasing fragmentation of the West Bank, including East Jerusalem, by way of a combination of policies and practices including, but not limited to: the wall; the creation of seam zones; checkpoints; zoning and planning restrictions; demolition of homes and forced evictions (particularly of Bedouin communities in Area C); revocation of residency rights; the designation of vast tracts of land in the West Bank as closed military zones

[339] Outposts are settlements which, although often established with some kind of Government support, are not officially recognized under Israeli law.

[340] A/63/326, A/HRC/13/53/Rev.1, A/65/331, A/HRC/16/72, A/66/358, A/HRC/20/32.

[341] See www.jpost.com/Opinion/Editorials/Settlements-arent-the-problem-330306.

or natural reserves; and the expropriation of land for settler agriculture or industrial zones, may irreversibly disrupt the contiguity of the West Bank, undermining a just and sustainable two-State solution.[342]

24. Peace Now, an Israeli NGO, called attention to "Bibi's settlements boom" in 2013, reporting that tenders had been published for 3,472 new units in settlements, and that plans had been promoted for 8,943 new settlement units in the eight months since the Netanyahu Government took office in March 2013.[343] Despite a brief and limited 10-month moratorium on settlement construction in 2010 during the last round of unsuccessful peace talks (which also demonstrated the ability of Israel to halt settlement activity if desired), Israel issued tenders for the construction of 5,302 housing units in the West Bank, including East Jerusalem, during the period from March 2009 to January 2013.[344]

25. The timing of announcements regarding settlement expansion has also been provocative, with the two most recent announcements coinciding with the first and second round of Palestinian prisoner releases by Israel in the context of the renewed peace negotiations that began in August 2013. The passage of time under the status quo has not been a neutral factor for Palestinians, as more "facts on the ground" are created daily, strengthening the position of Israel in its preferred mode of power-based negotiations (as opposed to negotiations based on rights and international law). Despite protestations over settlement activity by the United Nations, and notably also by the United States of America[345] and the European Union, Israel continues to use State power and resources to promote its defiant settlement policies. The Secretary-General has described Israel as playing a leading role in the construction and expansion of settlements (A/68/513, para. 3).

26. This latter factor is important to note if the removal of existing settlements were to occur as part of a peace agreement. Approximately half

---

[342] A/HRC/25/38, A/HRC/25/40, A/68/502 and A/68/513.

[343] See http://peacenow.org/Bibis%20Settlements%20Boom%20-%20March-November%20 2013%20-%20FINAL.pdf.

[344] See http://peacenow.org.il/eng/sites/default/files/summary-of-4-years-of-netanyahu-government.pdf.

[345] See www.haaretz.com/news/diplomacy-defense/1.556645; www.un.org/News/Press/ docs/2013/ sgsm15427.doc.htm.

of all settlements in the West Bank can be classified by type as either "quality of life," or a mixture of "quality of life/ideological," which tend to be inhabited by predominately secular or mixed settler populations.[346] Israel might be able to re-incentivize economic settlers, who were persuaded to move to the West Bank settlements through various government benefits and incentives, to re-settle to the west of the pre-1967 borders of Israel. However, it would have a more difficult time removing the more religious settlers who live in approximately 70 settlements across the West Bank, all the more so as population growth in the settlements (approximately 2.8 per cent) continues to outstrip population growth in Israel.[347] It also remains to be seen whether an emergent settler unity precludes implementing a future peace agreement based on inducing economic settlers to return to Israel. Certainly, it may be anticipated that ideological settlers would do their best to prevent such a division and the implementation of such an agreement.

27. A small minority within the ideologically motivated settlers has been responsible for most of the violence committed against Palestinian men, women and children and against their homes and properties. In the first 10 months of 2013, 361 incidents of settler violence were reported, including 87 resulting in the injury of Palestinians (compared to a total of 366 incidents in 2012).[348] Most of these incidents occurred in the Nablus, Ramallah and Hebron governorates. Settler violence is reinforced by a lack of accountability and the related failure of Israeli law enforcement forces to protect vulnerable Palestinian communities (A/68/513, paras. 42-52).

28. Housing demolitions and displacement of Palestinian communities also kept up with the settlement boom in 2013. From January to October 2013, 533 Palestinian homes and livelihood structures were demolished, including 205 residential structures, displacing 969 people, including 441 children. International donor-funded structures, paid for by taxpayers around

---

[346] Among 136 West Bank settlements listed by Peace Now, 25 settlements fall under the type "quality of life," 35 under the type "quality of life/ideological," 70 under the type "ideological" and six under the type "ultra-orthodox" (see http://peacenow.org.il/eng/content/settlements-and-outposts).

[347] Palestinian Centre for Human Rights submission to Special Rapporteur, 22 November 2013.

[348] See www.ochaopt.org/documents/ocha_opt_the_humanitarian_monitor_2013_11_25_english.pdf.

the world, were not spared from demolition, and 96 donor-funded structures, including residential, livestock-related and water and sanitation facilities in the West Bank were demolished by Israeli authorities.

29. Herding communities living in small villages in Area C have been particularly vulnerable to these Israeli practices. In 2013, the United Nations High Commissioner for Human Rights twice spoke out against the demolition of at least three Bedouin and herder communities in the northern Jordan Valley.[349] Violations by Israel of international law extend to actively preventing the provision of urgent humanitarian assistance from the international community to the affected Palestinian communities.[350]

The Future of Outposts

30. In July 2012, the Government-appointed committee to examine the state of construction in the West Bank, chaired by Supreme Court Justice (Ret.) Edmund Levy (the Levy Committee), issued its report on the legal status of Israeli settlements in the West Bank and, in particular, set forth recommended steps to regularize the construction of "illegal settlements" (outposts) in the West Bank (currently numbering over 100). It concluded that the international laws of occupation, including the Fourth Geneva Convention, did not apply to Israel's unique situation in Judea and Samaria (the name given the West Bank in internal Israeli discourse and signalling a claimed biblical attachment), and that Israelis had the legal right to settle in the West Bank despite the international consensus.

31. The conclusions of the Levy Committee not only reflected disregard of international law but also set forth a quasi-legal retroactive endorsement of outposts, formally unauthorized under Israeli law. In fact, the Committee determined that existing outposts were "carried out with the knowledge, encouragement and tacit agreement of the most senior political level, government ministers and the Prime Minister, and therefore such conduct is

---

349 See www.ohchr.org/EN/NewsEvents/Pages/DisplayNews.aspx?NewsID=13662&LangID=E and www.ohchr.org/EN/NewsEvents/Pages/DisplayNews.aspx?NewsID=13786&LangID=E.

350 www.ochaopt.org/documents/unhc_obstriction_humanitarian_assistance_english.pdf.

to be seen as implied agreement."[351] A previous report of 2005 by Talia Sasson, a former Chief State Prosecutor, concerning the illegal outposts had not gone so far as to implicate the senior-most political echelon of the country, but had found the World Zionist Organization (fully funded from the State Treasury), the Ministry of Construction and Housing, the Civil Administration in Judea and Samaria, and the Assistant to the Defense Minister complicit in the establishment of new unauthorized outposts, and exposed an unelected bureaucracy in charge of creating new outposts without political authorization or oversight.[352]

32. The Special Rapporteur notes that while Sasson's report labelled the outposts as illegal under Israeli law and recommended their dismantlement, developments on the ground since then have shown that successive Israeli Governments preferred to follow the approach endorsed post facto by the Levy Committee. Of 1,708 units constructed in West Bank settlements in the first half of 2013, 180 units were located in outposts (see A/HRC/25/38). In May 2013, Israel announced plans to legalize four outposts in the West Bank (in other words to recognize them as official settlements).[353] While the Netanyahu Government never adopted the Levy report, the Knesset Constitution, Law and Justice Committee is expected to debate the report early in December 2013, indicating that it is being taken seriously at the highest levels in Israel.[354]

"Demographic Balance" in East Jerusalem

33. The status of East Jerusalem remains one of the most contentious issues to be resolved in the Israeli-Palestinian conflict. It is worth recalling that in its resolution 478 (1980), the Security Council affirmed that the Basic Law of Israel proclaiming Jerusalem, including the annexed area, as the capital of Israel constitutes a violation of international law and does not

---

[351] See http://unispal.un.org/UNISPAL.NSF/0/D9D07DCF58E781C585257A3A005956A6.

[352] See www.mfa.gov.il/mfa/aboutisrael/state/law/pages/summary%20of%20opinion%20 concerning%20 unauthorized%20outposts%20-%20talya%20sason%20adv.aspx.

[353] See www.haaretz.com/news/diplomacy-defense/israel-to-legalize-four-west-bank-settlement-outposts-slated-for-demolition-1.524291.

[354] See www.jpost.com/Diplomacy-and-Politics/Knesset-panel-to-debate-Levy-Report-333137.

affect the application of the Fourth Geneva Convention in Palestine, including East Jerusalem.

34. For Palestinians living in East Jerusalem, their situation would not be as precarious if, despite the illegality of annexation, they were treated equally and afforded access to quality education, health care and housing. Instead, Palestinians living in East Jerusalem are regarded as "permanent residents" and subject to a gradual and bureaucratic process of ethnic cleansing.[355] This has consisted of revocation of residency permits, demolitions of residential structures built without Israeli permits (often virtually impossible to obtain),[356] and forced evictions of Palestinian families, in violation of the basic right to adequate housing, enshrined in the International Covenant on Economic, Social and Cultural Rights.

35. A 2013 report by the United Nations Conference on Trade and Development on the Palestinian economy in East Jerusalem detailed Israeli policies that have impeded the natural growth of the Palestinian economy. It also noted that Palestinians are made to pay high municipal taxes in return for poor services and disproportionately low public expenditure in East Jerusalem.[357] This has been particularly evident with respect to education, characterized by a shortage of classrooms, a high overall dropout rate of 13 per cent among Palestinian schools in East Jerusalem, and a general neglect of the Arab schooling system in comparison to their Jewish counterparts literally metres away in West Jerusalem.[358]

36. The situation in East Jerusalem today is a microcosm of the fragmentation of territory taking place across the West Bank. Israel actively seeks to undermine the Palestinian presence to serve its goal of preserving a Jewish majority in East Jerusalem. This has been a policy of Israel for decades, acknowledged by the Jerusalem Municipality, to maintain a demographic balance of approximately 70 per cent Jewish to 30 per cent Palestinian in Jerusalem.[359]

---

[355] A/65/331, para. 14, and A/HRC/20/32, para. 32.
[356] A/68/513, paras. 30–33.
[357] See http://unctad.org/en/PublicationsLibrary/gdsapp2012d1_en.pdf.
[358] See www.acri.org.il/en/2013/09/02/ej-edu-report-13.
[359] "EU Heads of Mission Jerusalem Report 2012."

37. Since 1996, an estimated 11,023 Jerusalem Palestinians have lost their resident status and right to live in occupied East Jerusalem.[360] During the period 2004–2013, 492 housing units were demolished in East Jerusalem, displacing 1,943 Palestinians. These figures account only for officially demolished housing units and do not include homes demolished by some owners after receiving a demolition order to avoid perverse heavy municipal penalties and demolition costs associated with the destruction of their own homes.[361]

38. The most problematic plan advanced in East Jerusalem in recent years has been the expansion of settlements and infrastructure around Har Homa, Gilo and Givat Hamatos, as well as the E1 settlement bloc to the east, which threatens to cut off East Jerusalem from the rest of the West Bank.[362] Eventual peace depends crucially on ensuring that Palestinian rights in East Jerusalem are not further jeopardized.

Corporate Complicity in International Crimes

39. Over the past two years, the Special Rapporteur focused attention on companies involved in business and financial activities related to the Israeli settlement enterprise as well as the possibility of corporate complicity in international crimes related to Israeli settlements in the West Bank, including East Jerusalem.[363]

40. The effort to focus on business activities in the settlements was made, in part, to bring a measure of accountability with respect to the emergent human rights obligations of companies in conformity with international law and the Guiding Principles on Business and Human Rights. The Special Rapporteur's intention was not only to provide a sound legal basis upon which to assess the complicity of businesses in international crimes related to the settlements, but also to clearly set out the risks and

---

[360] Submission to Special Rapporteur by the Civic Coalition for Palestinian Rights in Jerusalem (November 2013).

[361] At 30 November 2013 (www.btselem.org/planning_and_building/east_jerusalem_statistics).

[362] "EU Heads of Mission Jerusalem Report 2012."

[363] A/67/379, A/HRC/23/21, A/68/376.

associated costs in terms of reputation, as well as the potential legal consequences of doing business in the settlements.

41. The responses received from some of the 13 companies analysed in an earlier report (A/67/379) were mixed. Nonetheless, there have been a number of recent developments in relation to the involvement of other businesses involved in the settlements to indicate that public pressure and media attention does bring some ethical dividends, and has encouraged Governments to be more vigilant.

42. Some positive developments in this regard include Royal HaskoningDHV, a Dutch company, which announced in September 2013 its decision to terminate a contract with the Jerusalem Municipality to build a wastewater treatment plant in East Jerusalem.[364] In December, Vitens, a Dutch water utility company, decided to cut its ties with Mekorot, the Israeli national water company, citing concerns in relation to the adherence of international laws.[365] Earlier, in August 2013, the Swedish-Norwegian bank Nordea excluded Cemex, one of the companies taken up in the Special Rapporteur's earlier report, from its investment portfolio, due to its extraction of non-renewable natural resources from occupied Palestine.[366] Such examples should lead the way for more countries and companies to follow suit, as well as alerting Governments to their responsibility to urge companies subject to their authority to act in accordance with international law.

43. While due diligence on the part of businesses is an inherent aspect of corporate responsibility, Governments also have the obligation, as noted by the fact-finding mission on settlements, to take measures to ensure that they do not recognize an unlawful situation arising from the illegal activities of Israel.[367] In this regard, the European Union guidelines which establish that all agreements between Israel and the European Union for grants, prizes and financial instruments funded by the European Union must now

---

[364] See https://www.un.org/apps/news//story.asp?NewsID=45812&Cr=palestin&Cr1=.

[365] See www.jpost.com/Diplomacy-and-Politics/Dutch-firm-severs-ties-with-Mekorot-over-West-Bank-policy-even-as-Israel-Jordan-PA-sign-major-water-deal-334597.

[366] Palestinian BDS National Committee, submission to Special Rapporteur (November 2013).

[367] A/HRC/22/63, paras. 116–117.

unequivocally and explicitly indicate their inapplicability to the territories occupied by Israel in 1967 represents a step in the right direction.

44. The Special Rapporteur is also encouraged by the recent issuance by the Government of the United Kingdom of Great Britain and Northern Ireland of guidelines for businesses, which for the first time outline the risks of trading with Israeli settlements, and specifically warn of the legal and economic risks stemming from the fact that the Israeli settlements, according to international law, are built on occupied land and are not recognized as a legitimate part of the territory of Israel.[368]

Trade with the Settlements

45. The diligence shown by the European Union and some of its Member States regarding the responsibility of businesses operating in occupied Palestine naturally leads to the following question: Are the same human rights standards applied by countries when it comes to trade relations with the settlements? If the statements issued by the European Union and the United States protesting the expansion of settlements reiterate their illegality and illegitimacy, then steps should be taken to ensure that related actions also reflect a genuine commitment to human rights and respect for international law, for example by ceasing trade with the settlements starting with a ban on imports of settlement produce.

46. While produce originating in the Israeli settlements is not entitled to benefit from preferential tariff treatment under the European Union-Israel Association Agreement, fresh agricultural produce exported from the settlements — but falsely labelled as "made in Israel" — can still be found on many supermarket shelves across the European Union due to the voluntary nature of labelling requirements. Considering the fact that the European Union remains one of the most important trading partners for the settlements, with annual exports worth $300 million, a ban on settlement produce would have a significant impact. It should also not be forgotten that trade with settlements is linked to the violation of human rights with respect

---

[368] See www.theguardian.com/world/2013/dec/09/uk-government-warns-over-business-israeli-settlements.

to Palestinian communities denied access to fertile agricultural land, water and other natural resources.

47. So long as illegal settlements are supported through trade, statements protesting the expansion of settlements from the main trading partners of Israel will have little resonance on the ground, and third party States will continue to be associated with the violation of human rights in occupied Palestine.

IV. The Gaza Strip

48. In the space of six years since this Special Rapporteur assumed this mandate, the population of the Gaza Strip has lived through two major Israeli military operations (Cast Lead from December 2008 to January 2009 and Pillar of Defence in November 2012), and endured Israel's illegal blockade (in place since June 2007). Both conflicts inflicted disproportionate casualties and devastation on the Palestinian civilian population. This has been well documented by the United Nations.[369]

49. Since June 2013, the humanitarian situation in Gaza has worsened. In recent months, the destruction by the Egyptian authorities of most underground tunnels, which although problematic had been a lifeline to the residents, has had a particularly serious impact on the availability of fuel at affordable prices in Gaza. This has led to severe power shortages, resulting in shutdowns of sewage treatment facilities, and disruptions to specialized health services, such as kidney dialysis, operating theatres, blood banks, intensive care units and incubators, putting the lives of vulnerable patients in Gaza at risk.[370] The frequent closures of the Rafah crossing in recent months have generally prevented access to affordable health care in Egypt, which remains essential given the limitations of the Gaza health system.

50. The most egregious violations of human rights committed by Israel have been in its enforcement, using excessive force, of arbitrary access to restricted areas at sea and on land, profoundly affecting the lives of Palestinian fishermen and agricultural farmers and households dependent

[369] A/HRC/12/48, A/HRC/22/35/Add.1 and A/HRC/23/21.

[370] See www.ohchr.org/EN/NewsEvents/Pages/DisplayNews.aspx?NewsID=14028&LangID=E.

upon them. The more pervasive forms of human rights violations also linked to the blockade have been well documented by the Secretary-General (A/68/502), and include inter alia, severe restrictions on movement into and out of Gaza from Israel and adverse impacts on the rights of Palestinians in Gaza to education, health and work. In addition, severe export restrictions (and limitations on imports) undermine the potential of the Gaza economy, and accentuate the impoverished conditions that prevail in Gaza.[371] The recent refusal of Israel to allow exports from Gaza to the West Bank, despite a Dutch donation of a container security scanner, is emblematic of the denial of the right to development in Gaza, and undercuts claims by Israel that its actions are taken to serve genuine security concerns.[372]

V. The Question of Apartheid and Segregation

51. In 2011, the Special Rapporteur reiterated the call made by his predecessor in 2007, for a referral to the International Court of Justice for an advisory opinion on the question of whether "elements of the [Israeli] occupation constitute forms of colonialism and apartheid."[373] More precisely, he recommended that the Court be asked to assess the allegations that the prolonged occupation of the West Bank and East Jerusalem possess elements of "colonialism," "apartheid" and "ethnic cleansing" inconsistent with international humanitarian law in circumstances of belligerent occupation and unlawful abridgement of the right to self-determination of the Palestinian people.[374] Since no advisory opinion has been sought following the aforementioned reports of successive Special Rapporteurs, in the present report the Special Rapporteur assumes part of the task of analysing whether allegations of apartheid in occupied Palestine are well founded. He discusses Israeli policies and practices through the lens of the international prohibition of ethnic discrimination, segregation and apartheid.

---

[371] See www.cogat.idf.il/Sip_Storage/FILES/0/4320.pdf.
[372] See www.haaretz.com/news/diplomacy-defense/.premium-1.562465.
[373] A/HRC/16/72, para. 8, A/HRC/4/17, p. 3.
[374] A/HRC/16/72, para. 32(b).

Legal Framework

52. Apartheid is prohibited under international law, and Israel, as a State and an occupying Power, is bound by this prohibition. Under Protocol I additional to the Geneva Conventions, which is declaratory of international law and therefore widely regarded as universally binding, "practices of 'apartheid' and other inhuman and degrading practices involving outrages upon personal dignity, based on racial discrimination" are included as grave breaches.[375] Further, the International Law Commission has noted that Governments at the United Nations Conference on the Law of Treaties (1968) generally agreed that the prohibitions constituting peremptory norms included apartheid.[376] In addition, article 3 of the International Convention on the Elimination of All Forms of Racial Discrimination provides that "States Parties particularly condemn racial segregation and *apartheid* and undertake to prevent, prohibit and eradicate all practices of this nature in territories under their jurisdiction."[377] At the second universal periodic review of Israel in October 2013, South Africa recommended that Israel "prohibit policies and practices of racial segregation that disproportionately affect the Palestinian population in the OPT" (A/HRC/25/15, para. 136.202).

53. Apartheid involves the domination of one racial group over another, and some may argue that neither Israeli Jews nor Palestinians constitute racial groups per se. However, article 1 of the International Convention on the Elimination of All Forms of Racial Discrimination, in its definition of racial discrimination, makes it clear that race is in fact not the sole factor, but that racial discrimination may be based on "any distinction, exclusion, restriction or preference based on race, colour, descent, or national or ethnic origin." The Committee on the Elimination of Racial Discrimination has stressed that under the definition in article 1 "the Convention relates to all

---

[375] Art. 85(4)(c), A/HRC/16/72.

[376] Draft Articles on Responsibility of States for Internationally Wrongful Acts, with commentaries (2001), arts. 40–41 and commentaries.

[377] Regardless of the possibility that the Convention's inclusion of apartheid applies exclusively to South Africa, the Convention prohibits all forms of racial segregation. See Committee on the Elimination of Racial Discrimination, general recommendation No.19 (1995).

persons who belong to different races, national or ethnic groups or to indigenous peoples."[378]

54. The International Convention on the Suppression and Punishment of the Crime of Apartheid, in article 2, provides a detailed definition of the crime of apartheid, providing that it "shall include similar policies and practices of racial segregation and discrimination as practised in southern Africa," and applies to "inhuman acts committed for the purpose of establishing and maintaining domination by one racial group of persons over any other racial group of persons and systematically oppressing them." The Rome Statute of the International Criminal Court echoes these core elements (art. 7, para. 2(h)) and further specifies that for such acts to constitute "crimes against humanity" they must be "committed as part of a widespread or systematic attack directed against any civilian population, with knowledge of the attack" (art. 7, para. 1). Without prejudice to any possible differences in the elements of apartheid as an international crime and an internationally wrongful act, apartheid will be treated as a single concept for the purpose of the present report, which will be framed around the inhuman acts laid out in article 2(a)–(f) of the International Convention on the Suppression and Punishment of the Crime of Apartheid.[379]

Acts Potentially Amounting to Segregation and Apartheid

55. Article 2(a) concerns denial of the right to life and liberty of person, including by (i) murder; (ii) serious bodily and mental harm, infringement of freedom, and torture, and (iii) arbitrary arrest and illegal imprisonment. With respect to article 2(a)(i), continuing excessive use of force by Israeli security forces (ISF) and a lack of accountability for violations of international humanitarian law and international human rights law is well-documented by successive United Nations resolutions and reports.[380] Palestinians are killed as a result of regular Israeli military incursions into

[378] General recommendation No. 24 (1999), para. 1.

[379] Israel is not a party to the Convention and it is debated whether it was intended to apply exclusively to South Africa. Nonetheless, it continues to inform the prohibition of apartheid in international law.

[380] E.g., A/68/502, A/67/372, A/66/356, A/65/366, A/HRC/22/35; General Assembly resolution 67/118; and Human Rights Council resolutions 22/28 and 19/16.

occupied Palestine; lethal use of force against demonstrators; official endorsement of targeted killings; and large-scale military operations.[381]

56. According to B'Tselem, between 1987 and 2000 just under 1,400 Palestinians were killed by ISF.[382] After the year 2000, deaths of Palestinians caused by ISF accelerated, with more than 6,700 deaths, as at October 2013.[383] Of this number, over 3,100 were civilians not involved in hostilities. B'Tselem's statistics show that during Israel's "Cast Lead" operation in Gaza, of the 344 children reportedly killed, 318 did not take part in hostilities. During the same operation, of the 110 Palestinian women recorded as killed, two were police officers and the remaining 108 did not take part in the hostilities. During operation "Pillar of Defence," approximately 100 Palestinian civilians, a third of whom were children, were reportedly killed as a result of ISF actions (A/HRC/22/35/Add.1, para. 6).

57. Additional deaths were caused by the ISF policy of targeted killing, which resulted in the killing of 369 Palestinians during the period September 2000–December 2013. Moreover, on average, for every person killed as a target of ISF, one or two other persons have been killed in any given operation. Thus, during the same period, 453 Palestinians who were not targets were also killed.[384]

58. Individual accounts by former soldiers of the Israel Defense Forces (IDF), published by the Israeli NGO Breaking the Silence, bear witness to Israeli policy in respect to the occupied people: "'Prevention of terror' is the stamp of approval granted to any offensive IDF action in the Territories, obscuring the distinction between the use of force against terrorists and the use of force against civilians. In this way, the IDF is able to justify actions that intimidate and oppress the Palestinian population overall."[385]

59. Under a simple interpretation, the term murder, as referred to in the International Convention on the Suppression and Punishment of the Crime

---

[381] Russell Tribunal, *Findings* (2011), para.5.22.

[382] See www.btselem.org/statistics.

[383] Ibid.

[384] See www.btselem.org/statistics.

[385] *Israeli Soldier Testimonies 2000-2010*, p. 26 (www.breakingthesilence.org.il/testimonies/publications).

of Apartheid, signifies the unlawful taking of life. Therefore, the taking of lives — outside the limited circumstances in which international humanitarian law and international human rights law do not absolutely prohibit this — potentially constitutes an element of apartheid, in the context of a systematic and institutional regime in which these unlawful killings form part of acts carried out in order to maintain dominance over Palestinians. The relatively high proportion of civilian casualties caused by ISF in occupied Palestine is notable in this respect.

60. In regard to article 2(a)(ii) and (iii), detention by Israel of Palestinians is closely linked to the occurrence of torture and ill-treatment. According to the Prisoner Support and Human Rights Association, Addameer, in September 2013, there were some 5,000 Palestinian political prisoners, including 137 administrative detainees.[386] Many detainees are transferred to prisons in Israel, in violation of the Fourth Geneva Convention (art. 76).[387]

61. In 2012, the Committee on the Elimination of Racial Discrimination urged Israel to end administrative detention, which is discriminatory and constitutes arbitrary detention under international human rights law (CERD/C/ISR/CO/14-16, para. 27). Similar recommendations were made by a number of States during the most recent universal periodic review of Israel (A/HRC/25/15). The Committee further recommended that Israel ensure equal access to justice for all persons living in territories under its effective control, noting that Jewish settlers in occupied Palestine are subject to a civil law regime, while a military regime applies to Palestinians in the West Bank, including East Jerusalem.

62. Despite the absolute prohibition of torture,[388] Palestinians detained by Israel continue to be subjected to torture and ill-treatment (A/68/379).[389] Methods of torture and ill-treatment reportedly include: sleep deprivation; excessive use of handcuffs; beatings; verbal abuse; stress positions; solitary

---

386 See www.addameer.org/einside.php?id=9.
387 See www.addameer.org/etemplate.php?id=302.
388 Draft Articles.
389 A/68/379.

confinement; humiliation; and threats of killing, sexual assault and house demolitions, against the detainee or his or her family.[390]

63. In 1999 the Israeli High Court said that using certain methods of physical pressure for the purpose of "breaking" a detainee are unlawful and that interrogation methods must be fair and reasonable, and respectful of human dignity.[391] While representing an important recognition of the illegality of certain methods of torture employed against Palestinian detainees, the decision failed to outlaw torture by allowing the "ticking bomb" or "necessity" defence. According to Addameer, "necessity" is used by interrogators as a blanket defence with little to no accountability.[392] The Public Committee against Torture in Israel reported that of 701 formal complaints of torture submitted between 2001 and 2010, none resulted in a criminal investigation.[393]

64. Palestinian children are not exempt. In 2013, UNICEF concluded that "Ill-treatment ... appears to be widespread, systematic and institutionalized"[394] in the case of Palestinian children held in the Israeli military detention system. Israeli authorities seem to have taken some limited steps towards meeting the UNICEF recommendations,[395] including by piloting test summons in two West Bank areas instead of conducting frightening night arrests of children.[396] While this is clearly a needed development, it also shows just how basic the denial and lack of protection of Palestinian children's rights is under the Israeli military legal regime. By comparison, Israeli settler children in conflict with the law are subject to regular Israeli law. According to Defence for Children International, as at

---

[390] See www.addameer.org/etemplate.php?id=294 and www.stoptorture.org.il/en/skira1999-present.

[391] See www.btselem.org/torture/hcj_ruling.

[392] See www.addameer.org/etemplate.php?id=294.

[393] *Accountability Still Denied* (2012), p. 4 (www.stoptorture.org.il/files/PCATI_eng_web.pdf). The formal complaints may not be representative of the actual number of victims.

[394] *Children in Israeli Military Detention*, p. 1 (www.unicef.org/oPt/UNICEF_oPt_Children_in_Israeli_Military_Detention_Observations_and_Recommendations_-_6_March_2013.pdf).

[395] See www.unicef.org/oPt/UNICEF_oPt_Children_in_Military_Detention_Bulletin_No_1_October_2013.pdf.

[396] See also A/68/379 and CRC/C/ISR/CO/2-4.

October 2013, 159 Palestinian children were in Israeli military detention.[397] On average, around 700 children are detained and prosecuted per year, most commonly on charges of throwing stones.[398]

65. The regular denial by Israel of the right to life and liberty of significant numbers of Palestinians is reflected in its policies, laws and practices in occupied Palestine.

66. Article 2(b) refers to the imposition of living conditions calculated to cause a group's physical destruction in whole or in part. It seems unlikely that the policies, laws and practices of Israel can be said to have as their aim the physical destruction of the occupied people.[399]

67. Article 2(c) concerns measures calculated to prevent participation in the political, social, economic and cultural life of the country and the full development of a racial group, including and especially by denying them their rights to work, to education, to leave and to return to their country, to nationality, and to freedoms of movement and residence, opinion and expression, and peaceful assembly and association.

68. Violations of many of these rights have already been touched on in preceding sections. For instance the violations by Israel of the rights to work, education, freedom of movement and residence, and freedom of expression and assembly have been illustrated in the context of discussing the wall and its associated regime, and policies and laws related to the development of settlements, including in East Jerusalem. The rights to work, to freedom of movement, and to leave and return to one's country, are particularly relevant to Gaza. In the West Bank, the denial of rights to Palestinians is made possible by the existence of parallel legal systems operating in the same territory: one set of civil and criminal laws for Israeli settlers and another for Palestinian Arabs, subject to Israeli military orders, as well as other laws. While the Israeli High Court of Justice formally exercises judicial oversight of the Israeli administration in occupied Palestine, according to NGOs, case

---

[397] See www.dci-palestine.org/content/child-detainees.

[398] See www.addameer.org/etemplate.php?id=296.

[399] The United Nations has questioned whether Gaza will be a liveable place in 2020 ("*Gaza in 2020: A Liveable Place*?" 2012). Considering the situation in Gaza, the Russell Tribunal found that Israeli policies aimed at causing displacement of Palestinians, rather than their physical destruction.

law illustrates a trend whereby major policy decisions of government, e.g., relating to the wall and settlements, tend to be immune from judicial intervention, and that human rights and protection under international humanitarian law have not been adequately upheld by the High Court in its rulings.[400] The creation of Israeli legal zones for settlers and the resulting segregation was noted in the 2013 report by the independent fact-finding mission on settlements (A/HRC/22/63). The Committee on the Elimination of Racial Discrimination in 2012 expressed that it was "extremely concerned" at policies and practices amounting to de facto segregation and that it was "particularly appalled at the hermetic character of the separation of the two groups" (CERD/C/ISR/CO/14-16, para. 24).

69. It is clear that Israeli measures, in the form of policies, laws and practices, have the effect of preventing Palestinians from full participation in the political, social, economic and cultural life of Palestine and arguably also prevent their full development in both the West Bank and the Gaza Strip.

70. Article 2(d) refers to measures designed to divide the population along racial lines including by the creation of separate reserves and ghettos for the members of a racial group or groups, and the expropriation of landed property. The expropriation of Palestinian land is an obvious part of the expansion of settlements and of the construction of the wall. The fragmentation of Palestinian land and creation of separate reserves and enclaves, including the plans threatening to cut off East Jerusalem from the rest of the West bank, is well documented (A/HRC/22/63). The final conclusions of the Russell Tribunal on Palestine state: "Israel has through its laws and practices divided the Israeli Jewish and Palestinian populations and allocated them different physical spaces, with varying levels and quality of infrastructure, services and access to resources. The end result is wholesale territorial fragmentation and a series of separate reserves and enclaves, with the two groups largely segregated. The Tribunal heard evidence to the effect that such a policy is formally described in Israel as

---

[400] Information from Diakonia.

hafrada, Hebrew for 'separation'."[401] The Special Rapporteur has previously drawn attention to the dual system of roads in the West Bank, as a clear example of segregation, where Palestinians are largely relegated to alternative roads and forced to take long detours (A/HRC/16/72, paras. 20–22).

71. It seems incontestable that Israeli measures do divide the population of the Occupied Palestinian Territory along racial lines, create separate reserves for Palestinians and expropriate their land.

72. Article 2(e) refers to exploitation of labour. There exist historical reports[402] as well as current campaigns and reports[403] which address poor working conditions of Palestinian citizens working in Israel or in settlements. However, it is noted that there has been a sharp drop in Israeli use of Palestinian workers since the 1990s, especially as it is now impossible for Gazans to work in Israel and since in the West Bank the construction of the wall has further diminished the number of Palestinians working in Israel or for Israeli employers.[404]

73. Article 2(f) concerns persecution of those who oppose apartheid. This provision potentially relates to a wide range of human rights violations against Palestinians in the Occupied Palestinian Territory, who as a people desire self-determination and oppose the segregation, restrictions and discriminatory regime imposed by Israel on them. In this sense, the punitive response often meted out to those who demonstrate against the wall and its associated regime, or more generally oppose Israeli violations of human rights, arguably fall under this provision.

74. An individual case in point concerns the Palestinian human rights defender Issa Amro, who is a founder of the NGOs Youth Against Settlements and Hebron Defenders. In 2012, Mr. Amro was arrested and detained 20 times without charge.[405] At the time of writing, he had been

---

[401] Russell Tribunal, *Findings*, para.5.39.

[402] See http://unispal.un.org/UNISPAL.NSF/1ce874ab1832a53e852570bb006dfaf6/57c45a3dd0d46b 09802564740045cc0a?OpenDocument.

[403] See www.business-humanrights.org/Links/Repository/1023856, http://www.dci-palestine.org/documents/palestinian-children-invisible-workers-israeli-settlements.

[404] Russell Tribunal, *Findings*, para. 5.40.

[405] See www.ohchr.org/EN/NewsEvents/Pages/DisplayNews.aspx?NewsID=13626&LangID=E.

detained multiple times in 2013 and had been hospitalized, allegedly following a beating by ISF while in detention. In August 2013, a number of special rapporteurs, including this Special Rapporteur, expressed deep concern at the alleged ongoing judicial harassment, intimidation and abusive treatment of him. According to the Special Rapporteur on the situation of human rights defenders: "This is an unacceptable campaign of harassment, intimidation and reprisals against Mr. Amro, and other human rights defenders who peacefully advocate for the rights of Palestinians in the West Bank, including by cooperating with [United Nations] human rights bodies."[406]

75. An example of an Israeli citizen, belonging to the Druze minority, who has reportedly been imprisoned for his conscientious objection to serving in the Israeli army is Omar Saad. In an open letter to the Prime Minister and Minister of Defense he explained: "I couldn't imagine myself wearing military uniform and participating in the suppression of my Palestinian people." He asked: "How can I be a soldier standing at Qalandia checkpoint or any other checkpoint, after I experienced the injustices at these checkpoints? How can I prevent someone from Ramallah to visit his city, Jerusalem? How can I guard the apartheid wall? How can I be a jailer to my own people while I know that the majority of prisoners are freedom prisoners and seekers of rights and freedom?"[407]

76. It is strongly arguable that those who oppose Israeli measures amounting to apartheid risk persecution because of their opposition.

Systematic Oppression

77. None of the human rights violations discussed in the context of possibly constituting "inhuman acts" for the purpose of the International Convention on the Suppression and Punishment of the Crime of Apartheid or the Rome Statute can be said to be isolated events. Rather, their commission reflects systematic and discriminatory Israeli policies, laws and practices, which determine where in the occupied land Palestinians may or

---

[406] Ibid.
[407] See www.wri-irg.org/node/20565.

may not travel, live and work. Laws and policies have also institutionalized just how lightly a civilian Palestinian life may be weighed, when placed on the scales against claims of overarching security concerns, contrasting with the legal protection of the Israeli constitutional system given to unlawful Israeli settlers. The combined effect of the measures designed to ensure security for Israeli citizens, to facilitate and expand settlements, and, it would appear, to annex land, is *hafrada*, discrimination and systematic oppression of, and domination over, the Palestinian people.

VI. Concluding Remarks

78. Through prolonged occupation, with practices and policies which appear to constitute apartheid and segregation, ongoing expansion of settlements, and continual construction of the wall arguably amounting to de facto annexation of parts of the occupied Palestinian territory, the denial by Israel of the right to self-determination of the Palestinian people is evident. The Draft Articles on Responsibility of States for Internationally Wrongful Acts provide guidance as to the consequences of serious breaches of peremptory norms under international law. In this respect there is authority[408] to suggest that the following prohibitions have attained the status of peremptory norms: aggression through military occupation and imposition of military blockades on ports and coasts,[409] racial discrimination and apartheid, and torture. In addition, the right to self-determination itself has been recognized as a peremptory norm which applies *erga omnes*.[410]

79. Under article 40, paragraph 2, of the Draft Articles, for breaches of peremptory norms to be "serious" they must "involve a gross or systematic failure of the responsible State to fulfil the obligation." Without prejudice to an authoritative determination of whether the breaches of the discussed peremptory norms qualify as "serious," it is noted that the violations discussed in the context of the prolonged occupation appear deliberate, organized, institutionalized and longstanding. In the commentary, the International Law Commission considers it likely that competent

[408] Draft Articles, chap. III.
[409] General Assembly resolution 3314(XXIX).
[410] Draft Articles, chap. III, commentary.

international organizations, including the Security Council and the General Assembly will address such serious breaches. The implications for Member States for serious breaches of this nature include an obligation to cooperate to bring an end to breaches, and an obligation not to recognize or maintain the illegal situation.[411]

80. Finally, from the point of view of international criminal law, with the General Assembly's recognition of Palestinian statehood, the opportunity for Palestine to accept the jurisdiction of the International Criminal Court is now clear. While a declaration was lodged by the Palestinian Minister of Justice in 2009 purporting to accept its jurisdiction "for acts committed on the territory of Palestine since 1 July 2002,"[412] it seems the Court's decision of 3 April 2012 on the question of jurisdiction[413] had the effect of closing the preliminary examination.[414] An acceptance of jurisdiction would potentially bring a measure of accountability for key individuals, and address violations related to the crime of apartheid and other issues flowing from the more than 400 communications on crimes allegedly committed in Palestine, received by the Office of the Prosecutor of the International Criminal Court since 2009.[415]

VII. Recommendations

81. In this, his final report, the Special Rapporteur takes the opportunity to reiterate some past recommendations and add several new ones, namely that:

---

[411] *Id.*, art. 41.

[412] See www.icc-cpi.int/NR/rdonlyres/74EEE201-0FED-4481-95D4-C8071087102C/279777/20090122PalestinianDeclaration2.pdf.

[413] See www.icc-cpi.int/NR/rdonlyres/C6162BBF-FEB9-4FAF-AFA9-836106D2694A/284387/SituationinPalestine030412ENG.pdf.

[414] See www.icc-cpi.int/en_menus/icc/press%20and%20media/press%20releases/Documents/OTP%20Preliminary%20Examinations/OTP%20-%20Report%20%20Preliminary%20Examination%20 Activities%202013.PDF.

[415] See www.icc-cpi.int/en_menus/icc/structure%20of%20the%20court/office%20of%20the%20prosecutor/comm%20and%20ref/pe-cdnp/palestine/Pages/palestine.aspx.

(a) Palestinian legal rights, including the right of self-determination, be fully respected and implemented in attempts to reach a peaceful and just resolution of the conflict between these two peoples;

(b) The General Assembly request the International Court of Justice to issue an advisory opinion on the legal status of the prolonged occupation of Palestine, as aggravated by prohibited transfers of large numbers of persons from the occupying Power and the imposition of a dual and discriminatory administrative and legal system in the West Bank, including East Jerusalem, and further assess allegations that the prolonged occupation possesses legally unacceptable characteristics of "colonialism," "apartheid" and "ethnic cleansing";

(c) The Human Rights Council appoint an expert group to propose a special protocol to the Fourth Geneva Convention with the specific purpose of proposing a legal regime for any occupation that lasts for more than five years;

(d) The international community comprehensively investigate the business activities of companies and financial institutions registered in their own respective countries, which profit from the settlements of Israel and other unlawful Israeli activities, and take appropriate action to end such practices and ensure appropriate reparation for affected Palestinians. Member States should consider imposing a ban on imports of settlement produce;

(e) Future investigations consider whether other foreign corporate connections with unlawful occupation policies additional to settlements (e.g., separation wall, Gaza blockade, house demolitions, excessive use of force) should not be also deemed "problematic" under international law, and treated in a manner analogous to the recommendations pertaining to settlements;

(f) The Government of Israel cease expanding and creating settlements in occupied Palestine, start dismantling existing settlements and returning its citizens to the Israeli side of the Green Line, provide appropriate reparations for the damage due to settlement and related activity since 1967, and act diligently to protect Palestinians living under Israeli occupation from settler violence;

(g) The Government of Israel forthwith lift the unlawful blockade of Gaza, cease military incursions, allow Gazans to benefit fully from their natural resources situated within their borders or off the coast of Gaza, and take account of a deepening emergency in Gaza;

(h) The Human Rights Council pay increased attention to the failure by Israel to cooperate with the normal functioning of the United Nations by way of the Special Rapporteur on the situation of human rights in the Palestinian territories occupied since 1967,[416] and to the protection of Special Rapporteur from defamatory attacks diverting attention from substantive issues integral to the mandate.

---

[416] In 2013, the Special Rapporteur joined 71 other independent experts in an appeal to Member States to cooperate with their mandates (www.ohchr.org/EN/NewsEvents/Pages/DisplayNews.aspx? NewsID=14083&LangID=E).

REFERENCES[417]

Allison Henry, *Kant's Theory of Freedom* (Cambridge University Press, 1990).

Amato, A. D. 'It's a Bird, It's a Plane, It's *Jus cogens*' 6 *Connecticut Journal of International Law* (1990).

Anderson-Gold Sharon, *Unnecessary Evil: History and Moral Progress in the Philosophy of Immanuel Kant* (SUNY Press, 2001).

Andreopoulos George J. (ed.), *Genocide: Conceptual and Historical Dimensions* (Philadelphia, 1994).

Annacker C 'The Legal Régime of erga omnes Obligations in International Law' 46 *Austrian Journal of Public International Law* (1994), pp.131–66.

Anthony D'Amato 'The Moral Dilemma of Positivism', 20 *Valparaiso University Law Review* (1985-86), 43-53.

Aquila Richard E., *Matter in Mind: A Study of Kant's Transcendental Deduction*. (Indiana University Press, 1989).

Araujo, 'Anti-Personnel Mines and Peremptory International Law: Argument and Catalyst' 30 *Vanderbilt J Transnat'l L* (1997).

Arthur Naiman, '*9/11: The Simple Facts -- Why the Official Story can't Possibly be True'*, (US: Soft Skull Press, 2011).

[417] Mention here neither includes nor excludes mention in footnotes.

Arts Karin and Vesselin Popovski (eds.), *International Criminal Accountability and the Rights of Children* (Heidelberg: Springer, 2006), pp.37–52 and 53–65.

Bacevich Andrew J., *America's War for the Greater Middle East* (Random House, 2017).

Badar Mohamed Elewa, *The Concept of Mens Rea* (Hart Publishing, 2013).

Bassiouni, C. 'International Crimes: *Jus cogens* and *Obligatio Erga Omnes*' 59 *Law and Contemporary Problems* (1996) 63.

Bassiouni M. Cherif, Islam: Concept, Law and Word *Habeas Corpus*, 2 *Rutgers Camden Law Journal* (1970).

Bassiouni M. Cherif (ed.), *International Terrorism and Political Crimes* (1975).

Bassiouni M. Cherif, *Studies in Early Hadith Literature* (Indianapolis, 1978).

Bassiouni M. Cherif, 'Protection of Diplomats under Islamic Law', 74 *American Journal of International Law* (1980), pp.609-655.

Bassiouni M. Cherif, *'Sources of Islamic Law and the Protection of Human Rights' in Bassiouni*, the Islamic Criminal (1982).

Bassiouni M. Cherif, (ed.), *The Islamic Criminal Justice System* (London, Rome, New York, Oceana Publications, 1982).

Bassiouni M. Cherif, 'A Comprehensive Strategic Approach on International Cooperation for the Prevention, Control and Suppression of International and Transnational Criminality, Including the Establishment of an International Criminal Court', 15 *Nova Law Review* 353 (1991).

Bassiouni M. Cherif, 'Draft Statute of International Criminal Tribunal', 9 *Nouvellese Etudes Penales* (1993).

Bassiouni M. Cherif, *Crimes against Humanity in International law* (1999).

Bassiouni M. Cherif (ed.), *International Criminal Law* (US: Ocean Publication, 3 vols., 1999).

Bassiouni M. Cherif, *Introduction to International Criminal Law* (2005).

Bassiouni M. Cherif, 'International Recognition of Victims' Rights,' in Bassiouni (ed.), III *International Criminal Law* (2008), pp.655-701.

Bassiouni M. Cherif, 'The Discipline of International Criminal Law', in M. Cherif Bassiouni (ed.), *International Criminal Law*, Vol. 1 (2008), pp.5-40.

Bassiouni M. Cherif, 'The Subjects of International Criminal Law: Ratione Personae' in M. Bassiouni Cherif (ed.), *International Criminal Law*, Vol. 1 (2008) pp.41-70.

Bassiouni M. Cherif, *The Discipline of International Criminal Law,* in *International Criminal Law*, Vol. I (M. Cherif Bassiouni, ed., 2008).

Bassiouni M. Cherif, *Criminal Justice in the Time of War and Peace* (Cambridge University Press, Cambridge, 2014).

Bassiouni M. Cherif, *The Shariah and Islamic Criminal Justice in the Time of War and Peace* (Cambridge University Press, Cambridge, 2014).

Bassiouni M. Cherif and Benjamin B. Ferencz, *The Crime Against Peace and Aggression: From Its Origins to the ICC, in International Criminal Law*, vol. I, (M. Cherif Bassiouni, ed. 2008), pp.207-242.

Bassiouni M. Cherif and Christopher Blakesley, 'The Need for an International Criminal Court in the New International World Order', 25 *Vand. J. Transnat'l* 151 (1992).

Bassiouni M. Cherif and Daniel Derby, 'Final Report on the Establishment of an International Criminal Court for the Implementation of the Apartheid Convention and Other Relevant Instruments', 7 *Hofstra Law Review* 525 (1981).

Bassiouni M. Cherif and Ved P. Nanda (eds.), *A Treatise on International Criminal Law: Crimes and Punishment* (2 vols. 1975).

Baum L. M., 'Pursuing Justice in a Climate of Moral Outrage: An Evaluation of the Rights of the Accused in the Rome Statute of the International Criminal Court,' 19 *Wisconsin International Law Journal* (2001), 197.

Beattie J. M., *Policing and Punishment in London, 1660-1750: Urban Crime and the Limits of Terror* (Oxford: Oxford University Press, 2001).

Bekker P. M., 'The undefended accused/defendant: a brief overview of the development of the American, American Indian and South African Positions' *XXIV CILSA* (1991), pp.151-188.

Bellamy A., *Responsibility to Protect: the Global Effort to End Mass Atrocities* (Polity Press, Cambridge, 2009).

Bellamy R. (ed.), *C Beccaria, 'On Crimes and Punishments'*, (1995).

Benneh, E. Y. 'Sovereignty Immunity and International Crimes' 22 *Ghana Law Journal* (2002–2004), 112.

Bennett Jonathan, *Kant's Analytic* (Cambridge University Press, 1966).

Bennett Jonathan, *Kant's Dialectic* (Cambridge University Press, 1974).

Bennoune Karima, 'As-Salamu 'Alykum? Humanitarian Law in Islamic Jurisprudence', 15 *Michigan Journal of International Law* (1994), pp.605-643.

Benny Philip Berger, *Criminal Code of the Jews: According to the Talmud* (New Jersey: The Law Book Exchange, LTD., 2005).

Bernstein Richard J., *Radical Evil: A Philosophical Interrogation* (New York: Blackwell Publisher, 2002).

Bhutto Benazir, Reconciliation, Islam, Democracy, and the West (Simon & Schuster, 2008).

Bianchi A., 'Human Rights and the Magic of *Jus cogens*', 19 *European Journal of International Law* (2008), pp.491-508.

Bigi Giulia, 'Joint Criminal Enterprise in the Jurisprudence of the International Criminal Tribunal for the Former Yugoslavia and the Prosecution of Senior Political and Military Leaders: The Krajišnik Case' 14 Guyer Paul, *The Cambridge Companion to Kant* (1992).

Bigi Giulia, 'Joint Criminal Enterprise in the Jurisprudence of the International Criminal Tribunal for the Former Yugoslavia and the Prosecution of Senior Political and Military Leaders: The Krajišnik Case' 14 *Max Planck United Nations Yearbook* (2010), pp.51-83.

Bird Graham, *Kant's Theory of Knowledge* (Humanities Press, 1962).

Bix Brian, 'Natural Law: The Modern Tradition' in Jules Coleman and Schott Shapiro (eds.), *The Oxford Handbook of Jurisprudence and Philosophy of Law* (2002).

Bloxham Donald, *Genocide on Trial: War Crimes Trials and the Formation of Holocaust History and Memory* (2001).

Boerefijn Ineke, 'Towards a Strong System of Supervision: The Human Rights Committee's Role in Reforming the Reporting Procedure under Article 40 of the Covenant on Civil and Political Rights', *Human Rights Quarterly* 17.4 (1995), pp.766-793.

Boot Machteld, *Genocide, Crimes against Humanity, War Crimes: Nullum Crimen Sine Lege and the Subjective Matter of Jurisdiction of the International Criminal Court* (2002).

Bosly Henri D., 'Actualité du Tribunal International Pénal*', 1-2* h's.4 *Les Droit de Lowain* (1995), 3.

Bosworth-Smith R, *Mohammad and Mohammadanism* (London, 1889).

Boyle James D. A., ed., *Critical Legal Studies* (1992).

Boyle James, 'Is Subjectivity Possible? The Postmodern Subject in Legal Theory', 62 *University of Colorado Law Review* 489 (1991).

Browning Christopher, *The path to genocide: Essays on Launching the Final Solution* (2002).

Browning Don (eds.), *Universalism vs. Relativism: Making Moral Judgements in a Changing, Pluralistic, and Threatening World* (Rowman and Littlefield Publishers, United Kingdom, 2006).

Brownlie, Ian, *International Law and the Use of Force by States* (Oxford: Oxford University Press, 1996).

Brownlie Ian, *Principles of Public International Law* (Oxford: Clarendon Press, 5th ed., 1998).

Brunnée J., 'The Prohibition on Torture: Driving *Jus cogens* Home?' 104 *Proceedings of the Annual Meeting of the American Society of International Law* (2010).

Brunstetter Daniel R. and Arturo Jimenez-Bacardi, 'Clashing over Drones: The Legal and Normative Gap between the United States and the Human Rights Community', 19 (2) *International Journal of Human Rights* (2015), pp.176–198.

Buchanan Allen, 'Toward a Drone Accountability Regime', 29 (1) Ethics and International Affairs (2015), pp.15–70.

Burns Peter, 'An International Criminal Tribunal: The Difficult Union of Principle and Politics', 5 *Criminal Law Forum* (1994).

Byers M, 'Conceptualising the Relationship between *Jus cogens* and *Erga Omnes Rules*' 66 *Nordic Journal of International Law* (1997).

Byrd B. Sharon and Joachim Hruschka, *Kant and Law* (Ashgate, 2005).

Caenegem R. C. van, *European Law in the Past and the Future: Unity and Diversity over Two Millennia* (Cambridge: Cambridge University Press, 2001).

Cançado Trindade, A '*Jus cogens* in Contemporary International Law', UN Audiovisual Library, (http://www.un.org/law/avl).

Cannizzaro E., 'A Higher Law for Treaties?', in E. Cannizzaro (ed.),The Law of Treaties Beyond the Vienna Convention (2011).

Carlyle Tomas., *On Heroes, Hero-Worship, and the Heroic in History* (1841).

Carvin Stephanie, 'Getting Drones Wrong', 19 (2) *International Journal of Human Rights* (2015), pp.127–141.

Cassese A, 'For an Enhanced Role of *Jus cogens*' in Cassese, A (ed.), *Realizing Utopia* (2012).

Cassese Antonio (ed.), *The New Humanitarian Law of Armed Conflict* (Naples: Editoriale Scientifica, 1979).

Cassese Antonio, 'First Annual Report of the ICTY', *Yearbook* of *International Law Commission* (1994).

Cassese Antonio, *International Criminal Law* (Oxford: Oxford University Press, 2nd, ed., 2008).

Cassese, A. 'For an Enhanced Role of *Jus cogens*' in Cassese, A (ed.), *Realizing Utopia* (2012).

Charlesworth, H. 'Law-Making and the Sources' in Crawford, J and Koskenniemi (Eds.).

Chinkin C., '*Jus cogens*, Article 103 of the UN Charter and other Hierarchical Techniques of Conflict Solution' *Finnish Yearbook of International Law* (2006).

Chinkin C., '*Jus cogens*, Article 103 of the UN Charter and Other Hierarchical Techniques of Conflict Solution', 17 *Finnish Yearbook of International Law* (2008), pp.63-90.

Chossudovsky Michel, *War and Globalisation: The Truth Behind September 11 (*Global Outlook, *2002).*

Christian Wolff., *Jus Gentium Methodo Scientifica Pertractatum* translated by Joseph H. Drake (Oxford: Clarendon Press at London (1934).

Cicero, *De Finibus Bonorum et Malorum*, Book V, XXIII.

Clark Ramsey, *War Crimes – A Report on United States War Crimes against Iraq* (Maisonneuve Press, 1992).

Cohen Morris, 'Moral Aspects of the Criminal Law,' 49 *Yale Law Journal* (1949), pp.987-1026.

Coleman Francis, X. J., *The Harmony of Reason: A Study in Kant's Aesthetics*. (University of Pittsburgh Press, 1974).

Corten Olivier, 'La rébellion et le droit international: Le principe de neutralité en tension', 374 *Recueil des Cours: Académie de Droit International de la Haye* (2014), pp.53–312.

Coulson, N. J, *Conflict and Tensions in Islamic Jurisprudence* (University of Chicago Press, 1969).

Cox, J. Gray, *The Will at the Crossroads: A Reconstruction of Kant's Moral Philosophy* (University Press of America, 1984).

Crawford J. and S. Olleson 'The Continuing Debate on a UN Convention on State Responsibility' *54 ICLQ* (2005) 959–71.

Crawford J., *The ILC's Articles on State Responsibility: Introduction, Text and Commentaries* (CUP Cambridge 2002).

Cryer Robert, *Prosecuting International Crimes, Selectivity and the International Criminal Law Regime* (Cambridge University Press, Cambridge, 2005).

Cryer Robert, 'The Doctrinal Foundations of International Criminalization,' in *International Criminal Law*, Vol. 1 (M. Cherif Bassiouni, ed., 2008), pp.107-128.

D'Amato A., 'It's a Bird, It's a Plane, It's *Jus cogens'* (1990) 6 *Connecticut Journal of International Law, p.*1.

Danilenko G, 'International *Jus cogens*: Issues of Law-Making' 2 *European Journal of International Law* (1991).

David Eric, 'The Belgin Experince', in M. Cherif Bassiouni, *International Criminal Law*, Vol.III (Netherlands: Brill, 2008), pp.359-384.

Davis Michael C., Dietrich Wolfgang, Bettina Schoolman and Sepp.Dieter, *International Intervention in the Post-Cold War World: Moral Responsibility and Power Politics* (M.E. Sharpe, Inc., 2003).

de Hoog A. J. J., 'The Relationship between *Jus cogens*, Obligations *Erga Omnes* and International Crimes: Peremptory Norms in Perspective' 42

Österreichische Zeitschrift für öffentliches Recht und Völkerrecht (1991).

de Hoogh A., *Obligations erga omnes and International Crimes: A Theoretical Inquiry into the Implementation and Enforcement of the International Responsibility of States* (Kluwer The Hague, 1996).

de Wet Erika, 'The Prohibition of Torture as an International Norm of *Jus cogens* and its Implementation for National and Customary Law,' 15 (1) *European Journal of International Law* (2014), Vol. 15, No.1, 97-121.

de Wet, E. '*Jus cogens* and Obligations Erga Omnes' in de Wet, E and Vidmar (eds.), *J Hierarchy in International Law: The Place of Human Rights* (2012).

DeSon Jason S., 'Automating the Right Stuff? The Hidden Ramifications of Ensuring Autonomous Aerial Weapon Systems Comply with International Humanitarian Law', 72 *Air Force Law Review* (2015), pp.85–122.

Despland Michael, *Kant on History and Religion* (McGill-Queen's University Press, 1973).

Detmold M. J., *The Unity of Law and Morality: A Refutation of Legal Positivism* (Canada: Law Book Co. of Australasia, 1984).

Dhanapala Jayantha, *Under-Secretary-General for Disarmament Affairs United Nations, International Law, Security, and Weapons of Mass Destruction* (New York, 9 May 2002).

Dhokalia, 'Problems Relating to *Jus Cogens'*, in S. Agrawala (ed.), *Essays on the Law of Treaties* (1972).

Dickson Julie, *Evaluation and Legal Theory* (2001).

Don Paul and Jim Hoffman, Waking Up from Our Nightmare, the 9/11/01 Crimes in New York City (New York: I/R Press, 2004).

Drost Pieter Nicolaas, *The Crime of State: Genocide* (Original from Indiana University, 1959).

Dryer Douglas P., *Kant's Solution for Verification in Metaphysics* (Allen and Unwin, 1966).

Dugard John, 'Lifting the Guise of Occupation and Recourse to Action before the ICJ and ICC', *Palestine Yearbook of International Law,* Vol. 17, 2013–14, pp.9–27.

Duncan A. R. C., *Practical Reason and Morality* (Nelson, 1957).

Dupuy P. M., 'Reviewing the Difficulties of Codification: On Ago's Classification of Obligations of Means and Obligations of Result in Relation to State Responsibility' *10 EJIL* (1999), pp.371–85.

Dupuy, P. 'Some Reflections on Contemporary International Law and the Appeal to Universal Values: a Response to Marti Koskenniemi' 16 *European Journal of International Law* (2005), 131.

Duțu Mircea, Vespasian V. Pella (1897-1952): *Founder of International Criminal law, Promoter of the Unification of the Criminal Law, Architect of the International Criminal Justice* (Universul Juridic, Bucharest, 2012).

Eberle Edward J., 'The German Idea of Freedom', 10 *Orgon Review of Int'L Law* (2008), pp.1-76.

Edgeworth F. Y., *Mathematical Psychics: An Essay on the Application of Mathematics to the Moral Sciences*, (London: C. Kegan Paul & Co. 1881).

Emil L., 'Fackenheim, Kant and Radical Evil', in Immanuel Kant: *Critical Assessments.* 3 ed., Chadwick Ruth. (Routledge, 1992), 259-273.

Engelhardt Jordan, *The Pre-eminent State: National Dominance in the Effort to Try Saddam Hussein, Cornell Journal of International Law*, (2009).

Erakat Noura, *Justice for Some: Law and the Question of Palestine* (Stanford University Press, 2019).

Eric David, *Principes de Droit des Conflits Armés* (2nd, ed. 1999).

Ewald F., 'Unger's Philosophy: A Critical Legal Study' 5 *Yale Law Journal* 665(1988).

Ewing A. C., *A Short Commentary on Kant's 'Critique of Pure Reason'* (Methuen, 1978).

Falk Richard, 'The Accountability of Leaders: A Challenge to Civil Government and Society' in Jeremy Brecher, Jill Cutler, Smith Brendan, *In the Name of Democracy: American War Crimes in Iraq and Beyond (American Empire Project)*, (New York: Metropolitan Books, Henry Holt and Company, 2005).

Falk Richard, *The Vietnam War and International Law* (Princeton University Press, 1968).

Farmer John, *The Ground Truth: The Story Behind America's Defense on 9/11* (New York: Riverhead Books, 2009).

Fein Bruce, 'Hillary Clinton's 5 lies about Syria, Terror Threat', The *Washington Times* (25 October, 2016).

Ferencz Benjamin, *International Criminal Court* (2 vols. 1980).

Ferencz Benjamin, *An International Criminal Code and Court: Why They Stand and Where They're Going,* 30 *Columbia Journal of Transnational Law* (1992), 375.

Ferencz Benjamin B., 'Ending Impunity for the Crime of Aggression', 41 *Case W. Res. J* (2009), pp.281-290.

Finch George A., 'Draft Statute for an International Court', editorial comment 46 *American Journal of International Law* (1952), pp.89-98.

Finch George Augustus, 'The Nuremberg Trial and International Law,' 41 *American Journal of International Law* (1947), 20.

Finch George, 'Draft Statute for an International Criminal Court', 46 *American Journal of International Law* (1990), 67.

Findlay Escrito por Mark J., *International and Comparative Criminal Justice: A Critical Introduction* (Routledge, London, 2013).

Finnis John, *Fundamentals of Ethics* (1985).

Finnis John (ed.), *Natural Law* (1991).

Finnis John, *Aquinas: Moral, Political and Legal Theory* (1998).

Fischer-Lescano A. and G. Teubner, 'Regime Collision: The Vain Search for Legal Unity in the Fragmentation of Global Law', 25 *Michigan Journal of International Law* (2004), pp.999-104.

Fitzmaurice Gerald, 'The General Principles of International Law Considered from the Standpoint of the Rules of Law,' 92 *Recuel des Cours* (1957).

Focarelli C, 'Promotional *Jus cogens*: A Critical Appraisal of *Jus cogens*' Legal Effects' 77 *Nordic Journal of International Law* (2008), 429.

Fuller Lon Luvios, *The Morality of Law* (Virginia: Yale Law University, 2nd, ed., 1969).

Gardiner Gerald, *Capital Punishment as a Deterrent: And the Alternative* (London: Victor Gollancz, 1956).

Garland David; Randall McGowen; Michael Meranze, *America's Death Penalty: Between Past and Present* (2011).

Gavison Ruth (ed.), *Legal Philosophy: The Influence of H. L. A. Hart* (1987).

George Robert P., *Natural Law Theory: Contemporary Essays* (1994).

George Robert P. (ed.), *The Autonomy of Law: Essays on Legal Positivism* (1995).

Gideon Boas and William A. Schabas (eds.), *International Criminal Law Developments in the Case Law of the ICTY* (2005).

Glennon, M. J. "De l'Absurdité du Droit Impératif (*Jus cogens*)' 110 *Revue Générale de Droit International Public* (2006), 529.

Gómez Robledo, A "Le *Jus cogens* International: Sa Genése, sa Nature, ses Fonctions' 172, *Recueil des Cours de l'Académie de Droit International de la Haye* (1982), 9.

Gómez Robledo, A *El Ius Cogens Internacional (Estudio Histórico Crítico) (1982).*

Gottfried Martin, *Kant's Metaphysics and Theory of Science* (Manchester University Press, 1974).

Gram Moltke S. (ed.), *Kant: Disputed Questions* (Quadrangle, 1967).

Gray C., *International Law and the Use of Force* (2000).

Grayeff Felix, *Kant's Theoretical Philosophy* (Barnes & Noble, 1970).

Gross Michael L., 'Nonlethal Weapons, Non-Combatant Immunity, and the Principle of Participatory Liability', 47 *Case Western Reserve Journal of International Law* (2015), pp.201–216.

Grover Sonja, *Prosecuting International Crimes and Human Rights Abuses Committed against Children – Leading International Court Cases* (2010), pp.169–279.

Guyer Paul, *Kant and the Experience of Freedom* (Cambridge University Press, 1993).

Haas Jacob De, *History of Palestine - The Last Two Thousand Years* (USA: Macmillan, 1934).

Hacker P. M. S. and J. Raz, (eds.), Law, *Morality and Society: Essays in Honour of H. L. A. Hart* (1977).

Hakim Khalifa Abdul, *Fundamental Human Rights* (1952).

Hall W. A., *Treatise of International Law* (8th ed., 1924).

Hannikainen, L., *Peremptory norms (jus cogens) in international law: historical development, criteria, present status* (1988).

Harees Lukman, *The Mirage of Dignity on the highways of Human 'Progress': - the Bystanders Perspective* (2012).

Harle Vilho, *Ideas of Social Order in the Ancient World* (1998).

Harrit, Niels H. Jeffrey Farrer, Steven E. Jones, Kevin R. Ryan, Frank M. Legge, Daniel Farnsworth, Gregg Roberts, James R. Gourley, Bradley R. Larsen, *'Active Thermitic Material Discovered in Dust from the 9/11 World Trade Center Catastrophe'* in http://911review.com/evidence/wtcexplosives.html and www.benthamopen.org/pages/content.php?TOCPJ/2009/00000002/00000001/7TOCPJ.SGM.

Hart H. L. A., *Essays in Jurisprudence and Philosophy* (1985).

Hart H. L. A., *The Concept of Law* (1961).

Hart H. L. A., *The Concept of Law,* 2nd ed., (P. A. Bulloch and J. Raz, eds., 1994).

Hartnack Justus, *Kant's Theory of Knowledge* (Harcourt, Brace and World, 1967).

Hazlitt W., 'The New School of Reform: A Dialogue between a Rationalist and a Sentimentalist' (1826) in *The Complete Works of William Hazlitt*, 21 vols., ed. P. P. Howe (London: J. M. Dent and Sons, 1930–4), vol. 12, pp.179–95.

Heidegger Martin, *Kant and the Problem of Metaphysics* (Indiana University Press, 1962).

Hendeled C. W., (ed.), *The Philosophy of Kant and Our Modern World* (Liberal Arts, 1957).

Hersh Seymour M., *The Killing of Osama Bin Laden (2016).*

Higgins, 'Derogations under Human Rights Treaties' *BYIL* (1976–1977), 282.

Hoffe Otfried, *Immanuel Kant* (State University of New York Press, 1994).

Hoover Joseph, Moral Practices: Assigning Responsibility in the International Criminal Court, 76 *Law and Contemporary Problems* (2014), pp.263-86.

Hugo Adam Bedau, Paul G. Cassell, *Debating the Death Penalty: Should America Have Capital Punishment? The Experts on Both Sides Make Their Best Case* (2004).

Hugo Adam Bedau, Paul G. Cassell, *Debating the Death Penalty: Should America Have Capital Punishment? The Experts on Both Sides Make Their Best Case* (2004), David Garland; Randall McGowen; Michael Meranze, *America's Death Penalty: Between Past and Present* (2011).

Huntington Cairns, *Plato's Theory of Law*, 56 Harvard Law Review (1942), pp.559-587.

Husabø Erling Johannes and Ingvild Bruce, *Fighting Terrorism through Multilevel Criminal Legislation: Security Council Resolution 1373, the EU Framework Decision on Combating Terrorism and their Implementation in Nordic, Dutch and German Criminal Law* (Martinus Nijhoff Publishers, 2009).

Hutchings Patricia A. E., *Kant on Absolute Value* (Wayne State University Press, 1972).

Jacovides A., *Treaties Conflicting with Peremptory Norms of International Law and the Zurich-London 'Agreements'* (1966).

James *Paul, Jonathan Friedman, Globalization and Violence, Vol. 3: Globalizing War and Intervention (London: Sage Publications, 2006).*

Janis, M. W. 'The Nature of *Jus cogens*' 3 *Connecticut Journal of International Law* (1988) 59.

Jeffreys-Jones Rhodri, In Spies We Trust: The Story of Western Intelligence (Oxford: Oxford University Press, 2013).

Jevons W. S., *The Theory of Political Economy* (London: Macmillan and Co., 1871).

Jones Hardy E., *Kant's Principle of Personality* (University of Wisconsin Press, 1971).

Jørgensen, *The Responsibility of States for International Crimes* (OUP Oxford 2000).

Jori Mario (ed.), *Legal Positivism* (1992).

Kant Immanuel, *The Only Possible Argument in Support of a Demonstration of the Existence of God* (1763).

Kant Immanuel, *Answering the Question: What is Enlightenment?* (1784).

Kant Immanuel, *Critique of Judgment* (1790).

Kant Immanuel, *Critique of Pure Reason* (1781).

Kant Immanuel, *Prolegomena to Any Future Metaphysics* (1783).

Kant Immanuel, *Perpetual Peace, and Other Essays on Politics, History, and Morals* (1784).

Kant Immanuel, *Groundwork of the Metaphysic of Morals* (1785).

Kant Immanuel, *Metaphysical Foundations of Natural Science* (1786).

Kant Immanuel, *The Critique of Practical Reason* (1788).

Kant Immanuel, *Religion within the Bounds of Bare Reason* (1793).

Kant Immanuel, *Perpetual Peace: A Philosophical Sketch* (1795).

Kant Immanuel, *The Metaphysics of Morals* (1797).

Kant Immanuel, *Opus Postumum* (1995).

Kant Immanuel, 'Religion within the Limits of Reason Alone', in *Religion and Rational Theology*, ed. and transl. Allen Wood and George di Giovanni (Cambridge University Press, 1996), 93.

Kant Immanuel, *Practical Philosophy* (editor: Mary J. Gregor, 1999)

Kant Immanuel, *The Science of Right* (1790).

Kawasaki KYOJI, 'A brief Note on the Legal Effects of *Jus cogens* in International Law', 34 *Hitotsubashi Journal of Law and Politics* (2006), pp.27-43.

Kelsen Hans, 'Will the Judgement of the Nürenberg Trial Constitute a Precedent in International Law,' 1 *International Law Quarterly* (1947), 153.

Kelsen Hans, *What is Justice? Justice, Law and Politics in the Mirror of Science* (1957).

Kelsen Hans, *Pure Theory of Law* (transl. Maz Knight, 1967).

Kemal Salim., *Kant's Aesthetic Theory: An Introduction* (St. Martin's Press, 1992).

Kennedy D., 'Law and Ideology' 5 *Tikkun* (1988).

Kent Greenawalt, *Statutory and Common Law Interpretation* (Oxford: Oxford University Press, 2013).

Khadduri Majid, (ed.), *War and Peace in the Law of Islam* (Baltimore: The Johan Hopkins Press, 1955).

Khadduri Majid, (ed.), 'Islam and the Modern Law of Nations,' 50 *American Journal of International Law* (1956), pp.558-572.

Khadduri Majid, 'The Islamic Theory of International Relations and its Contemporary Relevance in Proctor' in J. Harris Protector, *Islam and International Relat*ions (New York, 1965), pp.24-39.

Khadduri Majid, (ed.), (transl.) *The Islamic Law of Nations: Shaybani's Siyar* (Transl. with an introduction, notes, and appendices, Baltimore, 1966).

Khadduri Majid, *Major Middle Eastern Problems in International Law* (1972).

King Martin Luther, *The Quest for Peace and Justice, a Nobel Lecture delivered by Martin Luther King in December* 11, 1964.

Kitcher Patricia, *Kant's Transcendental Psychology* (Oxford University Press, 1990).

Klein A., Theory for the Application of the Customary International Law of Human Rights by Domestic Courts 13 *Yale Journal of International Law* (1988).

Klein David F., 'A Theory for the Application of the Customary International Law of Human Rights by Domestic Courts,' 13 (2) *Yale Journal of International Law* (1988), pp. 332-365.

Klincewicz Michal, 'Autonomous Weapons Systems, the Frame Problem and Computer Security', 14 (2) *Journal of Military Ethics* (2015), pp.162–176.

Kolb, R. *Théorie du Jus cogens International: Essai de Relecture du Concept* (2001).

Kolb, Robert '*Jus cogens*, Intangibilité, Intransgressibilité, Dérogation 'Positive' et 'Négative' 109 *Revue Générale de Droit International Public* (2005), 305.

Kolb, R. 'Observations sur l'évolution du concept de jus cogens', *in* Revue générale de droit international public (2009), pp.837-850.

Komicker Uhlmann, E. M. 'The State Community Interests, *Jus cogens* and the Protection of the Global Environment: Developing Criteria for Peremptory Norms' *Georgetown International Environmental Law Review* (1998), 101.

Kornicker, 'State Community Interests, *Jus cogens* and Protection of the Global Environment' *11 Georgetown Int'l Environmental L Rev* (1998).

Koskenniemi M., 'Solidarity Measures: State Responsibility as a New International Order?' 72 *BYIL* (2001), pp.337–56;

Kress Claus, 'Aggression and the Use of Force in International Law', Proceedings of the 108th Annual Meeting of the American Society of International Law (2014), pp.325–346.

Kuper Leo, *International Action against Genocide* (Minority Rights Group Report No. 53, London, 1982).

Kuper Leo, *The Prevention of Genocide* (New Haven and London, 1985).

Lefenya Kesolofetse, 'Use of Explosive Weapons in Densely Populated Areas: Implications for International Humanitarian Law', *African Yearbook on International Humanitarian Law* (2014), pp.68–86.

Legal *Consequences of the Construction of a Wall in the Occupied Palestinian Territory* (I. C. J. Reports 2004).

Leiboff Marett and Mark Thomas, *Legal Theories in Principle* (2004).

Léon Victor Auguste Bourgeois, Léon Victor Auguste Bourgeois – Biography, Université d'Ottawa, available online at *aix1.uottawa.ca/~nstaman/alternatives/Nobels/TheNobelPeacePrize1920.doc*

Leonetti, 'Interprétation des traités et rêgles impératives du droit international général (*jus cogens*)', 24 *ÖZÖR* (1973).

Linderfalk Ulf, 'The Creation of *Jus cogens* – Making Sense of Article 53 of the Vienna Convention', Max-Planck-Institut für ausländisches öffentliches Recht und Völkerrecht (2011), pp.259-278.

Longobardo Marco, 'Some Developments in the Prosecution of International Crimes Committed in Palestine: Any Real News?' 35 *Polish Year Book of International Law* (2015), doi: 10.7420/pyoil2015d, pp. 109–138.

Luper-Foy, Steven 'Introduction: Global Distributive Justice' in Steven Luper-Foy (ed.), *Problems of International Justice* (London: Westview Press, 1988), pp.1-24.

Luvios Fuller Lon, *The Morality of Law* (Yale Law University, 2nd ed., 1969).

Lyons David, 'Moral Aspects of Legal Theory' in Kenneth Himma and Brian Bix (eds.) *Law and Morality* (2005).

MacGregor David, 'September 11 as 'Machiavellian State Terrorism', in Paul Zarembka, *The Hidden History of 9-11-2001* (New York: Seven Stories Press, 2008).

MacGregor Lorna, 'State Immunity and *Jus cogens*' 55 *International & Comparative Law Quarterly* (2006), 437.

Madsen Wayne, Jean-Charles and Guillaume Dasquie, *Forbidden Truth: U.S.-Taliban Secret Oil Diplomacy, Saudi Arabia and the Failed Search for bin Laden* (2002).

Majd Mohammad Gholi, *Great Britain & Reza Shah: The Plunder of Iran, 1921–1941*. University Press of Florida, 2001).

Majd Mohammad Gholi, *The Great Famine & Genocide in Iran: 1917-1919* (2nd ed., University Press of America, 2013).

Majd Mohammad Gholi, *Victorian Holocaust Iran in the Great Famine of 1869-1873* (Hamilton Books, 2018).

Majinge Charles Riziki, 'Peaceful Settlement of Disputes among States and the Rules of Regional Judicial Institutions in Africa' in Charles Riziki Majinge (ed.), *Rule of Law Through Human Rights and International Criminal Justice: Essays in Honour of Adama Dieng* (Cambridge: Cambridge Scholars publishing (Cambridge Scholars Publishing, 2015), pp.523-52.

MacIntyre Alasdair, *After Virtue: A Study in Moral Theory* (University of Notre Dame Press, 1982).

Malekian Farhad, *International Criminal Responsibility of States: A Study on the Evolution of International Responsibility of States with particular Emphasis on the Concept of Crime and Criminal Responsibility* (Stockholm, 1985).

Malekian Farhad, *System of International Law: Formation, Treaties, Responsibility* (Uppsala, 1987).

Malekian Farhad, *International Criminal Law: The Legal and Critical Analysis of International Crimes* (2 vols. 1991).

Malekian Farhad, *Condemning the Use of Force in the Gulf Crisis* (Almqvist & Wiksell International, 1st ed. (1992), 2nd ed. (1994).

Malekian Farhad, *The Concept of Islamic International Criminal Law, A Comparative Study* (Netherlands: Brill, 1994).

Malekian Farhad, *The Monopolization of International Criminal Law in the United Nations, A Jurisprudential Approach* (Almqvist Wiksell International, 1st ed., 1993), (2nd ed., 1995).

Malekian Farhad, 'International Criminal Responsibility: International Criminal Responsibility of Individuals' in M. Cherif Bassiouni, *International Criminal Law,* Vol. *Crimes* (2nd ed., New York: Transnational Publishers, 1999).

Malekian Farhad, 'Emasculating the Philosophy of International Criminal Justice in the Iraqi Special Tribunal', *Cornell International Law Journal*, 58/5 (2005) 675-725.

Malekian Farhad, *Prohibition Governing Child Soldiers Constituting an Integral Part of Jus cogens and Obligatio Erga Omnes*, XVII *World Congress of the International Association of Youth and Family Judges and Magistrates*, Belfast, Northern Ireland, 27 August – 2 September (2006).

Malekian Farhad, 'Armenian Genocide and the Questions of Responsibility of the Turkish Government,' *House of Commons Conference on the Armenian Genocide, Armenian Solidarity, British-Armenian All-Party Parliamentary Group, No Security Publication* (2007), pp.31-9.

Malekian Farhad, 'Mutilating the Philosophy of Justice in the Time of Armed Conflicts', *Contemporary Journal of International Criminal Law* (2007).

Malekian Farhad, *Documents on the Principles of International Human Rights* (Norstedts Juridik Student, 2007).

Malekian Farhad, 'The Functions of International Criminal Law and the Problem of Positivism and Neutralism Philosophy', *Contemporary Journal of International Criminal Law* (2007).

Malekian Farhad, 'The Miserable Wedding of Naturalism into Positivism,' 2 *ID EST Journal* (2009).

Malekian Farhad, 'The Homogeneity of International Criminal Court with Islamic Jurisprudence,' 9 (4) *International Criminal Law Review* (2009), pp.595-621.

Malekian Farhad, *Principles of Islamic International Criminal Law: A Comparative Search* (Netherlands: Brill & Nijhoff, 2011).

Malekian Farhad, 'Judging International Criminal Justice in the Occupied Territories,' 12 *International Criminal Law Review* (2012), 827–869.

Malekian Farhad, 'The Child as an Autonomous Subject of Justice' in Farhad Malekian, Kerstin Nordlöf, *Sovereignty of Children in Law* (Cambridge: Cambridge Scholars Publishing, 2012), pp.2-55.

Malekian Farhad, *Jurisprudence of International Criminal Justice* (Introduction by Professor Benjamin B. Ferencz, the former Prosecutor of the Nuremberg Tribunal (Cambridge: Cambridge Scholars Publishing, 2014).

Malekian Farhad, 'The Canon of Love against the Use of Force in Islamic and Public International Law: Part I: The Chamber of Love within Legal Discipline,' 15 *International Criminal Law Review*, 2015), pp.591-628.

Malekian Farhad, 'The Canon of Love against the Use of Force in Islamic and Public International Law: Part II: The Anatomy of Love against Violations,' 15 *International Criminal Law Review*, 2015), pp.861-895.

Malekian Farhad, 'Comparative Substantive International Criminal Justice', in Ronald Slye (ed.), *The Nuremberg Principles in Non-western Societies: A Reflection on their Universality, Legitimacy and Application* (2017), pp.10-44.

Malekian Farhad, 'Conundrums of *Jus cogens*: in International Criminal Law' (Part I), *Вісник Південного регіонального центру Національної академії правових наук України No. 12 Journal of the South regional Center of National Academy of Legal Sciences of Ukraine* (2017), pp.8-16.

Malekian Farhad, 'Conundrums of *Jus cogens:* In Case Law' (Part II), No.13 *Вісник Південного регіонального центру Національної академії правових наук України, No.13 Journal of the South regional Center of National Academy of Legal Sciences of Ukraine* (2017), pp.12-21.

Malekian Farhad, 'The Heaven of Justice with Love,' The *Journal of the Henry Martyn Institute* (2017), pp.5-29.

Malekian Farhad, 'The Laws Governing Crimes against Women Constituting *Obligatio Erga Omnes*' in David Wingeate Pike.

Malekian Farhad, *Corpus Juris* of Islamic International Criminal Justice (Newcastle: Cambridge Scholars Publishing, 2017).

Malekian Farhad, *Judgements of Love in Criminal Justice* (Germany: Springer: 2017).

Malekian Farhad, The Mirage of International Criminal Law: Kant Metaphysics of *Mens Rea* (Cambridge: Cambridge Scholars Publishing, 2018).

Malekian Farhad, *Trading Virginity of International Criminal Justice* (New York: Nova Sciences Publishers, 2019).

Malekian Farhad., *Islamic Law Justice Systems* in Albanese, vol. III vol., pp.1220-1225.

Malekian Farhad, *International Criminal Law of Children* (New York: Nova Sciences Publishers, 2021).

Malekian Farhad, *International Criminal Law: The Law of Somebodiness - The Law of Nobodiness* (New York: Nova Sciences Publishers, 2021).

Malekian Farhad, Kerstin Nordlöf, *Confessing the International Rights of Children: The Basic documents with Analysis* (Cambridge: Cambridge Scholars Publishing, 2012).

Malekian Farhad, Kerstin Nordlöf, *The Sovereignty of Children in Law* (Cambridge: Cambridge Scholars Publishing, 2012).

Malekian Farhad and Kerstin Nordlöf, 'International Legal Status of Children' in the *Encyclopaedia of Criminology & Criminal Justice* (United States: Wiley-Blackwell (5 volumes, 2013), vol.III, pp.1173-1178.

Malekian Farhad, Kerstin Nordlöf, *Prohibition of Sexual Exploitation of Children Constituting Obligation Erga Omnes* (Cambridge: Cambridge Scholars Publishing, 2013).

Manacorda Stefano, '*Cesare Beccaria e la pena dell'ergastolo'*, *Jus* (2015), pp.165–182.

Maxwell Max, 'A Socratic Perspective on the Nature of Human Evil', available online at http://www.socraticmethod.net/socratic_ essay_nature_of_ human_evil.htm.

May Lary *'Habeas Corpus as Jus cogens in International Law' 4 (3)* Criminal Law and Philosophy *(2010),* 249–265.

McInerny Ralph, 'Thomistic Natural Law and Aristotelian Philosophy' in John Goyette, Mark Latkovic and Richard Myers (eds.) *St Thomas Aquinas and the Natural Law Tradition: Contemporary Perspectives* (2004).

Mendus Susan, 'The Importance of Love in Rawls's Theory of Justice' 29 (1) *British Journal of Political Science* (1999), pp.57-75.

Meron Theodor, *The Humanization of International Law* (Netherlands: The Hague Academy, 2006).

Meron, T 'On Hierarchy of International Human Rights' 80 *American Journal of International Law* (1986), 1.

Meyssan Thierry, *11 September 2001: L'effroyable Imposture* (2002).

Mill J. S., *Collected Works of John Stuart Mill*, Gen. Ed. J. M. Robson, Toronto: University of Toronto Press, 1963-91).

Milmed Bella K., *Kant and Current Philosophical Issues* (New York University Press, 1961).

Mokhtar Ali, '*Nullum Crimen, Nulla Poena, Sine Lege*: Aspects and Prospects', 26 *Statute Law Review,* pp.41-55.

Muchnik Pablo, *Kant's Theory of Evil: An Essay on the Dangers of Self-love and the Aperiodicity of History* (Lexington Books, 2010).

Mueller Gerhard O.W., 'International Criminal Law: Civitas Maxima', 15 *Case Western Reserve Journal of International Law* (1985).

Murphy S., 'Nation-Building: A Look at Somalia', 3 *Tul J Int'l & Comp L* (1995).

Nafeez Mosaddeq Ahmed, 'Terrorism and Statecraft: Al-Qaeda and Western Covert Operations after the Cold War', in Paul Zarembka (ed.), pp.143-182.

Neal J., *Principles of Legislation: From the Ms. of Jeremy Bentham; … By M. Dumont … With Notes and a Biographical Notice of Jeremy Bentham and of M. Dumont*, Boston, MA: Wells and Lilly, 1830).

Newton Michael A., 'Back to the Future: Reflections on the Advent of Autonomous Weapons Systems', 47 (1) *Case Western Reserve Journal of International Law* (2015), pp.5–23.

Nieto-Navia, R. *International Peremptory Norms (Jus cogens) and International Humanitarian Law* (2011).

Nikam N. A. *Sense, Understanding and Reason* (Asia Publishing House, 1966).

Noone Gregory P.and Diana C. Noone, 'The Debate over Autonomous Weapons Systems', 47 (1) *Case Western Reserve Journal of International Law* (2015), pp.25–35.

O'Connell, '*Jus cogens*: International Law's Higher Ethical Norms' in Childress, DE III (ed.), *The Role of Ethics in International Law* (2012).

O'Connor Susan, 'Up in Arms: A Humanitarian Analysis of the Arms Trade Treaty and Its Application', 11 New Zealand Yearbook of International Law (2013), pp.73–105.

Ogletree Charles J., Austin Sarat, *The Road to Abolition? The Future of Capital Punishment in the United States* (2009).

Ogunfolu Adedokun and Oludayo Fagbemi, 'I Have a Drone: The Implications of American Drone Policy for Africa and International Humanitarian Law', 23 (1) *Revue Africaine de Droit International et Comparé* (2015), pp.106–128.

Oke Mim Kemal, 'The Ottoman Empire, Zionism and the Question of Palestine,' 14 *International Journal of Middle East Studies*, (1982).

Oliver C., 'Attorney-General of the Government of Israel v. Adolf Eichmann', 36 *Israeli Law Review* (1968).

Oliver Covey, 'The Attorney-General of the Government of Israel v. Eichmann', 56 (3) *The American Journal of International Law* (1962), pp.805-845.

Olson Peter M., 'The Lawfulness of Russian Use of Force in Crimea', 53 (1) *Revue de Droit Militaire et de Droit de la Guerre* (2014), pp.17–40.

O'Neill Onora, *Constructions of Reason: Explorations of Kant's Practical Philosophy* (Cambridge University Press, 1989).

Orakhelashvili A, *Peremptory Norms in International Law* (2006).

Orakhelashvili Alexander., 'The Impact of Peremptory Norms on the Interpretation and Application of United Nations Security Council Resolutions', 16 (1) *The European Journal of International Law* (2005), pp.59-88.

Pardo Pilar Villanueva Sainz-, 'Is International Criminal Law a living discipline?', 3:4 *The International Journal of Human Rights* (1999), pp.92-100.

Parish Matthew, *International criminal law – Justice or Mirage?* Transonflict (2013). http://www.transconflict.com/2013/05/international-criminal-law-justice-or-mirage-025/.

Paton Herbert James, *Kant's Metaphysic of Experience* (Humanities Press, 1961).

Patrides C. A. and Joseph Anthony Wittreich, *The Apocalypse in English Renaissance Thought and Literature: Patterns, Antecedents, and Repercussions* (Manchester University Press, 1984).

Patterson Dennis (ed.), *Postmodernism and Law* (1994).

Paulus A., '*Jus cogens* in a Time of Hegemony and Fragmentation', 74 *Nordic Journal of International Law* (2005), pp.297-334.

Paust, J., 'The Reality of *Jus cogens*', 7 *Connecticut Journal of International Law* (1991), 83.

Pella V. Vespasian, *La criminalité collective des états et le droit pénal de l'avenir*, Bucarest: Imprimerie de l'état, (1925).

Pella Vespasian, *Revue Internationale de Droit Penal* (1928).

Pella Vespasian V., *La Guerre-Crime et les Criminels de Guerre* (Paris, 1946).

Pella Vespasian V., *Plan for World Criminal Code*, 17 *Revue Internationale de Droit Penal* (1946).

Pella Vespasian V., *Fonctions Pacificatrices du Droit Pénal Supranational et Fin du Système Traditionnel des Traités de Paix*, 1 *Le Droit Internationale Public* (1947).

Pella Vespasian V., *Plan d'un Code Répressif Mondial,* 6 *Rewe International de Droit Pénal* 1948 (1955).

Pella Vespesian V., 'Towards an International Criminal Court', 44 *American Journal of International Law* (1950), 57.

Pellet A, 'Vive le crime! Remarques sur les degrés de l'illicité en droit international' in United Nations/International Law Commission (ed.), *International Law on the Eve of the Twenty-first Century: Views from the International Law Commission* (United Nations New York 1997), pp.287–315.

Pellet A, 'Comments in Response to Christine Chinking and in Defense of *Jus cogens* as the Best Bastion against the Excesses of Fragmentation' 83 *Finnish Yearbook of International Law* (2006).

Penrose Mary Margaret, 'Lest We Fail: The Importance of Enforcement in International Criminal Law *An Essay on the Nature and Immutability of Truth'*, 15 (2) *American University International Law Review* (1999), pp.321-394.

Peterson Jeremy, 'Unpacking Show Trials: Situating the Trial of Saddam Hussein', 48 *Harvard International Law Journal* (2007).

Plaw Avery and João Franco Reis, 'Learning to Live with Drones: Answering Jeremy Waldron and the Neutralist Critique', 14 (2) *Journal of Military Ethics*, 2015, pp.128–145.

Posner *Eric* A., A. O Sykes, *Economic Foundations of International Law* (Cambridge: Harvard University Press, 2013).

Power Jonathan, *Conundrums of Humanity: The Quest for Global Justice* (2007).

Protector J. Harris, *Islam and International Relati*ons (New York, 1965).

Quann Jack, 'Palestine Ambassador 'welcomes' Irelands Commitment after US Decision on Israel', available online at https://www.newstalk.com/news/palestine-ambassador-welcomes-irelands-commitment-us-decision-israel-926825.

Quigley John, 'The Palestine Declaration to the International Criminal Court: The Statehood Issue,' in: *Rutgers Law Record*, 35 (2009).

Quigley John, *The Statehood of Palestine*: *International Law in the Middle East Conflict* (Cambridge University Press, New York, 2010).

Ragazzi M. The Concept of International Obligations erga omnes (Clarendon Press Oxford 1997).

Ramadan Tariq, *Radical Reform: Islamic Ethics and Liberation* (Oxford: Oxford University Press, 2009).

Ramadan Tariq, *The Quest for Meaning, Developing a Philosophy of Pluralism* (London: Penguin, 2010).

Randall Kenneth C., 'Universal Jurisdiction under International Law' 66 *Texas Law Review* (1988).

Rawls Johan, *A Theory of Justice* (1971).

Rawls John, *A Theory of Justice* (1999).

Raz Joseph, *Ethics in the Public Domain: Essays in the Morality of Law and Politics* (Oxford: Oxford University Press, 1994).

Raz Joseph, *The Morality of Freedom* (1986).

Recognizing the Palestinian State on the 1967 Border & Admission of Palestine as a Full Member of the United Nations, PLO Negotiations Office, http://www.nad-plo.org (2011).

Rehman Javaid, *International Human Rights Law* (London and New York: Longman Pub Group, 2nd ed., 2010).

Reisman W. Michael, 'Legal Responses to Genocide and Other Massive Violations of Human Rights', 59 *Law and Contemporary Problems* (1996), 75.

Reiss Hans Siegbert, *Kant: Political Writings* (2003).

Report of the Independent Inquiry into the actions of the United Nations during the 1994 genocide in Rwanda, UN Doc S/1999/1257 (1999) [Rwanda Report].

Rinceanu, Johanna, 'Concept and Systematization of the Criminal Offense in Romania' in U. Sieber, S. Forster, & K. Jarvers (Eds.), *National Criminal Law in a Comparative Legal Context*, Vol. 3(1): Max-Planck-Institute Max-Planck-Institute für Ausländisches und Internationals Strafrecht (2011), pp.73–85.

Rinceanu Johanna, 'The principle of legality (*Nullum crimen sine lege*) in Romania' in U. Sieber, S. Forster, & K. Jarvers (Eds.), *National Criminal Law in a Comparative Legal Context, vol. 2* (1): Max-Planck-Institute für Ausländisches und Internationals Strafrecht, (2011), pp.89-101.

Rinceanu Johanna, 'Criminal Liability of Legal Persons in Romania' in *Riccardo Borsari, Responsabilita` da reato deli enti* (Padova: Padova University Press, 2016), pp.407–418.

Rishimawi Mona., 'A Reality or a Mirage: Judicial Review of Detention,' in Charles Riziki Majinge (ed.), *Rule of Law through Human Rights and*

International Criminal Justice: Essays in Honour of Adama Dieng (Newcastle: Cambridge Scholars publishing, 2015), pp.507-522.

Robertson Geoffrey, *Crimes against Humanity – The Struggle for Global Justice* (Penguin Books, 3rd ed., 2006).

Roméo Dallaire's, *Shake Hands with the Devil: The Failure of Humanity in Rwanda* (Carroll & Graf, New York, 2003).

Rosen Allen D., *Kant's Theory of Justice* (Ithaca, London: Cornel University Press, 1996).

Rosenstock R., 'An International Criminal Responsibility of States?', in United Nations/International Law Commission (ed.), *International Law on the Eve of the Twenty-First Century: Views from the International Law Commission* (United Nations New York, 1997), pp.265–85.

Rostow Eugene V., 'Palestinian Self-Determination: Possible Futures for the Unallocated Territories of the Palestine Mandate,' 5 *Yale Studies of World Public Order* (1978).

Ruys Tom, 'Of Arms, Funding and Non-Lethal Assistance: Issues Surrounding Third-State Intervention in the Syrian Civil War', 13 (1) *Chinese Journal of International Law* (2014), pp.13–53.

Ryngaert Cedric, *Jurisdiction in International Law* (Oxford: Oxford University Press, 2009), PP.42-84.

Ryngaert Cedtric, 'Territorial Jurisdiction Over Cross-frontier Offences: Revisiting a Classic Problem of International Criminal Law' 9 *International Criminal Law Review* 9 (2009), pp.187–209.

Sacirbey Muhamed, 'International Criminal Tribunal Born as Bastard?' The World Post', available (https://www.huffingtonpost.com/ambassador-muhamed-sacirbey/international-criminal-tribunals_b_3344169.html.

Sadat Carden Nadya Leila and S. Richard, 'The New International Criminal Court: An Uneasy Revolution,' 88 *Georgetown Law Journal* 581 (2000).

Sadat Leila Nadya, 'Competing and Overlapping Jurisdictions', Bassiouni, ed., *International Criminal* Law (2008).

Sadat Nadya Leila, Custom, 'Codification and Some Thoughts about the Relationship between the Two: Article 10 of the ICC Statute', 49 *DePaul Law Review* (2000), 909.

Sahovic Milan and William W. Bishop., 'The Authority of the State: Its Range with Respect to Persons and Places' in Max Sorensen, *Manual of Public International Law* (London: Macmillan, 1968), pp.311-380.

Salter William Mackintire, *Anarchy or Government? An Inquiry in Fundamental Politics* (1895).

Salter William Mackintire, *Ethical Religion* (1889).

Salter William Mackintire, *The conflict of the Catholic Church with the French republic* (1907).

Saner Hans, *Kant's Political Thought* (University of Chicago Press, 1973).

Sassoli, 'State Responsibility for Violations of Humanitarian Law', 84 *IRCR* (2002).

Saul, M. 'Identifying *Jus cogens* Norms: The Interaction of Scholars and International Judges', *Asian Journal of International Law* (2014) (forthcoming).

Schabas William A., *An Introduction to the International Criminal Court* (Cambridge University Press, 2011).

Schabas William A., *Genocide in International Law, the Crime of Crimes* (2000).

Schabas William A., *Genocide in International Law: The Crimes of Crimes* (Cambridge University Press, 2000 and 2009).

Schabas William A., Justice, 'Democracy and Impunity in Post Genocide Rwanda: Searching for Solutions to Impossible Problems', 7 *Criminal Law Forum* (1996).

Schabas William A., *The Abolition of the Death Penalty in International Law* (2002 and 2005).

Schabas William A., *The UN International Criminal Tribunals: The Former Yugoslavia, Rwanda and Sierra Leone* (Cambridge: Cambridge University Press, 2006).

Schabas William, *Abolition of the Death Penalty in International Law* (2002).

Schachter Oscar, *International Law in Theory and Practice* (1991).

Schwarzenberger Georg , *The Frontiers of International Law* (Stevens & Sons, Ltd, 1962).

Schwarzenberger Georg, 'The Problem of an International Criminal Law,' 5 *Current Legal Problems* (1950).

Schwarzenberger Georg., *International Jus cogens*?, 43 Tax. L. Rev (1965), p.476.

Scott L. Cummings, 'Introduction: What Good are Lawyers?' in Scott L. Cummings (ed.), Paradox of Professionalism Lawyers and the Possibility of Justice (2011).

Sevrine Knuche, 'State Immunity and the Promise of *Jus cogens*', *Northwestern Journal of International Human Rights (*2011), Vol. 9, No.2, pp.149-183.

Shaffer Thomas L., 'The Legal Ethics of Radical Individualism' 65 *Texas Law Review* (1997).

Shelton, D. 'Normative Hierarchy of International Law' 80 *American Journal of International Law* (1986), 1.

Sieber U., S. Forster, & K. Jarvers (Eds.), *National Criminal Law in a Comparative Legal Context*, Vol. 3(1): *Max-Planck-Institute Max-Planck-Institute für Ausländisches und Internationals Strafrecht* (2011).

Simma Bruno & Philip Alston, 'The Sources of Human Rights Law: Custom, *Jus cogens*, and General Principles' 90 *Australia Yearbook of International Law* (1992).

Simon William H., *The Practice of Justice: A Theory of Lawyers' Ethics* (1998).

Sinclair I., *The Vienna Convention on the Law of Treaties* (1986).

Smith Alic Halford, *Kantian Studies* (Greenwood Press, 1974).

Smith Norman Kemp, '*Commentary to Kant's 'Critique of Pure Reason''* (Humanities Press, 1962).

Smith T. S., *Lecture Delivered over the Remains of Jeremy Bentham, Esq., in the Webb-Street School of Anatomy & Medicine, on the 9th June, 1832* (London: Effingham Wilson, 1832).

Sowilet A., *The Problem of the Creation of a Permanent International Criminal Court* (1951).

Spiermann, 'Humanitarian Intervention as a Necessity and the Threat or Use of *Jus cogens*' 71 *Nordic Journal of International Law* (2002), 523.

Spooner Lysander, Natural Law; or the Science of Justice: A Treatise on Natural Law, Natural Justice, Natural Rights, Natural Liberty, and Natural Society; showing that all Legislation whatsoever is an Absurdity, a Usurpation, and a Crime. Part First. [1882], available online at http://oll.libertyfund.org/titles/spooner-natural-law-or-the-science-of-justice-1882 (Accessed: on 18 December 2017).

Stahn Carsten (ed.), *The Law and Practice of the International Criminal Court* (Oxford University Press, 2015).

Stern Robert, *Understanding Moral Obligation: Kant, Hegel, Kierkegaard* (Cambridge, Cambridge University Press, 2012).

Stigall Dan E., 'The French military Intervention in Mali, Counter-Terrorism, and the Law of Armed Conflict', 223 (1) *Military Law Review* (2015), pp.1–40.

Strawson P. F., *The Bounds of Sense: An Essay on Kant's 'Critique of Pure Reason'* (Methuen, 1966).

Sugarman David, ed., *Legality, Ideology and the State* (1985).

Suy, E 'Article 53: Treaties Conflicting with a Peremptory Norm of General International Law ('*jus cogens*')' in Corten, O and Klein, P (Eds.) *The Vienna Convention on the Law of Treaties: A Commentary Volume II* (2011).

Talmon S., 'The Duty Not to 'Recognize as Lawful' a Situation Created by the Illegal Use of Force or Other Serious Breaches of a *Jus cogens* Obligation: An Obligation without Real Substance?', in C. Tomuschat and J. M. Thouvenin (eds.), *The Fundamental Rules of the International Legal Order* (2005).

Thirlway H. W. A., *International Customary Law and Codification* (1972), pp.70-94.

Thornberry Patrick, *International Law and the Rights of Minorities* (Oxford, 1991), pp.57–109.

Thouvenin M. (eds.), *The Fundamental Rules of the International Legal Order* (2005).

Tomoko Yamashita 'Do *Jus cogens* Norms Invalidate State Immunity? International Restorative Justice and Japanese War Compensation Cases' Chinese (Taiwan) 31 *Yearbook of International Law and Affairs* (2013), pp.160-194.

Tomuschat, C. and Thouveinin, J. M. (eds.) *The Fundamental Rules of the International Legal Order: Jus cogens and Obligations* Erga Omnes (2006).

Tunkin G., *Soviet Theory of Sources of International Law, in Volkerrecht und Rechtsphilosophet: Internationale Festchrift for Stefan Verosta* (1980).

Vallejo Santiago Gonzalez, *Recognition of the State of Palestine and the Hypocrisy, Committee in Solidarity with the Arab Cause* (2011).

Vanhullebusch Matthias, 'The Arab League and Military Operations: Prospects and Challenges in Syria', 22 (2) International Peacekeeping (2015), pp.151–168.

Verdross, A. 'Forbidden Treaties in International Law: Comments on Professor Garner's Report on 'The Law of Treaties'' 31 *American Journal of International Law* (1937), 571.

Verdross, A. '*Jus Dispositivum* and *Jus cogens* in International Law' 60 *American Journal of International Law* (1966), 55.

Vest Hans, 'A Structure-Based Concept of *Genocidal* Intent', *Journal of International Criminal Justice* (2007), pp.781-797.

Vidmar, J. 'Rethinking *Jus cogens* after Germany v. Italy: Back to Article 53?' 60 *Netherlands International Law Review* (2013), 1.

Virally Michel, 'The *Sources of International Law', in* M. Sorenson, *Manual of Public International Law (*2nd ed., *1968*).

Virally, M. 'Réflexions sur le *Jus cogens*' 12 *Annuaire Français de Droit International* (1966), 5.

Vischer K. Robert, *Martin Luther King Jr. and the Morality of Legal Practice: Lessons in Love and Justice* (2014).

Vleeschauwer H. J., *The Development of Kantian Thought* (Nelson, 1962).

Waldock H., 'General Course on Public International Law', 106 *Recueil Des Course* (1962), pp.39-103.

Ward Keith, *The Development of Kant's View of Ethics* (Humanities Press, 1972).

Watson John, *The Philosophy of Kant Explained* (Garland, 1976).

Weatherhall Thomas, *Jus cogens International Law and Social Contract* (2015).

Weil, P. 'Towards Relative Normativity in International Law' 77 *American Journal of International Law* (1983).

Weinrib Ernest J., 'Law as a Kantian Idea of Reason', 87 *Columbia Law Review* (1987), pp.472-508.

Weisburd M., 'The Emptiness of the Concept of *Jus cogens*, As Illustrated by the War in Bosnia-Herzegovina', 17 *Michigan Journal of International Law* (1995-1996), pp.1-51.

Weiss T., *Military-Civilian Interactions: Humanitarian Crises and the Responsibility to Protect* (2nd ed., Rowman & Littlefield Publishers Inc, Lanham (MD), 2005).

Weller Marc, *Iraq and the Use of Force in International Law* (Oxford: Oxford University Press, 2010).

Wet De, 'The Prohibition of Torture as an International Norm of *jus cogens* and Its Implications for National and Customary Law', 15 *European Journal of International Law* (2004).

Whiteman, MM '*Jus Cogens* in International Law: With a Projected List' 7 *Georgia Journal of International and Comparative Law* (1977), p.609.

Williamson Myra, Terrorism, War and International Law, The Legality of the Use of Force Against Afghanistan in 2001 (London: Ashgate Publishing, 2009).

Wladyslaw Czaplinski, 'Concepts of *Jus cogens* and Obligations *Erga Omnes* in International Law in the Light of Recent Developments', 23 *Polish Yearbook of International Law* (1997–1998).

Wolff Christian, *Ius naturae et ius gentium* (Halle, 1740–46). Available online at http://oll.libertyfund.org/titles/vattel-the-law-of-nations-lf-ed.

Wolff R. P. (ed.), *Kant* (Doubleday, 1967).

Wood Allen W., *Kant's Moral Religion* (1970).

Wood Allen, *Kant's Ethical Thought* (Cambridge University Press, 1999).

Wright Quincy, 'Proposal for an International Criminal Court' 46 (1), *American Journal of International Law* (1952), pp.60-72.

Wright Quincy, 'The Scope of International Criminal Law: A Conceptual Framework', 15 *Virginia Journal of International Law* (1975).

Yoffie Adam G., 'Comment, The Palestine Problem: The Search for Statehood and the Benefits of International Law,' 36 Yale Journal of International Law (2011).

Zaman R., 'Playing the Ace? *Jus cogens* Crimes and Functional Immunity in National Courts', 17 *Australian International Law Journal* (2010), 53.

Zammito Johan, *The Genesis of Kant's Critique of Judgment* (University of Chicago Press, 1992).

Zarembka Paul, *The Hidden History of 9-11-2001* (New York: Seven Stories Press, 2008).

INDEX

#

11 September, 92, 183, 195, 326
11 September attacks, 92

A

Abbas, President Mahmoud, 91, 123
Abu Ghraib, 160, 168, 229
actus reus, x, 155, 176, 183, 187, 189, 195, 196, 208, 209, 214
additional protocol, 124, 128
additional protocols, 128
Advisory Opinion concerning the Legality of the Threat or Use of Nuclear Weapons, 132
Advisory Opinion of the Court, 131
Afghan governments, 106
Afghanis, 219
Afghanistan, 22, 58, 75, 159, 162, 165, 170, 223, 227, 229, 230, 237, 336
Afghans, 15, 18, 138
Africa, 113, 131, 227, 293, 322, 327
African, 321
African continent, 90
African National Congress, 59
African states, 90, 163
aggression, 55, 57, 58, 144, 159, 163, 164, 173, 180, 190, 198, 207, 209, 210, 225, 228, 244, 301, 306, 315, 321
aggressive apartheid, 53
Akayesu case, 95
Akayesu Judgment, 162, 176
Albania, 115, 170
Al-Bashir, 158
Alfredsson, Gudmundur, 157
Al-Quds(س /*Al-Quds*), , ix, 155, 167, 168, 171, 172, 198, 200, 201, 204, 205, 211, 212, 238, 239
Al-Quds/Jerusalem, ix, 155, 167, 168, 171, 172, 198, 200, 201, 204, 205, 211, 212, 238, 239
America, 10, 16, 22, 66, 158, 164, 232, 306, 311, 314, 315, 317, 318, 322
American citizens, 166
American Declaration of Human Rights, 179
American forces, 229
American people, 79, 81, 164
American Presidents, 229
American prisons, 80
American Service-Members' Protection Act, 165

American sovereignty, 166
American(s), xv, 53, 79, 80, 81, 85, 88, 107, 109, 110, 117, 156, 164, 165, 168, 179, 189, 207, 217, 229, 233, 307, 308, 310, 314, 315, 320, 321, 326, 327, 329, 333, 335, 336, 337
Amnesty International, 137
ANC, 60, 67
apartheid, 51, 52, 59, 67, 71, 74, 95, 148, 162, 175, 200, 218, 220, 234, 271, 274, 277, 279, 291, 292, 293, 295, 299, 300, 301, 302, 303, 306
Appeals Chamber, 139, 140
Aquinas, St. Thomas, 4, 315, 326
Arab, 53, 62, 66, 76, 78, 79, 91, 101, 102, 111, 113, 118, 125, 136, 157, 170, 171, 202, 203, 234, 245, 246, 247, 248, 252, 258, 259, 260, 261, 262, 263, 264, 266, 267, 268, 270, 271, 286, 335
Arab Charter on Human Rights, 111
Arab League, 118, 335
Arab nationalism, 79
Arab Peace Initiative, 101, 102, 136, 170, 203
Arab population, 125
Arab Spring, 76, 79
Arab states, 53, 76, 78
Arabia, 78, 167, 322
Arabic, 155, 234, 268
Arab-Israeli, 66, 234
Arabs, iv, 78, 81, 92, 235, 247, 252, 268, 297
Arian countries, 106
Aristotelian, 19, 326
Ashrawi, Hanan, 24, 55, 74, 124, 163
Assad family, 80
Assad, Bashar, 79, 80
Atlantic Charter, 158
Australia, 24, 46, 48, 53, 109, 126, 132, 171, 178, 203, 333

B

Bahrain, 53, 75, 170, 223, 225, 233
Balfour, xiv, 91, 92, 157, 159, 171, 210
Balfour Declaration, xiv, 91, 157, 159, 171, 210
Basque Homeland and Freedom, 59
Beijing Rules, 18
Belgium, 89, 170
Bentham, Jeremy, 2, 232, 326, 334
Bethlehem, 76, 265
Bible, 5
Biblical Code, vii, 4
Blair, Pime Minister Tony, 158
Bolton, John, 163
Bosnia, 94, 107, 171, 175, 203, 336
Bosnia and Rwanda, 175
Bourgeois, 321
Britain, 159
British authorities, 92
British Balfour Declaration, 91
British colonial power, xiv, 91, 205
British complicity, 92
British destroyers of traditional Palestinian land, 91
British diplomatic language, 91
British government, 66, 157, 233
British Mandate for Palestine, 90
British nationals, 233
British-occupied Palestinians territory, 157
Brownlie, Ian, 105, 309
Buddhists, 237
Bush, President George W., 65, 98, 158, 164, 229, 232

C

Cambodia, 65, 170
Cameron, Prime Minister David, 1, 52, 210

Canada, 46, 47, 48, 53, 119, 128, 171, 178, 203, 313
capital punishment, 150
capital punishment against children, 22
Catholic tradition, 4
CEDAW, 128
Cephalus, 26, 28
Cerkez cases, 208
Charter, 7, 26, 37, 38, 40, 49, 66, 68, 69, 71, 94, 95, 99, 103, 108, 117, 118, 131, 133, 141, 144, 158, 168, 169, 180, 181, 182, 199, 213, 220, 221, 222, 223, 226, 227, 244, 259, 266, 280, 311
Chávez, Hugo, 232
Chile, 59, 170
China, 22, 38, 102, 106, 132, 145, 170, 218, 226, 237
Chinese government, 132, 214
Chinese occupation of Tibet, 132
Chinkin, Christine, 180, 329
Christian history, 204
Christian thinkers, 5
Christian thought, 5
Christian(s), 4, 131, 157, 159, 160, 204, 265, 311, 337
Christianity, 155, 201
Churchill, Prime Minister Winston, 158, 159
CIA, 78, 79, 80
Cold War, 78, 79, 168, 312, 326
colonial powers, 91, 121
Commission of Human Rights, 54
Conundrums of Humanity, 71, 157, 329
Convention against Torture and Other Cruel, Inhuman or Degrading Treatment or Punishment, 125
Convention on Genocide, 58
Convention on the Children Rights, 54
Convention on the Elimination of All Forms of Discrimination against Women, 26, 124, 128
Convention on the Prevention and Punishment of the Crime of Genocide, 17, 40, 94, 95, 125
Convention on the Rights of Persons with Disabilities, 125
Convention on the Rights of the Child, 18, 22, 23, 26, 124
crimes against humanity, 15, 47, 48, 57, 64, 65, 136, 143, 144, 145, 147, 162, 164, 174, 175, 177, 180, 225, 293
Cuba, 38, 168, 170, 174, 202
Cuban, 59, 168
Cuban government, 168
Czech Republic, 46, 48, 53, 119, 171, 203
Czechoslovakia, 59, 245

D

Daesh, 183
de lege lata, 12, 173, 195, 197
Declaration of Independence of the United States, 204
Declaration of the United States, 174
Declaration on Human Rights, 206
Declaration on Principles of International Law concerning Friendly Relations and Co-operation among States, 117
Democratic Republic of the Congo, 107, 166, 171
Denmark, 24, 89, 170, 215, 237, 245
Deputy Legal Adviser at the Foreign and Commonwealth Office of the United Kingdom, 65
Draft Declaration on Rights and Duties of States, 72, 93
Drazen Erdemovic case, 64
Dulles, Allen, CIA Director, 78
Dutch, 124, 288, 291, 318
Dworkin, Ronald, 10

E

East *Al Quds*, 212
East Jerusalem, 46, 49, 50, 51, 77, 78, 99, 100, 106, 110, 125, 130, 131, 134, 135, 137, 142, 152, 153, 186, 200, 211, 271, 272, 273, 275, 277, 278, 279, 281, 282, 285, 286, 287, 288, 295, 297, 298, 303
East Timor, 107, 132, 171
East Timor Case, 132
Economic and Social Council, 212, 255
Egypt, xiv, 53, 75, 136, 159, 167, 170, 218, 223, 225, 233, 275, 290
Egyptian law of nations, 87
Egyptian policy, 167
El Salvador, 59, 171
erga omens, xv, 227
Ergo, 237
establishment of civilian settlements in the occupied West Bank, 154
Europe, 5, 47, 79, 81, 88, 157, 171, 211, 215, 219, 225, 234, 235
Europe lecture, 225
European Convention on Human Rights law, 233
European Court of Justice, 54
European criminal court, 231
European international lawyer, 89
European Jews, 168, 233
European law, 87, 88, 179, 310
European law of nations, 87
European members, 220
European nations, 231
European philosopher, 4
European politicians, 214, 217
European powers, 89
European states, 2, 62, 89, 90, 210, 211, 212, 214, 215, 216, 217, 218, 219, 222, 231, 233
European Union (EU), 63, 104, 156, 165, 211, 212, 225, 226, 241, 242, 273, 282, 287, 288, 289, 318
European(s), x, 2, 4, 23, 54, 59, 62, 63, 87, 88, 89, 90, 109, 120, 129, 141, 150, 163, 165, 168, 179, 207, 210, 211, 212, 213, 214, 215, 216, 217, 218, 219, 220, 222, 225, 231, 233, 238, 241, 242, 273, 282, 288, 289, 308, 310, 312, 314, 328, 336
Euskadi Ta Askatasuna, 59
ex post facto law, 139

F

Falk, Richard, 56, 271, 314
Farabundo Martí National Liberation Front, 59
Finland, 24, 38, 107, 170, 215
First World War, 232, 233
Fourth Geneva Convention, 76, 133, 154, 184, 201, 272, 273, 275, 276, 284, 286, 295, 303
France, xiv, 89, 91, 136, 170, 237
Franco Regime, 59
Frente Farabundo Martípara la Liberación Nacional, 59
Frente Revolucionario Antifascista y Patriota, 59
Frente Sandinista de Liberación Nacional, 59
Fulgencio Batista, 59

G

Gaza, 46, 48, 54, 55, 56, 57, 62, 63, 65, 66, 106, 110, 151, 152, 161, 163, 180, 182, 184, 185, 186, 191, 192, 193, 198, 209, 261, 262, 264, 271, 272, 274, 275, 290, 291, 294, 297, 298, 303, 304
Gaza authorities, 182, 191

Gaza Strip, 46, 48, 54, 55, 56, 57, 62, 65, 66, 106, 110, 151, 152, 182, 185, 186, 192, 193, 198, 271, 272, 274, 290, 298
Gaza War, 62
General Assembly, 14, 17, 48, 51, 52, 56, 57, 67, 71, 73, 76, 78, 98, 99, 100, 103, 104, 105, 111, 114, 116, 117, 118, 119, 120, 123, 125, 127, 128, 132, 133, 153, 167, 169, 170, 171, 180, 184, 187, 195, 202, 203, 204, 205, 207, 211, 212, 221, 230, 231, 232, 240, 243, 244, 245, 246, 249, 253, 254, 258, 271, 273, 275, 276, 280, 293, 301, 302, 303
General Assembly resolutions, 111, 120, 133, 276
Geneva Convention relative to the Protection of Civilian Persons in Time of War, 17, 49, 99, 131, 199, 272
Geneva Conventions, 18, 26, 54, 94, 124, 128, 137, 139, 174, 192, 292
Geneva Conventions of 1949, 54, 192
genocide, 1, 2, 8, 15, 16, 17, 47, 57, 59, 111, 129, 136, 144, 145, 163, 164, 174, 175, 176, 177, 179, 209, 210, 214, 215, 221, 225, 231, 234, 238, 239, 305, 309, 313, 321, 322, 330, 332
George, Lloyd, 157
German, 47, 107, 111, 115, 119, 215, 218, 219, 314, 318
German government, 47, 111, 215
German Nazism, 219
German-Polish Mixed Arbitral Tribunal, 107, 115
Germany, 14, 15, 17, 24, 43, 46, 47, 103, 111, 144, 170, 172, 215, 218, 233, 237, 324, 335
Germany against the Jews, 14, 43
Germany v. Italy
Greece Intervening, 103
Gilad Shalit, Israeli soldier, 191
God, 68, 160, 237, 238, 319
Goldstone report, 179, 183, 191
Goldstone, Richard, 55, 179, 182, 183, 191
Great Britain, x, 16, 91, 119, 211, 289, 322
Greek, 84, 219
Guinea-Bissau, 107, 171

H

Hague, 53, 90, 125, 138, 163, 165, 166, 229, 312, 326
Hague Invasion Act, 165
Hague Regulations, 90
Hamas, 106
Hammurabi, 229
Haspel, Gina, 229
Hebrew, 234, 268, 299
Helsinki Final Act, 118
Herodotus, 86
Herzegovina, 94, 107, 171, 203, 336
Historic Peace Agreement, 53
Hitchcock, Alfred, 232
Hitler, Adolf, 47, 157, 168, 171, 218
Holy City, 49, 50, 169, 170, 198, 199, 200, 203
Holy City of Jerusalem, 49, 169, 170, 198, 199, 200, 203
Holy Quran, 238
Holy See, 119
House of the Lord, 68
human rights, x, xi, xv, 54, 62, 77, 78, 104, 120, 129, 141, 143, 153, 156, 157, 172, 179, 180, 189, 194, 210, 215, 271, 272, 278, 283, 287, 293, 295, 303, 304, 307, 308, 309, 310, 313, 316, 317, 320, 322, 324, 326, 328, 330, 331, 333
Human Rights Committee, 62, 143, 309
Human Rights Committee of the Latin American, 143
Human Rights Council, xi, 77, 78, 153, 179, 180, 194, 271, 272, 278, 293, 303, 304

Human Rights Council resolution 31/36, 77, 78
human rights law, x, xv, 2, 7, 12, 14, 18, 19, 23, 24, 38, 39, 50, 51, 55, 63, 64, 70, 75, 81, 87, 89, 103, 104, 128, 130, 133, 136, 138, 141, 145, 161, 164, 172, 175, 177, 178, 179, 181, 185, 191, 195, 200, 206, 214, 215, 216, 218, 219, 225, 226, 227, 229, 233, 234, 235,237, 238, 241, 271, 272, 274, 293, 295, 330, 333
Human Rights Library, 157
Human Rights Watch, 54
humanitarian law, xv, 14, 42, 52, 71, 131, 132, 134, 135, 136, 141, 153, 157, 174, 180, 183, 184, 185, 191, 192, 195, 200, 201, 210, 229, 241, 271, 272, 274, 275, 291, 293, 295, 298, 308, 310, 313, 321, 327, 332
Humanitarian Law of Armed Conflict, 310
Hutu, 16, 161

I

ICCSL, 65
ICTR, 65, 95, 162
ICTY, 64, 65, 139, 310, 316
Illegal Israeli actions in Occupied East Jerusalem and the rest of the Occupied Palestinian Territory, 169, 170
Independent Commission for Human Rights, 191
India, 170, 237
Indian law of nations, 87
Inter-American Court of Human Rights, 239
International Convention on the Elimination of All Forms of Racial Discrimination, 21, 26, 125, 292
International Convention on the Rights of the Child, 54
International Convention on the Suppression and Punishment of the Crime of Apartheid, 125, 293, 295, 300
International Court of Justice (ICJ), ix, 50, 51, 52, 56, 57, 78, 84, 94, 95, 100, 103, 104, 105, 111, 115, 120, 121, 128, 130, 131, 132, 134, 145, 153, 156, 172, 173, 199, 200, 201, 207, 212, 239, 253, 254, 271, 273, 275, 276, 278, 280, 291, 303, 313
International Court of Justice Advisory Opinion, 51, 105, 130, 199, 201
International Court of Justice concerning *Jurisdictional Immunities of the State*, 103
International Court of Justice in The Hague, 120, 239
International Court of Justice's judgment, 111
International Covenant on Civil and Political Rights, 20, 23, 26, 41, 61, 125
International Covenant on Economic, Social and Cultural Rights, 20, 26, 125, 286
International Criminal Court (ICC), ix, 1, 26, 42, 56, 57, 65, 67, 81, 85, 93, 95, 104, 109, 126, 127, 133, 146, 147, 150, 151, 152, 156, 162, 163, 164, 165, 172, 177, 182, 190, 196, 209, 229, 233, 237, 238, 293, 302, 306, 308, 309, 313, 315, 317, 324, 329, 332, 334, 337
International Criminal Tribunal for Rwanda, 156, 161, 196
International Criminal Tribunal for the former Yugoslavia, 139, 196
International Humanitarian Law of Armed Conflict, 54
International Law Commission, 93, 178, 207, 292, 301, 310, 329, 331
international legal personality (ILP), viii, xiv, 38, 67, 73, 76, 83, 84, 85, 86, 87, 88, 89, 92, 93, 96, 97, 98, 99, 103, 105, 106,

120, 123, 130, 131, 163, 173, 178, 179, 202, 212, 213, 219, 222, 231, 239, 240
International Prosecutor's Office in Stockholm, 62
Iran, 16, 22, 59, 138, 170, 218, 322
Iranian, 22, 79, 80, 106
Iranian coup, 79
Iranian machinery of justice, 22
Iranian regimes, 80
Iranians, 14
Iraq, 22, 58, 59, 65, 66, 80, 92, 159, 160, 170, 223, 229, 230, 233, 237, 262, 311, 314, 325, 336
Iraq War, 59, 66
Iraqi generals, 80
Iraqi kids, 160
Iraqi population, 15
Iraqi(s), xiv, 1, 3, 15, 18, 80, 83, 138, 160, 177, 214, 219, 323
Islam, 80, 155, 157, 189, 196, 201, 307, 308, 320, 329
Islamic, 1, 4, 23, 76, 78, 80, 87, 102, 138, 150, 157, 159, 160, 162, 163, 167, 183, 189, 190, 191, 194, 195, 196, 201, 202, 206, 238, 241, 242, 306, 307, 308, 311, 319, 320, 323, 324, 325, 330
Islamic groups, 76
Islamic international criminal justice, 189, 196, 206, 324
Islamic international criminal law, 162, 163, 189, 190, 194, 195, 196, 202, 206, 325
Islamic international law, 206, 242
Islamic law, 87, 150, 189, 194, 307, 319, 325
Islamic law of nations, 87
Islamic nations, 202, 206
Islamic Republic of Iran, 138, 167
Islamic rules, 23, 160
Islamic state, 80, 183
Islamic thought, 5
Islamic world, 78, 201
Israel Ministry of Foreign Affairs, 154
Israel of settlements, 134, 153
Israeli actions in Occupied East Jerusalem, 52
Israeli armed, 46, 55, 209
Israeli armed forces, 46, 55, 209
Israeli authorities, 51, 55, 72, 130, 131, 172, 179, 200, 210, 211, 212, 277, 284, 296
Israeli forces, 151, 154
Israeli government, 18, 49, 52, 53, 60, 64, 68, 106, 121, 130, 131, 145, 147, 151, 152, 172, 179, 197, 198, 218, 228, 234, 235, 285
Israeli legal authorities, 133
Israeli military, 66, 76, 149, 290, 293, 296, 297
Israeli national law, 234
Israeli occupation, 76, 121, 125, 136, 151, 152, 170, 201, 203, 273, 303
Israeli Occupation Forces, 151
Israeli occupation of the Occupied Palestinian Territories, 125
Israeli occupying power, 148
Israeli officials, 142, 145, 146, 151
Israeli policies, 124, 286, 291, 297, 300
Israeli political interests, 66
Israeli populations, 51, 69
Israeli settlement, 73, 76, 77, 78, 99, 100, 133, 134, 135, 137, 142, 147, 148, 151, 153, 271, 272, 273, 281, 284, 287, 289
Israeli settlements, 73, 76, 77, 78, 99, 133, 137, 148, 153, 271, 272, 273, 281, 284, 287, 289
Israeli state, 62, 154, 171, 205, 235
Israeli state law, 235
Israeli troops, 126
Israeli-Palestinian conflict, 76, 103, 126, 285
Italy, 103, 145, 170, 335

J

Japan, 170, 227
Jeremiah, Prophet, 68, 69
Jerusalem, 45, 48, 49, 50, 71, 73, 75, 100, 103, 124, 135, 137, 142, 153, 155, 157, 167, 168, 169, 170, 174, 199, 200, 201, 202, 203, 212, 227, 238, 245, 246, 248, 250, 251, 252, 255, 256, 257, 258, 261, 263, 264, 265, 266, 267, 268, 269, 270, 276, 281, 285, 286, 287, 288, 300
Jessup, Philip, 114
Jesus Christ, 160
Jewish, xv, 56, 68, 91, 92, 138, 145, 157, 159, 171, 186, 204, 234, 242, 245, 246, 247, 248, 252, 258, 259, 263, 264, 265, 266, 267, 268, 270, 286, 295, 298
Jewish Diasporas, 91
Jewish interests, 92
Jewish population, 138
Jewish settlement, 234
Jews, xiv, 14, 15, 16, 17, 24, 47, 92, 111, 138, 144, 145, 157, 172, 207, 210, 212, 218, 219, 231, 237, 247, 252, 268, 292, 308
Johnson, Prime Minister Boris, 52
Jordan, 53, 75, 76, 125, 167, 170, 260, 284, 288, 314
Judaism, 68, 69, 155, 157, 201, 238
jus cogens, viii, ix, xv, 69, 70, 87, 94, 96, 104, 105, 109, 120, 128, 129, 130, 131, 138, 140, 141, 143, 144, 150, 178, 219, 239, 313, 316, 320, 321, 334, 336
justice, 156, 306, 307, 308, 314, 315, 319, 321, 322, 323, 324, 325, 326, 328, 329, 330, 331, 332, 333, 334, 335, 336

K

Kampala, 57
Kant, Immanuel, 6, 7, 9, 12, 14, 42, 43, 44, 163, 168, 195, 225, 305, 308, 309, 310, 311, 313, 314, 316, 317, 318, 319, 320, 325, 326, 327, 328, 330, 331, 332, 334, 336, 337
Khmer Rouge Tribunal, 65
Kierkegaard, 12, 334
King, Martin Luther, 2, 13, 235, 321, 336
Kordic, 208, 209
Kosovar population, 120
Kosovar territory, 121
Kosovo, 107, 120, 121
Kurdish, 138

L

La Cantuta, Fujimori case, 239
Lady Justice, 195
Latin America, 143, 227, 237
Latin American region, 143
Law of Nations, 112, 320
Law of Treaties, 310, 313, 333, 334, 335
League of Arab States, 101, 102
League of Nations, 18, 88, 91, 107, 115
Lebanese, 138, 264
Legal Consequences of the Construction of a Wall in the Occupied Palestinian Territory, 51, 105, 130, 199, 201, 321
Libya, 58, 75, 159, 170, 230
Libyan(s), 3, 14, 138
Lithuania, 46, 48, 53, 126, 170
London, 92, 94, 114, 163, 189, 306, 307, 308, 309, 311, 314, 315, 317, 318, 321, 330, 331, 332, 334, 336
Lund University, 157
Lutherpath, 89
Lysanias, 27

M

Madrid, 102, 136, 170, 203
Madrid Conference, 102
Malcolm X, xv, 235
Mandated Palestine, 171
Marshall Islands, 119, 203
McNair, Lord, 83
Mecca, 80
mens rea, ix, x, 7, 155, 167, 173, 174, 175, 176, 177, 179, 183, 187, 189, 190, 195, 196, 201, 202, 204, 206, 207, 208, 209, 237, 306, 325
Meron, Judge Theodor, 154
Micronesia, 119, 203
Middle Ages, 4
Middle East, xiv, 50, 52, 66, 78, 91, 92, 102, 124, 135, 137, 152, 167, 170, 173, 174, 199, 200, 202, 203, 216, 227, 240, 241, 306, 320, 327, 329
Middle East Peace Process and Personal Representative of the Secretary-General, 124
Mohammed, 238
Montevideo Convention, 105, 107, 110, 112
Muslim Brotherhood, 80
Muslim nations, 183
Muslim population, 56, 219
Muslim states, 201
Muslim(s), 56, 62, 79, 80, 92, 157, 159, 160, 183, 190, 201, 212, 219, 231, 237
Muslims groups, 92
Myanmar, 171, 219

N

Nassif, Philippe, 137
Nauru, 119, 203
Nazi law, 138
Nazi tyranny, 158
Nazi(s), 17, 18, 24, 47, 79, 138, 157, 158
Netanyahu, Benjamin, 53, 74, 158, 282, 285
Netherlands, 24, 46, 48, 53, 89, 170, 215, 237, 312, 325, 326, 335
New York Times, 79, 126
New Yorker, 80
New Zealand, 327
Nicaragua, 59, 170
Nigeria, 126, 170
non-Western states, 222
North Africa, 137
North America, 207, 232
North Korea, 38, 58
North Sea Continental Shelf, 115
Norway, 24, 46, 170, 215, 237
Norwegian, 39, 288
nullum crimen sine leg, 138, 139, 197, 309
Nuremberg, 47, 65, 156, 196, 197, 206, 210, 315, 322, 324
Nuremberg Principles, 196, 197, 206, 322

O

Obama, Barack President, 75, 158, 160
Occupied Palestinian Territory, 52, 77, 78, 99, 100, 125, 131, 142, 148, 151, 152, 153, 184, 185, 186, 194, 200, 275, 278, 280, 299
Occupied Palestinian Territory to the Human Rights Council, 194
occupied territory, 51, 137, 279, 281
Oppenheim, 89
Optional Protocol to the Convention on the Rights of the Child, 124
Oslo Accord, 46, 120, 124, 185
Ottoman Empire, 91, 270, 327
Ottoman Mandate, 90

P

pacta sunt servanda, viii, 57, 58, 59
Pakistan, 22, 170, 237
Palau, 46, 48, 53, 119, 203
Palestine in the United Nations, 53, 99, 101
Palestine Liberation Organization, 46, 60, 100, 101, 102, 123, 127
Palestine Liberation Organization (PLO), 46, 60, 67, 68, 75, 98, 100, 101, 102, 109, 118, 123, 124, 126, 127, 128, 330
Palestine refugees, 100, 103, 205
Palestinian and other Arab territories, 49, 199, 200
Palestinian Authority Security Forces, 134
Palestinian authority(ies), 101, 124, 134, 167, 191, 193, 212, 275
Palestinian Basic Law, 191
Palestinian case, 50, 227
Palestinian children, 151, 161, 296
Palestinian civilian deaths, 185
Palestinian civilians, 17, 133, 134, 142, 151, 153, 185, 191, 290, 294
Palestinian companies, 211
Palestinian government, 106, 107
Palestinian heritage, 204, 211
Palestinian homelands, 210
Palestinian homes, 72, 152, 284
Palestinian identity, 13
Palestinian land, 140, 148, 277, 298
Palestinian leadership, 123
Palestinian livelihood, 152
Palestinian membership, 13, 46, 47, 48, 70
Palestinian National Authority, 101, 120
Palestinian National Council, 111
Palestinian organisations, 211
Palestinian people, 51, 52, 74, 77, 100, 101, 102, 103, 119, 121, 124, 125, 127, 131, 142, 147, 149, 150, 153, 167, 186, 192, 193, 201, 202, 265, 271, 272, 274, 281, 291, 300, 301
Palestinian people to self-determination, 100, 102, 153
Palestinian political authority, 163
Palestinian population, 39, 46, 47, 48, 51, 53, 56, 58, 60, 66, 68, 81, 87, 92, 130, 131, 142, 148, 151, 152, 155, 168, 192, 216, 217, 218, 219, 222, 228, 233, 240, 279, 292, 294, 298
Palestinian President, 159
Palestinian prisoners, 124
Palestinian refugees, 75
Palestinian right, 16, 74, 119, 121, 224, 273, 287
Palestinian soil, ix, 156, 157
Palestinian sovereign state, 224
Palestinian state, xiv, 48, 73, 84, 86, 91, 96, 97, 101, 106, 109, 110, 119, 127, 128, 151, 302, 330
Palestinian statehood, xiv, 84, 91, 97, 110, 119, 128, 302
Palestinian territorial sovereignty, 205
Palestinian territories, 24, 51, 56, 69, 91, 110, 111, 119, 121, 125, 133, 174, 271, 273, 304
Palestinian territory, 51, 52, 73, 100, 102, 134, 135, 137, 149, 152, 153, 186, 200, 207, 276, 301
Palestinians, ix, xv, 14, 17, 18, 43, 46, 48, 50, 56, 62, 74, 91, 92, 109, 111, 118, 120, 127, 131, 132, 137, 144, 145, 146, 148, 149, 151, 152, 154, 163, 174, 184, 185, 186, 195, 201, 202, 207, 209, 210, 215, 216, 218, 219, 222, 223, 226, 227, 233, 235, 238, 271, 272, 273, 277, 278, 279, 281, 282, 283, 286, 287, 291, 292, 293, 294, 295, 297, 298, 299, 300, 303
Palestinians population, 50
Palme, 59, 60
Panama, 46, 48, 53, 119, 171, 203, 245
Panamanian draft, 93
Peace of Westphalia, 88

Permanent International Court, 53
Persian Gulf, 220, 227
Persian law of nations, 87
Petrograd, 92
Pinochet, Augusto, 59
Plato, 11, 20, 25, 26, 37, 219, 224, 318
PLO Executive Committee, 123, 126
Poland, 107, 171, 203
Polemarchus, 28, 29, 30, 32, 34, 35
Polydamas, 36
Power, Jonathan, 71, 157
Prague Spring, 59
President of the United States, 158, 167, 168, 202, 207, 227, 232
Prime Minister of Israel, 227
Prosecutor, 62, 138, 146, 147, 156, 162, 166, 180, 182, 285, 302, 324
Prosecutor of the International Criminal Court, 180, 182, 302
Prosecutor v. Mitar Vasiljević case, 138
Protocols of 1977, 54, 174

Q

Qatar, 53, 79, 170, 275
Qatari pipeline, 80
Quartet Roadmap, 134, 136, 203

R

ratione materiae, 139
Rawls, Johan, 9, 326, 330
Red Cross, 104, 184, 185, 206
Reference re Secessions of Quebec, 121
referral, 143, 146, 147, 148, 149, 150, 154, 291
Regulations Concerning the Laws and Customs of War on Land, 125
Reparations Case, 84
Report of the United Nations Fact Finding Mission on the Gaza Conflict, 55, 64, 71
Republic of Guinea, 51, 52
Republic of Korea, 126
Resolution 1723, 132
Resumed Tenth Emergency, 52
Revolutionary Antifascist Patriotic Front, 59
revolutionary governments, 97
Road Map of the Quartet, 51
Rome Statute, 26, 126, 127, 143, 146, 147, 149, 150, 154, 156, 164, 166, 182, 293, 300, 308
rule of humanity, 229
rule of law, xiv, 66, 164, 192, 197, 229, 273
rule of love, 212
rule of morality, 229
rule of mutual understanding, 229
rule of power, 164
rule of respect and love, 229
rule of weapons, 164
Russia, 107, 145, 167, 170, 177, 218, 226, 237
Russian government, 177
Russian(s), 15, 38, 79, 106, 136, 177, 327
Rwanda, 15, 16, 26, 126, 161, 171, 176, 203, 330, 331, 332, 333
Rwandan(s), xiv, 138, 175

S

Saddam Hussein's secular Ba'ath Party, 80
Samoa, 46, 48, 53, 171
Sandinista National Liberation Front, 59
Saudi Arabia, xiv, 22, 53, 75, 167, 170, 177, 217, 220, 225, 233, 322
Schwarzenberger, 333
Second World War, 16, 24, 38, 47, 88, 89, 92, 110, 111, 138, 144, 171, 215, 233
Secretary of State John Foster Dulles, 78

Secretary-General, 50, 78, 103, 136, 142, 180, 193, 199, 200, 205, 212, 244, 247, 276, 278, 282, 291, 313
Security Council, x, xiii, xv, 3, 7, 14, 17, 38, 39, 48, 49, 50, 51, 57, 65, 66, 67, 71, 73, 75, 76, 78, 81, 99, 102, 111, 115, 116, 119, 120, 125, 126, 130, 133, 139, 142, 144, 145, 147, 150, 153, 155, 168, 169, 170, 171, 172, 173, 174, 178, 180, 181, 182, 184, 193, 195, 198, 199, 202, 203, 207, 209, 210, 211, 212, 214, 220, 221, 222, 224, 228, 230, 231, 238, 244, 246, 247, 249, 276, 280, 285, 302, 318, 328
Security Council Resolution 478, 49
Security Council resolutions, 17, 49, 99, 111, 120, 147, 170, 171, 172, 193, 199, 202, 203, 211, 318
self-determination, viii, ix, 38, 39, 42, 47, 59, 61, 67, 68, 69, 71, 75, 76, 87, 92, 94, 99, 100, 103, 106, 113, 116, 117, 118, 121, 129, 131, 132, 145, 173, 204, 234, 271, 281, 291, 299, 301, 303, 331
Serbia, 120, 121, 170
Shukri-al-Quwatli, 79
Six-Day War, 46, 154, 198
Socrates, 25, 26, 27, 28, 29, 30, 32, 34, 35, 36, 37, 216, 224
Solomon Islands, 46, 48, 53, 171, 203
South Africa, 59, 60, 67, 131, 170, 179, 218, 220, 277, 279, 292, 293, 308
South African, 60, 67, 179, 308
Soviet treaty, 78
Soviet Union, 59
Spain, 59, 70, 89, 170
Special Coordinator, 124
Stalin, Joseph, 15
State of Palestine, 100, 101, 102, 113, 123, 124, 137, 142, 143, 145, 146, 147, 148, 149, 150, 152, 154, 335
state responsibility, 311, 313, 321, 332
Sudan, 22, 58, 170, 203
Sudani, 138
Sunni, 80, 81
Sunni-Shiite, 80
Supreme Court of Canada, 121
Swedish government, 39, 47, 54, 60, 62, 64, 70
Swedish International Prosecutor's Office, 63
Swedish legislation, 54
Swedish Prime Minister, 59, 60
Swedish Prime Minister Palme, 59
Swedish Prosecutor, 63
Swiss, 124, 128
Swiss Federal Council, 128
Switzerland, 171, 184
Sykes-Picot Agreement, xiv, 91
Syria, 79, 80, 81, 92, 159, 171, 223, 233, 264, 315, 335
Syrian Golan, 125
Syrian military officers, 79
Syrian people, 79
Syrian population, 217
Syrian(s), xiv, 3, 79, 80, 125, 138, 217, 219, 331

T

Tel Aviv, 75
Third Reich, 138, 145
Thomas Hobbes in *Leviathan*, 227
Thomism, 4
Thrasymachus, 34, 35, 36, 224, 225
Tibetan people, 132, 138
Tlaib, Rashida, 53
torture, 8, 61, 129, 144, 148, 150, 160, 168, 174, 175, 227, 229, 293, 295, 296, 301, 310, 312, 336
transparency between religions is at war with God, 238
Treaty of Versailles, xiii, 90
Trial Chamber of the ICTY, 64

Trump, President Donald, 53, 74, 76, 176, 204
Turkey, 79, 170, 275
Tutsi woman, 161

U

Uganda, 57, 171, 203
UN Charter, xiii, 75, 94, 113, 144, 174, 213, 218, 231, 311
UN Human Rights Office, 76, 77
UNESCO, 46, 47, 48, 55, 58, 64, 68, 71, 98, 111
UNESCO Cultural Heritage Charter, 111
UNGA, 127
Union of Soviet Socialist Republics, 38
United Arab Emeritus, 53
United Arab Emirates, xiv, 75, 167, 171, 225, 233
United Kingdom (UK), 309
United Nations (UN), 141, 309, 313, 325, 328, 329, 330, 331
United Nations Charter, 18, 37, 43, 66, 67, 98, 131, 141, 168, 173, 201, 207, 214, 216, 218, 219, 230
United Nations Convention against Corruption, 125
United Nations Educational, Scientific and Cultural Organization, 46
United Nations Fact Finding Mission on the Gaza Conflict, 180, 186, 194
United Nations High Commissioner for Human Rights, 181, 184, 185, 194, 284
United Nations Human Rights Council, 180
United Nations Partition Plan, 210
United Nations Report, 55
United Nations Security, 7, 41, 49, 95, 130, 133, 153, 168, 180, 181, 198, 215, 237, 328
United Nations Security Council (UNSC), 7, 41, 49, 95, 130, 133, 153, 156, 168, 171, 180, 181, 198, 214, 215, 228, 237, 328
United Nations Security Council Resolution, 49, 130, 198, 328
United Nations Standard Minimum Rules for the Administration of Juvenile Justice, 18
United Sates government, 205
United States Declaration, 167, 183
United States government, 137, 155, 158, 163, 169, 172, 195, 197, 198, 201, 202, 204, 209, 217, 218, 226, 237
United States Military Tribunal in Nuremberg, 90
United States of America (USA), xiv, 22, 24, 46, 47, 48, 49, 50, 52, 53, 59, 65, 66, 67, 70, 73, 75, 76, 87, 89, 90, 91, 92, 98, 99, 111, 114, 119, 124, 126, 127, 128, 130, 137, 145, 149, 155, 156, 158, 159, 160, 163, 164, 166, 167, 168, 169, 171, 172, 174, 177, 178, 183, 195, 196, 197, 198, 199, 200, 201, 202, 203, 204, 205, 207, 208, 209, 210, 217, 218, 220, 223, 226, 228, 229, 230, 232, 233, 234, 235, 237, 238, 282, 289, 306, 310, 311, 322, 327, 329
United States President, 52, 155
United States Secretary of State John Kerry, 124
Universal Declaration, 26, 40, 41, 104, 223
Universal Declaration of Human Rights, 26, 40, 104, 223
US intelligence agencies, 76, 229
US military personnel, 160
US soldiers, 159
use of force, xiii, xiv, 23, 39, 66, 70, 71, 72, 75, 106, 116, 117, 119, 121, 137, 145, 147, 148, 150, 155, 156, 159, 173, 183, 198, 207, 221, 231, 233, 241, 248, 293, 294, 303
USSR, 38, 39

V

Vanuatu, 46, 48, 171, 203
Vatican, 119
Venezuela, 166, 171, 232
Vienna Convention, 109, 124, 125, 128, 141, 310, 321, 333, 334
Vienna Convention on Consular Relations, 124
Vienna Convention on Diplomatic Relations, 124
Vienna Convention on the Law of Treaties, 125, 128, 333, 334
Vienna Declaration and Programme of Action, 118, 128
Vietnam, 15, 59, 160, 171, 223, 227, 314
Vietnam War, 59, 314
Vietnamese, xiv, xv, 3, 14

W

Wailing Wall, 238
Waldock, 336
Wallenberg, Raoul, 157
war crimes, 47, 48, 56, 57, 65, 84, 136, 137, 143, 144, 145, 147, 156, 163, 164, 174, 177, 180, 209, 225, 309, 311, 314
Washington, 75, 315
Welin, Katarina Johansson, 62, 63
West Bank, 46, 49, 72, 73, 76, 106, 110, 130, 137, 152, 154, 186, 198, 210, 271, 273, 274, 276, 277, 278, 281, 282, 283, 284, 285, 286, 287, 291, 295, 296, 297, 298, 299, 300, 303
West Bank and East Jerusalem, 73, 210, 291
Western, 316, 318, 326, 327
Western criminality, 222
Western intelligence agencies, 76
Western States, 78
Wilmshurst, Elizabeth, 65
World Bank, 101
World Conference on Human Rights, 118, 129

Y

Yazidis, 138
Yemen, 15, 22, 58, 170, 218, 230
Yemeni, 138, 217
Yemeni population, 217
Yemenis, xv, 219
Yugoslavia, 26, 94, 120, 156, 208, 308, 309, 333

Z

Zionist law, 138